The Greatest U.S. Navy Stories Ever Told

The Greatest U.S. Navy Stories Ever Told

UNFORGETTABLE STORIES OF COURAGE, HONOR, AND SACRIFICE

IAIN C. MARTIN

THE LYONS PRESS
An imprint of The Globe Pequot Press
Guilford, Connecticut

The Lyons Press is an imprint of The Globe Pequot Press.

10 9 8 7 6 5 4 3 2 1

Printed in the United States of America

ISBN-13: 978-1-59228-859-5

ISBN-10: 1-59228-859-6

The Library of Congress Cataloging-in-Publication Data is available on file.

This book is dedicated to the memory of my grandfathers—Karl Lukey, who volunteered for the British Merchant Marine at the age of fourteen, and John Blair Martin, a civilian engineer who worked with the Royal Navy and saw action at the Battle of Jutland.

Contents

Introduction: Origins	1	
Capture of HBM *Serapis* and *Countess of Scarbrough*	4	*John Paul Jones*
Proud New Frigates	18	*Nathan Miller*
Glory, from *A Rage for Glory*	33	*James Tertius de Kay*
The Battle of Lake Erie	47	*Cecil Scott Forester*
The USS *Constitution*	59	*James Fenimore Cooper*
From *White-Jacket*	68	*Herman Melville*
The *Merrimack* and the *Monitor*	76	*Captain Van Brunt, USN, and Franklin Buchanan, CSN*
Mobile Bay, from *Under Both Flags*	86	*Capt. H. D. Smith*
The Battle of Manila Bay, from *Autobiography of George Dewey*	110	*George Dewey*
From *The Terrible Hours*	131	*Peter Maas*
Sound General Quarters, from *At Dawn We slept*	140	*Gordon W. Prange*
The Galloping Ghost of the Java Coast	154	*Com. Walter G. Winslow*
Midway, from *How They Won the War in the Pacific*	170	*Edwin P. Hoyt*
First Blood, from *The Men of the Gambier Bay*	192	*Edwin P. Hoyt*
Hell Below, from *Take Her Deep!*	203	*Adm. I. J. Galantin*
The Capture of *U-505*	216	*Radm. Dan V. Gallery*
Kamikazes, from *The Battle of Okinawa*	233	*George Feifer*
In the Water: Gulf of Maine, from *Due to Enemy Action*	263	*Stephen Puleo*

USS *Consolation*, from *Quiet Heroes* **273** *Com. Frances Omori*

Nine Dragons, from *Brown Water, Black Berets* **285** *Thomas J. Cutler*

The Ballad of Whitey Mack, from *Blind Man's Bluff* **296** *Sherry Sontag and Christopher Drew*

Becoming a Jedi, from *Warrior Soul* **314** *Chuck Pfarrer*

Permissions Acknowledgments **327**

Introduction
Origins

Honor, Courage, and Commitment

The United States has always been first, and foremost, a maritime power. It is a nation whose origins were well suited to the task of building and sailing ships. The skilled colonials were masters of woodworking and ship design. Around them was the natural bounty of the world's greatest source of timber, hundreds of miles of shoreline with the best natural harbors in North America, and the fisheries of the Grand Banks—an inexhaustible supply of cod the British regarded as valuable as gold. Born of the greatest mercantile empire the world had yet seen, it was natural the Americans would reach to the sea as a means of supply, transport, and commerce.

It was not until the events of 1774–1775, when the bonds between sovereign and subjects were broken, the colonials were forced to look to their own maritime defense. In the French and Indian war of 1754–1763 they had aided the British at sea with privateers. Against the British, however, their former protectors were now the enemy, and in command of the greatest fleet to ever sail. It was imperative the colonies establish a defense, and a means to capture enemy supplies desperately needed for the war effort.

The American debate on naval matters was one of the first issues addressed by the Continental Congress. In August 1775, upon hearing of the sailing of two British supply ships headed for North America, a three man Naval Affairs Committee was established to outfit two armed vessels to capture the enemy ships. In October of the same year the committee was expanded to seven men with orders to oversee the construction and provision for four warships, one of thirty-six guns. The blue water Continental fleet never exceeded eighty ships of all types from 1775 to 1783. The colonies, however, commissioned over sixteen hundred privateers during the course of the revolution that were authorized by Congress.

Although the Navy failed to stop the British from raiding at will along the American coast or the capture of American merchant vessels at sea, the larger strategic results of American naval efforts contributed greatly to the final outcome. American ships took over six hundred British prizes worth over eighteen million dollars. Captured British supplies provided a vital source of military stores for George Washington's beleaguered army. In London, the effects of American privateers drove insurance rates upwards and eroded popular support for the war in Britain. Following the Treaty of Paris in 1783, however, the Continental Navy was disbanded.

American independence brought with it the first crisis in foreign affairs. The Barbary States of North Africa controlled the approaches to the Straights of Gibraltar. They demanded tribute from nations whose trade passed their shores. As a British colony, America had enjoyed the protection of the Royal Navy and free passage in the Mediterranean. Independence meant commercial access to the Mediterranean was closed and American ships became the targets of pirates and privateers around the world. Thus the Constitutional Convention in 1787 became the grounds for debate on the powers of government to commission and deploy naval forces.

James Madison and William B. Giles of Virginia led the opposition to the construction of a blue water navy. They argued that the proposed fleet of six ships would be too expensive and ineffectual at such a great distance. Sending American ships into European waters was sure to provoke a conflict with the major powers. Giles argued, "the sending of American armed ships into the midst of the fleets of Europe would certainly produce a quarrel . . . if an attempt is made to search our ships of war, like our merchantmen, it would infallibly produce a public affront, and consequent hostilities." This dubious result would create a "system of governing debts," which he saw as "the most refined system of tyranny . . . There is no devise which facilitates the expense and debts so much as a Navy."

Alexander Hamilton argued for the federalists, "There can be no doubt that the continuance of the Union under an efficient government would put it in our power, at a period not very distant, to create a navy which, if it could not vie with those of the great maritime powers, would at least be of respectable weight if thrown into the scale of either of two contending parties . . . A price would be set not only for our friendship, but upon our neutrality. By a steady adherence to the Union we may hope, erelong, to become the arbiter of Europe in America, and to be able to incline the balance of European competitions in this part of the world as out interest may dictate."

The bill to construct the frigates passed the House on March 10, 1794, by a vote of 50–39. President Washington signed it on March 27, "an act to provide a Naval Armament." The act provided for the purchase or construction of four 44-gun frigates and two of 36 guns. Until a Secretary of War was appointed in 1798, Henry Knox was entrusted to oversee their construction. Knox's liberal interpretation of his orders would set several precedents for the Navy. Knox wished to make this second American Navy permanent and worthy of respect among nations. Although his orders were to build frigates to deal with the Algerian threat he wished to "combine such qualities of strength, durability, swiftness of sailing and force as to render them equal if not superior, to any frigates belonging to any of the European powers."

Congress established the Department of the Navy on April 30, 1798. That July, the last of the first three warships of the permanent American Navy, the USS *United States,* the *Constellation,* and the *Constitution* had been launched. Designed by naval architects Joshua Humphreys and Josiah Fox, each was a masterpiece, rated to carry 44 guns yet possessing the speed to outsail any heavier warship. They entered service in time to see action in the Quasi War with France, serve against the Barbary States of North Africa, and engage the British Navy in the War of 1812. They became the first in a long line of ships and men that have protected the United States to this day.

Collected in this volume are the stories that best reflect the mission and spirit of the United States Navy from its earliest days to the present. The ships described here are more than machines to the nation that created them. They are ambassadors of state, sent to the far corners of the world and into harm's way, extending American influence and power where it is needed. As Marcus Goodrich would write, they are the towers erected by civilizations, set upon the sea to guard the approaches, manned by the toughest and most resolute crews, bound by traditions and dedication to their ship, crew, and above all victory. This book is dedicated to them.

—IAIN C. MARTIN

CLINTON, CONNECTICUT

FEBRUARY 2006

Capture of HBM *Serapis* and *Countess of Scarbrough*

JOHN PAUL JONES

I wish to have no connection with any ship that does not sail fast, for I intend to go in harm's way.

—Capt. John Paul Jones
November 16, 1778

John Paul Jones is a true American legend, viewed by many as the founding father of the American Navy. John Paul was born in Kirkcudbrightshire on the southern coast of Scotland, July 6, 1747. Apprenticed to a merchant at age thirteen, he went to sea in the brig *Friendship* to learn the art of seamanship. At twenty-one, he received his first command, the brig *John*. He became a successful merchant skipper in the West Indies trade, but was forced to emigrate to the British colonies in North America after the death of a crewmember John had flogged. Once in America he added "Jones" to his name. At the outbreak of the American Revolution, Jones was in Virginia where he cast his lot with the rebels, and on December 7, 1775, he was commissioned first lieutenant in the Continental Navy, serving aboard Commodore Esek Hopkins's flagship *Alfred*.

As First Lieutenant on *Alfred*, he was the first to hoist the Grand Union flag on a Continental warship. On November 1, 1777, he commanded the *Ranger*, sailing for France. On February 6, 1778, France signed a treaty with America, formally recognizing the independence of the new American republic. Sailing into Quiberon Bay eight days later, *Ranger* and Admiral La Motte Piquet's flagship exchanged gun salutes—the first time that the Stars and Stripes was officially recognized by a foreign government. His next war cruise of the English shore would see the capture of the HMS *Drake*, allowing Jones the honor of claiming the first defeat of an English combatant at sea.

Early in 1779, the French King gave Jones an ancient East Indiaman *Duc de Duras*, which Jones repaired, refitted, and armed with 32 guns. He renamed it *Bonhomme Richard* as a compliment to his patron Benjamin Franklin. Commanding four other ships and two French privateers, he sailed August 14, 1779, to raid English shipping.

On September 23, 1779, his ship engaged the HMS *Serapis* in the North Sea off Famborough Head, England. *Serapis* twice raked *Bonhomme Richard* with broadsides which cut her mainmast and holed her below the waterline, taking individual hits in return. *Bonhomme Richard* was burning and sinking, with her ensign shot away. The British commander asked if she had struck her colors. Jones has been quoted as saying, "Struck Sir? I have not yet begun to fight!" He then rammed *Serapis* and tied up to her, his marksmen in the rigging clearing the enemy decks so a boarding party was able to cross to *Serapis* and effect its capture. The following chapter is the actual report Captain Jones wrote to Benjamin Franklin following his triumphant return to port.

★ ★ ★ ★ ★

On Board the Ship of War Serapis, at Anchor
without the Texal in Holland, Octr. 3, 1779.

HONORED & DEAR SIR, When I had the honor of writing to you on the 11 August, previous to my departure from the Road of Groa, I had before me the most flattering prospect of rendering essential Service to the Common Cause of France and America. I had a full confidence in the Voluntary inclination & Ability of every Captain under my Command, to assist & Support me in my duty With cheerful Emulation ; & I Was persuaded that Every one of them Would pursue Glory in preference to intrest.

Whether I Was, or Was not deceived, Will best appear by a relation of Circumstances.

The Little Squadron under my orders, Consisting of the B. H. R., [Bonhomme Richard] of 40 guns ; the Alliance, of 36 guns ; the Pallas, of 32 guns ; the Cerf, of 18 guns ; and the Vengeance, of 12 guns ; joyned by two privateers, the Monsieur and the Granville, Sailed from the Road of Groa at Daybreak on the 14. of August ; the Same day We Spoke With a Large Convoy bound from the Southward to Brest.

On the 18 we retook a large Ship belonging to Holland, Laden Chiefly With brandy & Wine that had been destined from Barcelona for Dunkirk, and taken Eight days before by an English privateer. The Captain of the privateer, Monsieur, took out of this prize Such Articles as he pleased in the Night ; and the Next day being astern of the Squadron and to Windward, he actually wrote orders in his proper name, and Sent away the prize under one of his own officers. This, however, I Superseded by Sending her for L'Orient under my orders, in the Character of Commander in Chief. The Evening of the day following, the Monsieur Separated from the Squadron.

On the 20 We Saw and chaced a Large Ship, but could not overtake her, She being to Windward.

On the 21 We Saw and Chaced another Ship that Was also to Windward, & thereby Eluded our pursuit: The Same afternoon, We took a brigantine Called the Mayflower, Laden With butter and Salt provision, bound from Limerick in Ireland for London: this Vessel I immediately expedited for L'Orient.

On the 23d, We Saw Cap Clear and the S. W. part of Ireland. That afternoon, it being Calm, I sent Some armed boats to take a brigantine that appeared in the N. W. quarter. Soon after, in the Evening, it became necessary to have a boat ahead of the Ship to tow, as the helm Could not prevent her from Laying across the tide of flood, Which Would have driven us into a deep and dangerous bay, Situated between the Rocks on the South called the Skallocks, and on the North Called the Blaskats; the Ship's boats being absent, I Sent my own barge ahead to tow the Ship. The boats took the brigantine; She being Called the Fortune and bound with a Cargo of oil, blubber & staves, from Newfoundland for Bristol. This Vessel I ordered to proceed immediately for Nantes or St. Malo. Soon after Sun Set the villain who towed the Ship, cut the tow rope and decamped with my barge. Sundry Shot, Were fired to bring them too Without effect; in the mean time the master of the B. H. R., without orders, manned one of the Ship's boats, and With four Soldiers pursued the barge in order to stop the deserters. The Evenin Was then Clear and Serene, but the Zeal of that officer, [Mr. Cutting Lunt,] induced him to pursue too far, and a fog Which came on Soon afterwards prevented the boats from rejoyning the Ship, altho' I Caused Signal guns to be frequently fired. The fog and Calm Continued the next day till towards the Evening. In the afternoon Captain Landais came on board the B. H. R. and beheaved towards me with great disrespect, affirming in the most indelicate manner and Language, that I had lost my boats and people thro' my imprudence in Sending boats to take a prize! He persisted in his reproaches, though he Was assured by MM. de Weibert and de Chamillard, that the barge Was towing the Ship at the [time of] Elopement, and that she had not been Sent in pursuit of the prize. He was affronted, because I Would not the day before Suffer him to chace without my orders, and to approach the dangerous Shore I have already mentioned, Where he Was an entire Stranger, and When there Was [not] sufficient wind to govern a Ship. He told me that he Was the only American in the Squadron, and Was determined to follow his own opinion in chacing Where and When he thought proper, and in every other matter that Concerned the Service, and that if I continued in that Situation three days longer, the Squadron Would be taken, &c. By the advice of Captain de Cottineau, and With the free Consent and approbation of M. De Varage, I sent the Cerf in to reconnoitre the Coast, and Endeavour to take the boats and people, the next day, While the Squadron Stood off and on in the S.W. quarter, in the best possible Situation to intercept the Enemie's merchant Ships, whether outward or homeward bound. The Cerf had on board a pilot Well acquainted With the Coast, and Was ordered to Joyn me again before Night. I approached the Shore in the afternoon, but the Cerf did not appear; this induced me to Stand off again in the night in order to return and be rejoined by the Cerf the Next day ; but to my great Concern and disapointment, tho' I ranged the Coast along and hoisted our private Signal, neither the boats nor the Cerf joined me. The Evening of that day, the 26, brought with it Stormy Weather, With an appearance of a Severe gale from the S.W., yet I must declare I did not follow my own judgment, but Was led by the assertion Which had fallen from Captain Landais, When I in the evening made a Signal to Steer to the Northward and Leave that Station, Which I Wished to have occupied at Least a Week longer. The gale increased in the Night With thick Weather; to Prevent Separation, I carried a top Light and fired a gun Every quarter of an hour. I Carried, also, a Very moderate sail, and the Course had been Clearly pointed [out] by a Signal before night, yet With all this precaution, I found myself accompanied only by the Brigantine Vengeance in the morning, the Granville having remained astern with a prize. As I have since understood the tiller of the Pallas broke after midnight Which disenabled her from Keeping up, but no apology has yet been made in behalf of the Alliance.

On the 31, we saw the Flamie Islands situated near the Lewis, on the N.W. coast of Scotland; and the next morning, off Cap Wrath, We gave Chace to a Ship to Windward. at the Same time two Ships appearing in the

N.W. quarter, Which proved to be the Alliance and a prize Ship Which she had taken, bound, as I understood, from Liverpool for Jamaica. The Ship Which I Chaced brought too at noon. She proved the Union letter of Marque, bound from London for Quebeck, With a Cargo of naval Stores on account of government, adapted for the service of the British armed Vessels on the lakes. The public despatches Were lost, as the Alliance Very imprudently hoisted American Colours, though English colours were then flying on board the B. H. R. Captain Landais Sent a Small boat to ask Whether I Would man the Ship or [he] Should, as in the Latter Case he Would Suffer nor boat nor person from the B. H. R. to go near the prize. Ridiculous as this appeared to me, I yielded to it for the Sake of pease, and received the prisoners on board the B. H. R., While the prize was manned from the Alliance. In the afternoon another sail appeared, and I immediately made the Signal for the Alliance to chace, but instead of obeying, he Wore and Laid the Ship's head the other Way. The next morning I made a Signal to Speak with the Alliance, to Which no attention Was Shown. I then made Sail With the Ships in Company, for the second rendezvous, Which Was not far distant, and Where I fully Expected to be Joined by the Pallas and the Cerf.

The 2 of September We Saw a Sail at daybreak, and gave Chace ; that Ship proved to be the Pallas, and had met With no Success While Separated from the B. H. R.

On the 3 the Vengeance brought too a Small Irish brigantine, bound homewards from Norway. The Same Evening I Sent the Vengeance in the N. E. quarter to bring up the two prize Ships that appeared to me to be too near the Islands of Shetland, While with the Alliance and the Pallas, I Endeavoured to Weather Fair Isle, and to get into my Second rendezvous, Where I directed the Vengeance to join me With the three prizes. The Next morning, having Weathered Fair Isle, and not Seeing the Vengeance nor the prizes, I spoke the Alliance and ordered her to Steer to the Northward and bring them up to the rendezvous.

On the Morning of the 5 the Alliance appeared again, and had brought too two Very Small Coasting Sloops in ballast, but Without having attended properly to my orders of yesterday. The Vengeance Joined me Soon after, and informed me that in Consequence of Captain Landais' orders to the commanders of the two prize Ships, they had refused to follow him to the rendezvous. I am to this moment ignorant what orders these men received from Captain Landais, Nor Know I by Virtue of What authority he Ventured to give his orders to prizes in my presence and Without Either my Knowledge or approbation. Captain Ricot further informed me that he had burnt the prize brigantine, becasue that Vessel proved Leaky ; and I Was

Sorry to understand afterward that though the Vessel Was Irish property, the cargo Was Property of the Subjects of Norway.

In the Evening I Sent for all the Captains [to] Come on board the B. H. R., to Consult on future plans of operation. Captains Cottineau and Ricot obeyed me, but Captain Landais obstinately refused, and after sending me Various uncivil messages, Wrote me a Very Extraordinary Letter in answer to a Written Order, Which I had Sent him, on finding that he had trifled With my Verbal orders. The Next day a pilot boat came on board from Shetland, by Which means I received Such advices as induced me to change a plan Which I otherwise meant to have pursued, and as the Cerf did not appear at my Second rendezvous I determined to Steer towards the third in hopes of meeting her there.

In the afternoon a gale of Wind came on, which Continued four days Without intermission. In the Second night of that gale, the Alliance, With her two Little prizes, again Separated from the B. H. R. I had now with me only the Pallas and the Vengeance, yet I did not abandon the hopes of performing Some essential Service. The Winds Continued Contrary, So that We did not see the land till the Evening of the 13, When the hills of the Cheviot in the S. E. of Scotland appeared. The next day We Chased Sundry Vessels and took a Ship and a brigantine, both from the Firth of Edinburgh, Laden with coal. Knowing that there lay at anchor in Leith Road an armed ship of 20 guns, With two or three fine cutters, I formed an Expedition against Leith, Which I purposed to Lay under a Large contribution, or otherwise to reduce it to ashes. Had I been alone, the Wind being favorable, I Would have proceeded directly up the Firth, and must have Succeeded; as they lay there in a State of perfect indolence and Security, Which Would have proved their ruin. Unfortunately for me, the Pallas and Vengeance Were both at a considerable distance in the offing; they having chaced to the Southward ; this obliged me to Steer out of the Firth again to meet them. The Captains of the Pallas and Vengeance being Come on board the B. H. R., I Communicated to them my project, to Which many difficulties and objections Were made by them : At Last, however, they appeared to think better of the design after I had assured [them] that I hoped to raise a contribution of 200,000 pounds sterling on Leith, and that there was no battery of Cannon there to oppose our Landing. So much time, however, was unavoidably Spent in pointed remarks and Sage deliberation that Night, [that] the Wind became Contrary in the morning.

We continued Working to Windward up the Firth Without being able to reach the Road of Leith, till on the morning of the 17, When being almost Within Cannon Shot of the town, having Every thing in readiness for a descent, a Very Severe gale of Wind came on, and being directly Contrary, obliged us to bear away, after having in Vain Endeavoured for Some time to Withstand its Violence. The Gale Was so Severe, that one of the prizes that had been taken the 14 Sunk to the bottom, the Crew being With difficulty Saved. As the alarm had by this time reached Leith by means of a cutter that had Watched our motions that morning, and as the Wind Continued Contrary, (tho' more moderate in the evening) I thought it impossible to pursue the Enterprise With a good prospect of Success, Especially as Edinbourgh Where there is always a number of troops, is only a mile distant from Leith, therefore I gave up the project.

On the 19, having taken a Sloop and a brigantine in ballast, With a Sloop laden With building timber, I proposed another project to Mr. Cottineau, Which Would have been highly honorable tho' not profitable; many difficulties Were made, and our Situation Was represented as being the most perilous. The Enemy, he Said, Would Send against us a Superior force, and that if I obstinately Continued on the Coast of England two days longer, We Should all be taken. The Vengeance having chaced along Shore to the Southward, Captain Cottineau Said he Would follow her With the prizes, as I Was unable to make much Sail, having that day been obliged to Strike the main-top-mast to repair its damages; and as I afterward understood, he told M. De Chamillard that unless I joined them the next day both the Pallas and the Vengeance Would Leave the Coast. I had thoughts of attempting the Enterprise alone after the Pallas had made sail to join the Vengeance. I am persuaded even now, that I Would have Succeeded, and to the honor of my young officers, I found them as ardently disposed to the business as I could desire: nothing prevented me from pursuing my design but the reproach that Would have been Cast upon my Character, as a man of prudence, had the Enterprise miscarried, It Would have been Said, Was he not forewarned by Captain Cottineau and others?

I made Sail along Shore to the Southward, and next morning took a coasting Sloop in ballast, Which With another that I had taken the night before, I ordered to be Sunk. In the Evening, I again met With the Pallas and Vengeance off Whitby. Captain Cottineau told me he had Sunk the brigantine, and ransomed the Sloop, laden With building timber that had been taken the day before. I had told Captain Cottineau the day before, that I had no authority to ransom prizes.

On the 21 we saw and chaced two sail, of Flamborough Head, the Pallas chaced in the N. E. quarter, while the B. H. R. followed by the Vengeance chaced in the S. W. The one I chaced, a brigantine collier in ballast belonging to Scarborough, Was Soon taken, and Sunk immediately afterwards, as a fleet then appeared to the Southward. This was so late in the day that I Could not Come up With the fleet before Night; at Length, however, I got so near one of them, as to force her to run ashore, between Flamborought Head and the Spurn. Soon after I took another, a brigantine from holland belonging to Sunderland; and at DayLight the next morning, Seeing a fleet Steering towards me from the Spurn, I imagined them to be a convoy, bound from London for Leith, which had been for some time Expected, one of them had a pendant hoisted, and appeared to be a ship of force, they had not, however, Courage to Come on, but keept Back all Except the one Which Seemed to be armed, and that one also keept to Windward very near the land, and on the Edge of dangerous Shoals Where I could not With Safety approach.

This induced me to make a Signal for a pilot, and Soon afterward two pilot boats Came off; they informed me that the Ship that Wore a pendant Was an armed merchant Ship, and that a King's frigate lay there in Sight, at anchor Within the Humber, waiting to take under Convoy a number of merchant Ships bound to the northward. The pilots imagined the B. H. R. to be an English Ship of War, and consequently Communicated to me the private Signal Which they had been required to make. I Endeavoured by this means to decoy the Ships out of the port, but the Wind then changing, and With the tide becoming unfavourable for them, the deception had not the desired effect, and they Wisely put back. The Entrance of the Humber is Exceedingly difficult and dangerous, and as the Pallas was not in sight, I thought it not prudent to remain off the Entrance; i therefore Steered out again to join the Pallas off Flamborough Head. In the night We Saw and chaced two Ships, until 3 o'clock in the morning, When being at a Very Small distance from them, I made the private Signal of reconnoisance, Which I had given to Each captain before I Sailed from Groa. One half of the answer only Was returned. In this position both Sides lay too till dayLight, When the Ships proved to be the Alliance and the Pallas.

On the morning of that day, the 23, the brig from Holland not being in Sight, we chaced a brigantine that appeared Laying too to Winward. About noon We Saw and chaced a large ship that appeared Coming round Flamborough Head, from the Northward, and at the same time I manned and armed one of the pilot boats to send in pursuit of the brigantine, Which now appeared to be the Vessel that I had forced ashore. Soon after this a fleet of 41 Sail appeared of Flamborough Head, bearing N. N. E.; this induced me to abandon the Singl Ship Which had then anchored in Burlington Bay; I also Called back the pilot boat and hoisted a Signal for a general chace. When the fleet discovered us bearing down, all the merchant ships Crowded Sail towards the Shore. The two Ships of War that protected the fleet, at the Same time Steered from the land, and made the disposition for the battle. In approaching the Enemy I crowded Every possible Sail, and made the Signal for the line of battle, to Which the Alliance Showed no attention. Earnest as I Was for the action, I Could not reach the Commodore's Ship until Seven in the evening, being then within pistol shot. When he hailed the B. H. R., we answered him by firing a Whole broadside.

The battle being thus begun, Was Continued With unremitting fury. Every method was practised on both Sides to gain an advantage, and rake Each other; and I must Confess that the Enemie's Ship being much more manageable than the B. H. R., gained thereby several times an advantageous situation, in spite of my best endeavours to prevent it. As I had to deal With an Enemy of greatly Superior force, I was under the necessity of Closing with him, to prevent the advantage Which he had over me in point of manoeuvre.

It was my intention to lay the B. H. R. athwart the enemie's bow, but as that operation required great dexterity in the management of both Sails and helm, and Some of our braces being Shot away, it did not exactly succeed to my Wishes, the Enemie's bowsprit, however, came over the B. H. R.'s poop by the mizen mast, and I made both Ships fast together in that Situation, Which by the action of the Wind on the Enemie's Sails, forcer her Stern close to the B. H. R.'s bow, so that the Ships lay Square along side of each other, the yards being all entagled, and the cannon of Each Ship touching the opponent's Side. When this position took place it Was 8 o'clock, previous to which the B. H. R. had received sundry eighteen pounds Shot below the water, and Leaked Very much. My battery of 12 pounders, on Which I had placed my chief dependance, being Commanded by Lieut. Deal and Col. Weibert, and manned principally with American seamen, and French Volunteers, Were entirely silenced and abandoned. As to the six old eighteen pounders that formed the Battery of the Lower gun-deck, they did no Service Whatever: two out of three of them burst at the first fire, and killed almost all the men Who Were stationed to manage them. before this time too, Col. de Chamillard, Who Commanded a party of 20 soldiers on the poop had abandoned that Station, after having lost some of his men. I had now only two pieces of Cannon, nine pounders, on the Quarter deck that Were not silenced, and not one of the heavyer Cannon Was fired during the rest of the action. The purser, Mr. Mease, Who Commanded the guns on the Quarter deck, being dangerously Wounded in the head, I was obliged to fill his place, and With great difficulty rallied a few men, and Shifter over one of the Lee quarter-deck guns, So that We afterward played three pieces of 9 pounders upon the Enemy. The tops alone Seconded the fire of this little battery, and held out bravely during the Whole of the action; Especially the main top, Where

Lieut. Stack commanded. I directed the fire of one of the three Cannon against the main-mast, With double-headed Shot, While the other two Were exceedingly Well Served With Grape and Cannister Shot to Silence the Enemie's musquetry, and clear her decks, Which Was at last Effected. The Enemy Were, as I have Since understood, on the instant of Calling for quarters, When the Cowardice or treachery of three of my under officers induced them to Call to the Enemy. The English Commodore asked me if I demanded quarters, and I having answered him in the most determined negative, they renewed the battle with Double fury ; they Were unable to Stand the deck, but the fire of their Cannon, especially the lower battery, Which Was Entirely formed of 18 pounders, Was incessant, both Ships Were Set on fire in Various places, and the Scene was dreadful beyond the reach of Language. To account for the timidity of my three under officers, I mean the gunner, the carpenter, and the master-at-arms, I must observe that the two first Were Slightly Wounded, and as the Ship had received Various Shots under Water, and on of the pumps being Shot away, the Carpenter Expressed his fear that she Should Sin, and the other two concluded that She Was Sinking; Which occasioned the gunner to run aft on the poop without my Knowledge, to Strike the Colours. fortunately for me, a Cannon ball had done that before, by carrying away the ensign staff: he was therefore reduced to the necessity of Sinking, as he Supposed, or of Calling for quarter, and he preferred the Latter.

All this time the B. H. R. has Sustained the action alone, and the Enemy, though much Superior in force, Would have been Very glad to have got clear, as appears by their own acknowledgements, and by their having let go an anchor the instant that I laid them on board, by Which means they Would have escaped had I not made them well fast to the B. H. R.

At last, at half past 9 o'clock, the Alliance appeared, and I now thought the battle was at an End; but, to my utter astonishment, he discharged a broadside full into the stern of the B. H. R. We called to him for God's Sake to forbear firing into the B. H. R.; yet he passed along the off Side of the Ship and continued firing. There was no possibility of his mistaking the Enemie's Ship for the B. H. R., there being the most essential difference in their appearance and Construction; besides, it Was then full moon Light, and the Sides of the B. H. R. Were all black, while the Sides of the prizes Were yellow. yet, for the greater Security, I Shewed the Signal of our reconnoissance, by putting out three Lanthorns, one at the head, (Bow,) another at the Stern, (Quarter,) and the third in the middle, in a horizontal line. Every tongue Cried that he Was firing into the Wrong Ship, but nothing availed; he passed round, firing into the B. H. R.'s head, stern, and broadside, and by one of his Vollies Killed several of my best men, and mortally wounded a good officer on the forecastle. My Situation Was really deplorable. The B. H. R. received various Shot under Water from the Alliance; the Leack gained on the pump, and the fire increased much on board both Ships. Some officers persuaded me to strike, of Whose Courage and good sense I entertain an high opinion. My treacherous master-at-arms let Loose all my prisoners Without my Knowledge, and my prospect became gloomy indeed. I Would not, however, give up the point. The Enemie's main-mast begain to shake, their firing decreased, our Rather increased, and the British colours Were Struck at half an hour past 10 o'clock.

This prize proved to be the British Ship of War the Serapis, a New Ship of 44 guns, built on their most approved Construction, With two compleat batteries, one of them of 18 pounders, and Commanded by the brave Commodore Richard Pearson. I had yet two enemies to encounter far more formidable than the britons; I mean fire and Water. The Serapis Was attacked only by the first, but the B. H. R. Was assailed by both: there Was five feet Water in the hould, and Tho it Was moderate from the Explosion of so much gunpowder, yet the three pumps that remained Could With difficulty only Keep the Water from gaining. The fire broke out in Various parts of the Ship, in spite of all the Water that could be thrown to quench it, and at length broke out as low as the powder magazine, and Within a few inches of the powder. in that dilema, I took out the powder upon the deck, ready to be thrown overboard at the Last Extremity, and it was 10 o'clock the next day, the 24, before the fire Was entirely Extinguished. With respect to the situation of the B. H. R., the rudder Was Cut entirely off, the stern frame, and the transoms Were almost Entirely Cut away, the timbers, by the lower Deck especially, from the mainmast to the Stern, being greatly decayed with age, Were mangled beyond my power of description, and a person must have been an Eye-Witness to form a just idea of the tremendous scene of Carnage, Wreck, and ruin, that Every Where appeared. Humanity Cannot but recoil from the prospect of Such finished horror, and Lament that War Should produce Such fatal consequences.

After the Carpenters, as well as Capt. de Cottineau, and other men of Sense, had Well Examined and Surveyed the Ship, (Which Was not finished before five in the Evening,) I found every person to be Convinced that it Was impossible to keep the B.H.R. afloat so as to reach a port if the Wind Should increase, it being then only a Very moderate breeze. I had but Little time to remove my Wounded, which now became unavoidable, and Which Was effected in the Course of the night and the next morning. I Was determined to Keep the B. H. R. afloat, and, if possible, to bring her into port. For that purpose, the first lieutenant of the Pallas continued on board,

With a party of men to attend the pumps, With boats in Waiting ready to take them on board, in Case the Water Should gain on them too fast. The Wind augmented in the Night and the next day, on the 25, So that it Was impossible to prevent the good old Ship from Sinking. They did not abandon her till after 9 o'clock: the Water Was then up to the Lower deck; and a little after ten, I Saw With inexpressible grief the last glimpse of the B. H. R. No Lives were lost With the Ship, but it Was impossible to save the stores of any sort Whatever, I Lost even the best part of my Cloaths, books, and papers; and Several of my officers lost all their Cloaths and Effects.

Having thus Endeavoured to give a Clear and Simple relation of the Circumstances and Events that have attended the little armament under my com, I Shall freely Submit my Conduct therein to the Censure of my Superiors and the impartial public. I beg leave, however, to observe, that the force that Was put under my command Was far from being Well composed, and as the great majority of the actors in it have appeared bent on the pursuit of intrest only, I am Exceedingly sorry that they and I have been at all concerned. I am in the highest degree Sensible of the Singular attentions Which I have Experienced from the Court of France, Which I Shall remember With perfect gratitude until the End of my Life ; and Will always Endeavour to merit, while I Can, Consistent With my honour, Continue in the public Service. I must speak plainly. As I have been always honored With the full Confidence of Congress, and as I also flattered myself With Enjoying in Some measure the Confidence of the Court of France, I Could not but be astonished at the Conduct of M. de Chaumont, When, in the moment of my departure from Groa, he produced a paper, a Concordat, for me to Sign, in Common with the officers Whom I had Commissioned but a few days before. Had that paper, or Even a less dishonorable one, been proposed to me at the beginning, I would have rejected it With Just Contempt ; and the Word deplacement among others should have been necessary. I Cannot, however, Even now Suppose that he Was authorized by the Court to make Such a Bargain With me; Nor Can I Suppose that the minister of the marine meant that M. de Chaumont should Consider me merely as a Colleague With the Commanders of the other Ships, and Communicate to them not only all he Knew, but all he thought, respecting our destination and operations. M. de Chaumont has made me Various reproaches on account of the Expence of the B. H. R. wherewith I cannot think I have been justly chargeable. M. de Chamillard can attest that the B. H. R. Was at Last far from being well fitted or armed for War. If any person or persons Who have been charged With the Expense of that armament have acted Wrong, the fault must not be Laid to my charge. I had no authority to Superintend that armament, and the persons Who had authority Were So far from giving me What I thought necessary, that M. de Chaumont Even refused, among other things, to allow me Irons for securing the prisoners of War.

In Short, While my Life remains, if I have any Capacity to render good and acceptable Services to the Common Cause, no man Will Step Forth with greater cheerfulness and alacrity than myself, but I am not made to be dishonoured, nor can I accept of the half Confidence of any man living ; of Course I Cannot, Consistent With my honor and a prospect of Success, undertake future Expeditions, unless When the object and destination is communicated to me alone, and to no other person in the marine Line. In Cases Where troops are Embarked, a like confidence is due alone to their Commander in Chief. On no other Condition Will I ever undertake the Chief Command of a private Expedition; and when I do not Command in Chief, I have no desire to be in the secret.

Captain Cottineau Engaged the Countess of Scarborough and took her after an hour's action, while the B. H. R. Engaged the Serapis. The Countess of Scarborough is an armed ship of 20 six pounders, and Was Commanded by a King's officer. In the action, the Countess of Scarborough and the Serapis Were at a Considerable distance asunder ; and the Alliance, as I am informed, fired into the Pallas and Killed some men. If it Should be asked Why the Convoy Was Suffered to Escape, I must answer, that I Was myself in no condition to pursue, and that none of the rest Shewed any inclination, not even Mr. Ricot, who had held off at a distance to Windward during the Whole Action, and Witheld by force the pilot boat With my Lieutenant and 15 men. The Alliance too, Was in a State to pursue the fleet, not having had a Single man wounded, or a Single Shot fired at her from the Serapis, and only three that did execution from the Countess of Scarborough, at such a distance that one Stuck in the Side, and the other two just touched and then dropped into the Water. The Alliance killed one man only on board the Serapis. As Captain de Cottineau charged himself with manning and securing the prisoners of the Countess of Scarborough ; I think the escape of the Baltic fleet Cannot So Well be Charged to his account.

I should have mentioned, that the main-mast and mizen-top-mast of the Serapis fell overboard soon after the captain had come on board the B. H. R.

Upon the Whole, the captain of the Alliance has beheaved so Very Ill in Every respect, that I must complain loudly of his Conduct. He pretends that he is authorized to act independent of my command: I have been taught the Contrary ; but Supposing it to be so, his Conduct has been base and unpardonable. M. de Chamillard Will Explain the particulars. Either Captain Landais or myself is highly Criminal, and one or the other must be punished. I forbear to take any steps With him until I have the advice and approbation of your Excellency. I have been advised by all the officers of the Squadron to put M. Landais under arrest; but as I have postponed it So long, I Will bear With him a Little Longer until the return of my Express.

We this Day anchored here having, Since the action been tossed to and from by Contrary Winds. I Wished to have gained the Road of Dunkirk on account of our prisoners, but Was Overruled by the majority of my Colleagues. I Shall heasten up to Amsterdam, and there if I meet With no orders for my government, I Will take the advice of the French Ambassador. It is my present intention to have the Countess of Scarborough ready to transport the prisoners from hence to Dunkirk, unless it should be found more Expedient to deliver them to the English ambassador, taking his obligation to Send to Dunkirk, &c. immediately an Equal number of American prisoners. I am under Strong apprehensions that our object here will fail, and that thro' the imprudence of M. de Chaumont, who has Communicated Every thing he Knew or thought on the matter to persons Who Cannot help talking of it at a full table. This is the way he keeps State Secrets, tho' he never mentioned the affair to me.

I am ever, &c.
JNO. P. JONES.
His Excellency
BENJAMIN FRANKLIN,
ESQUIRE, &c. &c.

* * * * *

After the American Revolution, Jones served as a Rear Admiral in the service of Empress Catherine of Russia, but returned to Paris in 1790. He died in Paris at the age of 45 on July 18, 1792. He was buried in St. Louis Cemetery, which belonged to the French royal family. Four years later, France's revolutionary government sold the property and the cemetery was forgotten. American Ambassador Horace Porter began a systematic search for the grave in 1899. The burial place and Jones' body was discovered in April 1905. President Theodore Roosevelt sent four cruisers to bring it back to the U.S. On January 26, 1913, the remains of John Paul Jones were laid to rest in the crypt of the U.S. Naval Academy Chapel in Annapolis, Maryland.

Proud New Frigates

NATHAN MILLER

> Good discipline is considered by all who know anything of service as the vital part of a ship at war.
>
> —Captain Thomas Truxton

The Treaty of 1778 made France America's closest ally in the war for independence. It was the French fleet under Admiral Comte de Grasse that defeated the British in the Battle of the Chesapeake that sealed the fate of the British army at Yorktown in October 1781. The French Revolution of 1789 ended the close relationship America had enjoyed with Louis XVI. Debts the United States owed the French were denied after the revolutionary government came to power. In 1794 the United States signed the Jay Treaty with England further siding America with France's enemy. French privateers had been preying upon American merchant ships since the revolution began. Envoys from the U.S. government were sent to try and reach an accord in Paris. When those delegates were met with demands for tribute, negotiations with France ended. On July 7, 1798, the United States revoked all its former treaties with France and an undeclared naval war ensued.

Once again the fledgling American Navy was called into action. Captain Thomas Truxton commanded the frigate USS *Constellation* and would win fame and fortune for himself and his crew by defeating two French men of war including the frigate *L'Insurgente* on Febuary 9, 1799. Author Nathan Miller describes the history of this period and the classic engagement of the *Constellation* and *L'Insurgente* from his book *The Proud New Frigates.*

★ ★ ★ ★ ★

On the morning of September 20, 1797, while Britain was girding for an invasion, a new navy was making its appearance. A large and boisterous crowd had gathered at Edmund Hartt's shipyard in the North End of Boston to watch the launching of the U.S. Navy frigate *Constitution.* Shortly before noon, the tide reached flood, and Colonel George Claghorne, who had supervised the construction of the vessel, ordered the shoring timbers knocked out. A ragged cheer rose and then died. Instead of gliding gracefully into the water, the trim hull hung motionless on the ways. Claghorne ordered screw jacks and wedges applied to force the vessel to move, but she slid only a few feet before coming to a dead stop. Two days later another attempt was made to launch her, but this, too, ended in failure. Not until another month later, on October 21, 1797, did *Constitution* finally slip into the waters of Boston Harbor. A similar pattern of agonizingly fitful starts and stops marked the founding of the navy in which she served.

From the end of the War of Independence until the inauguration of George Washington as president in 1789, the United States had not been so much governed as maintained in caretaker status under the feeble Articles of Confederation enacted during the Revolution. There was no chief executive, and Congress functioned as little more than a council of ambassadors of an uneasy league of thirteen more or less sovereign republics. Funds were short, there was only a shadow of an army, and there was no navy at all. Moreover, most Americans had an inherent fear of a strong, centralized government, born out of the struggle for independence.

Once peace came, Yankee trading vessels carried the Stars and Stripes around the world. But no longer enjoying the protection of the British flag, they were prey for rapacious corsairs sailing from the Barbary states of Morocco, Algiers, Tunis, and Tripoli on the coast of North Africa. For two centuries these satrapies of the Ottoman Empire had levied tribute on the commerce of all nations. Unless paid bribes, they seized passing ships and enslaved their crews and passengers until they were ransomed. The Europeans paid the tribute, arguing only over the amount, not the principle. Britain and France could have ended these depredations, but allowed the pirates to operate against the trade of their rivals while their own ships were protected by their navies. Thus, the corsairs viewed the American merchant marine—the second largest in the world—as fair game because the new nation neither paid tribute nor possessed a navy to protect its ships.

In 1785, the year in which *Alliance,* the last ship of the Continental Navy, was sold, Algerian corsairs captured two American vessels and enslaved their crews. Thomas Jefferson and John Adams, the American ministers to Paris and London, respectively, who had the task of negotiating treaties with the Barbary states, agreed that in the long run it would be cheaper to organize a navy to protect American shipping than to pay tribute. This, said Jefferson, would provide the government "with the safest of all instruments of coercion." But, as Adams noted, prospects for such a service were not bright owing to the lack of funds and sectional rivalries similar to those that delayed formation of the Continental Navy at the start of the Revolution. Consequently nothing was done to resist the demands of these seagoing brigands.

The Constitution, which went into effect in 1789, authorized Congress to "to provide and maintain a navy," but during Washington's first term there was little discussion of the issue. In 1790 General Henry Knox, who as secretary of war dealt with such naval matters as these were, secured estimates of the cost of several frigates. The next year Secretary of State Jefferson recommended that a naval force be fitted out to deal with the Barbary pirates. The sole result of his recommendation and Knox's estimates was a Senate report suggesting that a navy be organized "as soon as the state of public finance will admit."

The eruption of war between Britain and France in 1793 brought matters to a head. A truce between Portugal and the Algerians, negotiated with British help, ended a Portuguese blockade of the Strait of Gibraltar that had kept the corsairs bottled up in the Mediterranean. Pirate ships suddenly swarmed into the Atlantic, and within two months captured eleven American ships and more than a hundred American sailors. Many Americans were convinced that the truce was part of a British plot to destroy American commerce with the Mediterranean. Britain claimed, however, that its Portuguese ally had lifted the blockade so she could use her ships for other purposes.

Reacting to the seizure of the American vessels, the House of Representatives approved, on January 2, 1794, a resolution stating that "a naval force adequate to the protection of the commerce of the United States against the Algerian corsairs ought to be provided." This resolution, approved by a margin of only two votes, was referred to a committee dominated by pronavy congressmen. Eighteen days later it recommended the construction of four frigates of forty-four guns and two ships of twenty guns at a total cost of six hundred thousand dollars. Debate on the resolution followed sectional lines. Northern and tidewater representatives supported creation of a navy; inland and southern members, with the exception of representatives of South Carolina mercantile interests, were opposed.

Opponents of the measure charged that a navy would only fatten the pockets of northern merchants, embroil the new nation in foreign adventures, be a drain on the public purse, and saddle the country with an ever-expanding naval establishment that would be a touchstone of tyranny. Supporters argued that if the nation had a navy it would no longer have to pay tribute or ransom, maritime insurance would be less costly, and inasmuch as a navy operated offshore, it could scarcely be an instrument of domestic tyranny. A navy, they said, would not only protect American commerce but also force the warring French and British to respect the nation's rights as a neutral.

This struggle over the navy was the first of a series of running battles between the newly emerging political parties that marked the early days of the republic. The Republicans, advocates of states' rights and southern agrarian interests and ancestors of today's Democrats, largely opposed the formation of a navy, while the Federalists, who favored a strong central government and were supported by the northern commercial interests, advocated a navy.

As finally approved on March 27, 1797, the Navy Act authorized the procurement of six frigates—four of forty-four guns and two of thirty-six guns—and provided for the number, pay, and rations of the officers and crews. But the measure contained a "poison pill." To ensure approval, its supporters accepted an amendment providing that work on the ships would be summarily halted if peace terms were concluded between the United States and the dey of Algiers. Shortly after the bill was passed—as if to emphasize the deep division over the navy—Congress authorized the expenditure of eight hundred thousand dollars to obtain a treaty with the Algerians and to ransom the American captives.

President Washington and General Knox decided to provide the navy with newly built ships rather than convert lubberly merchant vessels into warships. Writing to Joshua Humphreys, a prominent Philadelphia Quaker shipbuilder who had a hand in the design of the Continental Navy's first frigates, Knox suggested that "the vessels should combine such qualities of strength, durability, swiftness of sailing, and force, as to render them superior to any frigate belonging to the European powers." Lacking quantity, the new navy would emphasize quality. Several other men worked on the project, but the final designs were basically the work of Humphreys.

Longer, wider in beam, and with stout sides and fine lines, the larger of these vessels resembled cut-down ships of the line rather than any existing frigate. They were designed to outrun any ship they could not outfight and were intended as commerce raiders as well as combat vessels. Humphreys was influenced by French designs, but to strengthen his outsize ships, added original features, such as diagonal "riders," to the internal structure that had not been seen before. They had wider gangways on the spar deck, transforming it into an upper gun deck. Although the larger vessels were rated at forty-four guns, these "superfrigates" sometimes carried as many as sixty. Unlike the Royal Navy's standard thirty-two-gun frigate, which was armed with eighteen-pounders, the American vessels carried a main battery of twenty-four-pound guns on their gun decks and another complete tier of guns, usually carronades, on the spar, or flush upper deck, which made them virtual two-deckers.

To distribute the financial benefits of the construction program and to encourage popular support of the navy, the work of building and outfitting the ships was spread up and down the Atlantic coast to privately operated shipyards, establishing a pattern of distributing defense contracts for political reasons that has endured. *Congress,* of thirty-six guns, was built in Portsmouth, New Hampshire; *Constitution,* forty-four, at Boston; *President,* forty-four, at New York; *United States,* forty-four, at Philadelphia; *Constellation,* thirty-six, at Baltimore; and *Chesapeake,* forty-four, at Norfolk. Knox stipulated that the ships were to be built of live oak and red cedar, which were five times as durable as the white oak commonly used in America.

Work on the ships proceeded in fits and starts because there was no reserve of seasoned timber and because of a shortage of guns. Between three hundred and four hundred cannons were bought from British foundries to fill the gap. Unfortunately for the navy's advocates, a treaty was signed with the dey of Algiers in September 1795, and in compliance with the Navy Act of 1794, all work on the frigates was to be suspended immediately. President Washington strongly opposed the stoppage on grounds that it would be wasteful. While it was true that the cost of completing the ships would be higher than originally estimated, Washington noted, the price of peace was also high. It cost almost $1 million, including $525,000 in bribes and ransom, the gift to the Algerians of a custom-built thirty-six-gun frigate, and an annual tribute of $21,000 in naval stores. After considerable debate, Congress allowed the completion of two forty-fours and a thirty-six—*Constitution, United States,* and *Constellation.*

In the meantime, relations with France had become strained. Under the terms of the Treaty of Alliance of 1778, which brought the French into the

War of Independence, the United States agreed, in case of war between France and Britain, to help defend the French West Indies and throw open her ports to French privateers. The new French minister to the United States, Edmond Genêt, added to the tension through a series of unneutral acts, including arming privateers in American ports, meddling in domestic politics, and mounting filibustering expeditions against adjoining British and Spanish territory.

But with the Royal Navy dominating the sea lanes and with British troops, in defiance of the Treaty of Paris, occupying a line of forts along the western frontier, the new nation had no desire to risk a war with Britain by implementing the terms of the alliance, much to the anger of the French. Besides, America's sympathies were divided. Most ordinary Americans favored France because of their admiration for the French Revolution, while the more prosperous citizens, alarmed by the excesses of the revolutionary regime, sided with the British.

Yet no matter where their sympathies lay, the majority of Americans wanted to stay out of the war. Neutrality was profitable. Yankee farmers prospered as the French and British bid up the prices of foodstuffs and commodities. Shipowners reaped large profits carrying American goods to Europe, and gained a foothold in the trade with the French colonies in the Caribbean, from which they had been barred. To survive and prosper, the United States had to maintain a delicate balance between the belligerents. President Washington, who sympathized with the British, and Secretary of State Jefferson, who favored France, agreed that the Franco-American alliance of 1778 had outlived its usefulness and that neutrality was the best policy for the United States.

American anger was directed first at the British. Fighting for her life, Britain flatly refused to accept American arguments that neutral ships could trade freely with all the belligerents. The British contended that trade restricted in peacetime could not be open in time of war and seized goods carried in American ships from the Caribbean to France. Upward of 250 vessels may have been taken in the first year of the war. Moreover, Royal Navy captains used the right of search to impress likely hands into the king's service on grounds that they were really British subjects. It was a difficult thing to try to prove American citizenship in the face of a boarding party armed to the teeth and in search of prime seamen.

In 1794 Chief Justice John Jay, who was serving as a special envoy to Britain, negotiated a commercial treaty with the British. Under the terms of Jay's Treaty, the British relinquished the disputed frontier forts and opened the British home islands to American trade but gave no ground on American demands for the freedom of neutral trade. The treaty was unpopular in the United States, and Jay was hanged in effigy. Nevertheless, the agreement reduced tension between the two countries and the possibility that they might blunder into war. But reconciliation with the British complicated relations with France. The French Directory was aggrieved by Jay's treaty and tried to bully the United States into joining the war on their side. When the Americans refused, French commerce raiders harassed American shipping, seizing 312 vessels between October 1796 and June 1797.

As soon as John Adams, who had played a leading role in the organization of the Continental Navy, assumed the presidency on March 4, 1797, he called Congress into special session to deal with the crisis. "A Naval power, next to the militia, is the natural defense of the United States," he declared. Adams, a Federalist, sought authority to complete *Constitution, United States,* and *Constellation* and to procure several smaller vessels to help protect America's seaborne commerce. The Republicans, led by Jefferson, now vice president, suspected that Adams's request for approval of this naval program was but a step from a declaration of war against France and opposed the president's proposal. Nevertheless, with pronavy Federalist majorities in control of Congress, a new Navy Act was passed after acrimonious debate on July 1, 1797, enabling Adams to order the three frigates rushed to completion.

United States slid into the Delaware River on May 10. Work was speeded up on the other two ships, and *Constellation* was launched at Baltimore on September 7. After the two failures to get *Constitution* into the water, she joined the others six weeks later. Captains John Barry, Thomas Truxtun, and Samuel Nicholson, all veterans of the Continental Navy or successful privateersmen during the Revolution, had already been named to command the ships and helped supervise their construction. There were far more applicants for commissions in the new navy than berths, and would-be officers resorted to political influence to ensure appointment. The rules and regulations drafted by Adams for the Continental Navy were again put into effect. Building, arming, and maintaining the frigates cost about $2,510,730 from 1794 to 1798, but the savings in insurance charges paid by American shipowners during 1798 alone was estimated at $8,655,566—far more than the cost of the fleet.

In an attempt to head off a full-scale clash with France, Adams dispatched a three-man commission to Paris to negotiate an agreement with the Directory similar to the treaty Jay had reached with the British. For several months the commissioners were given the runaround, but just as they were packing up to return home, they were approached by three representatives of Charles Maurice de Talleyrand-Périgord, the apostate Catholic bishop who had become French foreign minister. These agents, accompanied by a woman—without whom no European intrigue was complete—demanded a $250,000 bribe for Talleyrand and a large loan to the French government as a prerequisite for negotiations. The Americans flatly rejected the proposal. One, Charles C. Pinckney, a South Carolina Federalist, is supposed to have declared, "No! No! Not a sixpence!," which was inflated into the patriotic "Millions for defense, but not one cent for tribute!"—even though the nation was paying tribute to the Barbary states.

When Adams issued a report in which the French agents were identified only as "X," "Y," and "Z," war fever swept the country. Although most leaders of the Federalist party wanted an all-out war with France so that New Orleans and Florida might be taken from France's ally Spain, Adams limited the struggle to a naval war. Beginning in early 1798, Congress appropriated new funds for the seemingly endless task of outfitting the three frigates already launched; ordered work resumed on the three left unfinished since the end of the Algerian crisis; and empowered the president to obtain an additional two dozen smaller ships. Logically, a declaration of a state of hostilities should have followed, but neither the United States nor France observed that formality. As a result, the two-and-a-half-year conflict that ensued was known as the Quasi-War.

The United States had acquired a navy—and a war in which it was to be used—but had no plans for deploying it. This was remedied on April 30, 1798, when Adams signed a bill creating the Department of the Navy. Benjamin Stoddert, a merchant and loyal Federalist living in Georgetown, then part of Maryland, was named the first secretary of the navy.[1] The choice was a good one. Stoddert was a wounded veteran of the Revolution, and later secretary to the Continental Board of War, predecessor of the War Department. Thus he was familiar with military logistics as well as ship design and construction, and had a smattering of knowledge of matters pertaining to the operation of a fleet. One officer called him "a man of few words." To assist him the new secretary had a chief clerk, Charles W. Goldsborough, who was to hold the post for almost fifty years; a half dozen junior clerks; and naval agents at the various ports to supervise construction and purchase supplies. In Philadelphia, the Navy Office, as it was commonly called, initially transacted its business at 139 Walnut Street and then at the corner of Eighth and Chestnut Streets.

[1]Adams's first choice, George Cabot of Boston, refused the post.

Under Stoddert's stewardship the U.S. Navy eventually grew to fifty-four vessels, including new vessels, converted merchantmen, revenue cutters, gifts from the patriotic citizens of seaport towns, and craft captured from the French. Navy yards were opened at Portsmouth, New Hampshire; New York; and Norfolk, Virginia. Stoddert also began work on a dozen seventy-four-gun ships, but they were never completed. At peak strength, "Stoddert's Navy" numbered about 750 officers and some 6,000 men, plus another 1,100 officers and men in the Marine Corps, which was established in July 1798. There was no difficulty in recruiting seamen because there were few privateers to compete for their services because French commerce was almost nonexistent. Unlike the Royal Navy, seaman signed on for a fixed enlistment, usually a year, commencing from the time when their ship left port. Able seamen were paid $17 a month—triple the rate in the British service.

Who were these men? Little information about them has survived, but certain conclusions can be drawn based on studies of merchant seamen at this time.[2] Most were young—running from the late teens to the late twenties—and remained at sea for only about fifteen years. Nearly 18 percent were black, probably freedmen, at a time when free blacks totaled only 2.5 percent of the American population. Blacks were allowed to enlist in the navy and were not segregated on board ship, although they were not accepted into the Marine Corps. Foreigners, especially English deserters from the Royal Navy, sometimes made up half the crews.

The French, blockaded for the most part in Brest and the Mediterranean by the Royal Navy, sent few large warships across the Atlantic. Instead they relied on a war against trade—the *guerre de course*—conducted by a handful of frigates and swarms of privateers. Commerce raiders darted out of Caribbean ports and plundered American shipping almost at will. Some were licensed by Victor Hugues, the "Caribbean Robespierre." To meet this threat, Stoddert concentrated his ships in coastal waters. Thus the story of the ensuing war is told not in heroic battles between great fleets but in the safe passage of convoys, the recapture of vessels taken by the French, and the driving off of commerce raiders from the major shipping lanes.

French privateer skippers were so brazen that they operated within sight of the American coast. In fact, the first prize captured by America's new navy was taken just outside Egg Harbor, New Jersey. She

[2]See Dye, "Early American Merchant Seafarers," *Proceedings* of the American Antiquarian Society 120. Also Bolster, *Black Jacks: African-American Seamen in the Age of Sail.*

was the twelve-gun schooner *La Croyable,* which had taken several Yankee vessels before being captured on July 7, 1798, by the twenty-gun sloop-of-war *Delaware,* to the surprise of the French captain, who was unaware that the Americans even had a navy. *Delaware* was a converted merchantman under the command of Captain Stephen Decatur Sr., an old privateersmen whose soon-to-be famous son was a midshipman on the frigate *United States.* Taken into the navy as *Retaliation,* the schooner was recaptured four months later by the French, and then again by the Americans.

These coastal operations allowed the captains of the new frigates to work out the problems inherent in any experimental design. Some officers were wary of these vessels because they thought them too large and too clumsy to handle easily, but with time and experience the ships achieved their full potential. Stoddert assigned twenty-one ships, including *United States, Constitution,* and *Constellation,* to the West Indies, with orders to "rid those seas . . . of French commissioned armed vessels. . . . We have nothing to fear but inactivity." By the end of 1798 the U.S. Navy had become so vigilant that the French retreated to the Caribbean.

Stoddert was convinced that concerted action by strong squadrons would be more effective than random patrols by one or two vessels, and organized his ships into four squadrons. Varying in size from three to ten ships, these units were commanded by Captains John Barry, Thomas Truxtun, Stephen Decatur Sr., and Thomas Tingley. To keep the ships on station as long as possible, without ruining their sailing qualities by loading them down with provisions or becoming dependent on the rapacious West Indies merchants, Stoddert sent out supply ships from the United States, and over time the U.S. Navy developed a long-legged capacity uncommon among the world's navies.

The assignment of these squadrons to the Caribbean brought the Americans into an area where war had been under way since 1793—and whether they liked it or not, they became unofficial allies of the British. The Royal Navy deployed four to five times more men-of-war in the West Indies than the U.S. Navy, and British ships chased and fought the same French cruisers and privateers. Both navies escorted each other's merchantmen, and exchanged recognition signals, while the American squadrons operated from British bases.

No man better personified the increasing professionalism and aggressive spirit of the fledgling navy than Thomas Truxtun, the captain of *Constellation.* Born on Long Island in 1755, he went to sea at age twelve. Three years later he was snatched from the deck of a merchantman and pressed into a British man-of-war. The youngster's abilities attracted the attention of his captain, who offered Truxtun the promise of advancement if he remained in the Royal Navy. Truxtun obtained his release, however, and by the time he was twenty had become a captain in the merchant service. During the War of Independence he captained several successful privateers and emerged from the conflict with a respectable fortune, which he invested with excellent results in the newly established China trade. Truxtun was not only a capable seaman but something of a scholar, too. In 1794, the same year in which he was commissioned a captain in the U.S. Navy, he published a treatise on navigation and wind currents. This was followed by books on signaling and naval tactics.

Under Truxtun's command, *Constellation* was a taut ship. Some of her crew, unused to the strict demands of the naval service, complained, but he was not a brutal man. Rather than having malefactors flogged, Truxtun preferred to withhold their rum rations.[3] One evening Midshipman David Porter was invited to dine with the captain and made the mistake of protesting the harsh treatment he had received from the captain and the frigate's first lieutenant, John Rodgers. He added that he was giving thought to resigning from the service.

"Why, you young dog!" Truxtun thundered. "If I can help it you shall never leave the navy! Swear at you? Damn it, sir—every time I do that you go up a round on the ladder of promotion! As for the first lieutenant's blowing up at you every day, why, sir, 'tis because he loves you and would not have you grow up a conceited young coxcombe. Go . . . and let us have no more whining."

Cruising alone off the island of Nevis at about noon on February 9, 1799, *Constellation* fell in with a large vessel that hoisted American colors as the Yankee frigate sailed up to inspect her. The stranger failed to respond to American and British recognition signals, and Truxtun was convinced she was a French man-of-war. As if to confirm his suspicions, the vessel broke out the French tricolor. She was *Insurgente,* a forty-gun frigate reputed to be one of the fastest ships in the French Navy. Although she carried four more guns than *Constellation,* her broadsides were less powerful. As the two vessels maneuvered for position, a sudden squall carried away the Frenchmen's main-topmast.

As soon as *Constellation*'s starboard guns began to bear on the enemy vessel, Truxtun unleashed a broadside into her. The French ship returned fire with spirit and swerved toward her adversary. "Stand by to

[3]One of the chief malcontents, Truxtun discovered, was an Englishman who proved to be one of the *Hermione* mutineers and was serving in *Constellation* under a false name. He was turned over to the Royal Navy and hanged.

board!" the French captain called to his men. Truxtun was alert to the danger, and his handier ship swept ahead of *Insurgente* and across her bow, pouring a murderous raking fire into her opponent's hull at close range. The battle raged for about an hour and a half, until the French vessel was a shambles. *Constellation* had just crossed her stern to rake her again when the French hauled down their colors.

A boarding party reported *Insurgente* "resembled a slaughter-house," with seventy of her crew dead or wounded. The French had fired high, and although *Constellation* was much cut up aloft, her total casualties were only one dead and two wounded.[4] *Insurgente* was taken into the U.S. Navy.[5] In his account of the action, Truxtun related that the French captain charged that "I have caused a War with France" and added, "if so, I am glad of it, for I detest Things being done by Halves."

Just about a year latter, *Constellation* engaged in another memorable battle. Following the encounter with *Insurgente,* Truxtun, dissatisfied with his vessel's sailing qualities, had altered her armament. The twenty-four-pound long guns of her main battery were replaced by eighteen-pounders, and to compensate for the loss of weight of metal, he substituted thirty-two-pound carronades for the long twelves on the quarterdeck. *Constellation* was now relatively weaker at long range but more powerful close in. She was sailing off Guadeloupe on February 1, 1800, when a lookout sighted a large ship on the horizon. Truxtun surmised that she was *Vengeance,* a fifty-four-gun French frigate, which he had been warned was in the area.

Although the French vessel outgunned *Constellation,* the enemy declined to give battle and clapped on all sail. Following a day-long chase that ran on into the darkness, the Yankee frigate closed with her. Night fell, and the men on both ships stood to their guns in the eerie light cast by the battle lanterns as the distance between the two vessels narrowed to little more than pistol shot. Without waiting to be hailed, the French fired first. *Constellation*'s guns, double-shotted at Truxtun's command, immediately replied with a broadside that slammed into *Vengeance*'s hull.

To make up for the deficiency in firepower, the American gun crews were ordered to "load and fire as fast as possible." In better trim than previously, *Constellation* repeatedly blocked attempts by the French to rake. Over the next five hours the two ships traded broadsides, and both suffered severe damage. The battle was "as close and obstinate an action as was ever

[4]The dead man was not a battle casualty but had been run through by Lieutenant Andrew Sterett—perhaps unnecessarily—for deserting his post at one of the guns.

[5]A year later, *Insurgente* was lost at sea with all her crew of 340 men.

fought between two ships of war," said an American officer. At close range, *Constellation*'s carronades wreaked havoc on her opponent.

Shortly before 1:00 A.M. Truxtun reported that "the Enemy's fire was completely silenced." Believing *Vengeance* had struck, he ordered *Constellation* laid alongside her, only to discover that his own mainmast was "totally unsupported by rigging." Truxtun broke off the action and made a last-minute effort to put up new rigging, but it was too late. The mast toppled into the sea, taking with it a midshipman and three topmen. In the confusion, the shattered French frigate limped off into the darkness, with her crew at the pumps. Before arriving at Curaçao, she lost her mainmast, foremast, and mizzen-topmast. An American prisoner reported that she had been hit nearly two hundred times, with several shots plowing through both sides of her hull. In his report the French captain described *Constellation* as a two-decker—quite a compliment to the fighting qualities of the Yankee frigate and her officers and men.

Before the Quasi-War petered out, several other American naval vessels gave a good account of themselves, especially the twelve-gun schooners *Enterprise* and *Experiment.* In a single cruise in 1800, *Enterprise* captured seven French armed vessels, including a large fourteen-gun privateer. Later that year she bagged thirteen more vessels along with three hundred prisoners. *Experiment* was almost as lucky, capturing two privateers as well as seizing several American merchantmen that had been taken by the French. The frigate *Boston,* of twenty-eight guns, pounded the French corvette *Berceau,* twenty-four, into submission in a vigorous five-hour fight in which both vessels were repeatedly forced to draw off for repairs. The American ascendancy in the Caribbean was reflected by a sharp drop in insurance rates for merchantmen traversing this area.

Having reaped such success, Stoddert settled on a more ambitious program of operations. Once the hurricane season hit the West Indies in 1799, he planned to send *Constitution* and *United States* to ravage the coast of France. The plan was a good one and might have produced dramatic results, but delays ashore prevented it from being carried out. Later, under the prodding of merchants doing business in the East Indies, the thirty-two-gun frigate *Essex,* built by public subscription by the citizens of Essex County, Massachusetts, was ordered to escort a convoy to Java, cruise for privateers in Sunda Strait, and then return home with another convoy. Under the command of Captain Edward Preble, she was the first American warship to cross the equator, double the Cape of Good Hope, and show the flag in the East Indies. U.S. Navy ships also supported the Haitian revolutionary regime of Toussaint L'Overture in his battles with the French for the island's freedom.

In the meantime, President Adams had begun negotiations with France for an end to hostilities. Leaders of the Federalist Party wished the war to continue, but Adams unselfishly put the nation's welfare above that of his party. Even though he fully realized that peace would result in the collapse of the Federalists' popularity and probably cost him reelection, he pressed ahead with the negotiations. Seven months of talks ended when the French, who recognized that the conflict was driving the United States into the arms of Britain, gave up their insistence that the Treaty of Alliance of 1778 was still in force and accepted the American view of neutral rights. On the other side, the United States dropped its claim for twenty million dollars in reimbursements for damages inflicted on American commerce. The settlement was unpopular, and as Adams had foreseen, he was defeated by Thomas Jefferson in 1800. But he was unbowed and regarded the successful conclusion of the war and the abrogation of the 1778 treaty as triumphs of his presidential team.

Before the Federalists relinquished control of the government, they took steps to protect the navy from the budgetary ax certain to be swung by the incoming Republican administration. On March 3, 1801, the day before the new president was inaugurated, Congress approved an act providing for a peacetime naval establishment. Based on Secretary Stoddert's recommendations, it authorized the president to dispose of the fleet but ordered the retention of the following frigates: *United States, Constitution, President, Chesapeake, Philadelphia, Constellation, New York, Boston, Adams, Essex, John Adams,* and *General Greene.* Six of the ships to be retained were to be kept in commission, while the rest were to be laid up.

With exception of 9 captains, 36 lieutenants, and 150 midshipmen, all the officers were to be dismissed from the service with four months' pay, although Stoddert had recommended the formation of a reserve of officers on half pay, following the practice of the Royal Navy. Frigates on active duty were allowed only two-thirds of their usual complements. These reductions were drastic, but as Charles Goldsborough said, "the existence of the [naval] establishment could be preserved by no other means than by reducing it to its lowest possible scale."

Nevertheless, for the U.S. Navy, the undeclared naval war with France had been a success. While some of the American commanders left over from the Continental Navy had proved superannuated, many had served with distinction. American ships and seamen had proven their worth in battle and provided protection for American trade. Benjamin Stoddert, with only a minimal staff and resources, had effectively established the navy as a fighting force with some claim to permanence. In all these activities, however, the U.S. Navy's secret ally was the Royal Navy, whose blockade of Europe denied the French Navy free movement to the theater of war in the Caribbean.

★ ★ ★ ★ ★

The Quasi-War ended with the Treaty of Mortefontaine that made for the return captured ships and established reparations to the owners. It also re-opened trade between the United States and France that would later be the cause for dispute with Great Britain leading into the War of 1812. Captain Thomas Truxton retired from the Navy in 1800.

Glory, from *A Rage for Glory*

JAMES TERTIUS DE KAY

> Our country! In her intercourse with foreign nations,
> may she always be in the right; but our country, right or wrong.
> —Captain Stephen Decatur

Stephen Decatur came from the ranks of able seamen of the U.S. Navy. In the Quasi-War against France he displayed such ability he was promoted to lieutenant in 1799. His chance for glory would come two years later with the arrival of Thomas Jefferson to the White House. For many years the United States had been paying tribute to the Barbary states of Algiers, Tunis, and Tripoli to allow American ships safe passage through the Mediterranean. Having just established a permanent navy to fight the French, Jefferson refused to continue the tributary payments to the Barbary pirates. A state of war with Tripoli followed, and Jefferson dispatched a small fleet of frigates under Edward Preble to protect American interests in the region. They blockaded ports and made raids along the enemy coast.

In October 1803, the USS *Philadelphia* ran aground while patrolling outside Tripoli harbor and its captain and crew taken hostage. Stephen Decatur led a small detachment of sailors, disguised as Arabs on a captured vessel that had been taken into the U.S. Navy and renamed the *Intrepid*, on a night raid into Tripoli harbor. Their mission was to board the *Philadelphia* and set her on fire to deny her use by the enemy. It was a courageous event British Admiral Lord Nelson is said to have later called "the most bold and daring act of the age." Tertius de Kay wrote the acclaimed biography of Stephan Decatur, *A Rage for Glory,* and in the following chapter describes the famous raid.

★ ★ ★ ★ ★

On Tuesday, November 1, 1803, Decatur once again passed through the Pillars of Hercules and into the Mediterranean, dropping anchor in Gibraltar after a notably uneventful crossing of thirty-four days from Boston. It had been a little over six months since he had hastily left for home to escape arrest on the charge of murder. Now he was returning in temporary command of the spanking new brig *Argus,* of eighteen guns, and carrying with him thirty thousand dollars in gold and silver for the use of the American squadron and its new commodore, Edward Preble.

Decatur remained in Gibraltar for two weeks, occupied in turning over the *Argus* to his friend and superior, Lieutenant Isaac Hull, and assuming command of the older and smaller schooner *Enterprise,* of twelve guns. It was not until November 12 that Commodore Preble arrived in the harbor on board his flagship, the *Constitution,* and Decatur was able to report to him in person. He had already heard stories from the other officers of the squadron of Preble's determination to bring the war directly to the Tripolitanians, and was much encouraged by the meeting. Preble was an irascible, strongly opinionated Down-East Yankee who made no effort to curb his short temper or hide his aggressive nature. His fighting spirit contrasted sharply with that of his two predecessors, and Decatur and the squadron's other junior officers took heart.

But no sooner had Preble arrived than he disappeared again, setting sail the next day to deliver the American consul to Algiers. Before departing he ordered Decatur to meet him at the new American command post at Syracuse, where he planned to put together his campaign against Yusuf Karamanli. What neither Decatur nor Preble knew at the time was that a disaster had just occurred a thousand miles to the east that would drastically alter the balance of power in the Mediterranean and render all the American commodore's war plans irrelevant.

On October 31, the day before Decatur's arrival at Gibraltar, Captain William Bainbridge was returning the frigate USS *Philadelphia* to her blockading position off the stormy shores of Tripoli. For several days the wind had been blowing strongly from the west, and had driven the ship a considerable distance off station. Now Bainbridge was taking advantage of a fair breeze to run her down toward the town again.

Around nine o'clock in the morning, with the minarets of Tripoli just visible on the horizon, lookouts spotted a vessel inshore and to windward, standing for the harbor. Bainbridge was eager to overhaul the stranger—there was prize money to be made from such captures—but he was initially reluctant to take his deep drafted ship into uncharted waters that might well mask dangerous shoals. But the temptation of a possible capture was too strong to resist, and eventually Bainbridge overcame his doubts and decided to risk it. He gave the orders to make sail and give chase.

Another captain might have been more cautious, but William Bainbridge had his own reasons for taking a more aggressive course. In his five years of active duty he had somehow managed to compile the most woefully lackluster record of any officer in the navy, and he was eager to clear his reputation.

Soon after receiving his commission as a lieutenant, he had been put in command of the USS *Retaliation*. She was subsequently taken by the French, and Bainbridge became the first American naval officer forced to strike his flag to an enemy.

An even greater humiliation lay in store a year later, when he was given command of a frigate, the USS *George Washington,* with orders to deliver an annual tribute of gold and naval stores to the dey of Algiers. After Bainbridge discharged his cargo the dey demanded the use of his ship to carry an embassy to the ruler of the Ottoman Empire in Constantinople. Bainbridge vigorously refused, protesting that American warships could not be used as common freighters by foreign potentates. But Bainbridge had made the mistake of mooring his ship under the guns of the dey's shore batteries. If he attempted to raise anchor and depart in defiance of the dey's demands, his frigate would be blown out of the water. As the realization of his tactical blunder finally became clear, Bainbridge was forced to change his tune. Reluctantly, he gave in and agreed to do the dey's bidding. After loading an exotic cargo of wild animals, harem slaves, and diplomatic representatives into the *George Washington,* the dey then added insult to injury by insisting that Bainbridge replace the American flag at the main truck with the Algierian standard. Again Bainbridge protested, but again he was forced to capitulate. Once more an American officer had been forced to strike his colors, and once more that officer was William Bainbridge.

The navy forgave him in both instances, but Bainbridge was sensitive to the fact that he now had two formidable black marks against his name, and if he wanted to wipe them away it behooved him to improve his record. It was almost certainly such a mind-set that impelled him to take an unwarranted risk that morning, and to give chase to an otherwise unimportant Arab trader.

Bainbridge quickly discovered that chasing that particular quarry and overhauling her were two quite different things. After a frustrating two hours in pursuit, the *Philadelphia* had made only the barest headway, and a little before eleven o'clock, seeing no other chance of overtaking the stranger in the short time that remained before she reached the safety of the enemy harbor, he opened fire with his eighteen-pounders. He continued firing for almost an hour, but it was at long range, and his men scored no hits. Bainbridge continued to be anxious about having committed his ship to uncharted waters and ordered three separate leadsmen to make constant soundings, to insure the frigate did not run aground. The leadsmen regularly reported depths of anywhere from seven to ten fathoms—roughly forty to sixty feet—as the water shoaled or deepened. The *Philadelphia*'s normal draft was eighteen and one-half feet forward and twenty and one-half feet aft, so the ship seemed in no danger.

By half past eleven the two vessels had moved considerably to the west and the town of Tripoli now lay in plain sight about three miles distant. Bainbridge, concerned that he was still in uncharted waters, decided to give up the chase. He ordered the helm aport to haul her directly off the land and into deeper water, but it was already too late. Even as the ship was coming up fast to the wind, and before she had lost any of her way, she struck a hidden reef and shot up on it, lifting the suddenly motionless frigate five to six feet out of the water.

The disaster had come upon them so quickly that it took a moment for those on the quarterdeck to absorb just how hopeless their situation had suddenly become. To be stranded on such a coast, in plain sight of the enemy and with no other vessel to bring aid, was nothing short of calamitous.

Bainbridge watched the Arab vessel he had so recently been chasing double the edge of the shoal and sail safely into the harbor, apparently interested only in escaping. But others had heard the American guns, and now nine Tripolitanian gunboats came out to investigate. The situation was perilous in the extreme, and Bainbridge recognized there was not a moment to be lost. The little Arab gunboats might appear insignificant in comparison to the looming frigate, but they would be able to attack with impunity as soon as they understood that the *Philadelphia* was immobilized.

In a desperate attempt to lighten ship, the crew began smashing open the water casks and pumping out the flooded hold, and throwing almost all the guns overboard, leaving only a few for defense. The anchors were the next to go, along with the huge, heavy cables that held them. Bainbridge ordered his men to chop down the foremast, which went crashing into the sea, carrying with it all its sails and rigging. But the ship remained stubbornly embedded in the sandy shoal.

By now the Tripolitanian gunboats had come within range, and tentatively opened fire. The Americans answered with the few guns that remained in the ship. For the moment, they were enough to keep the enemy boats at a respectful distance. As yet, the Arabs had no inkling of the desperate conditions on board the *Philadelphia*. The business of lightening the frigate continued for several hours.

By midafternoon it finally occurred to the Tripolitanians that they had the upper hand. They grew bolder and crossed the stern of the frigate, taking a position on her starboard quarter where they could fire at will, while it was impossible for the *Philadelphia* to bring a single gun to bear.

Night was coming on. With every passing minute the gunboats grew still bolder. Other boats were seen approaching from the town. Bainbridge, after consulting with his officers, saw no recourse but surrender, to save the lives of his people. He ordered the ship's signal books destroyed and the ship scuttled. The magazine was drowned, holes were bored in the ship's bottom, the pumps choked. About five o'clock he signaled his surrender. Any captain must lose heart at such a time, but one can only imagine Bainbridge's feelings, knowing that this was now the third time an American warship had been forced to strike her colors, and on all three occasions he was the man responsible.

Commodore Preble did not learn of the loss of the *Philadelphia* until November 24, three weeks after it occurred, when his flagship fell in with the Royal Navy frigate *Amazon* off the coast of Sardinia, and British officers apprised him of all the sorry details. In a single staggering blow Preble had lost half his frigates and a full quarter of his firepower. All his carefully developed plans for humbling Tripoli were suddenly thrown into confusion, and the future of his squadron's Mediterranean cruise looked decidedly grim.

Losing the ship was bad enough, but there were other distressing ramifications that vastly increased Preble's problems. The bashaw now held over three hundred new hostages and could demand almost any ransom within his imagination. He would now be encouraged to continue fighting no matter what the cost. The United States could not ignore the suffering of its own people, and would be forced to take him seriously.

The British had still worse news for Preble. The scuttling of the *Philadelphia* had been handled so hastily and imperfectly that, when a storm raised the water level a few days after the grounding of the vessel, the Tripolitanians had been able to float her off the sandbar on which she had foundered, patch her up, and bring her within the protection of the harbor forts. Then they went back and fished up her guns from where they had been cast overboard and restored them to their carriages, and once more the *Philadelphia* rode proudly on the waves. All she needed was a new foremast and she could become the most powerful vessel in Yusuf Karamanli's fleet, ready to cruise against the Americans as soon as the mild season returned. In the meantime, she lay at anchor in the middle of Tripoli harbor, the most valuable prize ever taken by the Barbary pirates.

"It distresses me beyond description," Preble wrote grimly to the secretary of the navy. "Would to God that the officers and crew of the *Philadelphia* had one and all determined to prefer death to slavery."

Shortly after hearing the dire news, Preble shaped course for his base at Syracuse. Off Cape Passaro he fell in with Decatur's *Enterprise,* bound for the same destination, and in the course of a courtesy visit to the flagship, Preble told Decatur of the *Philadelphia*'s fate. The two vessels arrived in Syracuse in company, and not long afterward they left again, once more in company, headed for Tripoli to reconnoiter the *Philadelphia*.

Once off the North African coast, Decatur left the deep-drafted *Constitution* safely out to sea and ran the little *Enterprise* close in to the coast to scout the harbor and determine the position of the *Philadelphia*. The sight of the frigate, dwarfing every other warship around her, and lying directly under the protection of the bashaw's land batteries, was a sobering vision. Decatur was much moved by the sight. He had strong personal ties to the ship. As a youth he had witnessed her construction only a few city blocks from his home. Later, his father had served as her first captain. Now, suddenly disgraced, she belonged to his country's enemies, ready to be turned into the most formidable terror in the Mediterranean. Having made note of the *Philadelphia*'s location and of the vessels guarding her, he returned to the open sea to fall in with the waiting Preble. After reporting to the commodore, he made a suggestion. He asked to be allowed to take the *Enterprise* into the harbor and destroy the *Philadelphia.* Preble was sympathetic—Decatur's aggressive spirit matched his own—but he rejected the idea as too hazardous. Still, he agreed that some such plan would have to be worked out, and promised Decatur that since he was the first to make the offer, he should be the one to carry it out.

It was during this brief scouting expedition that an apparently minor piece of good fortune fell the Americans' way, when they managed to overhaul and capture the *Mastico,* a small four-gun ketch of sixty or seventy tons, with seventy Tripolitanians on board, including forty-two slaves. She was an older vessel that had already seen much service, and was not likely to bring much in the way of prize money. But at the moment neither Preble nor Decatur was much interested in prize money. They saw a more valuable use for her. She was indistinguishable from hundreds of coastal traders in the western Mediterranean, and could sail into Tripoli harbor without anyone taking notice. She would be the means by which they would destroy the *Philadelphia*.

Once back in Syracuse, Preble had his carpenters examine the *Mastico*. They reported her basically sound and the commodore, using his discretion as squadron commander, bought her into the American navy and renamed her *Intrepid*. Over the month of January 1804, plans for the raid were worked out in greatest secrecy, for fear that word might get back to the bashaw. Winter was the stormy season in the Mediterranean, and the weather continued foul throughout the month. It was not until February 3, 1804, that Preble judged conditions favorable to send the little *Intrepid* in.

As soon as he had his orders, Decatur mustered the crew of the *Enterprise*—most of whom had no inkling of the secret preparations that had been going on for weeks—and outlined the plan that he and Preble had developed for the *Intrepid*. He warned them of the dangers involved, which were very real, and called for volunteers. Without hesitation, every member of the ship's company, officers, men, and boys, stepped forward in a body. The unquestioning enthusiasm of his crew to volunteer for such a hazardous mission remains one of the most telling aspects of the whole venture. It speaks volumes about Decatur's style of leadership, the high morale of his men, and their great trust in him.

Later that day, from the quarterdeck of the *Constitution*, Commodore Preble watched the little *Intrepid* sail off in company with the brig *Siren*, which would serve as her support vessel. The venture was dangerous, and possibly harebrained to boot, but the destruction of the *Philadelphia* was critical to the mission of the squadron, and for all the perils involved it was the best idea that anyone could come up with. He could only hope that not too many brave men would die in the endeavor. "I shall hazard much to destroy her," he wrote to the secretary of the navy, "it will undoubtedly cost many lives, but it must be done."

Preble had bestowed upon Stephen Decatur the greatest gift that was within his power to grant. Now he would see what the young man would do with it.

Late in the afternoon of February 16, 1804, a weatherbeaten ketch, similar to any number of Arab and Maltese traders plying the coast of North Africa, made her way toward the eastern entry of Tripoli harbor. She appeared in need of caulking and a coat of paint, and there was nothing about her to excite the curiosity of the sentries on the guard boats and in the forts that protected the harbor. The nondescript character of the ketch, and the fact that she aroused not the least interest, was just as well for those on board, for had the Tripolitanians been aware of the true nature of the vessel, they would most certainly have made short work of her.

Near her helm stood two men in native dress. They were Stephen Decatur and a Sicilian pilot named Salvadore Catalano, who had been recruited for the venture because he was familiar with the harbor and spoke the patois used by the sailors along the North African coast. There were perhaps another five or six crewmen in native dress visible along with the pair at the helm, but altogether they represented only a small fraction of the boat's company. A dozen or so men lay prone on the deck, hidden behind the bulwarks, and down below another sixty or so volunteers, armed to the teeth, were making the best of it among the water casks and hogsheads of combustibles crammed into the noisome hold.

As night closed in there was still enough light for Decatur to make out the town of Tripoli, two miles to the west, a collection of sun-bleached forts and minarets dominated by the bashaw's palace. In the heart of the harbor loomed the ship they had come to destroy. The *Philadelphia* was moored in such a way as to serve as the harbor's principal defense. She bristled with twenty-eight eighteen-pounder long guns and sixteen thirty-two-pounder carronades. Decatur had to assume that all the guns were loaded and that there might be as many as two hundred Tripolitanians on board, since it would take at least that number to fight the guns. He knew there were another 115 heavy guns in the forts surrounding the harbor and probably fifty more on the cruisers and galleys that lay at anchor within range of the *Philadelphia.*

The Americans hidden in the little *Intrepid* were fully aware of the dangers surrounding them. Their chances of death, dismemberment, and slavery were probably far higher than their chances of a safe return to base, but there was such a glorious aura of derring-do about the enterprise, such a sense that they were participants in a grand storybook adventure, that it buoyed their spirits and crowded out any fears that might otherwise have sapped their enthusiasm.

Decatur had drilled his crew repeatedly on the particulars of each man's assignment—where he was to go once they boarded the *Philadelphia,* what he was to accomplish, how he was to do it. For all his zeal, there must have been a part of Decatur that recoiled at the idea of destroying such a ship. Almost certainly, during the weeks of planning for the raid, he would have at least considered the possibility of trying to save the *Philadelphia,* of manning her helm and bearing her away in triumph from under the noses of the enemy, that she might fight another day. But just as certainly he would have recognized that such a romantic scheme was totally out of the question. The ship was dismantled, and her bowsprit and foremast gone. Under the best conditions, the mouth of the harbor was a difficult passage for such a large ship, and it would have taken a dozen or more whaleboats to tow her to sea. The only practical solution was to burn her.

Behind the *Intrepid,* hovering near the horizon beyond the mouth of the harbor, lay the American brig *Siren,* of sixteen guns, commanded by Decatur's old friend Charles Stewart. Stewart had disguised his vessel as a trader, so as not to attract attention. The original plan, as worked out in Syracuse, had called for a number of the *Siren*'s crewmen to join the *Intrepid* and augment her fighting force. But earlier that day, when the two vessels had first come within sight of Tripoli, it had been important to keep the *Siren* at a distance from the *Intrepid,* so that she would not be seen to be in any way connected with Decatur's ketch. As darkness fell, the wind, which was light from the north-northwest, prevented the *Siren* from closing in as quickly as had been hoped, and by seven o'clock, Decatur decided he could wait no longer. He would have to go it alone and forgo the extra fighters. He ordered Catalano to enter the harbor between the reef and the shoals, and then explained the change in plans to his men, closing with a quotation from *Henry V:* "The fewer men, the greater share of honor." Decatur was by his own admission no scholar, but it is typical of him that he was intimately familiar with the one Shakespeare play that dealt so specifically with honor and its many ramifications, a subject of paramount importance to him.

The original plan called for the attack to take place at ten o'clock, but Decatur had so often experienced the uncertainty of the weather on the North African coast that when he found the wind, which was now light from the north-northwest, cooperating with his plans, he ordered his helmsman to steer boldly onward, directly toward the *Philadelphia,* now visible in ghostly silhouette, illuminated by the cool glow of a crescent moon.

Around nine o'clock the breeze shifted to the northeast and became very light, but proved strong enough to bring them within two hundred yards of the *Philadelphia.* It was now half past nine, and the setting moon, still visible above the horizon, gave them enough light to see that the ship's ports were open, and her guns run out, and that there were a number of sailors on the spar deck. It had been Decatur's intention to run in under her bows and board over the forecastle, but the shift in the wind meant they would have to improvise.

When they got within a hundred yards of the *Philadelphia,* the wind died completely, and they were momentarily dead in the water. The huge bulk of the *Philadelphia* was blocking any wind and leaving the little *Intrepid* becalmed. Eventually the breeze picked up from the opposite quarter, still very light. The change brought the two vessels nearly parallel to each other at a distance of little more than twenty yards, their heads in the same direction, and the *Intrepid* abreast of the larboard gangway of the *Philadelphia.* Some ten or twelve Tripolitanian sailors were looking over the ship's hammock rail.

The ketch was almost within an oar's length of the frigate when there was a sudden warning call from high above in the *Philadelphia,* ordering her to keep away. Catalano answered, explaining that she was a Maltese boat, and had lost her anchors in the late gale under Cape Mesurado. He asked permission to run a warp to the frigate, and ride by her until the following morning when they could get new anchors from shore. The man on the *Philadelphia,* who seemed to be in charge, considered the matter briefly, and then agreed.

He was curious about the brig that had stood in the offing most of the day—the Americans knew he was referring to the *Siren*—and asked Catalano if he knew anything about her. The Sicilian told him that she was the *Transfer,* a former British man-of-war that had been purchased for the Tripolitanians at Malta, and whose arrival was anxiously expected. The man in the *Philadelphia* seemed pleased with the information.

During the conversation, the wind shifted still again, and once more left the ketch, helpless and motionless, right under the frigate's guns. Fortunately, the *Intrepid*'s small boat was still in tow. Crewmen from the ketch, disguised in the same manner as Decatur and Catalano, clambered into it with as little show of haste as possible, and took a line from the *Intrepid* and made it fast to one of the ring bolts of the *Philadelphia*'s fore chains. The unsuspecting Tripolitanians, in a spirit of cooperation, manned one of their own boats and brought a line from the after part of their ship to the *Intrepid*'s boat, gave it to the Americans, who made gruff but incoherent murmurs of thanks, and brought the line back to their ketch. Then those men hidden behind the *Intrepid*'s bulwark began slowly to haul in the rope, bringing them gradually nearer their prey.

Every man on board the *Intrepid* knew precisely where he was to go once they boarded. None of them carried firearms. In accordance with Preble's written orders, they were to "carry all by the sword." The commodore did not want the noise of pistols or muskets to alert those on shore.

As the moment for boarding grew imminent, each man concentrated on the fury to come. Boarding a ship—particularly at night—calls for an extreme form of hand-to-hand combat, not only dangerous but chaotic, the sort of fighting where plans can change in the flick of a saber, and where the confusion of bodies and blades can baffle and terrify even the hardiest of souls. The Americans were dressed in Arab disguises, and in the dark it would be easy to make fatal mistakes. The only means of identification was the watchword "Philadelphia." That alone might save a man from being slaughtered by his own friends.

Whether it was the unusual rapidity of the approach of the *Intrepid* that aroused suspicion or whether the Tripolitanians noted the movement of shadowy figures on the deck is not known, but just as the ketch was on the point of touching there was a startled cry from the *Philadelphia,* "Americanos! Americanos!" Catalano panicked and shouted "Board, Captain, board!" but Decatur saw there was still more than six feet of open water between the two vessels and shouted, "No orders to be obeyed but that of the commanding officer!" His instantaneous response undoubtedly prevented what would have been a debacle. Moments later as the *Intrepid* touched the *Philadelphia,* he shouted "Board!" and sixty men, led by Decatur and Midshipman Charles Morris, scrambled over the channels and rail and up onto the *Philadelphia*'s spar deck, and through the gunports onto the main deck below.

Despite the alarm from the *Philadelphia* the surprise was complete, and the terrified Tripolitanians made only a feeble resistance. A few of the more coolheaded managed to remove the tampions from some of the guns, but they never got a chance to fire them. The deadly sabers and tomahawks of the Americans proved irresistible. Decatur first led an attack on the large number of the crew that had gathered on the forecastle. All those who did not jump into the sea were killed. The lower decks were cleared with the same ruthless dispatch, and in five minutes, the ship was in the hands of her attackers.

Despite Preble's ban on firearms, there was no way to stop either side from yelling, and the noise of the fight raised the alarm on shore and in the cruisers and boats lying nearby. The situation remained perilous, and the Americans expected a bombardment at any moment. There was a hurried call for the combustibles, which were instantly passed up from the ketch and distributed to the gun room berths, the cockpit, the berth deck rooms, and the forward storerooms. The men were supplied with short lengths of sperm oil candles, and at a shouted order from Decatur they set fire to the combustibles. The oily rags and old ropes roared instantly into a blaze, and flames began spilling wildly out of the spar deck hatchways and gunports. So rapidly did the flames spread that the little *Intrepid* was in danger of catching fire as well. Decatur, making sure that everyone was off the burning frigate, was the last to leave, leaping into the rigging of the ketch as she swung away from the blazing *Philadelphia.*

It had taken only about twenty minutes to capture the frigate, set her on fire, and return on board the *Intrepid.* Not a single American life had been lost, and only one man slightly wounded. Some twenty Tripolitanians had been killed outright. Undoubtedly others, who had hidden themselves below decks, died in the flames, while some of those who leaped into the sea probably drowned. At least one boat full of enemy sailors escaped in safety to the town. Only one prisoner was captured. After being severely wounded, he jumped on board the *Intrepid,* where his life was spared by Surgeon Lewis Heerman.

The expedition had been a spectacular success so far, but they were by no means out of danger. Sparks and fragments of fiery canvas floated about everywhere, threatening to ignite the additional barrels of highly flammable combustibles on the *Intrepid*'s quarterdeck. The first order of business was to get away from the burning frigate, but as they raised the jib to catch the wind, the ketch was suddenly sucked back toward the inferno. The huge blaze was devouring all the air around it and creating a vacuum that threatened to pull the *Intrepid* into the fire. It was only by frantic use of the sweeps that they managed to escape from the holocaust they had risked their lives to ignite.

Once safely out of reach of the fire they faced a new danger. The batteries on shore and the cruisers in the harbor began firing at the retreating ketch, but the Americans, intoxicated with their own gallantry, seemed oblivious to the danger. One of the participants, Midshipman Morris, remembered the scene over fifty years later in his memoirs. "While urging the ketch onwards with sweeps, the crew were commenting upon the beauty of the spray thrown up by the shot between us and the brilliant light of the ship, rather than calculating any danger that might be apprehended from the contact."

The sight of the burning *Philadelphia,* in the middle of the small harbor, must have been breathtaking. "The appearance of the ship was indeed magnificent," Morris remembered. "The flames in the interior illuminated her ports and, ascending her rigging and masts, formed columns of fire, which, meeting the tops, were reflected into beautiful capitals."

The town itself was equally spectacular to see. The castles, forts, and minarets were all lit up by the splendor of the conflagration, and shone like an illustration out of the *Arabian Nights.*

The *Philadelphia*'s loaded guns were in the midst of the fire, and as their metal heated, they fired haphazardly from either side. Her starboard battery, which was aimed directly at the shore, smashed blindly into walls and doorways. When the frigate's anchor cables burned through and parted, the *Philadelphia* drifted slowly and grandly toward the town, an aimless funeral pyre and a hazard to every vessel in its path.

The breeze picked up and moved the *Intrepid* toward the harbor mouth, but the guns from the forts and the warships in the harbor continued firing. The shot fell thickly about her, but with little accuracy. One ball passed through her topgallant sail, the only hit. Near the entrance to the harbor, the *Intrepid* was met by the boats from the *Siren,* and together the victorious Yankees made good their escape. By six in the morning the two vessels were forty miles north of Tripoli. From the deck of the *Siren,* the light from the burning frigate was still visible.

Two days later both vessels returned in triumph to Syracuse and an ecstatic Commodore Preble. He ordered a glorious celebratory dinner for the heroes, and within days the raid was the talk of the Mediterranean. When Admiral Nelson heard the story on board his flagship *Victory* off Toulon, he roared with laughter and pronounced it "the most bold and daring act of the age."

Commodore Preble wasted no time in getting off a recommendation to the secretary of the navy. "Lieutenant Decatur is an officer of too much value to be neglected. The important service he has rendered in destroying an enemy's frigate of forty guns, and the gallant manner in which he performed it, in a small vessel of only sixty tons and four guns, under the enemy's batteries, surrounded by their corsairs and armed boats, the crews of which stood appalled at his intrepidity and daring, would, in any navy in Europe, insure him instantaneous promotion to the rank of post captain. I wish, as a stimulus, it could be done in this instance; it would eventually be of real service to our navy. I beg earnestly to recommend him to the President that he may be rewarded according to his merit."

It would take many weeks for the news of Decatur's triumph to reach America, but when it finally arrived his life would change forever. From that day on, presidents would seek out his company. Strangers, speaking in deferential tones, would point to him on the street. At gatherings, voices would drop and conversations pause when he entered a room. Every schoolchild in America would know his name, and countless little boys would reenact the burning of the *Philadelphia* and vie for the privilege of leading the boarding party. Stephen Decatur, still only twenty-five years old, had found the fame and potential immortality for which he had so long yearned. For the rest of his life, he would be a man apart.

★ ★ ★ ★ ★

Decatur's successful raid made him a national hero and he was promoted to captain. He would serve with distinction in the War of 1812 and return to the Barbary Coast again in 1815 to fight the second and final war against the pirate kingdoms. Decatur would go on to serve as Navy Commissioner between 1816–1820. He was mortally wounded in a duel in 1820. Five U.S. Navy ships have since been named in his honor.

The Battle of Lake Erie

CECIL SCOTT FORESTER

> We have met the enemy and they are ours;
> two ships, two brigs, one schooner and one sloop.
> —Commodore Oliver Hazard Perry

The War of 1812 was a time of few great victories for the United States. It is best remembered by Americans today for the creation of the Star Spangled Banner. Originally written as a poem by Francis Scott Key, it describes the siege of Fort McHenry at the entrance to Baltimore harbor in September 1814. Naval artillery pounded the fort through the night. Only when dawn arrived on the following day did people see the American flag still flying—the Americans had refused to surrender, and the British withdrew. It was a glorious moment for the United States in a costly and unsuccessful war.

Two years earlier a confederation of allies in Congress under Henry Clay convinced President James Madison and most of Congress to declare war on Britain for seizing American ships at sea, impressments of American citizens into the Royal Navy, and the refusal to surrender forts in the Northwest Territories promised at the Treaty of Paris in 1783. The war, however, was a disaster from the start. In 1812, the regular army consisted of fewer than 12,000 men. Congress authorized the expansion of the army to 35,000 men, but the service was voluntary and unpopular, and there was an almost total lack of trained and experienced officers. The American attempts to invade Canada ended in failure as war raged across the frontier.

On the Canadian frontier, control of the Great Lakes was required to move men and supplies for offensive actions. As the Americans fell back from their first invasion of Canada, British forces were poised to strike into the states of Michigan, Ohio, Pennsylvania, or western New York. Control of the lakes had to remain in American hands to prevent the British from advancing. Commodore Oliver Hazard Perry, by his own request, was given command of naval forces on Lake Erie. At the port of Erie he secretly commissioned a small fleet of nine ships, only to discover that enemy ships had established a blockade. C. S. Forester describes the campaign from his highly regarded book, *The Age of Fighting Sail.*

★ ★ ★ ★ ★

While Yeo and Chauncey were feebly contending for the mastery of Lake Ontario, the command of Lake Erie above them was held by the British by a small superiority of force which any minor accident or any success by the Americans in the shipbuilding race could change into an inferiority. At the western end of the lake General William Henry Harrison faced General Procter; the mobility of both depended on water communication down the lake. Oliver Hazard Perry arrived in early 1813 to take command of the American naval forces; Captain R. H. Barclay, R.N., arrived in June of the same year to take command of the British naval forces—one British captain had already imperiled his career by refusing the appointment. Perry enjoyed the advantage that at least some of his necessary supplies could reach him via Pittsburgh; everything that Barclay needed had to travel via Ontario. Perry was a man of energy, and his shipbuilders were men of ingenuity; the concluding months of the winter saw construction proceeding apace at his shipyards. They were queer ships which were taking shape there, built of green timber, shallow of draft, and held together by wooden pegs; although wooden pegs were freely used in normal contemporary ship construction, the shortage of nails on Lake Erie compelled their use there for construction at points where nails were considered essential in seagoing ships. There were lake schooners which could barely carry their armament, not being designed for such concentrated and lofty loads, and which were likely to upset when their guns were fired. Even the ships built with fighting in mind were flimsy in construction on account of the haste with which they were built as well as on account of the shortages—they represented a compromise between delay and security—and their necessarily shallow draft made them even more uninhabitable than ordinary ships of war and more perilous to fight in. They were armed with whatever guns could be dragged over the endless trails and floated along the endless waterways that connected Presqu'ile with the foundries on the eastern seaboard; Cockburn's bold exploit in the summer of 1813 when his landing party destroyed the foundry at Frenchtown came too late, for Perry had by that time collected the guns which won the battle, borrowed from the army as well as supplied by the navy, and dragged up French Creek during fortunate freshets.

Seamen to man them could come only from the Ontario fleet, which Chauncey was striving to maintain at an equality with Yeo's. The importance of the command of Ontario was so obvious that Chauncey dared not part with many men; Perry, engrossed with his own problems, was inclined to at tribute Chauncey's reluctance to timidity or jealousy or something even worse, and at the crisis of the campaign was held back from resigning his command only by a remarkable display of firmness on the part of the Secretary of the Navy.

On the English side the difficulties were of the same nature and even more acute. Everything for use on Erie had to come from Ontario; there was no alternative line of communication whatever, and at the farthest end of the difficult line was Procter with an army and a horde of Indians who had to be fed and supplied. The briefest loss of command of the lake meant serious trouble at its western end, where Harrison could at least keep his army together in a threatening attitude without American command of the lake. Barclay, arriving in the spring—he encountered some difficulty in making his way along Ontario at the time of Chauncey's temporary command of that lake—was kept aware of this by ceaseless complaints and warnings from Procter, as well as from Prevost, the commander in chief; but Barclay stood in exactly the same situation to Yeo as Perry did to Chauncey, and Yeo proved to be even more reluctant to part with men or material than Chauncey was. The building program initiated on the British side was less ambitious than the American program; there was only the ship-rigged *Detroit* under construction, and guns for her could not be coaxed from Yeo on any terms. She was necessarily built without her designers knowing what armament she was to carry, and the armament she eventually received was largely made up from field artillery borrowed from Procter, supplemented by whatever else could be found—there were six different types of cannon among the nineteen guns she carried, with a complication of the ammunition supply in action that can hardly be imagined.

Barclay, as has been said, met with even more difficulty in persuading Yeo to part with seamen than did Perry with Chauncey, and another of Barclay's troubles was of a nature that Perry hardly encountered; most of the seamen under his command were Canadians, not too ready to submit to naval routine, and their numbers in any case were astonishingly small. Indeed, it is very much to Barclay's credit that he succeeded in winning the devotion of the motley force under his command.

The misfortunes that befell Barclay were to a considerable extent the result of his own personal errors. They began almost immediately after his arrival. On his very first voyage he crossed the lake to intercept the vessels set free by the American advance in the Niagara peninsula, and he failed to do so. There was thick weather, and the American ships clung to the shallows and reached Presqu'ile. Perhaps the failure to destroy them on their passage was excusable, but Barclay was aware that they were going to make the attempt—he had seen with his own eyes what was happening at Niagara—and it is hard to believe that with diligence and vigilance he could not have detected them.

Even now there were opportunities to restore the balance already disturbed. Presqu'ile was not a very secure base; its militia garrison was unreliable, seamen were lacking and the shipyard workers discontented and weakened by disease. Two powerful ships of war were under construction there which would confer superiority on Perry even after *Detroit* should be completed. The importance of these two ships can best be understood when it is realized that their entry into service trebled Perry's strength and certainly made him twice as strong as Barclay without *Detroit*. There were the same advantages to be gained from a blow at Presqu'ile as had offered themselves a few weeks before to Chauncey regarding an attack on Kingston. Barclay was aware of them, but he did not succeed in gaining Procter's co-operation.

Procter employed the mobility conferred on him by the last fleeting weeks of the British command of the lake to make an attack on Fort Meigs; the attack failed, despite the fact that Procter cut up a relieving force and inflicted terrible loss. The troops and siege equipment employed at Fort Meigs could have been far more usefully employed at Presqu'ile, but the full realization of the fact dawned upon Procter and Barclay only after the moment had passed; it would take time to prepare a fresh expedition, and when that time had elapsed Presqu'ile was regarded as too strong to be meddled with—perhaps not a correct conclusion.

Yet there was still another opportunity, even after Perry's two new ships were launched at Presqu'ile. They had to be brought out onto the lake, and there was a bar to be passed, for Presqu'ile suffered under that disadvantage; the vessels had to be lighted to a draft of five feet, not only emptied of guns and stores, but hoisted over by means of "camels," and during their passage they would be utterly defenseless. Barclay could not help being aware of Perry's difficulty; he could have guessed it if he did not hear about it through spies or careless gossip, and it was to his obvious advantage to be ready to attack the American ships as they passed the bar, helpless and unarmed. As long as he maintained his squadron within striking distance of Presqu'ile and kept the place under observation, Perry would not dare move. Barclay's actions showed that he understood the situation. He arrived off Presqu'ile on July 20 and watched the place. As it happened, he was not even imposing delay upon Perry at that moment, because the final reinforcement of seamen which Chauncey had brought himself to spare was on its way and Perry had decided not to move until it arrived.

American accounts lay stress on the vulnerability of Presqu'ile at this moment and suggest that Barclay had only to send in his boats to destroy the whole American squadron, but they do not make sufficient allowance for Barclay's numerical weakness. He had less than four hundred men on board, and he could not have scraped together a landing force of as many as two hundred men. Perry had guns mounted on the beach, and his ships had their batteries on board. Even before Perry's reinforcements arrived, and even though the regular American soldiers had been recalled and the militia were worthless, Barclay would have had no chance of success in a landing without troops to aid him, and he had no troops because Procter was now meditating a further futile offensive, against Sandusky.

The other side of the argument is that if Barclay took no action his situation was bound to deteriorate, so that the most desperate attempt could be justified. Even if an attack by brute force was hopeless, there might have been other means employed. It might have been possible for a boat to creep in under cover of darkness to attempt to set the anchored ships on fire—not a promising line of attack, but anything would have been better than inaction; the present peril was obvious, and ultimate disaster was likely.

What little opportunity Barclay had for offensive action was greatly diminished within four days of his arrival off Presqu'ile, for the reinforcements from Chauncey began to come in at last, a hundred and thirty seamen whose quality Perry deplored, but men at least—and men who, as the event was to prove, were prepared to face enormous losses. Their presence made it more necessary still that Barclay should maintain his close watch over Presqu'ile, and he did not do so.

The motives that carried Barclay away from his blockading position are impossible to discover at this late time; they were not stated in any of the documents surviving or in the records of the official inquiries held after the event. It can only be said that on the day that the last of

Chauncey's reinforcements arrived the Americans, looking out across the lake, could see no sign of Barclay. He had sailed away. Perhaps his motley crews were restive; perhaps his own patience had been exhausted by ten days of waiting. Perhaps he was running short of food; provisions were continually in short supply on the British side even when they commanded the lake, but if lack of food forced Barclay to retire he was to blame—a shortage in ten days' time should have been foreseen and provided for. It may have been any other kind of trouble; with those makeshift ships and makeshift crews anything might happen, of a nature no one can guess at nowadays.

With the coast clear, Perry plunged into the business of getting his ships out over the bar; the necessity had been foreseen and arrangements already made. Barclay sailed on July 30. On the night of August 1 the movements started; during August 2 they continued. The weather was kind, but the lake was not—the depth on the bar had diminished from five feet to four. There was a perilous moment when the first of the big ships grounded and had to be refloated. They worked through the night, and by the morning of August 4 she was over the bar together with the smaller vessels, and her guns and ammunition were being hurried on board. At that moment Barclay's sails appeared over the horizon again. It was Barclay's last chance. He might have attacked forthwith. The Americans could not have been in very good order, and their second large ship was still within the bar. But all Barclay could see was that they were in "a most formidable state of preparation," and he turned away. On August 6 Perry took his fleet out on its first cruise, and Barclay was not there to oppose him. He was sheltering at Malden, waiting for his own big ship to be completed.

And Perry was growing stronger yet, for another hundred seamen arrived from Chauncey; it is hard to overestimate the magnitude of the sacrifice Chauncey was making, because it was at this very time that he and Yeo were in presence on Ontario, facing each other with approximately equal forces. Chauncey was taking a serious risk, for a disaster to him on Ontario could nullify any gains won by a victory on Erie. Perry remained unappreciative; he could hardly spare sympathy for Chauncey when he was bitterly conscious that his own fleet was inadequately manned by any normal standard. Harrison found him more men—a hundred Kentucky riflemen, volunteering for an adventure that must have been a novelty even to those adventurous figures.

Perry commanded the lake. He swept down it to Malden, looking at the British ships inside, returning more than once from his usual anchorage in the Bass Islands, thirty miles from the British base and dominating the narrow western end of the lake. No British vessels could venture through the blockade that he instituted; the British, cut off at the far end, were immediately conscious of the resultant shortages. Even Barclay's own men were put on reduced rations during the weary days while the new ship was being fitted out. The British military position was in the gravest peril, and it could be restored only by the reconquest of the command of the lake. Nothing else would make it possible to transport the daily twenty thousand rations needed by the troops, by the Indians and their families, and by the sailors cooped up there; it was of no importance that the tactical situation still gave the British naval command of the straits of Detroit and of Lake Huron, for all that wilderness to the westward produced no flour, and cattle in insufficient quantity. Barclay could come out and fight or he could abandon his ships and carry off his crews with the British army in its retreat, and he made the obvious choice. His newest ship was ready for service just in time, when the flour remaining in store was on the point of exhaustion. He sailed out from Malden on September 10 in a desperate mood.

Oliver Perry at twenty-eight was a man of strong emotions, fiery and energetic and yet with that vein of sentiment that often makes itself evident in such men. His last big ship was about to be launched at the moment when the dreary news reached the Lakes that *Chesapeake* had been captured and that Lawrence was dead. Perry was deeply moved, caught up in the wave of emotion that was sweeping through much of the United States. His new ship was christened *Lawrence* at her launching. Press and public were repeating the words "Don't give up the ship," which the dying Lawrence had breathed as he was carried below. The expression caught Perry's fancy too. He had a blue flag made on which the words were sewn in white, after the fashion of the flag Lawrence had hoisted in Boston; the existence of this flag is worth remembering. The slogan would not commend itself to modern experts in propaganda; it was negative and not positive; by its very wording it admitted the possibility that the ship might be given up; and it could hardly fail to remind the public that the ship, in the end, had actually been given up. It might instill a mood of desperate resignation, but that is a dangerous mood from the point of view of the propagandist, who would fear lest the resignation might eventually combine with the despair to induce apathy. But it was to serve its purpose at that moment; certainly it was a more appealing battle cry than "Free Trade and Sailors' Rights," with its windy suggestion of legal and economic arguments.

Perry's second large ship was the *Niagara,* named for the recent successes won while Chauncey held the command of Ontario; the third largest, and much less important, was the *Caledonia,* the vessel that had been captured from the British by the prompt and vigorous action of Elliott the preceding autumn. In addition Perry had a number of schooners which were to play an important part in the battle to come, but the two large vessels comprised two thirds or more of his fighting strength. Perry enjoyed five weeks of command of the lake before the day of battle; it was a long enough period to exercise his crews, and it was also long enough to enable him to make his plans for the coming action, especially as he was able to form a close estimate of the force that would be opposed to him. Possibly he thought too long over his plans; possibly they were too rigid; possibly his exact information tempted him to be too mathematical about the battle; possibly his orders were worded too strictly to allow of the flexibility necessary in an action between fleets with its unpredictable conditions of wind and weather; possibly Perry did not exert himself to win the wholehearted devotion of his next senior officer, Elliott, who had once been senior officer on Lake Erie, who had distinguished himself by the capture of *Caledonia,* and who now found himself under the command of Perry, who—as was known—owed his appointment to the representations of the senior senator from Rhode Island and had no distinguished fighting record behind him. These were all small factors, but, acting together, they came near to losing the battle.

Barclay's biggest ship was the *Detroit*—named after the British victory—comparable in size with *Lawrence* and *Niagara,* but far inferior in force. He had the *Queen Charlotte* (the last *Queen Charlotte* had been the three-decker flagship of the Mediterranean fleet, destroyed by fire at Leghorn), smaller but more adequately armed although still greatly inferior to *Niagara,* and smaller vessels inferior in total weight of metal to Perry's. Arithmetically his squadron may have been two thirds as strong as the American squadron, certainly not more. The arithmetic is complicated by the differing proportion of long guns and carronades, and still more by the fact that it is impossible to arrive at exact figures regarding the number of men on each side fit for duty. Certainly the numerical odds that Barclay came out to fight were considerably greater than those Nelson faced at Trafalgar, and Barclay was no Nelson, as recent events had already shown. Nor was Perry a Villeneuve, as the battle was to prove.

On September 10 the chances of the weather favored America. The wind that brought Barclay down upon Perry (and that might have imposed upon the latter a roundabout exit from his harbor that would have delayed the battle) shifted at the right moment to enable Perry to come out, and with the weather gauge. He could bear down with the wind abeam and enter at once into action. He could see Barclay's two large ships stationed in the British line with a smaller vessel ahead, astern, and in between, and Perry's orders and order of sailing allotted *Lawrence* to fight *Detroit* and *Niagara* to fight *Queen Charlotte.*

As soon as the battle began Perry and the Americans faced the tactical problem which had plagued attacking fleets ever since they first formed in line. Were they to follow their leader so that the heads of the two lines would come together first, with the respective rears still far apart, or was each ship to make the best of her way into action against her opposite number? The first method might give the fleet to leeward the chance of doubling upon the leading attacking ships, and certainly might lead to indecisive action; the second was more difficult to put into practice. Even Lord Howe, a disciplinarian and a tactician, had not succeeded in bringing all his ships into close action at the Glorious First of June. And when there was doubt as to which method was in the admiral's mind, and when that doubt was increased by the memory of the rigid convention of the line ahead, there was likely to be indecision and disorder, as Byng found in the unlucky action that cost him his life. And when one of the subordinate officers is sulky or stupid, disaffected or resentful, there is likely to be entirely disjointed action. This was Mathews' experience in 1744, when he engaged without any assistance whatever from his second-in-command, Lestock, who could still plead—as he actually did at his court-martial—that he had obeyed his orders to the letter.

Perry in the *Lawrence* found himself in close action with the British squadron, while Elliott in the *Niagara*—representing at least a third of the American strength—was still at long range. The battle was ferociously contested, both sides enduring losses of proportions that in many previous battles had ended the fighting. Barclay's Canadians and soldiers and handful of seamen stood to their guns with a bravery that was equaled only by Perry's Kentuckians and soldiers and handful of seamen. Along the line there were local superiorities and inferiorities, where in one case there was distant action with long guns against carronades and in another close action with carronades against long guns. The *Detroit*'s guns were not equipped with locks. Apparently she had no port-fires, even, and the guns were fired by snapping pistols over loose powder piled in the touchholes. They were served bravely enough, and effectively enough, in any event. Even in small vessels the Americans had a superiority and made good use of it, one or two of the gunboats being employed in the most effective manner for such craft, raking the larger British vessels with their long guns from good tactical positions ahead and astern, although in the end the inexperienced crews mishandled their artillery and overcharged their hot guns, so that *Scorpion*'s gun leaped from its carriage and fell down the hatchway, while one of *Ariel*'s guns burst.

In the heat of the battle Barclay's second large ship, the *Queen Charlotte,* moved up in the line and brought her guns to bear on the *Lawrence* in addition to those of the *Detroit.* Perry's flagship was shot to pieces; one credible estimate states her losses in killed and wounded as 80 percent of her total crew; the wounded had to be summoned back from the cockpit to help handle the ship. On the British side the losses were heavy; in the two big ships the captain and lieutenants were all killed or wounded, Barclay (who had lost an arm at Trafalgar eight years before) being wounded in five places. From a statistician's point of view it is a pity that no analysis of the nature of the British casualties has been preserved, for it would be informative regarding what proportion of hits was scored by the Kentucky riflemen; but there is the negative evidence of the absence of British complaints in the matter, and it is not unreasonable to conclude that small arms played a very minor part in the battle.

The vital point was that Perry survived, unhurt. If he had fallen along with the four fifths of the men around him, this battle of Lake Erie might conceivably have ended in a bloody reverse for the Americans. The fact that he survived, the fact that in the midst of all the din and destruction he kept his head clear while his fighting spirit was at fever pitch, saved the day. Elliott in *Niagara* was still at long—and ineffective—range. There can be no doubt about the fact, even though the possible explanations are numerous enough. There was the fluky wind, there were Perry's orders, there was the fact that *Niagara*'s next ahead, the *Caledonia,* was slow and unhandy, and Elliott was under orders to keep in line with her. There was the possibility that *Caledonia,* badly handled, had actually balked *Niagara*'s efforts to get into action. The most obvious explanation is that Elliott, resentful of being under Perry's command (or perhaps of some imagined slight), chose to interpret his orders to the letter and hung back in consequence. No actual proof has ever been put forward of this, and it is far too grave a charge to be accepted without proof. But so matters stood; more than two hours after the fighting began, *Niagara* was still only distantly engaged, while *Queen Charlotte* had pushed into the heart of the battle and the American flagship was being overwhelmed.

Perry decided to transfer himself to the *Niagara.* There were numerous precedents for such action—in the Anglo-Dutch wars both British and Dutch admirals had frequently shifted their flags in the heat of battle from disabled or beaten ships. He started off on the long pull; it was as fortunate for America that the *Lawrence* still possessed a boat that would float as it was that Perry had not been hit. He took with him his "Don't give up the ship" flag, which may explain the British accusations that Perry absconded from his ship after it had surrendered; if that flag had been flying during the action and had then been hauled down for Perry to take with him, the British had grounds for thinking the surrender took place then, especially as the *Lawrence* actually struck immediately after Perry left her.

The firing died away. The Stars and Stripes had been hauled down in the *Lawrence.* The disabled British *Hunter* was drifting off to leeward; so was the *Lady Prevost.* The small craft were still exchanging occasional shots. Guns were being fired from *Detroit* and *Queen Charlotte* at Perry's boat, but they missed—Perry was luckier than Sir Edward Spragge, who had been killed in exactly the same circumstances in action with Van Tromp. There was some small cheering in the British ships, but the men were weary; *Detroit* and *Queen Charlotte* fell foul of each other, disabled as they were, and it was no easy matter to separate them, for the men were without officers. The expectation, even the certainty, among the British was that *Niagara* would lead the schooners astern of her away from the battle, acknowledging defeat and leaving the British in possession of the field of battle and of their hard-won prize.

Perry had nothing of the sort in mind. He boarded *Niagara;* the fluky wind was strengthening, which had made his pull all the longer. There were no recriminations at that moment; both Perry and Elliott were determined to see the battle through. Perry took command of the *Niagara;* Elliott set off by boat to bring the schooners along as well. The wind remained favorable, and the British, exhausted and leaderless, saw the *Niagara,* fresh and uninjured, bearing down upon them. Despite the strain of the past hours Perry was still in good fighting condition and handled *Niagara* excellently—it might almost be said cold-bloodedly. He swept round the bows of *Detroit* and *Queen Charlotte,* raking them with his broadside of nine carronades; Elliott brought up the gunboats to fire into their sterns; *Caledonia,* still in good fighting condition, closed in as well. British resistance ended abruptly; *Detroit* and *Queen Charlotte* could only surrender; *Lawrence* was recaptured; *Lady Prevost,* unmanageable with her rudder shot away, hauled down her colors under the fire of *Niagara's* guns; so did *Hunter; Chippeway* and *Little Belt* tried to struggle away but were caught by the fresh gunboats and compelled to surrender. It was annihilation, disaster as complete as the French had experienced at San Domingo or Cape Ortegal, more complete than the Nile.

Perry kept his head as clear in the moment of victory as he had done in the heat of battle. General Harrison on shore must be informed that the Americans had undisputed command of the lake, and Perry did not lose an hour. "We have met the enemy and they are ours," he wrote. Those words told Harrison that his army was free to move forward, that the British army could only retreat. Within three weeks of the battle, despite the damage received there and further damage suffered in a storm, Perry had troops on board to ferry across the narrow end of the lake, and Procter was in full retreat, with his army starving. He could not, or would not, retreat fast enough. Overtaken by Harrison's forces, he turned to fight and was badly beaten, his forces almost annihilated. Tecumseh, the leader of his Indian allies, fell in the fighting, and his death and the British defeat meant the practical cessation of dangerous Indian hostility to the Americans. Detroit was in American hands again; American soil was clear of British invaders; an American army was established on Canadian soil; American mastery of Lake Erie was undisputed; and along with all this, to the clear-thinking mind, American expansion to the Northwest was an obvious certainty.

★ ★ ★ ★ ★

Control of Lake Erie would remain in American hands for the rest of the war and assist with American victories in Canada in 1813. Perry's victory would help raise American morale when it was desperately needed.

The USS *Constitution*

JAMES FENIMORE COOPER

We felt that the eyes of the country were upon us and
that every thing within the bounds of possibility was expected.

—Assheton Y. Humphreys
Acting Chaplain, USS *Constitution,* December 1814

The USS *Constitution* was launched in 1797 from Hartt's shipyard in Boston as one of six frigates authorized for construction by the Naval Act of 1794. Designed by American shipbuilders Joshua Humphreys and Josiah Fox, the new American frigates were intended to serve as the capital ships for the United Sates. They were built from live Georgian oak timbers up to seven inches thick to ensure a longevity four times greater than ships made from white oak. The construction also featured a unique diagonal cross-bracing of the ship's skeleton and copper-plated hulls. Inspired by French heavy frigate designs, the new ships delivered firepower that enabled their commanders to fight any ship of up to 64 guns and a speed that allowed them to outsail anything they couldn't fight.

Humphrey's design outlined what American Naval strategy would require; to raid and harass the enemy versus a ship of the line engagement and arms race with European nations. The *Constitution* would enter service in time to defend American shores in the Quasi-War with France and was designated flagship for the Mediterranean squadron under Captain Edward Preble. Her nickname "Old Ironsides" came from a battle with the HMS *Guerriere* on August 19, 1812, off the coast of Nova Scotia, when British cannon balls bounced harmlessly off her thick oak timbers. Her greatest and last combat action came on February 20, 1815, under Capt. Charles Stewart when the *Constitution* was 180 miles from Madeira in an engagement with two British men-of-war, *Cyane* (24 guns) and *Levant* (18 guns). This two-against-one fight began as the sun was setting. Through superb sail handling and tactics, Stewart swiftly closed on *Cyane* and dealt her tremendous damage to her masts and rigging. The *Constitution* then fired on *Levant* hard enough to put her out of action temporarily, during which time the *Cyane* was forced to surrender. After putting a prize crew in the *Cyane*, Stewart turned his attention again to the *Levant*, chasing and firing into her until she also surrendered.

James Fenimore Cooper wrote the first history of the American Navy published in 1839. It is still considered one of the greatest accounts from the Age of Sail. In the following chapter he describes the last wartime cruise of the USS *Constitution* and her encounter with the HMS *Levant* and *Cyane.*

★ ★ ★ ★ ★

When Commodore Bainbridge gave up the command of the *Constitution 44*, in 1813, that ship was found to be so decayed as to require extensive repairs. Her crew was principally sent upon the lakes, a new one entered, and the command of her was given to Captain Charles Stewart. The ship, however, was not able to get to sea until the winter of 1814, when she made a cruise to the southward, passing down the coast, and running through the West Indies, on her way home, where he fell in with *La Pique 36*, which ship made her escape by going through the Mona passage in the night. Previously to her return the *Constitution* captured the *Pictou 14*, a man-of-war schooner of the enemy. Reaching the American coast, she was chased into Marblehead by two English frigates, the *Junon* and *Tenedos*. Shortly after she went to Boston. In this cruise, the *Constitution* made a few prizes, in addition to the schooner.

On the 17th of December, the *Constitution* again left Boston, and ran off Bermuda; thence to the vicinity of Madeira, and into the Bay of Biscay. After this, she cruised some time in sight of the Rock of Lisbon, making two prizes, one of which was destroyed, and the other sent in. While in the vicinity of Lisbon, she made a large ship and gave chase, but before her courses were raised, one of the prizes just mentioned, was fallen in with, and while securing it, the strange sail disappeared. This vessel is understood to have been the *Elizabeth 74*, which, on her arrival at Lisbon, hearing that the *Constitution* was off the coast, immediately came out in pursuit of her; but Captain Stewart had stood to the southward and westward, in quest of an enemy said to be in that direction.

On the morning of the 20th of February, the wind blowing a light levanter, finding nothing where he was, Captain Stewart ordered the helm put up, and the ship ran off southwest, varying her position, in that direction, fifty or sixty miles. At 1 P.M., a stranger was seen on the larboard bow, when the ship hauled up two or three points, and made sail in chase. In about twenty minutes the stranger was made out to be a ship; and half an hour later, a second vessel was seen farther to leeward, which at two was also ascertained to be a ship. The *Constitution* kept standing on, all three vessels on bowlines, until fur, when the nearest of the strangers made a signal to the ship to leeward, and shortly after he kept away and ran down towards his consort, then abut three leagues under his lee. The *Constitution* immediately squared away, and set her studding-sails, alow and aloft. No doubt was now entertained of the strangers being enemies; the nearest ship having the appearance of a small frigate, and the vessel to leeward that of a large sloop of war. The first was carrying studding-sails on both sides, while the last was running off under short canvass, to allow her consort to close. Captain Stewart believed it was their intention to keep away, on their best mode of sailing, until night, in the hope of escaping; and he crowded every thing that would draw, with a view to get the nearest vessel under his guns. About half-past four, the spar proving defective, the main royal-mast was carried away, and the chase gained. A few guns were now fired, but finding that the shot fell short, the attempt to cripple the stranger was abandoned.

Perceiving, at half-past five, that it was impossible to prevent the enemy from effecting a junction, the *Constitution*, then a little more than a league distant from the farthest ship, cleared for action. Ten minutes later, the two chases passed within hail of each other, came by the wind with their heads to the northward, hauled up their courses, and were evidently clearing to engage. In a few minutes both ships suddenly made sail, close by the wind, in order to weather upon the American frigate, but perceiving that the latter was closing too fast, they again hauled up their courses, and formed on the wind, the smallest ship ahead.

At 6 P.M., the *Constitution* had the enemy completely under her guns, and she showed her ensign. The strangers answered this defiance, by setting English colors, and five minutes later, the American ship ranged up abeam of the sternmost vessel, at the distance of a cable's length, passing ahead with her sails lifting, until the three ships formed nearly an equilateral triangle, the *Constitution* to windward. In this masterly position the action commenced, the three vessels keeping up a hot and unceasing fire for about a quarter of an hour, when that of the enemy sensibly slackened. The sea being covered with an immense cloud of smoke, and it being now moonlight, Captain Steward ordered the cannonading to cease. In three minutes the smoke had blown away, when the leading ship of the enemy was seen under the lee-beam of the *Constitution*, while the sternmost was luffing, as if she intended to tack and cross her wake. Giving a broadside to the ship abreast of her, the American frigate threw her main and mizzen-topsails with topgallant-sails set, flat aback, shook all forward, let fly her jib-sheet, and backed swiftly astern, compelling the enemy to fill again to avoid being raked. The leading ship now attempted to tack, to cross the *Constitution*'s fore-foot, when the latter filled, boarded her fore-tack, shot ahead, forced her antagonist to ware under a raking broadside, and to run off to leeward to escape from the weight of her fire.

The *Constitution* perceiving that the largest ship was waring also, wore on her keel, and crossing her stern, raked her with effect, though the enemy came by the wind immediately, and delivered his larboard broadside; but as the *Constitution* ranged up close on his weather quarter, he struck. Mr. Hoffman, the second lieutenant of the *Constitution*, was immediately sent to take possession; the prize proving to be the British ship *Cyane 24*, Captain Falcon.

In the meantime, the ship that had run to leeward had been forced out of the combat by the crippled condition of her running rigging, and to avoid the weight of the *Constitution*'s fire. She was ignorant of the fate of the *Cyane*, but at the end of about an hour, having repaired damages, she hauled up, and met the *Constitution* coming down in quest of her. It was near nine before the two ships crossed each other on opposite tacks, the *Constitution* to windward, and exchanged broadsides. The English ship finding her antagonist too heavy, immediately bore up, in doing which she got a raking discharge, when the *Constitution* boarded fore-tack and made sail, keeping up a most effective chasing fire, from her two bow guns, nearly every shot of which told. The two ships were so near each other, that the ripping of the enemy's planks was heard on board the American frigate. The former was unable to support this long, and at 10 P.M. he came by the wind, fired a gun to leeward, and lowered his ensign. Mr. W. B. Shubrick, the third lieutenant, was sent on board to take possession, when it was found that the prize was the *Levant 18*, the Honorable Captain Douglas.

During this cruise, the *Constitution* mounted 52 guns; and she had a complement of about 470 men, all told; a few of whom were absent in a prize. The *Cyane* was a frigate-built ship, that properly rated 24 guns, though she appeared as only a 20 in Steele's list, mounting 22 thirty-two-pound carronades on her gun-deck, and 10 eighteen-pound carronades, with two chase guns, on her quarterdeck and forecastle; making 34 in all. The *Levant* was a new ship, rating 18, and mounting 18 thirty-two-pound carronades, a shifting eighteen on her topgallant forecastle, and two chase guns; or 21 in all. There were found in the *Cyane*, 169 prisoners, of whom 26 were wounded. The precise number slain on board her is not known; Captain Steward, probably judging from an examination of the musterbook, computing it as 12, while the accounts given by the English publications differ, some putting the killed at only 4 and others at 6. It was probably between the two estimates. Her regular crew was about 185, all told, and there is no reason to believe that it was not nearly, if not absolutely full. Captain Stewart supposes it to have been 130, all told; but it appears by a statement published in Barbadoes, where some of her officers shortly after went, that there were good many supernumeraries in the two vessels, who were going to the Western Islands, to bring away a ship that was building there. Captain Stewart supposed the *Levant* to have had 156 men in the action, of whom he believed 23 to have been killed, and 16 wounded. The first estimate may have been too high, though the truth can probably never be known. It is believed that no English official account of this action has ever been published, but the Barbadoes statement makes the joint loss of the two ships, 10 killed, and 28 wounded; other English accounts raise it as high as 41 in all. It may have been a little less than the estimate of Captain Stewart (although his account of the wounded must have been accurate), but was probably considerably more than that of the English statements. The *Constitution* had 3 killed, and 12 wounded, or she sustained a total loss of 15 men. By 1 A.M., of the 21st, she was ready for another action. Although it was more than three hours and a half, from the time this combat commenced, before the *Levant* struck, the actual fighting did not occupy three-quarters of an hour. For a night action, the execution on both sides was unusual, the enemy firing much better than common. The *Constitution* was hulled oftener in this engagement, than in both her previous battles, though she suffered less in her crew than in the combat with the *Java*. She had not an officer hurt.

The manner in which Captain Stewart handled his ship, on this occasion, excited much admiration among nautical men, it being an unusual thing for a single vessel to engage two enemies, and escape being raked. So far from this occurring to the *Constitution*, however, she actually raked both her opponents, and the manner in which she backed and filled in the smoke, forcing her two antagonists down to leeward, when they were endeavoring to cross her stern or fore-foot, is among the most brilliant maneuvering in naval annals.

It is due to a gallant enemy to say, that Captain Douglas commanded the respect of the Americans, by his intrepid perseverance in standing by his consort. Although the attempt might not have succeeded, the time necessarily lost in securing the *Cyane*, gave him an opportunity to endeavor to escape, that he nobly refused to improve.

Captain Stewart proceeded with his two prizes to Port Praya, where he arrived on the 10th of March. Here a vessel as engaged as a cartel, and more than a hundred of the prisoners were landed with a view to help fit her for sea. Saturday, March 11th, 1815, a little after meridian, while the cutter was absent to bring the cartel under the stern of the frigate, the sea was covered with a heavy fog, near the water, and there was a good deal of haze above, but in the latter, the sails of a large ship were visible. She was on a wind, looking in-shore, and evidently stretching towards the roads. The first lieutenant, Mr. Shubrick, reported the circumstance to Captain Stewart. This officer believing that the strange sail would prove to be an English frigate or an Indiaman, directed the lieutenant to return on deck, call all hands, and get ready to go out and attack her. As soon as this order was given, the officer took a new look at the stranger, when he discovered the canvass of two other ships rising above the bank of fog, in the same direction. These vessels were evidently heavy men-of-war, and Captain Stewart was immediately apprised of the fresh discovery. That prompt and decided officer did not hesitate an instant concerning the course he ought to take. Well knowing that the English would disregard the neutrality of any port that had not sufficient force to resist them, or which did not belong to a nation they were obliged to respect, he immediately made a signal for the prizes to follow, and ordered the *Constitution*'s cable to be cut. In 10 minute after this order was issued, and in 14 after the first ship had been seen, the American frigate was standing out of the roads, under her three topsails.

The cool and officer-like manner in which sail was made and the ship cast, on this occasion, has been much extolled, and not an instant having been lost by hurry or confusion. The prizes followed with promptitude. The northeast trades were blowing, and the three vessels passed out to sea about gun-shot to windward of the hostile squadron, just clearing East Point. As the *Constitution* cleared the land, she crossed topgallant-yards, boarded her tacks, and set all the light sails that would draw. The English prisoners on shore, took possession of a battery, and fired at her as she went out. As soon as the American ships had gained the weather beam of the enemy, the latter tacked, and the six vessels stood off to the southward and eastward, carrying everything that would draw, and going about ten knots.

The fog still lay so thick upon the water as to conceal the hulls of the strangers, but they were supposed to be two line-of-battle ships, and a large frigate, the vessel most astern and to leeward, being the commodore. The frigate weathered on all the American ships, gaining on the *Levant* and *Cyane*, but falling astern of the *Constitution*; while the two larger vessels, on the latter's lee quarter, held way with her. As soon as clear of the land, the *Constitution* cut adrift two of her boats, the enemy pressing her too hard to allow of their being hoisted in. The *Cyane* was gradually dropping astern and to leeward, rendering it certain, if she stood on, that the mostly weatherly of the enemy's vessels would soon be alongside of her; and at 10 minutes past one, Captain Steward made a signal for her to tack. This order was obeyed by Mr. Hoffman, the prize-master; and it was now expected that one of the enemy's ships would go about, and follow him; a hope that was disappointed. The *Cyane* finding that she was not pursued, stood on until she was lost in the fog, when Mr. Hoffman tacked again, anticipating that the enemy might chase him to leeward. This prudent officer improved his advantage, by keeping to windward long enough to allow the enemy to get ahead, should they pursue him, when he squared away for America, arriving safely at New York on the 10th of April following.

The three ships of the enemy continued to chase the *Constitution* and *Levant*. As the vessels left the land the fog lessened, though it still lay so dense on the immediate surface of the ocean, as to leave Captain Steward in doubt as to the force of his pursuers. The English officers on board the *Constitution* affirmed that the vessel that was getting into her wake was the *Acasta 40*, Captain Kerr, a twenty-four-pounder ship, and it was thought that the three were a squadron that was cruising for the *President*, *Peacock*, and *Hornet*, consisting of the *Leander 50*, Sir George Collier, *Newcastle 50*, Lord George Stuart, and the *Acasta*; the ships that they subsequently proved to be. The *Newcastle* was the vessel on the lee-quarter of the *Constitution*, and by half-past two the fog had got so low, that her officers were seen standing on the hammock-cloths, though the line of her ports was not visible. She now began to fire by divisions, and some opinion could be formed of her armament, by the flashes of her guns, through the fog. Her shot struck the water within a hundred yards of the American ship, but did not rise again. By 3 P.M., the *Levant* had fallen so far astern, that she was in the very danger from which the *Cyane* had so lately been extricated, and Captain Stewart made her signal to tack also. Mr. Ballard immediately complied, and 7 minutes later the three English ships tacked, by signal, and chased the prize, leaving the *Constitution* standing on in a different direction, and going at the rate of eleven knots.

Mr. Ballard finding the enemy bent on following the *Levant*, with the *Acasta* already to windward of his wake, ran back into Port Praya, and anchored, at 4 o'clock, within 150 yards of the shore, under a strong battery. The enemy's ships had commenced firing, as soon as it was seen that the *Levant* would gain the anchorage, and all three now opened on the prize. After bearing the fire for a considerable time, the colors of the *Levant* were hauled down. No one was hurt in the prize, Mr. Ballard causing his men to lie on the deck, as soon as the ship was anchored. The English prisoners in the battery, also fired at the *Levant*.

Sir George Collier was much criticized for the course he pursued on this occasion. It was certainly a mistake to call off more than one ship to chase the *Levant*, though the position of the *Leander* in the fog, so far to leeward and astern, did not give the senior officer the best opportunities for observing the course of events. There was certainly every prospect of the *Acasta*'s bringing the *Constitution* to action in the course of the night, though the other vessels might have been left so far astern, as still to render the result doubtful.

Whatever may be thought of the management of the enemy, there can be but one opinion as to that of Captain Stewart. The promptitude with which he decided on his course, the judgment with which he ordered the prizes to vary their courses, and the steadiness with which the *Constitution* was commanded, aided in elevating a professional reputation that was already very high.

This terminated the exploits of the gallant *Constitution*, or Old Ironsides, as she was affectionately called in the navy; Captain Stewart, after landing his prisoners at Maranham, and learning at Porto Rico, that peace had been made, carried her into New York, about the middle of May. In the course of two years and nine months, this ship had been in three actions, had been twice critically chased, and had captured five vessels of war, two of which were frigates, and a third frigate-built. In all her service, as well before Tripoli, as in this war, her good fortune was remarkable. She never was dismasted, never got ashore, or scarcely ever suffered any of the usual accidents of the sea. Though so often in battle, no very serious slaughter ever took place on board her. One of her commanders was wounded, and four of her lieutenants had been killed; two on her own decks, and two in the *Intrepid*; but, on the whole, her entire career had been that of what is usually called a "lucky ship." Her fortune, however, may perhaps be explained in the simple fact, that she had always been well commanded. In her two last cruises she had probably possessed as fine a crew as ever manned a frigate. They were principally New England men, and it has been said of them, that they were almost qualified to fight the ship without her officers.

★ ★ ★ ★ ★

Captain Stewart had eighteen men killed and wounded; his two opponents suffered around eighty casualties. On the return voyage home his small flotilla ran into a British squadron that retook the *Levant*. The *Constitution* and *Cyane* returned safely to New York on May 15, 1815. The *Cyane* was purchased into the U.S. Navy and became the USS *Cyane*. For his victories, Stewart received a gold medal from Congress, and the crew was awarded considerable prize money.

From *White-Jacket*

HERMAN MELVILLE

> To produce a mighty book, you must choose a mighty theme. No great and enduring volume can ever be written on the flea, though many there be that have tried it.
>
> —Herman Melville

Herman Melville was one of the greatest writers on the age of sail in the English language. The authenticity of his narratives came from an early life serving on whalers and with the U.S. Navy in the Atlantic and the South Pacific. *White Jacket* was written from his memories of service as an ordinary seaman for fourteen months on the American frigate *United States* returning from the Pacific. The book is a detailed description of life aboard a man-of-war, and a social commentary for the cause of humanitarian justice. It is part autobiographical and part epic fiction. In the following chapter, Melville describes his role and how the crew aboard an American man-of-war is organized by its officers for duty and action at sea.

★ ★ ★ ★ ★

> Conceive him now in a man-of-war;
> with his letters of mart, well armed,
> victualed, and appointed,
> and see how he acquits himself.
> —FULLER'S "Good Sea-Captain"

NOTE. In the year 1843 I shipped as "ordinary seaman" on board of a United States frigate then lying in a harbor of the Pacific Ocean. After remaining in this frigate for more than a year, I was discharged from the service upon the vessel's arrival home. My man-of-war experiences and observations have been incorporated in the present volume.

NEW YORK, MARCH, 1850.

CHAPTER I.
THE JACKET.

It was not a *very* white jacket, but white enough, in all conscience, as the sequel will show.

The way I came by it was this.

When our frigate lay in Callao, on the coast of Peru—her last harbor in the Pacific—I found myself without a *grego*, or sailor's surtout; and as, toward the end of a three years' cruise, no pea-jackets could be had from the purser's steward: and being bound for Cape Horn, some sort of a substitute was indispensable; I employed myself, for several days, in manufacturing an outlandish garment of my own devising, to shelter me from the boisterous weather we were so soon to encounter.

It was nothing more than a white duck frock, or rather shirt: which, laying on deck, I folded double at the bosom, and by then making a continuation of the slit there, opened it lengthwise—much as you would cut a leaf in the last new novel. The gash being made, a metamorphosis took place, transcending any related by Ovid. For, presto! the shirt was a coat!—a strange-looking coat, to be sure; of a Quakerish amplitude about the skirts; with an infirm, tumble-down collar; and a clumsy fullness about the wristbands; and white, yea, white as a shroud. And my shroud it afterward came very near proving, as he who reads further will find.

But, bless me, my friend, what sort of a summer jacket is this, in which to weather Cape Horn? A very tasty, and beautiful white linen garment it may have seemed; but then, people almost universally sport their linen next to their skin.

Very true; and that thought very early occurred to me; for no idea had I of scudding round Cape Horn in my shirt; for *that* would have been almost scudding under bare poles, indeed.

So, with many odds and ends of patches—old socks, old trowser-legs, and the like—I bedarned and bequilted the inside of my jacket, till it became, all over, stiff and padded, as King James's cotton-stuffed and dagger-proof doublet; and no buckram or steel hauberk stood up more stoutly.

So far, very good; but pray, tell me, White-Jacket, how do you propose keeping out the rain and the wet in this quilted grego of yours? You don't call this wad of old patches a Mackintosh, do you?—you don't pretend to say that worsted is water-proof?

No, my dear friend; and that was the deuce of it. Waterproof it was not, no more than a sponge. Indeed, with such recklessness had I bequilted my jacket, that in a rain-storm I became a universal absorber; swabbing bone-dry the very bulwarks I leaned against. Of a damp day, my heartless shipmates even used to stand up against me, so powerful was the capillary attraction between this luckless jacket of mine and all drops of moisture. I dripped like a turkey a roasting; and long after the rain storms were over, and the sun showed his face, I still stalked a Scotch mist; and when it was fair weather with others, alas! it was foul weather with me.

Me? Ah me! Soaked and heavy, what a burden was that jacket to carry about, especially when I was sent up aloft; dragging myself up step by step, as if I were weighing the anchor. Small time then, to strip, and wring it out in a rain, when no hanging back or delay was permitted. No, no; up you go: fat or lean: Lambert or Edson: never mind how much avoirdupois you might weigh. And thus, in my own proper person, did many showers of rain reascend toward the skies, in accordance with the natural laws.

But here be it known, that I had been terribly disappointed in carrying out my original plan concerning this jacket. It had been my intention to make it thoroughly impervious, by giving it a coating of paint, But bitter fate ever overtakes us unfortunates. So much paint had been stolen by the sailors, in daubing their overhaul trowsers and tarpaulins, that by the time I—an honest man—had completed my quiltings, the paint-pots were banned, and put under strict lock and key.

Said old Brush, the captain of the *paint-room*—"Look ye, White-Jacket," said he, "ye can't have any paint."

Such, then, was my jacket: a well-patched, padded, and porous one; and in a dark night, gleaming white as the White Lady of Avenel!

CHAPTER II.
HOMEWARD BOUND.

"All hands up anchor! Man the capstan!"

"High die! my lads, we're homeward bound!"

Homeward bound!—harmonious sound! Were you *ever* homeward bound?—No?—Quick! take the wings of the morning, or the sails of a ship, and fly to the uttermost parts of the earth. There, tarry a year or two; and then let the gruffest of boatswains, his lungs all goose-skin, shout forth those magical words, and you'll swear "the harp of Orpheus were not more enchanting."

All was ready; boats hoisted in, stun' sail gear rove, messenger passed, capstan-bars in their places, accommodation-ladder below; and in glorious spirits, we sat down to dinner. In the ward-room, the lieutenants were passing round their oldest port, and pledging their friends; in the steerage, the *middies* were busy raising loans to liquidate the demands of their laundress, or else—in the navy phrase—preparing to pay their creditors *with a flying fore-topsail*. On the poop, the captain was looking to windward; and in his grand, inaccessible cabin, the high and mighty commodore sat silent and stately, as the statue of Jupiter in Dodona.

We were all arrayed in our best, and our bravest; like strips of blue sky, lay the pure blue collars of our frocks upon our shoulders; and our pumps were so springy and playful, that we danced up and down as we dined.

It was on the gun-deck that our dinners were spread; all along between the guns; and there, as we cross-legged sat, you would have thought a hundred farm-yards and meadows were nigh. Such a cackling of ducks, chickens, and ganders; such a lowing of oxen, and bleating of lambkins, penned up here and there along the deck, to provide sea repasts for the officers. More rural than naval were the sounds; continually reminding each mother's son of the old paternal homestead in the green old clime; the old arching elms; the hill where we gambolled; and down by the barley banks of the stream where we bathed.

"All hands up anchor!"

When that order was given, how we sprang to the bars, and heaved round that capstan; every man a Goliath, every tendon a hawser!—round and round—round, round it spun like a sphere, keeping time with our feet to the time of the fifer, till the cable was straight up and down, and the ship with her nose in the water. "Heave and pall! unship your bars, and make sail!"

It was done: barmen, nipper-men, tierers, veerers, idlers and all, scrambled up the ladder to the braces and halyards; while like monkeys in Palm-trees, the sail-loosers ran out on those broad boughs, our yards; and down fell the sails like white clouds from the ether—topsails, top-gallants, and royals; and away we ran with the halyards, till every sheet was distended.

"Once more to the bars!"

"Heave, my hearties, heave hard!"

With a jerk and a yerk, we broke ground; and up to our bows came several thousand pounds of old iron, in the shape of our ponderous anchor.

Where was White-Jacket then?

White-Jacket was where he belonged. It was White-Jacket that loosed that main-royal, so far up aloft there, it looks like a white albatross' wing. It was White-Jacket that was taken for an albatross himself, as he flew out on the giddy yard-arm!

CHAPTER III.
A GLANCE AT THE PRINCIPAL DIVISIONS, INTO WHICH A MAN-OF-WAR'S CREW IS DIVIDED.

Having just designated the place where White-Jacket belonged, it must needs be related how White-Jacket came to belong there.

Every one knows that in merchantmen the seamen are divided into watches—starboard and larboard—taking their turn at the ship's duty by night. This plan is followed in all men-of-war. But in all men-of war, besides this division, there are others, rendered indispensable from the great number of men, and the necessity of precision and discipline. Not only are particular bands assigned to the three *tops*, but in getting under weigh, or any other proceeding requiring all hands, particular men of these bands are assigned to each yard of the tops. Thus, when the order is given to loose the main-royal, White-Jacket flies to obey it; and no one but him.

And not only are particular bands stationed on the three decks of the ship at such times, but particular men of those bands are also assigned to particular duties. Also, in tacking ship, reefing top-sails, or "coming to," every man of a frigate's five-hundred-strong, knows his own special place, and is infallibly found there. He sees nothing else, attends to nothing else, and will stay there till grim death or an epaulette orders him away. Yet there are times when, through the negligence of the officers, some exceptions are found to this rule. A rather serious circumstance growing out of such a case will be related in some future chapter.

Were it not for these regulations a man-of-war's crew would be nothing but a mob, more ungovernable stripping the canvas in a gale than Lord George Gordon's tearing down the lofty house of Lord Mansfield.

But this is not all. Besides White-Jacket's office as looser of the main-royal, when all hands were called to make sail; and besides his special offices, in tacking ship, coming to anchor, etc.; he permanently belonged to the Starboard Watch, one of the two primary, grand divisions of the ship's company. And in this watch he was a maintop-man; that is, was stationed in the main-top, with a number of other seamen, always in readiness to execute any orders pertaining to the main-mast, from above the main-yard. For, including the main-yard, and below it to the deck, the main-mast belongs to another detachment.

Now the fore, main, and mizen-top-men of each watch—Starboard and Larboard—are at sea respectively subdivided into Quarter Watches; which regularly relieve each other in the tops to which they may belong; while, collectively, they relieve the whole Larboard Watch of top-men.

Besides these topmen, who are always made up of active sailors, there are Sheet-Anchor-men—old veterans all—whose place is on the forecastle; the fore-yard, anchors, and all the sails on the bowsprit being under their care.

They are an old weather-beaten set, culled from the most experienced seamen on board. These are the fellows that sing you "*The Bay of Biscay Oh!*" and "*Here a sheer hulk lies poor Torn Bowling!*" "*Cease, rude Boreas, blustering railer!*" who, when ashore, at an eating-house, call for a bowl of tar and a biscuit. These are the fellows who spin interminable yarns about Decatur, Hull, and Bainbridge; and carry about their persons bits of "Old Ironsides," as Catholics do the wood of the true cross. These are the fellows that some officers never pretend to damn, however much they may anathematize others. These are the fellows that it does your soul good to look at;—hearty old members of the Old Guard; grim sea grenadiers, who, in tempest time, have lost many a tarpaulin overboard. These are the fellows whose society some of the youngster midshipmen much affect; from whom they learn their best seamanship; and to whom they look up as veterans; if so be, that they have any reverence in their souls, which is not the case with all midshipmen.

Then, there is the *After-guard*, stationed on the Quarterdeck; who, under the Quarter-Masters and Quarter-Gunners, attend to the main-sail and spanker, and help haul the main-brace, and other ropes in the stern of the vessel.

The duties assigned to the After-Guard's-Men being comparatively light and easy, and but little seamanship being expected from them, they are composed chiefly of landsmen; the least robust, least hardy, and least sailor-like of the crew; and being stationed on the Quarter-deck, they are generally selected with some eye to their personal appearance. Hence, they are mostly slender young fellows, of a genteel figure and gentlemanly address; not weighing much on a rope, but weighing considerably in the estimation of all foreign ladies who may chance to visit the ship. They lounge away the most part of their time, in reading novels and romances; talking over their lover affairs ashore; and comparing notes concerning the melancholy and sentimental career which drove them—poor young gentlemen—into the hard-hearted navy. Indeed, many of them show tokens of having moved in very respectable society. They always maintain a tidy exterior; and express an abhorrence of the tar-bucket, into which they are seldom or never called to dip their digits. And pluming themselves upon the cut of their trowsers, and the glossiness of their tarpaulins, from the rest of the ship's company, they acquire the name of "*sea-dandies*" and "*silk-sock-gentry*."

Then, there are the *Waisters*, always stationed on the gun-deck. These haul aft the fore and main-sheets, besides being subject to ignoble duties; attending to the drainage and sewerage below hatches. These fellows are all Jimmy Duxes—sorry chaps, who never put foot in ratlin, or venture above the bulwarks. Inveterate "*sons of farmers*," with the hayseed yet in their hair, they are consigned to the congenial superintendence of the chicken-coops, pig-pens, and potato-lockers. These are generally placed amidships, on the gun-deck of a frigate, between the fore and main hatches; and comprise so extensive an area, that it much resembles the market place of a small town. The melodious sounds thence issuing, continually draw tears from the eyes of the Waisters; reminding them of their old paternal pig-pens and potato-patches. They are the tag-rag and bob-tail of the crew; and he who is good for nothing else is good enough for a *Waister*.

Three decks down—spar-deck, gun-deck, and berth-deck—and we come to a parcel of Troglodytes or "*holders*," who burrow, like rabbits in warrens, among the water-tanks, casks, and cables. Like Cornwall miners, wash off the soot from their skins, and they are all pale as ghosts. Unless upon rare occasions, they seldom come on deck to sun themselves. They may circumnavigate the world fifty times, and they see about as much of it as Jonah did in the whale's belly. They are a lazy, lumpish, torpid set; and when going ashore after a long cruise, come out into the day like terrapins from their caves, or bears in the spring, from tree-trunks. No one ever knows the names of these fellows; after a three years' voyage, they still remain strangers to you. In time of tempests, when all hands are called to save ship, they issue forth into the gale, like the mysterious old men of Paris, during the massacre of the Three Days of September: every one marvels who they are, and whence they come; they disappear as mysteriously; and are seen no more, until another general commotion.

Such are the principal divisions into which a man-of-war's crew is divided; but the inferior allotments of duties are endless, and would require a German commentator to chronicle.

We say nothing here of Boatswain's mates, Gunner's mates, Carpenter's mates, Sail-maker's mates, Armorer's mates, Master-at-Arms, Ship's corporals, Cockswains, Quarter-masters, Quarter-gunners, Captains of the Forecastle, Captains of the Fore-top, Captains of the Main-top, Captains of the Mizen-top, Captains of the After-Guard, Captains of the Main-Hold, Captains of the Fore-Hold, Captains of the Head, Coopers, Painters, Tinkers, Commodore's Steward, Captain's Steward, Ward-Room Steward, Steerage Steward, Commodore's cook, Captain's cook, Officers' cook,

Cooks of the range, Mess-cooks, hammock-boys, messenger boys, cot-boys, loblolly-boys and numberless others, whose functions are fixed and peculiar.

It is from this endless subdivision of duties in a man-of-war, that, upon first entering one, a sailor has need of a good memory, and the more of an arithmetician he is, the better.

White-Jacket, for one, was a long time rapt in calculations, concerning the various "numbers" allotted him by the *First Luff*, otherwise known as the First Lieutenant. In the first place, White-Jacket was given the *number of his mess*; then, his *ship's number*, or the number to which he must answer when the watch-roll is called; then, the number of his hammock; then, the number of the gun to which he was assigned; besides a variety of other numbers; all of which would have taken Jedediah Buxton himself some time to arrange in battalions, previous to adding up. All these numbers, moreover, must be well remembered, or woe betide you.

Consider, now, a sailor altogether unused to the tumult of a man-of-war, for the first time stepping on board, and given all these numbers to recollect. Already, before hearing them, his head is half stunned with the unaccustomed sounds ringing in his ears; which ears seem to him like belfries full of tocsins. On the gun-deck, a thousand scythed chariots seem passing; he hears the tread of armed marines; the clash of cutlasses and curses. The Boatswain's mates whistle round him, like hawks screaming in a gale, and the strange noises under decks are like volcanic rumblings in a mountain. He dodges sudden sounds, as a raw recruit falling bombs.

Well-nigh useless to him, now, all previous circumnavigations of this terraqueous globe; of no account his arctic, antarctic, or equinoctial experiences; his gales off Beachy Head, or his dismastings off Hatteras. He must begin anew; he knows nothing; Greek and Hebrew could not help him, for the language he must learn has neither grammar nor lexicon.

Mark him, as he advances along the files of old ocean-warriors; mark his debased attitude, his deprecating gestures, his Sawney stare, like a Scotchman in London; his—"*cry your merry, noble seignors!*" He is wholly nonplussed, and confounded. And when, to crown all, the First Lieutenant, whose business it is to welcome all new-comers, and assign them their quarters: when this officer—none of the most bland or amiable either—gives him number after number to recollect—246—139—478—351—the poor fellow feels like decamping.

Study, then, your mathematics, and cultivate all your memories, oh ye! who think of cruising in men-of-war.

The *Merrimack* and the *Monitor*

CAPTAIN VAN BRUNT, USN, AND
FRANKLIN BUCHANAN, CSN

> The combat of the *Merrimack* and the *Monitor* made the greatest change in sea-fighting since cannon fired by gunpowder had been mounted on ships. . . .
>
> —Winston Churchill, *History of the English-Speaking Peoples*

The USS *Monitor* was the first in a new class of steam-driven ironclad warships named after her. They rode low in the water, with several heavy guns housed in a central turret. The ship was double hulled and heavily armored. Designed by John Ericsson, the *Monitor* was built in New York and commissioned on February 25, 1862. Slow and cumbersome to sail, the *Monitor* still represented the next level of technology in naval warfare, being one of the first warships powered by steam with heavy iron armored plate and a revolving turret with two eleven-inch Dahlgren smoothbore shell guns, the heaviest weapons available at the time. The mission for Union ironclads was to engage the Confederate ironclads and bombard southern forts and land forces.

The USS *Monitor* was destined to make history on her very first sortie when she encountered the Confederate ironclad CSS *Virginia* at Hampton Roads on March 9, 1862. It was the first engagement between two ironclad warships. The *Virginia* was formerly the USS *Merrimack*, a steam frigate burned to the waterline and sunk at the dock in Norfolk when the Union abandoned the port. Confederate engineers raised the hull and rebuilt the ship as a casemate ironclad ram with sloping plate armor and ten guns, a seven-inch pivot-mounted rifle at each end and a broadside battery of two six-inch rifles and six nine-inch smoothbores. Equally unwieldy as the *Monitor* at sea, she was nevertheless a serious threat to Union warships manning the blockade of southern ports.

On the morning of March 8, 1862, the *Virginia* and two other Confederate steamships, the CSS *Jamestown* and *Patrick Henry*, sailed from Norfolk navy yard to engage the frigates USS *Cumberland*, the *Congress,* and *Minnesota,* stationed offshore as part of the naval blockade. The *Virginia* rammed the *Cumberland* with the specially built iron ram at her bow, sinking the enemy vessel, and then turned her guns on the *Congress* forcing her to surrender. The *Minnesota*, meanwhile, had run aground and remained trapped against the bottom. The shallow water prevented the *Virginia* from getting close enough to finish her off before the day ended and the Confederate ironclad retreated to port.

During the night, the *Monitor* arrived from New York setting the stage for one of the greatest naval duels of all time. When the *Virginia* sortied once more the following day to destroy the *Minnesota*, the *Monitor* placed itself in between the *Virginia* and the stranded warship. The following passages are from the after action reports taken from both sides. The first is from Capt. Van Brunt who commanded the USS *Minnesota* and had a ringside view of the action. The second is from Flag Officer Franklin Buchanan who commanded the CSS *Virginia* and James River Squadron.

Report of Captain Van Brunt, U.S. Navy, Commanding the steam frigate USS *Minnesota*.

U.S.S. MINNESOTA, *March 10, 1862.*

SIR: On Saturday, the 8th instant, at 12:45 P.M., three small steamers, in appearance, were discovered rounding Sewell's Point, and as soon as they came into full broadside view I was convinced that one was the iron-plated steam battery *Merrimack,* from the large size of her smoke pipe. They were heading for Newport News, and I, in obedience to a signal from the senior officer present, Captain J. Marston, immediately called all hands, slipped my cables, and got underway for that point to engage her. While rapidly passing Sewell's Point the rebels there opened fire upon us from a rifle battery, one shot from which going through and crippling my mainmast. I returned the fire with my broadside guns and forecastle pivot. We ran without further difficulty within about 1½ miles of Newport News, and there, unfortunately, grounded. The tide was running ebb, and although in the channel, there was not sufficient water for this ship, which draws 23 feet. I knew that the bottom was soft and lumpy, and endeavored to force the ship over, but found it was impossible so to do.

At this time it was reported to me that the *Merrimack* had passed the frigate *Congress* and run into the sloop of war *Cumberland,* and in fifteen minutes after I saw the latter going down by the head. The *Merrimack* then hauled off, taking a position, and about 2:30 P.M. engaged the *Congress,* throwing shot and shell into her with terrific effect, while the shot from the *Congress* glanced from her iron-plated sloping sides without doing any apparent damage. At 3:30 P. M. the *Congress* was compelled to haul down her colors. Of the extent of her loss and injury you will be informed from the official report.

At 4 P.M. the *Merrimack, Jamestown,* and *Patrick Henry* bore down upon my vessel. Very fortunately the iron battery drew too much water to come within a mile of us. She took a position on my starboard bow, but did not fire with accuracy, and only one shot passed through the ship's bow.

The other two steamers took their position on my port bow and stern, and their fire did most damage in killing and wounding men, inasmuch as they fired with rifled guns; but with the heavy gun that I could bring to bear upon them I drove them off, one of them apparently in a crippled condition. I fired upon the *Merrimack* with my pivot 10-inch gun without apparent effect, and at 7 P.M. she too hauled off and all three vessels steamed toward Norfolk. The tremendous firing of my broadside guns had crowded me farther upon the mud bank, into which the ship seemed to have made for herself a cradle. From 10 P.M., when the tide commenced to turn flood until 4 A.M., I had all hands at work with steam tugs and hawsers, endeavoring to haul the ship off of the bank, but without avail, and, as the tide had then fallen considerably, I suspended further operations at that time. At 2 A.M. the iron battery *Monitor,* Commander [Lieutenant] John L. Worden, which had arrived the previous evening at Hampton Roads, came alongside and reported for duty, and then all on board felt that we had a friend that would stand by us in our hour of trial.

At 6 A.M. the enemy again appeared, coming down from Craney Island, and I beat to quarters, but they ran past my ship and were heading for Fortress Monroe, and the retreat was beaten to allow my men to get something to eat. The *Merrimack* ran down near to the Rip Raps, and then turned into the channel through which I had come. Again all hands were called to quarters, and when she approached within a mile of us I opened upon her with my stern guns and made signal to the *Monitor* to attack the enemy. She immediately ran down in my wake, right within the range of the *Merrimack,* completely covering my ship as far as was possible with her dimensions, and, much to my astonishment, laid herself right alongside of the *Merrimack,* and the contrast was that of a pigmy to a giant. Gun after gun was fired by the *Monitor,* which was returned with whole broadsides from the rebels with no more effect, apparently, than so many pebblestones thrown by a child. After a while they commenced maneuvering, and we could see the little battery point her bow for the rebels, with the intention, as I thought, of sending a shot through her bow porthole; then she would shoot by her and rake her through her stern. In the meantime the rebel was pouring broadside after broadside, but almost all her shot flew over the little submerged propeller, and when they struck the bomb-proof tower the shot glanced off without producing any effect, clearly establishing the fact that wooden vessels can not contend successfully with ironclad ones; for never before was anything like it dreamed of by the greatest enthusiast in maritime warfare. The *Merrimack,* finding that she could make nothing of the *Monitor,* turned her attention once more to me. In the morning she had put a 11-inch shot under my counter near the water line, and now, on her second approach, I opened upon her with all my broadside guns and 10-inch pivot a broadside which would have blown out of the water any timber-built ship in the world. She returned my fire with her rifled bow gun with a shell, which passed through the chief engineer's stateroom, through the engineer's mess room, amidships, and burst in the boatswain's room, tearing four rooms all into one in its passage, exploding two charges of powder, which set the ship on fire, but it was promptly extinguished by a party headed by my first lieutenant; her second went through the boiler of the tugboat *Dragon,* exploding it and causing some consternation on board my ship for the moment, until the matter was explained. This time I had concentrated upon her an incessant fire from my gun deck, spar deck, and forecastle pivot guns, and was informed by my marine officer, who was stationed on the poop, that at least fifty solid shot struck her on her slanting side without producing any apparent effect. By the time she had fired her third shell the little *Monitor* had come down upon her, placing herself between us, and compelled her to change her position, in doing which she grounded, and again I poured into her all the guns which could be brought to bear upon her. As soon as she got off she stood down the bay, the little battery chasing her with all speed, when suddenly the *Merrimack* turned around and ran full speed into her antagonist. For a moment I was anxious, but instantly I saw a shot plunge into the iron roof of the *Merrimack;* which surely must have damaged her. For some time after the rebels concentrated their whole battery upon the tower and pilot house of the *Monitor,* and soon after the latter stood down for the Fortress Monroe, and we thought it probable that she had exhausted her supply of ammunition or sustained some injury. Soon after the *Merrimack* and the two other steamers headed for my ship, and I then felt to the fullest extent my condition. I was hard and immovably aground, and they could take position under my stem and rake me. I had expended most of my solid shot and my ship was badly crippled and my officers and men were worn out with fatigue, but even then, in this extreme dilemma, I determined never to give up the ship to the rebels, and, after consulting my officers, I ordered every preparation to be made to destroy the ship after all hope was gone to save her. On ascending the poop deck I observed that the enemy's vessels had changed their course and were heading for Craney Island. Then I determined to lighten the ship by throwing overboard my 8 inch guns, hoisting out provisions, starting water, etc. At 2 P.M. I proceeded to make another attempt to save the ship, by the use of a number of powerful tugs and the steamer *S. R. Spaulding*, kindly sent to my assistance by Captain Tallmadge, quartermaster at Fortress Monroe, and succeeded in dragging her half a mile distant, and then she again was immovable, the tide having fallen. At 2 A.M. this morning I succeeded in getting the ship once more afloat, and am now at anchor opposite Fortress Monroe.

It gives me great pleasure to say that during the whole of these trying scenes the officers and men conducted themselves with great courage and coolness.

I have the honor to be, your very obedient servant,

G. J. VAN BRUNT,

Captain, U. S. Navy,
Commanding Frigate Minnesota.

Hon. GIDEON WELLES,

Secretary of the Navy,
Washington, D.C.

Report of Flag-Officer Buchanan, Commander of CSS *Virginia* and the James River Squadron, C.S. Navy.

NAVAL HOSPITAL, *Norfolk, March 27, 1862.*

SIR: Having been confined to my bed in this building since the 9th instant, in consequence of a wound received in the action of the previous day, I have not had it in my power at an earlier date to prepare the official report, which I now have the honor to submit, of the proceedings on the 8th and 9th instant, of the James River Squadron under my command, composed of the following-named vessels: Steamer *Virginia,* flagship, 10 guns; steamer *Patrick Henry,* 12 guns, Commander John R. Tucker; steamer *Jamestown,* Lieutenant Commanding J. N. Barney, 2 guns; and gunboats *Teaser,* Lieutenant Commanding W. A. Webb, *Beaufort,* Lieutenant Commanding W. H. Parker, and *Raleigh,* Lieutenant Commanding J. W. Alexander, each 1 gun; total, 27 guns.

On the 8th instant, at 11 A.M., the *Virginia* left navy yard, Norfolk, accompanied by the *Raleigh* and *Beaufort,* and proceeded to Newport News to engage the enemy's frigates *Cumberland* and *Congress,* gunboats, and shore batteries. When within less than a mile of the *Cumberland,* the *Virginia* commenced the engagement with that ship with her bow gun, and the action soon became general, the *Cumberland, Congress,* gunboats, and shore batteries concentrating upon us their heavy fire, which was returned with great spirit and determination. The *Virginia* stood rapidly on toward the *Cumberland,* which ship I had determined to sink with our prow, if possible. In about fifteen minutes after the action commenced we ran into her on starboard bow; the crash below the water was distinctly heard, and she commenced sinking, gallantly fighting her guns as long as they were above water. She went down with her colors flying. During this time the shore batteries, *Congress,* and gunboats kept up their heavy concentrated fire upon us, doing us some injury. Our guns, however, were not idle; their fire was very destructive to the shore batteries and vessels, and we were gallantly sustained by the rest of the squadron.

Just after the *Cumberland* sunk, that gallant officer, Commander John R. Tucker, was seen standing down James River under full steam, accompanied by the *Jamestown* and *Teaser.* They all came nobly into action, and were soon exposed to the heavy fire of shore batteries. Their escape was miraculous, as they were under a galling fire of solid shot, shell, grape, and canister, a number of which passed through the vessels without doing any serious injury, except to the *Patrick Henry,* through whose boiler a shot passed, scalding to death four persons and wounding others. Lieutenant Commanding Barney promptly obeyed a signal to tow her out of the action. As soon as damages were repaired, the *Patrick Henry* returned to her station and continued to perform good service during the remainder of that day and the following.

Having sunk the *Cumberland,* I turned our attention to the *Congress.* We were some time in getting our proper position, in consequence of the shoalness of the water and the great difficulty of managing the ship when in or near the mud. To succeed in my object I was obliged to run the ship a short distance above the batteries on the James River, in order to wind her. During all the time her keel was in the mud; of course she moved slowly. Thus we were subjected twice to the heavy guns of all the batteries in passing up and down the river, but it could not be avoided. We silenced several of the batteries and did much injury on shore. A large transport steamer alongside of the wharf was blown up, one schooner sunk, and another captured and sent to Norfolk. The loss of life on shore we have no means of ascertaining.

While the *Virginia* was thus engaged in getting her position for attacking the *Congress,* the prisoners state it was believed on board that ship that we had hauled off; the men left their guns and gave three cheers. They were soon sadly undeceived, for a few minutes after we opened on her again, she having run on shore in shoal water. The carnage, havoc, and dismay caused by our fire compelled them to haul down their colors and to hoist a white flag at their gaff and half-mast another at the main. The crew instantly took to their boats and landed. Our fire immediately ceased, and a signal was made for the *Beaufort* to come within hail. I then ordered Lieutenant Commanding Parker to take possession of the *Congress,* secure the officers as prisoners, allow the crew to land, and burn the ship. He ran alongside, received her flag and surrender from Commander William Smith and Lieutenant Pendergrast, with the side arms of those officers. They delivered themselves as prisoners of war on board the *Beaufort,* and afterward were permitted, at their own request, to return to the *Congress* to assist in removing the wounded to the *Beaufort*. They never returned, and I submit to the decision of the Department whether they are not our prisoners. While the *Beaufort* and *Raleigh* were alongside the *Congress*, and the surrender of that vessel had been received from the commander, she having two white flags flying hoisted by her own people, a heavy fire was opened on them from the shore and from the *Congress,* killing some valuable officers and men. Under this fire the steamers left the *Congress,* but as I was not informed that any injury had been sustained by those vessels at that time, Lieutenant Commanding Parker having failed to report to me, I took it for granted that my order to him to burn her had been executed, and waited some minutes to see the smoke ascending her hatches. During this delay we were still subjected to the heavy fire from the batteries, which was always promptly returned.

The steam frigates *Minnesota* and *Roanoke* and the sailing frigate *St. Lawrence* had previously been reported as coming from Old Point, but as I was determined that the *Congress* should not again fall into the hands of the enemy, I remarked to that gallant officer Flag-Lieutenant Minor, "That ship must be burned." He promptly volunteered to take a boat and burn her, and the *Teaser,* Lieutenant Commanding Webb, was ordered to cover the boat. Lieutenant Minor had scarcely reached within 50 yards of the *Congress* when a deadly fire was opened upon him, wounding him severely and several of his men. On witnessing this vile treachery, I instantly recalled the boat and ordered the *Congress* destroyed by hot shot and incendiary shell. About this period I was disabled and transferred the command of the ship to that gallant, intelligent officer, Lieutenant Catesby Jones, with orders to fight her as long as the men could stand to their guns.

The ships from Old Point opened their fire upon us. The *Minnesota* grounded in the north channel, where, unfortunately, the shoalness of the channel prevented our near approach. We continued, however, to fire upon her until the pilots declared that it was no longer safe to remain in that position, and we accordingly returned by the south channel (the middle ground being necessarily between the *Virginia* and *Minnesota,* and *St. Lawrence* and the *Roanoke* having retreated under the guns of Old Point), and again had an opportunity of opening upon the *Minnesota,* receiving her heavy fire in return, and shortly afterwards upon the *St. Lawrence,* from which vessel we also received several broadsides. It had by this time become dark and we soon after anchored off Sewell's Point. The rest of the squadron followed our movements, with the exception of the *Beaufort,* Lieutenant Commanding Parker, who proceeded to Norfolk with the wounded and prisoners as soon as he had left the *Congress,* without reporting to me. The *Congress,* having been set on fire by our hot shot and incendiary shell, continued to burn, her loaded guns being successively discharged as the flames reached them, until a few minutes past midnight, when her magazine exploded with a tremendous report.

The facts above stated as having occurred after I had placed the ship in charge of Lieutenant Jones were reported to me by that officer.

At an early hour next morning (the 9th), upon the urgent solicitations of the surgeons, Lieutenant Minot and myself were very reluctantly taken on shore. The accommodations for the proper treatment of wounded persons on board the *Virginia* are exceedingly limited, Lieutenant Minor and myself occupying the only space that could be used for that purpose, which was in my cabin. I therefore consented to our being landed on Sewell's Point, thinking that the room on board vacated by us could be used for those who might be wounded in the renewal of the action. In the course of the day Lieutenant Minor and myself were sent in a steamer to the hospital at Norfolk.

The following is an extract from the report of Lieutenant Jones of the proceedings of the *Virginia* on the 9th:

> At daylight on the 9th we saw that the *Minnesota* was still ashore, and that there was an iron battery near her. At 8 [o'clock] we ran down to engage them (having previously sent the killed and wounded out of the ship), firing at the *Minnesota* and occasionally at the iron battery. The pilots did not place us as near as they expected. The great length and draft of the ship rendered it exceedingly difficult to work her. We ran ashore about a mile from the frigate and were backing fifteen minutes before we got off. We continued to fire at the *Minnesota*, and blew up a steamer alongside of her, and we also engaged the *Monitor*, sometimes at very close quarters. We once succeeded in running into her, and twice silenced her fire. The pilots declaring that we could get no nearer the *Minnesota*, and believing her to be entirely disabled, and the *Monitor* having to run into shoal water, which prevented our doing her any further injury, we ceased firing at 12 [o'clock] and proceeded to Norfolk.
>
> Our loss is 2 killed and 19 wounded. The stem is twisted and the ship leaks. We have lost the prow, starboard anchor, and all the boats. The armor is somewhat damaged; the steampipe and smokestack both riddled; the muzzles of two of the guns shot away. It was not easy to keep a flag flying. The flagstaffs were repeatedly shot away. The colors were hoisted to the smokestack and several times cut down from it.
>
> The bearing of the men was all that could be desired; their enthusiasm could scarcely be restrained. During the action they cheered again and again. Their coolness and skill were the more remarkable from the fact that the great majority of them were under fire for the first time. They were strangers to each other and to the officers, and had but a few days' instruction in the management of the great guns. To the skill and example of the officers is this result in no small degree attributable.

To that brave and intelligent officer Lieutenant Catesby Jones, the executive and ordnance officer of the *Virginia*, I am greatly indebted for the success achieved. His constant attention to his duties in the equipment of the ship; his intelligence in the instruction of ordnance to the crew, as proved by the accuracy and effect of their fire, some of the guns having been personally directed by him; his tact and management in the government of raw recruits; his general knowledge of the executive duties of a man-of-war, together with his high-toned bearing, were all eminently conspicuous, and had their fruits in the admirable efficiency of the *Virginia*. If conduct such as his (and I do not know that I have used adequate language in describing it) entitles an officer to promotion, I see in the case of Lieutenant Jones one in all respects worthy of it. As flag-officer I am entitled to someone to perform the duties of flag-captain, and I should be proud to have Lieutenant Jones ordered to the *Virginia* as lieutenant-commander, if it be not the intention of the Department to bestow upon him a higher rank.

While in the act of closing this report I received the communication of the Department, dated 22nd instant, relieving me temporarily of the command of the squadron for the naval defenses of James River. I feel honored in being relieved by the gallant Flag-Officer Tattnall.

I much regret that I am not now in a condition to resume my command, but trust that I shall soon be restored to health, when I shall be ready for any duty that may be assigned to me.

Very respectfully,

FRANKLIN BUCHANAN,
Flag-Officer.

Hon. S. R. MALLORY,
Secretary of the Navy.

★ ★ ★ ★ ★

The engagement of March 9, was inconclusive as neither side could overcome the other. Yet the Union was not dislodged from Hampton Roads and the blockade continued, giving a strategic victory to the U.S. Navy. The CSS *Virginia* was run aground and burned on May 11, 1862, to prevent her from falling into enemy hands as the Confederacy abandoned the Norfolk area. The USS *Monitor* foundered in heavy seas off Cape Hatteras in December 1862. She became the prototype, however, for the *Monitor* class, which proved very successful as a river gunboat design that would see action on the James and Mississippi rivers. Naval warfare would never be the same as iron warships had proven to be nearly indestructible when matched against wooden steamships.

Mobile Bay, from *Under Both Flags*

CAPT. H. D. SMITH

Damn the torpedoes! Full speed ahead!
—Admiral David G. Farragut

At the outset of the American Civil War, the United States Navy established a blockade of Confederate ports in order to cut off the Confederacy's supply and trade. Unable to challenge the Union at sea, the South relied on fast, nimble blockade runners to break free of the Union warships and return with the desperately needed weapons and supplies. In order to defeat the Confederacy, it was necessary to capture the port of New Orleans and eliminate the use of other ports from which blockade runners were sailing. Admiral David Farragut forced the surrender of New Orleans in April 1862 by a daring run up the Mississippi past two enemy forts through a gauntlet of heavy fire. With it he achieved a devastating blow to the Confederate war effort as their greatest port and control of the Mississippi fell to the Union.

The center of blockade running shifted to Mobile, Alabama, which by 1864 was the last operating port on the Gulf coast east of the Mississippi. Admiral Farragut returned in August with a fleet of eighteen ships. The mission was to close the port by defeating the Confederate forts Jackson and Gaines protecting the mouth of the bay. The attacking force was also challenged by a well placed minefield that forced them to sail through a narrow channel to enter the bay. A small flotilla of four Confederate warships awaited them in the bay under the command of Admiral Franklin Buchanan, including the formidable ironclad CSS *Tennessee*. Captain H. D. Smith of the U.S. Revenue Marine was with Farragut throughout the battle. The following chapter is his narration of the fighting at Mobile Bay.

★ ★ ★ ★ ★

CONFEDERATES RAM *TENNESSEE*

An incident relative to a blockade runner, not found in any naval history, is well worthy of mention here as illustrative of the life and perils encountered by officers and men comprising the Federal navy.

On the night of August 1st, an English blockade runner, favored by circumstances, ran through the fleet, but was pressed so closely by pursuing gunboats that, running too near to the land, her keel took the bottom at a point close under the guns of Morgan. Farragut was much annoyed by the circumstance, and ordered an expedition to be formed, composed of two boats from each ship, amounting to one hundred men, who, under cover of darkness, pulled in for the beach. At three o'clock they returned, reporting that they could not find the wreck. Farragut summoned his aid, Lieutenant Watson:

"Watson, take my barge and a dozen men; go in there and destroy that blockade runner."

Watson required no second bidding; he loved such work. The larger expedition retired chagrined, while the crew of the barge, with white covers on their caps to distinguish them from the enemy, armed with cutlasses and revolvers, pulled at a swinging stroke straight for the entrance to the Confederate works. The fort loomed up through the darkness, stern and forbidding, while a sharp lookout for the hull of the blockader was maintained. She was discovered by a keen-eyed young topman, lying in the deep shadows of an angle of the fort. There was no delay or nonsense about it; no appealing to the men to fight manfully. There was no occasion for that with the men of the *Hartford*. The barge was headed direct for her, the men boarding just forward of the starboard paddle-box. The demoralized crew were driven in all directions, many seeking safety in flight ashore, giving the alarm to the garrison. With dextrous hands the sailors strewed combustibles in various parts of the vessel, and placing a large tank of powder in the midst of the machinery, the torch was applied. Fort Morgan had now opened a plunging fire, and as the barge pulled off shore, flames burst from all portions of the doomed craft, revealing a company of soldiers advancing at a double-quick down the broad beach. But the game had slipped through their fingers. The shot from the fort made the water boil and foam around the barge, but none struck her, and as the first red streaks of dawn tinged the east, Watson reported his mission to the admiral as accomplished.

The morning of Friday, August 5th, long before day, the boatswain's shrill pipes summoned "all hands!" and "up all hammocks!" Coffee and hardtack were served to the men, while in the cabin, the admiral, Drayton, and Palmer were partaking of a light and early breakfast. Daylight was breaking, with appearances of rain, which, however, had no effect upon the spirits of the men. The wind was west-southwest, in the most favorable quarter for blowing the smoke of the guns on Fort Morgan, and Farragut expressed his satisfaction at the favorable outlook.

Acting Rear-Admiral Bailey, who led the fleet at the passage of the Mississippi forts and who then commanded the East Gulf squadron, had written to his old chief, "Nothing will please me more than to hoist once more the square red flag, and lead the van of your squadron into Mobile Bay, to the capture of Forts Morgan and Gaines, as well as the city. Put me down for two chances, as the jackass said to the monkey at the lion's ball."

But yellow fever broke out in his squadron, he was stricken down with it himself, and it was not deemed prudent to have the vessels of the two commands brought into contact.

Generals Canby and Granger had visited the *Hartford*, and made arrangements that all the troops that could be spared should co-operate with the fleet. There were not enough men to invest both forts, so a body of troops, at Farragut's suggestion, were landed on Dauphin Island, covered by the guns of the *Conemaugh*, Lieutenant-Commander De Krafft.

At four o'clock the wooden ships formed in double column, lashed in pairs, in the following order, the first-mentioned of each pair being the starboard vessel:

Brooklyn, Captain James Olden.
Octarora, Lieutenant-Commander C. H. Greene.
Hartford (flagship), Fleet-Captain Percival Drayton.
Metacomet, Lieutenant-Commander J. E. Jouett.
Richmond, Captain Thornton A. Jenkins.
Port Royal, Lieutenant-Commander Bancroft Gherardi.
Lackawanna, Captain J. B. Marchand.
Seminole, Commander Edward Donaldson.
Monongahela, Commander J. H. Strong.
Kennebec, Lieutenant-Commander W. P. McCann.
Ossipee, Commander W. E. LeRoy.
Itasca, Lieutenant-Commander George Brown.
Oneida, Commander J. R. Madison Mullany.
Galena, Lieutenant-Commander C. H. Wells.

The *Brooklyn* was appointed to lead because she had four chase-guns and apparatus for picking up torpedoes. The four monitors, *Tecumseh*,

Commander T. A. M. Craven; *Manhattan*, Commander J. W. A. Nicholson; *Winnebago*, Commander Thomas H. Stevens; and *Chickasaw*, Lieutenant-Commander G. H. Perkins, formed a line abreast of the four leading ships, and between them and Fort Morgan.

At half-past five Farragut rose from the table, holding in his hand a cup of hot tea, which he was still sipping. He glanced for a moment at Drayton, who, quiet and thoughtful, watched the movements of his superior. "We may as well get under way," he said. Drayton saluted and left the cabin. In one minute answering signals came from the whole fleet, and at six A.M. the ships were all formed in line, moving up the main ship channel, toward the forts, with the Stars and Stripes flying from every masthead and peak. At half-past six the boom of a gun from the *Tecumseh* announced the opening of the ball, and Fort Morgan promptly responded. The *Tecumseh*, with the lion-hearted Craven, had been the last to join the fleet, and was the first to perish on that eventful August morning.

The forts had the advantage, pouring in a raking fire for over half an hour before the ships could get their broadsides to bear, driving the gunners from the barbette and water batteries.

The *Hartford* steamed ahead slowly, coming within short range of the fort before receiving a shot from one of the guns. The order to fire was eagerly awaited, and when it came the old flagship trembled from truck to keelson.

The quarter-deck was occupied by Captain Drayton, with officers of the staff standing conveniently near. At the wheel were three old and reliable seamen, thoroughbreds in every sense of the word, who had been in every engagement known to the vessel, and whose courage and skill were beyond all doubt or question. Their names were McFarland, Wood, and Jassin. Knowles, the signal quartermaster, precise and methodical in his department, walked backward and forward, never for a moment allowing the exciting scenes being enacted about him to divert his attention from his duty.

A great deal has been written relative to the position of Farragut in the Mobile fight, and the incident of being lashed to the rigging has occasioned considerable controversy. Certainly, no question concerning the post occupied by Farragut could arise among those who were on board the flagship and witnessed the engagement.

In the port main-rigging, a few ratlines above the sheer-pole, where he could clearly observe all that was transpiring about him, stood Farragut. In the top was stationed Freeman, his pilot, who bravely piloted the flagship and the fleet behind it through shoals and hidden dangers, when to ground might have brought defeat, as assuredly it would death to those exposed to the fort's scathing fire. And yet, but a few years since, this trusty veteran and servant of Farragut sought in vain for a pilot's berth on some government vessel, ultimately meeting death, in his old age, alone, an inmate of a negro's hut—a pauper, with not even the necessaries of life at hand to soothe his last wretched hours on earth.

As the smoke increased, rolling above and around the admiral, he mounted the main-rigging higher and higher, until his head was on a level with the buttock band. At that point, Captain Drayton, fearing some accident might occur, sent Knowles with a piece of new lead line to make the admiral more secure.

The honest old sailor, in speaking of the incident, in 1880, at which time he was quartermaster on the U. S. Steamer *Phlox*, stationed at the Naval Academy, expressed himself as follows:

"Pilot Freeman, who was apt to talk too much, I know very well; but that man Baldwin, who yarns it about the admiral and puts him in the *starboard main-rigging,* under the top, he does not know what he is writing about. I was chief quartermaster of the *Hartford* and the man that lashed the admiral to the rigging, and I ought to know something about it.

"When we got up close to the forts, I heard Mr. Kimberly, the executive officer, tell Mr. Watson, our flag-lieutenant, to have a rope passed around the admiral. I was busy at the time with some signal flags for the monitors, when I was ordered to go up the port main-rigging and put a rope around the admiral. I cut a fathom or two from a new lead line which was lying on the deck, went up the ratlines to where the admiral was standing, with opera-glasses in his hand, just under the buttock shrouds, and made the forward end of the line fast. As I took the after end around the admiral, he passed the remark that the rope was not necessary, but I went on and made the after end secure. I don't think he noticed the rope around him, as we were square abreast of Fort Morgan, and it was pretty hot work; but when the ships got clear of the forts, the admiral had to cast the rope adrift before he could come down."

Regarding the assertion made by Brownell in his poem, "The Bay Fight," where he puts the admiral "high in the mizzen shroud," and for which he has been severely criticized, the incident will be hereafter alluded to.

The painting by Page was presented to the Grand Duke Alexis by the citizens of New York, on the occasion of his visit to this country, the presentation speech being made by General Dix. It at present hangs on the walls of the Czar's winter palace.

A great deal of interesting testimony on the much disputed episode is in possession of the writer, but to introduce it all would add nothing to the interest of the battle. It can be produced, however, if it should ever be wanted.

The scene on the deck of the *Hartford* was now one of bustle and extreme animation. Guns were being worked as rapidly as possible; every officer and man was busy; powder boys were rushing from point to point; marines, drawn up in double lines, were loading and firing with as much precision as though on the parade ground; while shot shivered and tore the timbers beneath their feet, shells burst above, filling the air with whizzing particles, mingled with splinters torn from sides, bulwarks, and masts, varying from the length of a match to a piece of cord-wood. Men were falling; blood was everywhere, with shrieks, moans, and groans rising above the din, thud, and roar of battle. The fire from the Confederate gunboats now began to tell, while the solid shot from the *Tennessee*, weighing one hundred and ten pounds, produced a terrible effect. In the foretop of the *Hartford* was a howitzer, under the management of half a dozen sailors, throwing grape and canister into the water battery in front of the fort, doing good service and assisting largely in driving the gunners from their pieces.

The entire fleet was now engaged, with answering shot and shell from the Confederate gunboats, both parties contending for victory, with the old *Hartford* forging very closely upon the dividing line, marking the decisive point in the battle. A shell burst between the two forward guns, in charge of Lieutenant Tyson, killing and wounding fifteen men. A 120-pound shell, from a Blakely rifle, on the Confederate gunboat *Selma*, struck the main-mast, but did not explode; another struck the foremast, while a solid shot, coming through a bow-port, struck a gunner on the neck, shaving his head from the body as quickly as though done with a knife. One poor fellow lost both legs by a round shot; as he fell, he threw up both arms, both of which were carried away by whizzing missiles, which seemed to fill the air.

There was no skulking on that bloody deck, covered with shreds and patches of poor humanity. Men and boys toiled at the guns, shoulder to shoulder; black and white were there, with no thought of social superiority or pre-eminence troubling their brains. No; the smell of blood and the sight of dear friends crushed and mangled about them, filled their hearts with but one desire, stifling all thoughts or sentiments of fear—victory! Triumph over their foes and revenge for the dear blood already spilled—that was what nerved their arms and cleared their eyes, and whenever a telling shot was sent true to its mark, the wild cheers of the *Hartford*'s crew would ring out above the roar of the guns. The bodies of the dead were placed in a long row on the port side, so as not to interfere with the working of the guns, while the wounded were sent below until the surgeon's quarters could contain no more. From an elevated position it was easy to trace the course of every shot, both from the guns of the flagship and from the hostile fleet.

At half-past seven the *Tecumseh* was well up with the fort, having the *Tennessee* on the port beam. The monitor's guns had been loaded with steel shot and sixty pounds of powder, which at that time was the heaviest that had been attempted. Craven knew that the eyes of all the fleet were upon him. It was his great opportunity, and his chivalrous nature yearned for a fair trial of strength with the formidable ram and her famous commander. The fire from the fort was scarcely noticed as the monitor steamed toward her adversary, drawing ahead of the *Brooklyn*, the other monitors following Craven closely. As they drew near the buoy, Craven, from the pilot-house, saw it so close in line with the beach that he said to his pilot, "It is impossible that the admiral means for this vessel to go inside the buoy; I cannot turn my ship." At the same moment the *Tennessee*, which up to that time had lain to the eastward of the buoy, went ahead to the westward of it, and Craven, either fearing she would elude him or unable to restrain his eagerness to commence the combat, gave the order "starboard," heading the *Tecumseh* straight for the ram. She had gone but a few yards, with all hands awaiting the order to fire, when one or more torpedoes exploded under her. She lurched from side to side, careened violently over, and went down, bows first, her screw plainly visible in the air for a moment to all on the *Tennessee*, who awaited her onset, less than two hundred yards off, on the other side of the fatal line. The monitor sank beneath the surface, carrying within her iron walls Craven and one hundred and twenty men, helplessly imprisoned. Had the course of the monitor been directed thirty feet more to the eastward, she would have escaped the danger. The pilot leaped from the pilot-house, and half a dozen sailors in the turret managed to jump through the ports. Farragut, from his post in the port main-rigging, hailed Jouett, who was standing on top of the pilot-house of the *Metacomet*, to know if he had a boat that he could send to pick up the survivors. Jouett had anticipated the order, and a boat in charge of Ensign H. C. Neilds, a volunteer officer, was about leaving the port quarter of the gunboat. She pulled round the *Hartford*'s stern and broadside, across the bows of the *Brooklyn*, toward the wreck, when the pilot, John Collins, and nine of the crew were saved. While on his way, Neilds, who was steering the boat, noticed that the flag was not flying, and, removing it from its cover, unfurled it in the face of friend and foe. The ensign of the forecastle division of the *Hartford*, seeing the boat without a flag, and thinking only of torpedoes, was training his rifled gun upon it when he was stopped just in time, as he was about to pull the lockstring. The *Hartford* had passed on when Neilds had picked up the survivors, and, after putting them on board the *Winnebago*, he pulled down to the *Oneida*, where he served during the rest of the action.

The pilot of the *Tecumseh*, John Collins, stated that at the moment of the explosion he was standing with Captain Craven in the iron tower or pilot-house, directly over the turret. Seeing the inevitable fate of the vessel, Craven and the pilot scrambled down into the turret and met at the foot of the iron ladder, leading to the top of the turret through a narrow scuttle, the only exit now left for escape from the doomed vessel. At that point Craven drew back in a characteristic way and said, "After you, pilot." "There was nothing after me," said Mr. Collins. "When I reached the topmost round of the ladder the vessel seemed to drop from under me."

Farragut had witnessed the frightful fate of the *Tecumseh*, at the same time the *Brooklyn* stopped causing the admiral a great deal of uneasiness. A moment's hesitation might lose him the battle, and to press on might result in sending fleet, guns and all to the bottom of the bay. Farragut himself, in alluding to the subject afterwards, admitted that the sinking of the *Tecumseh* and the stopping of the *Brooklyn* looked as though all of his plans were to be thwarted, and he was at a loss whether to advance or to retreat. In this extremity his natural impulse was to appeal to heaven for guidance, and he offered up this prayer: "O God, who created and gave me reason, direct me what to do. Shall I go on?" And it seemed as if in answer a voice commanded him to "go on!"

When the *Tecumseh* sank, the *Brooklyn* was about a hundred yards astern of her and a little outside; the *Hartford* between one and two hundred yards from the *Brooklyn*, on her port quarter. The admiration of Farragut and his officers was excited, as they passed the *Winnebago*, in witnessing Commander Stevens walking from point to point, between the turrets, giving his directions as unconcernedly as though at anchor in some quiet harbor.

Suddenly the *Brooklyn* and her consort stopped, and then began to back, coming down upon the *Hartford*. At the same time their bows fell off toward the fort and they soon lay nearly athwart the channel. "What is the matter with the *Brooklyn*—has she water enough?" demanded Farragut of his pilot. "Plenty and to spare, sir," was the answer. The *Hartford* was forced to sheer, lapping the *Brooklyn* on the port quarter, while the guns were silenced.

"What's the trouble on board the *Brooklyn*?" came from the flagship.

"Torpedoes ahead!" was the answer.

"D——n the torpedoes!" shouted Farragut. "Four bells, Captain Drayton; go ahead! Jouett, full speed!"

The order to take the lead was received by all on board with loud cheers, which in turn were taken up by the other vessels.

Though the delay had been short, the order to go ahead came none too soon. The *Richmond* had to sheer to avoid collision with the flagship, and all vessels in turn were compelled to stop, their guns partially silenced, while the fire from the enemy's batteries increased, if anything. It was their opportunity.

Clearing the *Brooklyn*, the flagship dashed ahead, and had gained nearly a mile lead before the line could be straightened, but she had cleared the torpedo ground, her broadside guns were again in full play, and Farragut, with his blue flag fluttering above his head, pushed on ahead and alone, with the exception of the *Metacomet*, lashed alongside, and her gallant, impetuous commander, who was a host in himself.

The following lines well describe this heroic action of the lamented Craven:

"After you, pilot," he grandly said,
And proudly stayed his dauntless tread,
Till up the ladder the pilot crept,
And softly from the turret stepped.
Alas! no after was there for him,
Waiting in turret so close and grim.
Each throb of time with peril fraught,
Weightier growing by doubt distraught,
As the eager flood with gurgling sound,
And rush and roar fast flowed him round.
Fainter and fainter the morning beams
Shimmered through tower in fitful gleams;
Darker and darker grew turret and tower,
Surging and plunging with fateful power;
Faster and faster the torn hulk filled,
A moment more and all was stilled—
For oh! the waters, with pitiless thrall,
Over grand Craven threw their pall,
And shrouded in iron, he sank to rest,
Enshrined indeed, forever blest.
On swept the fleet midst flame and smoke
And thundering roar and cannon stroke,
But the bubbles that rose to the surface brim
Were the last of earth that told of him.
Oh! beauteous bay that saw such bloom

Of valor's flower its deeps illume;
A grace like that by Sidney sealed,
Refulgent ray from Zutphen's field,
Stay not your joys with saddening tear,
As flow your tides about his bier,
But leave to the gulf's aye restless surge
The murmurous chant of ceaseless dirge;
For down the years with freshing glory,
Resplendent glows the lustrous story,
And calling to deeds of likest fame,
Immortal crowns grand Craven's name.

THAT AUGUST MORNING

The fleet under Farragut carried the heaviest guns afloat. Their total weight of metal was 14,246 pounds, and they threw at a broadside 9,288 pounds. The *Tennessee* at one discharge could throw 600 pounds, and the remainder of the Confederate craft about 900.

Buchanan fully expected to meet the *Tecumseh*, whose fifteen-inch guns had been loaded with sixty pounds of powder and cylindrical flat-headed steel bolts that it was supposed would penetrate the armor of the *Tennessee*. At that time sixty pounds was the maximum charge for fifteen-inch guns, the largest guns afloat or known to naval warfare. It was afterwards found they could stand one hundred pounds, with a proportionate gain of velocity and battering power.

Before going into action, Admiral Buchanan addressed his officers and men, saying: "Now, men, the enemy is coming, and I want you to do your duty; and you shall not have it to say, when you leave this vessel, that you were not near enough to the enemy, for I will meet them and then you can fight them alongside of their own ships; and if I fall, lay me on one side and go on with the fight, and never mind me, but whip and sink the Yankees or fight until you sink yourselves, but do not surrender."

Buchanan kept his eyes fixed upon the *Tecumseh*, whose flat raft of a hull and ominous-looking turret were with every passing second creeping closer to him. Buchanan had passed the order not to fire until the vessels were in contact and the attention of all men riveted upon the monitor, who, with helm put hard-a-starboard, dashed straight at the *Tennessee*, regardless of the chain of torpedoes of which he had been warned by Farragut. The vessels were not more than a hundred yards apart, when a muffled explosion was heard. A column of water like a fountain shot up from the sea; the monitor lurched heavily, her head settled, her stern went up in the air so that her revolving-screw could be plainly seen, and then she settled beneath the surface in thirty seconds. A cheer rang out from the garrison of Fort Morgan, who imagined that a shot from one of their guns had brought about the catastrophe. A week afterwards, when the divers went down to examine the wreck, they found nearly all the crew at their posts as they sank. The chief engineer, Farron, who had been married in New York only two weeks before and who had received from the flagship's mail his letters while the line was forming, stood with one hand upon the revolving-bar of the turret engine and in the other an open letter from his bride, which his sightless, staring eyes seemed to be reading. He was an invalid, but left his bed at the Pensacola hospital in order to be at his post.

Lieutenant A. D. Wharton, who had command of the forward division of the *Tennessee*, states that when the *Hartford* passed the *Brooklyn* and led the fleet into the bay, she passed square across the ram's bow and not more than 200 yards distant. The seven-inch rifle in the bow of the ram was loaded with a percussion shell, and Wharton congratulated himself that he would have the pleasure of sinking Farragut's flagship under the batteries of Fort Morgan, and that her destruction would defeat the Yankee fleet. He took the lock string from the captain of the gun, taking a long and deliberate aim, giving the commands, "Raise! steady! ready! fire!" He was confident that the shell would tear a hole in the *Hartford*'s side big enough to sink her in a few minutes. It did make a large opening, but it was above the waterline, and the flagship passed majestically on, her sides ablaze with fire from her terrible guns. The keel of the *Hartford* struck several torpedo cases, and the primers were heard to snap; but the admiral's good star shone over him. They had become so corroded by action of the salt water that not one of them exploded, and the fleet passed safely through the net-work of danger to which the *Tecumseh* had fallen a victim.

At half-past eight o'clock the fleet of Farragut's was well into Mobile Bay and past the guns of Fort Morgan. Again had the great admiral proved his ability to run and maneuver his fleet in the face of powerful shore batteries, passing them successfully as he had at New Orleans, Vicksburg, and Port Hudson. Fort Morgan was now out of the fight, but Buchanan with his ram, backed by the gunboats *Selma*, *Gaines*, and *Morgan*, was still lively and full of fight, as the *Hartford* found to her cost when she took the lead.

The three Confederate gunboats took up positions close on the starboard bow of the *Hartford* as she crossed the torpedo line, raking her with a galling fire from their rapidly served seven and eight-inch rifled guns. Keeping ahead of the flagship, they used mainly their stern guns at a range not exceeding 1,000 yards, and their fire was the perfection of artillery practice. One shot from the *Selma* killed ten men and wounded five at guns numbers one and two, while that division was strewn with the bodies of the dead and wounded, and fragments of the bodies were hurled on to the deck of her consort, the *Metacomet*.

Buchanan, through the dense smoke, caught a glimpse of Farragut's blue flag as it floated from its lofty perch. He smiled grimly as he pictured to himself that emblem lowered and humbled, and the ship sinking 'neath the feet of its master. He would give him a taste of the iron ram's quality, which Farragut affected to despise. Everything was in favor of the ram, for the *Hartford* was still some distance in advance of the column and could look for no assistance from her consorts. The ram dashed at its antagonist, but failed to reach the mark. Shots were exchanged, and the Confederate admiral continued down the bay to meet the advancing Federal fleet. Had the ram kept on, it could hardly have failed to sink the *Hartford*, for the channel was narrow, with no opportunity for sheering. The ram endeavored in succession to ram the *Brooklyn*, the *Richmond*, and the *Lackawanna*, but owing to the manner in which they were handled, Buchanan was foiled. But what he missed with his iron prow was more than made up for with his heavy broadsides. He rasped alongside the quarter of the *Kennebec*, putting a shell on her berth deck, killing an officer and four men. He next lodged a couple of shots into the *Ossipee*, and then swung around under the stern of the *Oneida*, into which vessel he discharged two broadsides, disabling two guns, carrying away rigging, and robbing Commander Mullany of an arm.

The last few moments the *Hartford* was under fire of the forts, batteries, and gunboats, was the warmest work the old flagship had ever encountered. Every man on her broad deck appeared to be in motion, and so intent upon his particular line of duty that scarcely a word was spoken. The carefully trained guns seemed imbued with life as they sped in and out of the spacious ports. The hurried run of powder boys and shellmen from the magazines at the stairways and fire-hatches, with supplies for their guns, gave an air of apparent confusion on the deck. The roar of the heavy guns was so great that it was impossible to distinguish the tones of human voices. Occasionally, the peculiar scream of shot passing in close proximity caught the attention of the men, while the bursting of shell and quick snapping crash of flying timber hummed through the air. The cut, frayed rigging swayed wildly to and fro from aloft, and the men, with faces smeared and begrimed with powder, toiled steadily on, peering through the thick pall of battle, watching for the flash and glare of the enemy's guns, and firing in that direction. One gun's crew was entirely swept away, remaining silent until re-manned by men from other portions of the ship. A sailor, fearfully wounded, turned and writhed in the cot used for lowering the wounded to the surgeon's quarters. He fell a distance of thirty feet and his sufferings were at an end. Bulwarks, masts, ropes, guns, and carriages were all more or less smeared with blood and pieces of the human body, over which there was no time to ponder, think, or even grow pale. Captain Drayton and Lieutenant Watson were on the quarter-deck, close observers of all that was passing, and whether fighting or conversing, Watson's face was seldom seen without a pleasant smile, a feature peculiar to him.

Kimberly, the executive officer, speaking-trumpet in hand, walked slowly forward aft the main-deck, seemingly on hand at the very spot where his presence was most required. In caring for the wounded and disposing of the dead, he was tender and careful, looking after all the details as calmly and coolly as though death was miles away, instead of lurking above, below, and all around him.

The *Selma*, which had been handled with great ability, was still annoying the flagship, causing Jouett to manifest great impatience, finding it almost impossible to curb his ardor. The *Metacomet* was the fastest vessel in the fleet, and as yet, in all the shifting phases of the great fight, he had been held in restraint, with no opportunity to measure swords with the foe. Three times he had asked the admiral for permission to leave the side of the *Hartford* and tackle the *Selma*, but the admiral's answer was, "Wait a little longer." At last the flagship emerged from the channel into the deep water of the bay. Then came the signal: "Gunboats, chase enemy's gunboats;" and with a loud and hearty "Ay, ay, sir!" Jouett seized a hatchet and, in common with his axemen, helped to cut asunder the lashings. Farragut waved his hands to Jouett, whose enthusiasm and courage he much admired, and with three hearty cheers rising from the *Metacomet*'s crew, they steamed at full speed in pursuit of the *Selma*, who for some time had been having the fun all her own way.

A heavy rain and wind squall had swept in from the gulf, completely obscuring, for a short interval, objects both afloat and on shore. The *Morgan*, in her anxiety to escape the coming wrath, ran aground, but floated as the squall cleared up, and steamed for protection under the guns of Fort Morgan.

During the mist and uncertainty accompanying the rush of wind and rain, the Federal gunboat was dashing ahead at full speed, while the commander was looking after the effective serving of the forward pivot gun.

"We are shoaling our water, sir," remarked the executive. "I am afraid we shall take the bottom, as we draw twelve feet of water."

"Never mind, sir, never mind. Keep her going," replied Jouett, as he sighted the piece. But the prudent executive quietly ordered a quartermaster to take the lead, and the next instant "Fifteen feet!" was announced. That was all right, and the engine never ceased in its powerful workings. "Fourteen feet!" was the next report. "Thirteen feet!" came sharp and clear from the steady old seaman. The situation was becoming serious! The men glanced quickly at one another, while the officers kept their eyes fastened upon their commander, who turned coolly from the gun, saying, as he walked aft: "Call that man in from the lead. He makes me nervous."

Lieutenant Murphy, commanding the *Selma*, attempted to escape under cover of the fogs, but his vessel was too slow to escape the *Metacomet*. At nine o'clock, by which time the sky was clear again, Jouett was forging across the bow of his antagonist, his battery trained upon the gunboat. Their guns rang out; *Comstock*, the executive officer, and four men fell, to rise no more, and Murphy himself was wounded. Jouett and his boarders were mustering to complete their work at close quarters, when the *Selma*'s flag disappeared in token of submission. In tow of the *Metacomet*, she was carried back to the *Hartford*. The gunboat *Gaines* meanwhile had been chased on shore, under the guns of Fort Morgan, where the torch was applied, the crew seeking shelter inside the fort. The ram, with colors flying and ports closed, had also retired under the shadow of the fort, and the roar of battle died away. Farragut, supposing that the fighting was over for the time being, had anchored about three miles up the bay, signaling his fleet to follow his motions. All hands were at once engaged in clearing the wreck, washing the blood from the decks, and cleansing the ship throughout, while the wounded were made as comfortable as circumstances would permit. The boilers were relieved in part of the great pressure of steam, while the fires were allowed to assume much smaller proportions. Preparations were made as rapidly as possible to give the tired, hungry survivors some breakfast, and stewards and cooks, with fresh uniforms, clean hands and faces, white aprons and jackets in lieu of cutlass, revolver, and cartridge-box, bustled briskly about, with orders flying thick and fast from caterers of messes.

Such of the officers as could be spared from the deck and posts of duty hastened to the wardroom to ascertain how it had fared with friends and messmates who were dead and who had survived. One, Ensign Heginbotham, of the admiral's staff, was mortally wounded. Lieutenant Adams was slightly wounded; all the rest had escaped unhurt. Of the crew, twenty-eight mangled bodies were lying in a ghastly row on the port side of the deck, with twenty-five wounded below. Out of the eighteen officers in the wardroom, strange to state, but one was fatally hurt. Each congratulated the other upon his good fortune, and around the mess-table such a handshaking and exchange of hearty good-will the wardroom had never witnessed before.

Swords, caps, accoutrements of all kinds had been piled hurriedly in one corner of the wardroom, while the grateful aroma of strong, freshly-made coffee pervaded the apartment. In the midst of it all the sharp, piercing tones of Executive Kimberly were heard calling all hands to quarters, and a messenger boy, his young face all aglow with excitement, hurried into the officers' midst with the words, "Gentlemen, the ram is coming!"

Every officer and man repaired to his post, anxious to have the affair decided, for no rest could be expected while the *Tennessee* remained afloat with the Confederate ensign flying over her.

Farragut and Buchanan were of equal rank in the old navy, Farragut being the senior, having entered the service December 10, 1810, and Buchanan on January 28, 1815. Both received a captain's commission on September 14, 1855. At the outbreak of the Rebellion, Farragut was waiting orders at Norfolk. Buchanan had command of the Washington Navy Yard. He resigned his commission when the Massachusetts troops were attacked in the streets of Baltimore, expecting that Maryland, his native State, would at once secede. Failing in his expectations, he petitioned to recall his resignation, but was refused.

The parapets of the forts were lined with Confederate soldiers, who were beyond range of the guns, and as spectators were greatly interested in the coming contest. Single-handed, the ram, which was believed to be invulnerable, was running straight for the Federal fleet as fast as her powerful double engines could propel her. The monitors, slow and unwieldy, could offer little or no resistance to her approach, and Farragut, who placed his chief dependence upon his stout wooden walls, at once prepared to accept the gauge of battle so bravely thrown at his feet. That the spectators from the forts expected to see the *Tennessee* whip in detail the Yankee fleet there can be but little doubt, and more than one stout heart on board the Federal vessels beat apprehensively as the distance between the rival admirals lessened.

Farragut stood with his arms folded, his eyes riveted upon the ram, his features bearing a stern expression. With a rapid, nervous movement the great captain unbuttoned his frock-coat, and, turning to his fleet captain, said: "He is after me. Let him come on. Admiral for admiral, flagship for flagship! I'll fight him while I have a gun left or a man to ram home the charge."

Buchanan's previous experience with wooden vessels, when he commanded the Merrimac in Hampton Roads, gave him confidence and strong hopes of winning an easy victory, for the *Tennessee* was far superior to his former command. But he had antagonists keenly alive to every chance and fluctuation of battle; the vessels, though wooden, were not helplessly anchored, and, above all, there was a ruling master spirit, which, had it been present at Hampton Roads, might have registered a far different result from that won by the astute Confederate admiral.

From the poop of the *Hartford* Farragut watched the approach of the ram, while from the spanker gaff of the flagship fluttered the signal, "Attack the enemy." Cables were slipped, all anxious to lead in the action, but the *Monongahela*, with her iron prow, was foremost in the race, and at once rushed at the ram full speed. It had been Farragut's intention, after serving breakfast to the officers and men, to seek the *Tennessee* in her lair and bring her out to a conclusion, as the advantages of daylight were far in excess of what possibly could have been at night. Buchanan, by his spirited action, had simply anticipated his antagonist's intentions by an hour at most. Under the guns of the fort an opportunity to inspect damages was afforded. A narrow examination revealed a few dents in the armor, and a portion of the smoke-stack carried away. With this slight exhibit, as a result of the heavy fire sustained from the Federal fleet, Buchanan smiled exultantly, and summoning Captain Johnston communicated to him his resolution to once more engage the fleet. "Follow them up, Johnston," he said, "we can't let them off that way." It has been stated that Buchanan was advised not to make his second attack. It was one vessel pitted against three ironclads and fourteen wooden ships. But the iron will and determined courage of the man was proof against all argument. He realized that he was alone, that his squadron had disappeared, that the forts could render him no assistance, but he felt that his vessel was more than a match for a dozen wooden ships; as for the monitors, he knew not their strength, but would not yield until he had squarely tested their merits.

Some fortunate accident might occur—torpedoes possibly rid him of another ironclad—a panic demoralize the Federals through the loss of their vaunted flagship and great leader, who viewed with such scorn the iron plating and swinging shutters of the newly-created iron men-of-war. The battle might yet be won, defeat turned into victory, Mobile saved from disaster and humiliation, and the forts and defences restored to their lost prestige and strength.

Animated with sentiments that caused his cheeks to flush and eyes sparkle, the old warrior answered his advisers: "Let those retire who wish to. I will either be killed or taken prisoner, and now I am in the humor I will have it out at once."

Steadily the *Tennessee* approached the Federal fleet, which was under way. Not a living being could be seen on board the ram. Every port was closed; the colors waved from a short flag-staff aft; an indescribable air of superiority pervaded the huge vessel, as singly and alone she faced the entire force, as if conscious of her superior strength and resources.

Then ensued one of the most remarkable naval battles the world had ever known, unsurpassed in any age for bravery and fierceness.

THE ADMIRAL'S TRIUMPH

The *Monongahela*, with her iron prow and under a full head of steam, was the first vessel of the Federal fleet to try issues with the Confederate champion. But the *Tennessee* paid no attention to the attack, merely putting her helm to port, which caused the *Monongahela* to strike her a glancing blow. It crushed the stern and crumbled the iron prow of the wooden ship, who received from the ram two shots that pierced her through and through, while the shot from the nine-inch guns rolled harmlessly off the sloping sides of the ironclad. The *Chickasaw* sent one of her solid bolts after her, but no harm resulted. The next vessel to meet the ram was the *Lackawanna*, which succeeded in striking her antagonist at right angles at the after end of the casemate. The concussion was great, but the effect on the ram was scarcely noticeable, while the wooden vessel had her timbers crushed in for a distance of three feet above the water's edge to five feet below. After striking, the two swung head and stern alongside of each other. Two shots from the ram passed through the bow of the unlucky craft whose guns had been pivoted on the opposite side, and but one nine-inch shell was expended on the *Tennessee*. This struck one of her port shutters, which was distant about twelve feet, destroying it and driving some of the fragments into her casemate. A few of the enemy were seen through the ports, making insulting gestures and using opprobrious language. Both sailors and marines opened upon them with rifles and revolvers; even a spittoon and a holy-stone were thrown by the indignant sailors from the deck of the *Lackawann*a, before the vessels finally cleared each other. As the smoke drifted to leeward, Buchanan discovered the *Hartford* coming bows on at full speed. It was the opportunity he had been looking for. There was a clear space between the opposing flagships, and Buchanan felt positive of his ability to send Farragut and his walls of oak, shattered, crushed, beaten, to the bottom of the bay. Up to the commencement of the war they had been warm friends; now each was hoping for the overthrow of the other, and had Buchanan possessed the same degree of dogged determination as his former associate, it is possible both flagships might have terminated their career in the furious onset. Had the ram struck fair, with her power and momentum, she would have forced her way to the foremast of the *Hartford*, and unable to extricate herself from the shattered frigate would have sunk side by side with her antagonist. But it was ordered otherwise: the *Tennessee* swerved, struck a glancing blow on the port bow, injuring the frigate but slightly, and the two vessels grated and rasped sullenly by each other.

Buchanan now met with a vexatious turn of fortune which no good seamanship or precaution could have avoided. He could not have wished for a more favorable opportunity to try his powerful guns on his wooden rival, and the order was at once passed to "give it to her!" But one gun after another in rapid succession missed fire, the primers failed to explode except at one gun, which sent a shell through the berth-deck, above the water-line, killing five men and wounding eight—the last hostile shot that ever was fired at the old flagship. The muzzle of the gun was so close that the powder blackened the ship's side. It was the most unfortunate moment of the combat for Buchanan; his would-be victim glided from his side, pouring in a broadside of solid shot as a parting salute, which merely dented the ram's armor and bounded harmlessly into the air.

While the *Hartford* was about to ram the *Tennessee*, Farragut sprang into the port mizzen-rigging in order to overlook the maneuver. He was a conspicuous target, in his uniform, for either a rifle or a pistol ball. Lieutenant Watson, his aid, who observed his peril, begged him not to remain in so exposed a position; but he remained that he might better observe the impending collision. Watson picked up a piece of rope off the poop and made a turn around his body, securing the end to the mizzen shrouds. In this position the admiral remained until the two ships separated; so that Brownell, in his poem of the "Bay Fight," does not err very badly in making use of the line and putting the admiral "high in the mizzen shroud."

Captain Drayton during the ramming was on the top-gallant forecastle, and catching a glimpse of Buchanan's head above the hatch on the casemate, cried: "Infernal traitor, are you afraid of a wooden ship?" and shook his marine glasses in a threatening manner. Lieutenant Watson at the same time fired his revolver at him, which warm reception Buchanan acknowledged by prudently disappearing. So close were the two vessels that Farragut from his position could easily have jumped to the deck of the ram. The ram now dropped astern and was immediately taken in hand by the rest of the fleet, while the *Hartford* circled around to obtain a favorable position for renewing her fight.

It was a reception Buchanan had not calculated upon receiving. He had hoped for a different state of affairs, with his iron prow carrying panic and destruction through the wooden fleet as at Hampton Roads; and the spectators from the forts began to doubt seriously that the iron ram was so much of a prodigy, after all. At any rate, there was no appearance or prospect of victory appearing on the banner of the ironclad. The flagstaff and its shot-riddled flag had long since disappeared, to be replaced by another lashed to a boat-hook thrust through the grating that covered the casemate. The rattle of the nine-inch shot on the sloping sides of the ram made the stout craft quiver and tremble, while the shocks from the huge wooden vessels ramming him demoralized and disheartened the crew. They were rapidly losing faith in the unwieldy monster, and loudly muttered their dissatisfaction.

Lieutenant Wharton, of the *Tennessee*, in speaking of the effect of the monitor's fire, thus describes it:

> "The *Monongahela* was hardly clear of us when a hideous-looking monster came creeping up on our port side, whose slowly-revolving turret revealed the cavernous depths of a mammoth gun. 'Stand clear of the port side!' I shouted. A moment after a thunderous report shook us all, while a blast of dense sulphurous smoke covered our port holes, and 440 pounds of iron, impelled by sixty pounds of powder, admitted daylight through our side, where, before it struck, there had been over two feet of solid wood, covered with five inches of solid iron. This was the only fifteen-inch shot that hit us fair. It did not come through; the inside netting caught the splinters, and there were no casualties from it. I was glad to find myself alive after that shot."

As the *Hartford* turned to renew her attack on the ram, she steamed in front of the *Lackawanna*, which had already pointed for the *Tennessee*, and was running down upon her at full speed. Thick clouds of smoke were eddying about, and the *Lackawanna*, discovering the *Hartford* too late, reversed her engine, putting her helm hard-a-starboard. The force of the blow was broken, but she struck the flagship two guns forward of the mizzen-rigging, knocking two ports into one, throwing two guns over on deck, carrying away the rail to the mizzen-rigging, and cutting the *Hartford* down nearly to the water's edge. The collision carried consternation and alarm to the *Hartford*'s men, who imagined that the flagship had received her death-blow, and that from the hands of a friend. "Save the admiral!" was the cry that resounded along the deck, but that official, cool as ever, had sprung into the starboard mizzen-rigging, looked over the side of the ship, and finding there were still a few inches of splintered planking left above the water's edge, instantly ordered the ship ahead again at full speed, after the ram.

The three monitors had now arrived in position, and were paying undivided attention to the *Tennessee*, which still pluckily continued the fight. The *Chickasaw* ranged up under the stern of the ram, firing as rapidly as her huge guns would permit, while the *Winnebago* and *Manhattan* remained on either quarter. The *Hartford* proceeded to repair damages inflicted by the *Lackawanna*, and was soon reported ready. Farragut was anxious to remain in close proximity to the ram, and never, in any of his previous battles, had exhibited so much anxiety.

The *Ossipee*, *Lackawanna*, *Monongahela*, and *Hartford* were all preparing to run down the ram under full heads of steam, while Buchanan, with closed ports, moved slowly ahead, receiving the thundering blows from the monitor's fifteen-inch guns without once replying to their fire. Feebly and laboriously the bows of the *Tennessee* were turned toward Fort Morgan, and it was apparent that the champion of the South was sorely beset. Like a knight of old, encased in well-tried armor, surrounded by enemies, with all hope gone and everything lost save honor and reputation, receiving blow after blow upon armor dented and gaping with wounds, yet disdaining to surrender, to such might be likened the plight Buchanan found himself in. The ram had been shorn of all her glory, naught remaining but her sloping casemates as a target for the guns of the Union fleet. Her smoke-stack had disappeared, flagstaff and ensign had succumbed, steering gear shot away, and several of her port shutters jammed, preventing the working of her guns. Many of her plates had been started by the eleven-inch shot of the *Chickasaw*, while the smashing of her shield by the *Manhattan*'s bolt added materially to the ram's distress.

The gun-deck was filled by smoke escaping from the stump of the pipe, and the heat was so great that the men, although many of them had stripped to the waist, were in great distress.

Urged on by desperation, Admiral Buchanan had descended to the gun-deck and taken personal charge of the battery. He was a brave man, had always been successful in whatever he had undertaken, and had been held in high estimation by the department previous to the Rebellion. He organized the Naval Academy; co-operated in landing the troops at Vera Cruz, and was one of the leading spirits of the navy at the capture of San Juan d'Ulloa; he was among the first to step foot on the soil of Japan in the expedition of Commodore Perry; and later was honored by the President with the position of commandant of the navy yard at Washington. He had an extensive acquaintance in the service, and should have known the character of the men pitted against him well enough to have considered his task hopeless in conquering such men as Farragut and his rugged lieutenants. Once on the gun-deck, Buchanan sent for a machinist to back out the pivot pin of a jammed stern-post shutter, in order that the gun might be brought into action again, when a shot struck the casemate just outside of where the man was sitting, and the concussion shivered him into atoms as minute as sausage meat; his remains were shoveled into fire-buckets. The same shot started an iron splinter that struck Buchanan and fractured his leg, compelling him to be carried below.

The responsibility of command now devolved upon Captain Johnston, who found that the ram could revolve her screw and use three guns if a foe passed in front of their muzzles, but she could not be steered, and was therefore practically at the mercy of her adversaries. From the pilot-house he listened to the incessant battering kept up on the after end of the shield, which was now so thoroughly shattered that it was a question of a very short time when it must succumb, exposing the gun-deck to a raking fire. He beheld each Federal ship either cannonading the *Tennessee* or preparing to ram her. It had been fifteen minutes since she had discharged a gun, while with every moment her armor was growing weaker under the tremendous hammering to which she was being subjected. Filled with regret, Johnston sought the side of Buchanan, communicating to him the true state of affairs.

"Do the best you can, Johnston, and when all is done, surrender," was the reply, as he groaned with pain on his bed of torture.

The *Ossipee* was within a few yards of the ram when LeRoy saw the white flag fluttering from the *Tennessee*. He stopped his engines, backing hard to avoid collision. LeRoy and Johnston were old shipmates, and their meeting was marked by warmth and hearty good feeling. Johnston formally surrendered the ram to Commander LeRoy, and his sword and that of Admiral Buchanan were afterwards delivered to Farragut.

The appearance of the white flag was hailed by cheers from all the sailors of the fleet, and many a long breath of satisfaction was indulged in as they viewed the fruits of their valor. The fleet anchored where it had fought, with the *Tennessee* in their midst, a prize crew on board, and the Stars and Stripes flying from an improvised flagstaff. Thus terminated the great naval contest, leaving Farragut victor in the most desperate battle he had ever been in—as he expressed it—since the famous fight in the old *Essex*.

The *Hartford* was a sorry-looking vessel. She had been struck twenty times by shot and shell, her punishment having been very severe; but in two hours time, all hands working with a will, the marks of the great battle were almost obliterated. The *Richmond* passed the forts under cover of an impenetrable cloud of smoke, escaping the torrent of shot and shell encountered by the balance of the fleet. When the surgeon's report was handed to the captain, "two men slightly wounded," he was indignant. "What!" he cried, "only two wounded; is that all? How is it there are none killed? They will think at home that this vessel was not in the fight!" An old sailor suggested the propriety of killing two of the after-guard sweepers to swell the report.

Fort Morgan refused to surrender, and steps were at once taken to bring the garrison to terms. Army and navy worked in unison, and a battery of four nine-inch guns were landed from the *Hartford* to assist the army, Lieutenant Tyson having charge of them. At daylight on the 23d, the bombardment of the fort began from the shore batteries, the monitors and ships inside the Bay of Mobile and those outside, and no hotter shelling was ever maintained for twenty-four hours. It brought the fort speedily to terms, and with the disappearance of the flag from the ramparts, Farragut remained undisputed master of Mobile Bay and its approaches. It was the crowning event of his illustrious career.

The admiral, in alluding to the engagement, expressed himself as follows: "It was the hardest earned victory of my life, and one momentous to the country, over the ram *Tennessee*. I always said I was the proper man to fight her, because I was one of those who believed I could do it successfully. I was certainly honest in my convictions and determined in my will, but I did not know how formidable the *Tennessee* was."

The two admirals did not meet. Farragut sent his fleet surgeon, J. C. Palmer, on board to attend to him, and there is no question but that he saved Admiral Buchanan's leg, if not his life. It had been proposed by the Confederate fleet surgeon to resort to amputation, but upon examination Dr. Palmer declined to have the operation performed; and for his skillful management of the case received grateful acknowledgments in after years from Buchanan. The *Metacomet* conveyed him and other Confederates, under a flag of truce, to Pensacola, where in the hospital every care and attention was bestowed upon the wounded Confederates. Buchanan after the war was president of the Maryland Agricultural College. He died at "The Rest," his splendid residence in Maryland, May 1874.

In no battle during the war did the sailors exhibit greater courage and determination than in the battle of Mobile Bay, especially when the

Tennessee made her attack upon the fleet. Men on the *Hartford* who were so seriously wounded that they could not stand would crawl back to their guns, anxious to encourage, with their last breath, their comrades whom they could no longer assist. Men with the pallor of death on their faces essayed to cheer when they heard that the *Tennessee* had struck her flag, and with the knowledge would turn in their hammocks to die contentedly—knowing that to the last they had served their country well. To quote from a celebrated Union admiral:

> "It is not always in the excitement of battle that these heroic acts are noticed, and many officers thought enough of their sailors to mention those who had especially distinguished themselves. The medal of honor was as much as they could expect, but these badges were as much prized as were the decorations which Napoleon served out to his brave soldiers after a victory. It is not the value of the medal, for it is only made of copper; it is the fact that a sailor's services are noticed that makes him the happiest of men, and he treasures the mementos of his services with care and pride."

Admiral Farragut, in relation to the question of attacking Mobile, expressed himself as follows:

> "As this is the last of my work, I expect a little respite, unless the Government want the city of Mobile, which I think is bad policy. It would be an elephant, and take a large army to hold it; and besides, all the traitors and rascally speculators would flock to that city and pour into the Confederacy the wealth of New York. If the Government wish it taken, they must send the means to hold it. I must confess I don't like to work in seven and nine feet of water, and there is no more within several miles of Mobile. The enemy has barricaded the channel with forts, piles, and sunken vessels. Now, you know I am in no way diffident about going anywhere in the *Hartford*; but when I have to leave her and take to a craft drawing six feet of water, I feel badly."

On the 27th of August, Farragut wrote to the Department, stating that his health was failing and that he wanted rest. It had been the intention of the Department to assign him to the command of the Fort Fisher expedition, and orders to that effect were made out on September 5, 1864, but in deference to the admiral's wishes they were revoked and Admiral Porter's name substituted. The action of the Department in giving Rear-Admiral Porter the command instead of Farragut was much commented upon and never fully understood by the country, which had learned to appreciate the noble qualities of Farragut and gave him its unstinted confidence. Secretary Welles has stated that "the great admiral always regretted—though on his account I did not—that he had reported his physical sufferings and low state of health before any orders were received or even issued."

After a short visit to Pensacola and New Orleans the *Hartford* sailed for New York, where her crew were discharged at the Brooklyn Navy Yard, December 24, 1864. Of the 380 men that formed her crew when she sailed from Philadelphia three years before, but forty remained. During that period Farragut had fought eleven battles. Some of the ship's company had deserted, many had succumbed to the malarial diseases common to the Mississippi River, and the balance were killed or wounded in battle. Of the officers but three remained—Admiral Farragut, Lieutenant Watson, and Lieutenant Tyson.

At the Brooklyn Navy Yard, Farragut bade a final adieu to his well-beloved and battle-scarred ship that with him had shared his perils, his triumphs, and final success. Her staunch timbers bore him from Southern seas to the snow-clad North, where a grateful nation bestowed upon him another laurel, a fresh honor worthily won, a commission as vice-admiral, bearing date December 23, 1864. It was a Christmas gift that the old sailor might well view with pride and satisfaction. As senior rear-admiral, Farragut hoisted a plain square blue flag at New Orleans, on the main masthead of the *Hartford*. Afterwards the flag was shifted to the mizzen; thence, on his promotion to vice-admiral, it waved from the fore; and on his elevation to full admiral, July 25, 1866, it floated again high up on the main.

★ ★ ★ ★ ★

Mobile would remain in Confederate hands, but the port would no longer serve blockade runners. The defeat of Atlanta earlier that July, along with Farragut's victory at Mobile Bay served President Lincoln well in the 1864 election. The Confederate ironclad *Tennessee* was promptly taken into the Union Navy as USS *Tennessee*. With her combat damage quickly repaired, she was employed during operations to capture Fort Morgan later in August.

The Battle of Manila Bay, from *Autobiography of George Dewey*

GEORGE DEWEY

You may fire when you are ready Gridley.
—Admiral George Dewey aboard the *Olympia*, May 1, 1998

In January 1898, the battleship USS *Maine* was sent to Havana to protect American interests during the long-standing revolt of the Cubans against the Spanish government. Many in Congress wished to see an end to Spanish rule in Cuba, and saw a chance for the United States to increase its influence and power by occupying Spain's colonial territories in Cuba and the Philippines. All that was needed was an event to rally the American people to action.

That event came on the night of February 15, 1898, when the forward gunpowder magazines of the *Maine* exploded, killing nearly three-quarters of her crew as she sank in minutes. Those in the media and Congress were quick to blame the Spanish by means of sabotage. War was declared on Spain in April when it refused to withdraw its forces from Cuba. "Remember the *Maine*!" became a resounding battle cry of the Americans.

In the Pacific, the Asiatic fleet was under the command of Commodore George Dewey. He was a graduate of the U.S. Naval Academy in 1858 and had served as a lieutenant under Admiral David Farragut in the American Civil War, seeing action at Mobile Bay and along the Mississippi River. On April 27, 1898, he sailed out from China with orders to attack the Spanish at Manila Bay. He arrived at the mouth of the bay late the night of April 30, and the following morning he gave the order to attack at first light. The following chapter is taken from Dewey's memoirs of the events of that day.

★ ★ ★ ★ ★

THE BATTLE OF MANILA BAY

Manila Bay is a spacious body of water opening out from a narrow entrance between high headlands and expanding toward a low-lying country until it has a navigable breadth of over twenty miles. On either side of the inlet are high volcanic peaks densely covered with tropical foliage, while in the passage itself lie several islands. The principal islands, Corregidor and Caballo, divide this entrance into two channels, known as Boca Grande, the great mouth, and Boca Chica, the little mouth.

Boca Chica has a width of two miles, while Boca Grande would have double this if it were not for the small island of El Fraile. This, being some distance off the main-land, practically reduces the breadth of Boca Grande to about three miles. Corregidor and Caballo are high and rocky, effectually commanding both entrances, while El Fraile, though smaller, is large enough to be well fortified and to aid in the defense of the broader channel.

No doubt the position is a strong one for defensive batteries, but the Spaniards, in keeping with their weakness for procrastination, had delayed fortifying the three islands until war appeared inevitable. Then they succeeded in mounting sufficient guns to have given our squadron a very unpleasant quarter of an hour before it met the Spanish squadron, provided the gunners had been enterprising and watchful.

Examination of these batteries after their surrender on May 2 showed that there were three 5.9-inch breech-loading rifles on Caballo Island, three 4.7-inch breech-loading rifles on El Fraile rock, and three 6.3-inch muzzle-loading rifles at Punta Restinga, commanding the Boca Grande entrance, which our squadron was to use; three 8-inch muzzle-loading rifles on Corregidor, three 7-inch muzzle-loading rifles at Punta Gorda, and two 6.3-inch breech-loading rifles at Punta Lasisi, commanding the Boca Chica entrance. The complement manning these batteries, as given by the official papers found in the commandant's office at Cavite Arsenal, was thirteen officers and two hundred and forty-six men. While the muzzle-loaders were relatively unimportant, the six modern rifles commanding the Boca Grande, at a range of a mile and a half, if accurately served, could deliver a telling fire.

A cable received from our consul-general at Singapore the day before we left Mirs Bay stated that the Boca Grande channel had been mined. His information was from the steamer *Isla de Panay,* which had just arrived at Singapore from Manila. This agreed with the accounts of Consul Williams, and with those of merchant-captains from Manila who had recently arrived in Hong Kong.

This subject of mines had been fully discussed in the conferences of myself and staff and the captains of our ships. We decided that submarine mines in Boca Grande might safely be considered a negligible quantity. First, the depth of water rendered the planting of submarine mines in Boca Grande, except by experts of much experience, a matter of great difficulty; secondly, either contact or electrical mines would deteriorate so rapidly in tropical waters as to become ineffective in a short time after being placed; and, thirdly, all agreed that the many reports of warnings to vessels, of notices that the passage was dangerous, of compulsory pilotage, and of spectacular zigzag courses appeared suspiciously like a cry of "wolf," intended to have its due effect upon a presumptuous enemy.

It was a similar course of reasoning, I recalled, that opened the Suez Canal during the Arabi Pasha rebellion. Hundreds of merchant-steamers had been blocked at the entrance to the canal in the fear of mines said to have been planted by the Egyptians, when an Italian man-of-war under the command of a torpedo expert (late Vice-Admiral Morin, minister of marine) appeared. He said that the Egyptians had hardly skill enough to lay mines properly, and if these had been laid as long as reported they were probably innocuous. So he steamed through the canal in spite of warning, and thus raised a blockade that had lasted for weeks.

The city of Manila lies upon the eastern side of Manila Bay, some twenty-five miles from the entrance, with the headland of Sangley Point and the naval station of Cavite five miles nearer. At all these places there were shore batteries, which added materially to the problem that our squadron had to solve. The batteries on the water-front of the city had thirty-nine heavy guns, four 9.4, four 5.5, two 5.9, two 4.7 breech-loading rifles; nine 8.3 muzzle-loading mortars; eighteen 6.3 muzzle-loading rifles; and eight breech-loading Krupp field-pieces. At Sangley Point was a battery with two 5.9 breech-loading rifles and at Canacao one 4.7 breech-loading rifle. These three guns and three of the Manila batteries fired on our ships during the engagement. It will be noted that four guns of the Manila batteries being over 9-inch were larger calibre than any on board our ships.

Before reaching the entrance to Manila Bay there is another bay which might be made an invaluable aid to the protection of the capital and its harbor from naval attack. This is Subig Bay, situated thirty miles to the northward of Corregidor and directly upon the flank of any enemy threatening Manila. With this strategic point effectively occupied, no hostile commander-in-chief would think of passing it and leaving it as a menace to his lines of communication. But with it unoccupied the way was clear.

The Spaniards had inaugurated a small naval reservation at Olongapo, the port of Subig, and at various times appointed boards of officers to report upon the strategic advantages of the situation. So emphatic were the recommendations of these boards in favor of Subig as a naval station in place of Cavite that the change might have been made except for the strong social and official opposition, which preferred life in the capital to comparative exile in a provincial port. Therefore, the fortification of the bay had been neglected; and although at the last moment there was a nervous attempt to improvise defences, so little was done that when, on April 26, the Spanish admiral finally realized that Subig Bay was the strongest point for the defence of his fleet and of Manila, and accordingly sailed from Cavite for Subig, he found, upon arrival, that comparatively nothing had been accomplished and that the position was untenable.

Only twenty-four hours before the arrival of our scouts he got under way and steamed back to Cavite.[6] In his official report he writes feelingly of his disgust that no guns had been mounted and that the entrance had not been mined. He was in error about the mines, however. A Spanish officer assured the executive officer of the *Concord* that eighty mines had been planted in the entrance to Subig Bay. Some fifteen others which the Spaniards had neglected to plant were found later by our officers in the Spanish storehouse at the Subig Bay naval station. In order to get their powder the insurgents had pulled up many of the eighty that had been planted.

So far as our squadron is concerned, no doubt if we had entered Subig Bay we should have found the mines there as negligible a quantity as those which had undoubtedly been planted in Manila Bay and its entrance.[7] I simply mention their existence to show the state of misinforma-

---

[6]Amazingly, a Spanish naval commission headed by Capitán del Frigata Don Julio del Rio had predicted this course of events seven years earlier. The capitán's 1891 report on the inadequacy of Manila's defenses said, in part: "The enemy admiral, if he finds Subig empty, will then stand in for Manila. Where is our squadron? If it is at Cavite he attacks the arsenal and our squadron which is almost motionless suffers helplessly until its annihilation is complete" (quoted in Ronald Spector, *Admiral of the New Empire,* p. 53). This, of course, is precisely what happened in 1898, and to add insult to injury, the hapless Capitán del Rio was present at the Battle of Manila Bay to see his predictions realized.

[7]Lieutenant John M. Ellicott, U.S.N., who was one of the officers of the *Baltimore*, in his article upon "The Defences of Manila Bay," published in the *Proceedings of the U.S. Naval Institute*, June 1900, says: "In the face of all evidence the existence of mines at the entrance to the bay can scarcely be doubted. A chart was captured at Cavite next morning with lines of torpedoes marked on it in Boca Chica, and off San Nicolas Shoal, and with marginal memoranda about the spacing and number of mines. In the articles of capitulation signed

tion in the Spanish admiral's mind about his own resources. He naively adds, in continuing his report, that under the circumstances his vessels could not only have been destroyed if found in Subig Bay, but that, owing to the great depth of water, they would have been unable to save their crews in case of being sunk. What a singular lack of morale and what a strange conclusion for a naval officer!

A comparison of the relative strength of the two squadrons about to be engaged may easily be made by consulting Appendix A, which, however, does not mention some twenty-five small gun-boats not brought into action, but which might have been transformed into torpedo-launches for night attack or defence of the entrance to the bay. In action we had six ships to the Spaniards' seven, but we were superior in class of vessel and in armaments.

We had fifty-three guns above the 4-inch calibre and the Spaniards thirty-one; fifty-six guns under 4-inch to the Spaniards' forty-four; eight torpedo-tubes to the Spaniards' thirteen; officers and men, 1,456 to the Spaniards' 1,447. It will be seen that, in keeping with American naval precedent, we were much more heavily armed in ratio to our personnel than the enemy. Neither side had any armored ships and both fought with brown powder. The fact that we were not armored made the heavy guns of the Spanish batteries, if they were brought to bear on us, a serious consideration.

As for the batteries noted in the *Olympia*'s official log as having fired on us during the battle and verified after the surrender, they were two 6.3-inch muzzle-loaders and three 9.4-inch from the Manila batteries; two 5.9-inch from the Sangley Point battery; and one 4.7-inch from the Canacao battery. All except the two muzzle-loaders mentioned were modern breech-loading rifles.

As we cruised southward after leaving Mirs Bay, the weather was such that we could continue the preparation of crews and ships for action by drilling the men again in battle drills and their stations in case of fire, and for repairing injuries to the ships by shell-fire, while we built barricades of canvas and iron to shield the gun crews, protected the sides and ammunition hoists with lengths of heavy sheet chain faked up and down

---

by the Governor of Corregidor it was stated that mines existed in Boca Grande. The testimony of nearly every Spanish officer interviewed by the writer after the fall of Manila was to the same effect. If these mines were contact mines they had become innocuous from barnacles or sea-weed or badly adjusted moorings; if they were electro-controlled the firing devices had not been installed or were defective." [Author's note]

over a buffer of awnings, and threw overboard much extra wood-work which, while essential to comfort in time of peace, might become ignited in an engagement. Had the Spaniards disposed of their wood-work their ships would have burned less fiercely both at Manila and at Santiago.[8] At night all lights were extinguished except one on the taffrail to denote position, and even this was so carefully screened as to be visible only from directly astern. The presence of the squadron on the waters was denoted alone by the dark forms of the ships and the breaking of phosphorescence at their bows and in the wake of their propellers.

Now, Consul Williams, when he came on board just before our departure from Mirs Bay, had brought news which was anything but encouraging. It upset my preconceived ideas, as I had counted upon fighting in Manila Bay. Just as the consul was leaving Manila he had learned of the sailing of the Spanish squadron for Subig Bay. Thus Admiral Montojo at the last moment seemed to have realized the strategic advantage of Subig over Manila, which we had hoped he would fail to do. When we sighted land near Cape Bolinao early on the morning of May 30, the *Boston* and *Concord* were signalled to proceed at full speed to reconnoitre Subig Bay.

Later, some of our officers declared that they heard the sound of heavy guns firing in the direction which the *Boston* and *Concord* had taken. Though I could not hear any firing myself, I sent the *Baltimore* to support the two scouts if necessary, and to await the rest of the squadron at the entrance to the bay.

As the day broke the coast of Luzon, which had been indefinitely seen on the horizon, appeared clearly in outline. We kept at a distance of three or four miles as we cruised slowly, keeping our speed to that of our slowest vessel, the collier *Nanshan*. In the hope of obtaining news we overhauled some of the fishing-boats in our path, but they knew nothing of the movements of the Spanish squadron. At 3:30 in the afternoon the three ships which had been sent ahead as scouts were sighted at the entrance to the bay. I waited very anxiously for their signal. When it came, saying that no enemy had been found, I was deeply relieved. I remember that I said to Lamberton, "Now we have them."

---

[8]The ever-skeptical Ronald Spector casts some doubt on these smug statements: "Only aboard the *Olympia* did the woodwork remain in place. 'The commodore knew best what we were up against,' recalled one sailor, 'and we didn't tear out anything, just covered it [woodwork] with canvas and splinter nets.' There was some grumbling among the crew about the danger of fire, but Dewey, who had seen many battles, was not about to be panicked into sacrificing all his creature comforts" (*Admiral of the New Empire*, p. 56).

The distance from Subig Bay to Corregidor was only thirty miles. As we had decided to run past the batteries at the entrance to Manila Bay under cover of darkness, we slowed down and finally stopped. All the commanding officers were signalled to come on board the flag-ship. When they were in my cabin, and Wildes, of the *Boston,* and Walker, of the *Concord,* had corroborated in person the import of their signals that there were no Spanish vessels in the vicinity, I said:

"We shall enter Manila Bay to-night and you will follow the motions and movements of the flagship, which will lead."

There was no discussion and no written order and no further particulars as to preparation. For every preparation that had occurred to us in our councils had already been made. I knew that I could depend upon my captains and that they understood my purposes. My position in relation to my captains and to all my officers and crews was happy, indeed, by contrast with that of the unfortunate Montojo, who tells in his official report of how, upon arriving at Subig Bay on the night of April 25 with six of his ships, he found that none of his orders for the defence of the bay had been executed. The four 5.9-inch guns which should have been mounted a month previously were lying on the shore; yet in landing-drill our men have often mounted guns of equal calibre on shore in twenty-four hours. Aside from the planting of the mines which have been mentioned and the sinking of three old hunks at the eastern entrance of the bay, nothing had been done.

Soon after his arrival at Subig on the 28th Admiral Montojo received the following cable from the Spanish consul at Hong Kong:

"The enemy's squadron sailed at 2 P.M. from Mirs Bay, and according to reliable accounts they sailed for Subig to destroy our squadron and then will go to Manila."

A council of war was held, and the captains of the Spanish ships unanimously voted to return to Manila rather than, as their own consul had expressed it, be destroyed where they were. So on the morning of the 29th the Spanish squadron steamed back to Cavite. The attitude of the commanding officers must have been the attitude of the personnel. Any force in such a state of mind is already half beaten. The morale of his squadron, as revealed by Montojo's report after the battle, bore out my reasoning before the war had begun, that everywhere the Spaniards would stand upon the defensive. This must mean defeat in the end, and the more aggressive and prompt our action the smaller would be our losses and the sooner peace would come.

When my captains, after receiving their final orders on board the flag-ship, had returned to their own ships, the squadron resumed its course to Corregidor. As the gloom of night gradually shut out the details of the coast, the squadron steamed quietly on toward the entrance of Manila Bay with all lights masked and the gun crews at the guns. By degrees the high land on either side loomed up out of the darkness, while the flag-ship headed for Boca Grande, which was the wider but comparatively little used channel. A light shower passed over about eleven o'clock and heavy, cumulus clouds drifting across the sky from time to time obscured the new moon. The landmarks and islands were, however, fairly visible, while compass bearings for regulating our course could readily be observed.

It was thirty-six years since, as executive officer of the *Mississippi,* I was first under fire in the passage of Forts Jackson and St. Philip under Farragut, and thirty-five years since, as executive officer, I had lost my ship in the attempted passage of the batteries of Port Hudson. Then, as now, we were dependent upon the screen of darkness to get by successfully, but then I was a subordinate and now the supreme responsibility was mine.

If the guns commanding the entrance were well served, there was danger of damage to my squadron before it engaged the enemy's squadron. If the Spaniards had shown enterprise in the use of the materials which they possessed, then we might have expected a heavy fire from the shore batteries. One who had military knowledge did not have to wait for the developments of the Russo-Japanese War to know how quickly modern guns of high velocity and low trajectory may be emplaced and how effective they may be, when fired from a stationary position, against so large a target as a ship. Had the batteries search-lights they could easily locate us, while we could locate them only by the flash of their guns.

When we were ten miles from Boca Grande we judged, as we saw signal lights flash, that we had already been sighted either by small vessels acting as scouts or by land lookouts. El Fraile was passed by the flag-ship at a distance of half a mile and was utilized as a point of departure for the course up the bay clear of the San Nicolas Shoals. When El Fraile bore due south (magnetic) the course was changed to northeast by north. We were not surprised to find the usual lights on Corregidor and Caballo Islands and the San Nicolas Shoals extinguished, as this was only a natural precaution on the part of the Spaniards.

There were no vessels, so far as we could see, cruising off the entrance, no dash of torpedo-launches which might have been expected, no sign of life beyond the signalling on shore until the rear of the column, steaming at full speed, was between Corregidor and El Fraile.

As we watched the walls of darkness for the first gun-flash, every moment of our progress brought its relief, and now we began to hope that we should get by without being fired on at all. But about ten minutes after midnight, when all except our rear ships had cleared it, the El Fraile battery opened with a shot that passed between the *Petrel* and the *Raleigh.* The *Boston, Concord, Raleigh,* and *McCulloch* returned the fire with a few shots. One 8-inch shell from the *Boston* seemed to be effective. After firing three times El Fraile was silent. There was no demonstration whatever from the Caballo battery, with its three 6-inch modern rifles, no explosion of mines, and no other resistance. We were safely within the bay. The next step was to locate the Spanish squadron and engage it.

Afterward we heard various explanations of why we were not given a warmer reception as we passed through. Some of the officers in the El Fraile battery said their dilatoriness in opening fire was due to the fact that their men were ashore at Punta Lasisi and could not get off to their guns in time after they heard of the squadron's approach. An eye-witness on Corregidor informed me that our squadron was perfectly visible as it was passing through the entrance, but for some extraordinary reason the commanding officer gave no orders to the batteries to open fire.

Perhaps the enemy thought that he had done all that was necessary by cutting off the usual lights on Corregidor and Caballo Islands and San Nicolas Shoals for guiding mariners, and he expected that without pilots and without any knowledge of the waters we would not be guilty of such a foolhardy attempt as entering an unlighted channel at midnight.

Once through the entrance, as I deemed it wise to keep moving in order not to be taken by surprise when the ships had no headway, and as, at the same time, I did not wish to reach our destination before we had sufficient daylight to show us the position of the Spanish ships, the speed of the squadron was reduced to four knots, while we headed toward the city of Manila. In the meantime the men were allowed to snatch a little sleep at their guns; but at four o'clock coffee was served to them, and so eager were they that there was no need of any orders to ensure readiness for the work to come.

Signal lights, rockets, and beacon lights along the shore, now that we were sure of grappling with the enemy, no longer concerned us. We waited for dawn and the first sight of the Spanish squadron, which I had rather expected would be at the anchorage off the city of Manila. This seemed naturally the strong position for Admiral Montojo to take up, as he would then have the powerful Manila battery, mounting the guns which have already been enumerated, to support him. But the admiral stated in his report that he had avoided this position on account of the resultant injury which the city might have received if the battle had been fought in close proximity to it.

The *Nanshan* and *Zafiro,* as there was no reserve ammunition for either to carry, had been sent, with the *McCulloch,* into an unfrequented part of the bay in order that they should sustain no injury and that they might not hamper the movements of the fighting-ships. When we saw that there were only merchantmen at the Manila anchorage, the squadron, led by the flag-ship, gradually changed its course, swinging around on the arc of a large circle leading toward the city and making a kind of counter-march, as it were, until headed in the direction of Cavite. This brought the ships within two or three miles of shore, with a distance of four hundred yards between ships, in the following order: *Olympia* (flag), *Baltimore, Raleigh, Petrel, Concord,* and *Boston.*

About 5:05 the Luneta and two other Manila batteries opened fire. Their shots passed well over the vessels. It was estimated that some had a range of seven miles. Only the *Boston* and *Concord* replied. Each sent two shells at the Luneta battery. The other vessels reserved their fire, having in mind my caution that, in the absence of a full supply of ammunition, the amount we had was too precious to be wasted when we were seven thousand miles from our base. My captains understood that the Spanish ships were our objective and not the shore fortifications of a city that would be virtually ours as soon as our squadron had control of Manila Bay.

With the coming of broad daylight we finally sighted the Spanish vessels formed in an irregular crescent in front of Cavite. The *Olympia* headed toward them, and in answer to her signal to close up, the distance between our ships was reduced to two hundred yards. The western flank of the Spanish squadron was protected by Cavite Peninsula and the Sangley Point battery, while its eastern flank rested in the shoal water off Las Pinas.

The Spanish line of battle was formed by the *Reina Cristina* (flag), *Castilla, Don Juan de Austria, Don Antonio de Ulloa, Isla de Luzón, Isla de Cuba,* and *Marqués del Duero.*

The *Velasco* and *Lezo* were on the other (southern) side of Cavite Point, and it is claimed by the Spaniards that they took no part in the action. Some of the vessels in the Spanish battle-line were under way, and others were moored so as to bring their broadside batteries to bear to the best advantage. The *Castilla* was protected by heavy iron lighters filled with stone.

Before me now was the object for which we had made our arduous preparations, and which, indeed, must ever be the supreme test of a naval officer's career. I felt confident of the outcome, though I had no thought that victory would be won at so slight a cost to our own side. Confidence was expressed in the very precision with which the dun, war-colored hulls of the squadron followed in column behind the flag-ship, keeping their distance excellently. All the guns were pointed contantly at the enemy, while the men were at their stations waiting the word. There was no break in the monotone of the engines save the mechanical voice of the leadsman or an occasional low-toned command by the quartermaster at the conn, or the roar of a Spanish shell. The Manila batteries continued their inaccurate fire, to which we paid no attention.

The misty haze of the tropical dawn had hardly risen when at 5:15, at long range, the Cavite forts and Spanish squadron opened fire. Our course was not one leading directly toward the enemy, but a converging one, keeping him on our starboard bow. Our speed was eight knots and our converging course and ever-varying position must have confused the Spanish gunners. My assumption that the Spanish fire would be hasty and inaccurate proved correct.

So far as I could see, none of our ships was suffering any damage, while, in view of my limited ammunition supply, it was my plan not to open fire until we were within effective range, and then to fire as rapidly as possible with all of our guns.

At 5:40, when we were within a distance of 5,000 yards (two and one-half miles), I turned to Captain Gridley and said:

"You may fire when you are ready, Gridley."

While I remained on the bridge with Lamberton, Brumby, and Stickney, Gridley took his station in the conning-tower and gave the order to the battery. The very first gun to speak was an 8-inch from the forward turret of the *Olympia,* and this was the signal for all the other ships to join the action.

At about the time that the Spanish ships were first sighted, 5:06, two submarine mines were exploded between our squadron and Cavite, some two miles ahead of our column. On account of the distance, I remarked to Lamberton:

"Evidently the Spaniards are already rattled."

However, they explained afterward that the premature explosions were due to a desire to clear a space in which their ships might maneuver.

At one time a torpedo-launch made an attempt to reach the *Olympia,* but she was sunk by the guns of the secondary battery and went down bow first, and another yellow-colored launch flying the Spanish colors ran out, heading for the *Olympia,* but after being disabled she was beached to prevent her sinking.

When the flag-ship neared the five-fathom curve off Cavite she turned to the westward, bringing her port batteries to bear on the enemy, and, followed by the squadron, passed along the Spanish line until north of and only some fifteen hundred yards distant from the Sangley Point battery, when she again turned and headed back to the eastward, thus giving the squadron an opportunity to use their port and starboard batteries alternately and to cover with their fire all the Spanish ships, as well as the Cavite and Sangley Point batteries. While I was regulating the course of the squadron, Lieutenant Calkins was verifying our position by crossbearings and by the lead.

Three runs were thus made from the eastward and two from the westward, the length of each run averaging two miles and the ships being turned each time with port helm. Calkins found that there was in reality deeper water than shown on the chart, and when he reported the fact to me, inasmuch as my object was to get as near as possible to the enemy without grounding our own vessels, the fifth run past the Spaniards was farther inshore than any preceding run. At the nearest point to the enemy our range was only two thousand yards.

There had been no cessation in the rapidity of fire maintained by our whole squadron, and the effect of its concentration, owing to the fact that our ships were kept so close together, was smothering, particularly upon the two largest ships, the *Reina Cristina* and *Castilla*. The *Don Juan de Austria* first and then the *Reina Cristina* made brave and desperate attempts to charge the *Olympia,* but becoming the target for all our batteries they turned and ran back. In this sortie the *Reina Cristina* was raked by an 8-inch shell, which is said to have put out of action some twenty men and to have completely destroyed her steering-gear. Another shell in her forecastle killed or wounded all the members of the crews of four rapid-fire guns; another set fire to her after orlop; another killed or disabled nine men on her poop; another carried away her mizzen-mast, bringing down the ensign and the admiral's flag, both of which were replaced; another exploded in the after ammunition-room; and still another exploded in the sick-bay, which was already filled with wounded.

When she was raised from her muddy bed, five years later, eighty skeletons were found in the sickbay and fifteen shot holes in the hull; while the many hits mentioned in Admiral Montojo's report, and his harrowing description of the shambles that his flag-ship had become when he was finally obliged to leave her, shows what execution was done to her upper works. Her loss was one hundred and fifty killed and ninety wounded, seven of these being officers. Among the killed was her valiant captain, Don Luis Cadarso, who, already wounded, finally met his death while bravely directing the rescue of his men from the burning and sinking vessel.

Though in the early part of the action our firing was not what I should have liked it to be, it soon steadied down, and by the time the *Reina Cristina* steamed toward us it was satisfactorily accurate. The *Castilla* fared little better than the *Reina Cristina*. All except one of her guns was disabled, she was set on fire by our shells, and finally abandoned by her crew after they had sustained a loss of twenty-three killed and eighty wounded. The *Don Juan de Austria* was badly damaged and on fire, the *Isla de Luzón* had three guns dismounted, and the *Marqués de Duero* was also in a bad way. Admiral Montojo, finding his flag-ship no longer manageable, half her people dead or wounded, her guns useless and the ship on fire, gave the order to abandon and sink her, and transferred his flag to the *Isla de Cuba* shortly after seven o'clock.

Victory was already ours, though we did not know it. Owing to the smoke over the Spanish squadron there were no visible signs of the execution wrought by our guns when we started upon our fifth run past the enemy. We were keeping up our rapid fire, and the flag-ship was opposite the center of the Spanish line, when, at 7:35, the captain of the *Olympia* made a report to me which was as startling as it was unexpected. This was to the effect that on board the *Olympia* there remained only fifteen rounds per gun for the 5-inch battery.

It was a most anxious moment for me. So far as I could see, the Spanish squadron was as intact as ours. I had reason to believe that their supply of ammunition was as ample as ours was limited.

Therefore, I decided to withdraw temporarily from action for a redistribution of ammunition if necessary. For I knew that fifteen rounds of 5-inch ammunition could be shot away in five minutes. But even as we were steaming out of range the distress of the Spanish ships became evident. Some of them were perceived to be on fire and others were seeking protection behind Cavite Point. The *Don Antonio de Ulloa,* however, still retained her position at Sangley Point, where she had been moored. Moreover, the Spanish fire, with the exception of the Manila batteries, to which we had paid little attention, had ceased entirely. It was clear that we did not need a very large supply of ammunition to finish our morning's task; and happily it was found that the report about the *Olympia*'s 5-inch ammunition had been incorrectly transmitted. It was that fifteen rounds had been fired per gun, not that only fifteen rounds remained.

Feeling confident of the outcome, I now signalled that the crews, who had had only a cup of coffee at 4 A.M., should have their breakfast. The public at home, on account of this signal, to which was attributed a nonchalance that had never occurred to me, reasoned that breakfast was the real reason for our withdrawing from action.[9] Meanwhile, I improved the opportunity to have the commanding officers report on board the flag-ship.

There had been such a heavy flight of shells over us that each captain, when he arrived, was convinced that no other ship had had such good luck as his own in being missed by the enemy's fire, and expected the others to have both casualties and damages to their ships to report. But fortune was as pronouncedly in our favor at Manila as it was later at Santiago. To my gratification not a single life had been lost, and considering that we would rather measure the importance of an action by the scale of its conduct than by the number of casualties we were immensely happy. The concentration of our fire immediately we were within telling range had given us an early advantage in demoralizing the enemy, which has ever been the prime factor in naval battles. In the War of 1812 the losses of the *Constitution* were slight when she overwhelmed the *Guerrière* and in the Civil War the losses of the *Kearsarge* were slight when she made a shambles of the *Alabama.* On the *Baltimore* two officers (Lieutenant F. W. Kellogg and Ensign N. E. Irwin) and six men were slightly wounded. None of our ships had been seriously hit, and every one was still ready for immediate action.

In detail the injuries which we had received from the Spanish fire were as follows:

The *Olympia* was hulled five times and her rigging was cut in several places. One six-pound projectile struck immediately under the position where I was standing. The *Baltimore* was hit five times. The projectile which wounded two officers and six men pursued a most erratic course. It entered the ship's side forward of the starboard gangway, and just above the line of the main deck, passed through the hammock-netting, down through the deck planks and steel deck, bending the deck beam in a wardroom state-room, thence upward through the after engine-room coaming, over against the cylinder of a 6-inch gun, disabling the gun, struck and exploded a box of three-pounder ammunition, hit an iron ladder, and finally, spent, dropped on deck. The *Boston* had four unimportant hits, one causing a fire which was soon extinguished, and the *Petrel* was struck once.

At 11:16 A.M. we stood in to complete our work. There remained to oppose us, however, only the batteries and the gallant little *Ulloa.* Both

---

[9]Dewey was also afraid to let potential enemies know that he was having problems with ammunition at Manila. When his acting "aide," journalist and ex-naval officer Joseph L. Stickney, suggested that the news dispatches refer to the temporary withdrawal as a "breakfast break," Dewey readily agreed for security reasons.

opened fire as we advanced. But the contest was too unequal to last more than a few minutes. Soon the *Ulloa,* under our concentrated fire, went down valiantly with her colors flying.

The battery at Sangley Point was well served, and several times reopened fire before being finally silenced. Had this battery possessed its four other 6-inch guns which Admiral Montojo had found uselessly lying on the beach at Subig, our ships would have had many more casualties to report. Happily for us, the guns of this battery had been so mounted that they could be laid only for objects beyond the range of two thousand yards. As the course of our ships led each time within this range, the shots passed over and beyond them. Evidently the artillerists, who had so constructed their carriages that the muzzles of the guns took against the sill of the embrasure for any range under two thousand yards, thought it out of the question that an enemy would venture within this distance.

The *Concord* was sent to destroy a large transport, the *Mindanao,* which had been beached near Bacoor, and the *Petrel,* whose light draught would permit her to move in shallower water than the other vessels of the squadron, was sent into the harbor of Cavite to destroy any ships that had taken refuge there. The *Mindanao* was set on fire and her valuable cargo destroyed. Meanwhile, the *Petrel* gallantly performed her duty, and after a few shots from her 6-inch guns the Spanish flag on the government buildings was hauled down and a white flag hoisted. Admiral Montojo had been wounded, and had taken refuge on shore with his remaining officers and men; his loss was three hundred and eighty-one of his officers and crew, and there was no possibility of further resistance.

At 12:30 the *Petrel* signalled the fact of the surrender, and the firing ceased. But the Spanish vessels were not yet fully destroyed. Therefore, the executive officer of the *Petrel,* Lieutenant E. M. Hughes, with a whaleboat and crew of only seven men, boarded and set fire to the *Don Juan de Austria, Isla de Cuba, Isla de Luzón, General Lezo, Coreo,* and *Marqués de Duero,* all of which had been abandoned in shallow water and left scuttled by their deserting crews. This was a courageous undertaking, as these vessels were supposed to have been left with trains to their magazines and were not far from the shore, where there were hundreds of Spanish soldiers and sailors, all armed and greatly excited. The *Manila,* an armed transport, which was found uninjured after having been beached by the Spaniards, was therefore spared. Two days later she was easily floated, and for many years did good service as a gun-boat. The little *Petrel* continued her work until 5:20 P.M., when she rejoined the squadron, towing a long string of tugs and launches, to be greeted by volleys of cheers from every ship.

The order to capture or destroy the Spanish squadron had been executed to the letter. Not one of its fighting-vessels remained afloat. That night I wrote in my diary: "Reached Manila at daylight. Immediately engaged the Spanish ships and batteries at Cavite. Destroyed eight of the former, including the *Reina Cristina* and *Castilla*. Anchored at noon off Manila."

As soon as we had sunk the *Ulloa* and silenced the batteries at Sangley Point, the *Olympia*, followed by the *Baltimore* and *Raleigh*, while the *Concord* and *Petrel* were carrying out their orders, started for the anchorage off the city. The Manila batteries, which had kept up such a persistent though impotent firing all the early part of the day, were now silent and made no attempt to reopen as our ships approached the city.

Consul Williams was sent on board a British ship moored close inshore near the mouth of the Pasig River, with instructions to request her captain to be the bearer of a message to the Spanish captain-general. This message was taken ashore at 2 P.M., in the form of a note to the British consul, Mr. E. H. Rawson-Walker, who, after the departure of Mr. Williams, had assumed charge of our archives and interests, requesting him to see the captain-general, and to say to him, on my behalf, that if another shot were fired at our ships from the Manila batteries we should destroy the city. Moreover, if there were any torpedo-boats in the Pasig River they must be surrendered, and if we were allowed to transmit messages by the cable to Hong Kong the captain-general would also be permitted to use it.

Assurance came promptly that the forts would not fire at our squadron unless it was evident that a disposition of our ships to bombard the city was being made. This assurance, which was kept even during the land attack upon the city, some three months later, led me to drop anchor for the first time since we had entered the bay. From the moment that the captain-general accepted my terms the city was virtually surrendered, and I was in control of the situation, subject to my government's orders for the future. I had established a base seven thousand miles from home which I might occupy indefinitely. As I informed the secretary of the navy in my cable of May 4, our squadron controlled the bay and could take the city at any time. The only reason for awaiting the arrival of troops before demanding its surrender was the lack of sufficient force to occupy it.

In answer to the other points of my message, the captain-general, Don Basilio Augustin Davila, said that he knew of no torpedo-boats in the river, but that if there were any his honor would not allow him to surrender them. As there were none, he was quite safe in making this reservation, which did not affect the main fact, that his capital was under our guns. He refused my request about the cable. As a result he found himself cut off from all telegraphic communication with the outside world on the next morning, because I directed the *Zafiro* to cut the cable.

As the sun set on the evening of May 1, crowds of people gathered along the water-front, gazing at the American squadron. They climbed on the ramparts of the very battery that had fired on us in the morning. The *Olympia's* band, for their benefit, played "La Paloma" and other Spanish airs, and while the sea-breeze wafted the strains to their ears the poor colonel of artillery who had commanded the battery, feeling himself dishonored by his disgraceful failure, shot himself through the head.

During the mid-watch that night a steam-launch was discovered coming off from Manila. The crews went to quarters and search-lights and guns were trained upon her until she approached the *Olympia,* when she was allowed to come alongside. A Spanish official was on board. He desired permission to proceed to Corregidor to instruct the commanding officer that none of the batteries at the entrance to the bay were to fire on our ships when passing in or out. Permission was granted and he was told to return the following morning. When he came he was put on board the *Raleigh,* which was sent, with the *Baltimore* as escort, to demand the surrender of all the defences at the entrance to the bay. The surrender was made and the garrisons disarmed. The next day I had the *Boston* and *Concord* land parties, who disabled the guns and brought their breech-plugs off to the ships. All the ammunition found, as it was of a calibre unsuited to any of our guns, was destroyed.

Meanwhile, to my surprise, on the morning of May 2, the Spanish flag was seen to be again flying over the Cavite arsenal. Captain Lamberton was sent at once to inquire what it meant, and to demand a formal surrender. He went over to Cavite in the *Petrel,* and upon leaving her to go on shore gave instructions that in case he did not return within an hour she was to open fire on the arsenal. Upon landing he found the Spanish soldiers and sailors under arms, and in answer to his inquiry, what was meant by this and by the hoisting of the Spanish colors, he was informed by the Spanish commandant, Captain Sostoa, that the colors had been lowered the day before only as token of a temporary truce. Captain Lamberton's reply to this evasive excuse was an ultimatum that if the white flag were not hoisted by noon he would open fire.

Captain Sostoa then asked for time in which to refer the matter to Madrid, and this being refused, for time to refer it to the authorities at Manila. But he was informed that only an unconditional surrender of officers, men, and arms would be considered. Captain Lamberton then returned to the *Petrel,* and at 11:35 the white flag was hoisted by the order of

Admiral Montojo; and it was this order, peculiarly enough, and not the loss of his squadron, that led to his court-martial upon his return to Spain. Shortly afterward all the Spanish officers and men evacuated the place. Possibly imperfect knowledge of each other's language by Captain Lamberton and Captain Sostoa led to a misunderstanding of our terms by the Spaniards. In a way this was fortunate for us, as we were in no position to take care of prisoners. We had what we needed: possession of the arsenal, with its machinery, workshops, and supplies, as a base for future operations.

It was not until May 4, however, when all the aftermath of the details of the victory had been cared for, that I found it convenient to send the *McCulloch* to Hong Kong to transmit to Washington the complete news of what the squadron had accomplished, where already many misleading reports had been received from Spanish sources. Before the cable was cut the captain-general, in a communication to his government, had acknowledged his severe loss, yet intimated that the American squadron had been repulsed; while other cables affirmed that our casualties were heavy.[10]

But the newspapers of May 2 had had a brief announcement of the victory, one of which had been sent by the operator at the Manila cable station before the cable was cut. Senator Redfield Proctor, of Vermont, who had been responsible for my assignment to the command of the Asiatic Squadron, felt that he had a personal cause for jubilation, and on the morning of the 2d he wrote the following note, in his characteristic vein, to President McKinley:

"I feel well this morning.

"You may remember that you gave, at my earnest request, the direction to Secretary Long to assign Commodore Dewey to the Asiatic Squadron. You will find you made no mistake; and I want to say that he will be as wise and safe, if there are political duties devolving on him, as he is forcible in action. There is no better man in discretion and safe judgment. We may run him against you for President. He would make a good one."

The President now gave me the same rank of acting rear-admiral that Captain Sampson, commanding the North Atlantic Squadron, had al-

---

[10]"Last night, April 30, the batteries at the entrance to the port announced the arrival of the enemy's squadron, forcing a passage under the obscurity of the night. At daybreak the enemy took up position, opening with a strong fire against Fort Cavite and the arsenal. Our fleet engaged the enemy in a brilliant combat, protected by the Cavite and Manila forts. They obliged the enemy with heavy loss to manoeuvre repeatedly. At nine o'clock the American squadron took refuge behind the foreign shipping on the east side of the bay." (Cablegram of the Spanish captain-general to Madrid, May 1, 1898.) [Author's note]

ready received. Congress passed a vote of thanks to the squadron commander, its officers and men, and all anxiety for the safety of the Pacific coast was relieved. One of the most gratifying cables was this: "Every American is your debtor. Roosevelt."

Now until many weeks later, when the mails began to arrive, did I fully realize how the victory had electrified the whole United States. One of the first congratulatory letters received I particularly prize. It was written by my old friend John Hay, then ambassador to England, in the delightful phrase of which he was a master. He spoke of the "mingled wisdom and daring" of our entrance into the bay, which has always seemed to me as fine a compliment as any naval officer could receive.

The victory had put a stop to the talk of European intervention. It had set a pace to be followed in the operations on the Atlantic coast and had checked the mendacious slanders about our navy which had been circulated broadcast throughout continental Europe. There were reports of utter lack of discipline and that our crews were entirely foreign mercenaries. Perhaps, in comparison with some foreign navies, we lacked the etiquette of discipline, which is immaterial if the spirit of discipline exists. We had the spirit—efficient, dependable, and intelligent. "The man behind the gun" was not a foreigner. With the development of the new navy the percentage of American-born seamen had rapidly increased. It was about eighty per cent in my squadron.

In his war proclamation, April 23, 1898, the Spanish captain-general had declared that the North American people were "constituted of all the social excrescences." He spoke of us as a "squadron manned by foreigners possessing neither instruction nor discipline," which was "unacquainted with the rights of property" and had come "to kidnap those persons whom they consider useful to man their ships or to be exploited in agricultural or industrial labor. . . . Vain designs! Ridiculous boastings! . . . They shall not profane the tombs of your fathers, they shall not gratify their lustful passions at the cost of your wives' and daughters' honor, or appropriate the property your industry has accumulated as a provision for your old age."

The author of this proclamation, I was told, was not the captain-general himself, but the Archbishop of Manila, who as head of the church in the Philippines was *ex officio* a member of the general council of the colony. Some months later I had the pleasure of entertaining him on board the *Olympia*. In his honor I had the ship's company paraded. As he saw the fine young fellows march past his surprise at their appearance was manifest.

"Admiral, you must be very proud to command such a body of men," he said finally.

"Yes, I am," I declared; "and I have just the same kind of men on board all the other ships in the harbor."

"Admiral, I have been here for thirty years," he concluded. "I have seen the men-of-war of all the nations, but never havé I seen anything like this" (as he pointed to the *Olympia*'s crew).

In view of the language of the proclamation, I considered this generous admission very illuminating.

But better than winning the esteem of foreigners was winning that of our own people. They could have had none too great confidence in their navy at the outbreak of the war, or else there would not have been such a popular cry to have the Atlantic coast guarded against possible ravages by Cervera's squadron.

It was the ceaseless routine of hard work and preparation in time of peace that won Manila and Santiago. Valor there must be, but it is a secondary factor in comparison with strength of material and efficiency of administration. Valor the Spaniards displayed, and in the most trying and adverse circumstances. The courageous defence made by all the vessels of the Spanish squadron, the desperate attempt of the *Reina Cristina* to close with the *Olympia,* and the heroic conduct of her captain, who, after fighting his ship until she was on fire and sinking, lost his own life in his attempt to save his wounded men, can only excite the most profound admiration and pity.

But what might not have been accomplished had this courage been properly directed and had there been appreciation of the importance of preparation? For three months war had been imminent, and although the Spanish government was highly reprehensible for its unaccountable inertia, and Spanish indolence and climatic influences must bear their share of blame, nothing can excuse the Spanish authorities in the Philippines for neglecting to utilize the materials of defence already in their possession.

The approach of our squadron had been reported from Bolinao in the morning and from Subig in the afternoon the day before the battle, yet the Spanish admiral that very evening left his flag-ship and went over to Manila, five miles distant, to attend a reception given by his wife. He was driving back to Cavite by carriage at the same hour that our squadron was passing through the Boca Grande. Many of his officers, following his example, passed the night ashore and were seen returning to their ships early on the morning of the battle, after the firing had actually begun.

To us it seems almost incomprehensible that the guns of Caballo and Corregidor and Punta Restinga failed to fire on our ships; that when our vessels were hampered by the narrow waters of the entrance there was no night attack by the many small vessels possessed by the Spaniards; and that during the action neither the *Isla de Cuba* nor the *Isla de Luzón,* each of them protected by an armored deck and fitted with two torpedo-tubes, made any attempt to torpedo our ships.

Naturally, the Spanish government attempted to make a scapegoat of poor Admiral Montojo, the victim of their own shortcomings and maladministration, and he was soon afterward ordered home and brought before a court-martial. It was some satisfaction to know that a factor in influencing the court in concluding that he had fulfilled his duty in a courageous manner was a letter from me testifying to his gallantry in the action, which I was glad to give in response to his request.[11]

★ ★ ★ ★ ★

Dewey returned home a national hero and was promoted to Rear Admiral and was made Admiral of the Navy in 1899 by an act of Congress. He is the only person in the history of the United States to attain that rank, the highest in the Navy. President William McKinley placed the Philippines under American control placing the country on a course of Pacific expansion, and into conflict with the rising empire of Japan.

[11]For a detailed, nuts-and-bolts account of the navigation, gunnery, range-finding, signaling, and tactics at Manila, see Lieutenant C. G. Calkins, "Historical and Professional Notes on the Naval Campaign of Manila Bay in 1898," U.S. Naval Institute *Proceedings* (June 1899), pp. 267–87.

From *The Terrible Hours*

PETER MAAS

Like the destroyer, the submarine has created its own type of officer and man with language and traditions apart from the rest of the service, and yet at the heart unchangingly of the Service.
—Rudyard Kipling

Submariners are a special breed among sailors of all navies. The unique dangers of diving below the surface of the ocean create a situation where the survival of all depends on the actions of each man. The sea is unforgiving. One fault, one simple mistake, could mean the loss of the boat with no chance of escape. It makes the bonds of comradeship especially close aboard submarines, and crews are profoundly loyal to their captain, their boat, and each other.

The early submarines were particularly dangerous as new designs and technologies were put to trial. Such was the case with the USS *Squalus* (SS-192), a diesel-electric submarine built at the Portsmouth Navy Yard, Portsmouth, New Hampshire, and commissioned there on March 1, 1939. On a test dive off the Isle of Shoals on May 23, 1939, she suffered a catastrophic failure of a sea valve that sent her 240 feet to the bottom, partially flooded and unable to surface. The thirty-three surviving crew members were trapped, and faced a certain death by asphyxiation if they could not be reached. In his *New York Times* best seller, author Peter Maas describes the moment of the accident aboard the *Squalus*.

★ ★ ★ ★ ★

At the sudden cry from Kuney that the engine rooms were flooding, everyone in the control room froze, hypnotized by the Christmas tree board.

It was still unaccountably green.

This could not be happening! There was a moment of complete stupefaction on every face, the kind experienced by men who are absolutely certain that what is coming to pass could not possibly be. Yet it was.

Somehow, the dreadful thing was upon them. Despite what the control board was registering, the big main air-induction valve leading back to the now dormant diesels had failed to close or, if it did, had opened again. With ferocious force, tons of sea were shooting into the engine rooms. It was as if a huge fire hydrant, wide open, had suddenly gone berserk. The fluttering sensation that Naquin had felt seconds ago was the rush of air being shoved violently forward by the ocean as it burst into the after compartments of the *Squalus*.

Naquin was the first to recover. "Blow all main ballast!" he shouted.

The words were barely out of his mouth before Walter Doyle called out, "Blow bow buoyancy!"

The still-mesmerized control room crew came to and scrambled into action. Al Prien, the machinist's mate manning the levers for the valves and vents during the dive, had already closed the ballast tank air-escape vents. Close by, Carol Pierce, who had bled air into the boat to make doubly sure it was watertight as the dive commenced, now slammed home the lever that would blow 3,000 pounds per square inch of air into the bow buoyancy tank. The air from his number 1 bank blasted off. Inside the control room, it made a soft whooshing sound. An instant later, he sent more pressurized air rushing into the main ballast tanks to drive the sea from them.

Two gunner's mates, Gene Cravens and Gavin Coyne, operating the bow and stern dive planes, immediately put them at hard rise.

Prien, having closed the ballast-tank air vents, stared down at the level that should have shut the main inductions. He clenched it, knuckles white, and tried to yank it farther toward him. but it wouldn't budge. It had gone as far as it could go.

Charles Kuney stood transfixed, his hands clapped over his phone receivers, pressing them tighter to his ears. The last thing he had heard from the after compartments was a desperate scream, "Take her up! Take her up!" Kuney couldn't tell which compartment the scream had come from.

The *Squalus* shuddered.

At eighty feet, for a tantalizing tick in time, she hung suspended between ocean floor and surface. Then she seemed to respond to the blowing of her ballast tanks. Her bow tilted upward. She even rose a little, her nose perhaps just breaking through the waves above. But the growing weight in her tail was too much. Inexorably, she began to slide stern first into the black depths of the North Atlantic.

The steep pitch of the *Squalus* came so suddenly that only by clinging to his number 1 periscope and bracing himself against the steel well of the second periscope directly behind him did Naquin remain on his feet. This was crazy, he kept thinking. How was it possible?

As Pierce was sending emergency blasts of air into the ballast tanks, Harold Preble rushed to his aid. Hanging on to the base of the gyroscope with one hand, the Portsmouth yard's test superintendent knelt beside Pierce and tried to activate a reserve cylinder of air to clear the tanks faster. He had to use a wrench to get the valve open. He was still struggling with it when a column of water hit him in the back of his neck, flattening him. Both Pierce and Chief Roy Campbell were struck by the same stream. Pierce, stumbling over Preble, grabbed the wrench and finished the job. But it didn't make any difference.

Campbell picked up Preble. Then he reached overhead to shut off a pipe in the ventilation system from which the water had shot out. By now the sea had found its way into the maze of pipes that ran the length of the *Squalus*. In the control room, jets of saltwater sprayed from a dozen different places. The men worked frantically to close them off, seizing hold of whatever they could to stay upright.

Behind him, Chief Campbell heard an ominous hissing. He traced it to two toilet closets in the rear of the control room on the starboard side. Campbell groped through a billowing mist. It was coming out of a drainage line in the second closet. He had trouble turning the handwheel that would stop the leak because of the new packing around it. But finally he succeeded. Then he turned off every other valve he could find.

Across from Campbell, alone in his cubicle, radioman Powell was in the process of stowing his transmitter after sending the second dive message to Portsmouth when water gushed out of an air-supply blower in front of him. Powell reached for a valve in the pipe that he thought might stop the flow. Before he got to it, the water suddenly dwindled to a dribble. Powell figured that someone in the after battery must have closed another valve down the line. He sealed his anyway, and trying to maintain his balance, he staggered into the control room proper to find out what was happening. Overhead, the lights flickered, flared briefly and went out. The emergency lights came on, then they also began to flicker.

In the forward torpedo room, Lieutenant Nichols ordered Lenny de Medeiros to close the watertight door to the forward battery moments after learning that the engine rooms were flooding. As he did, he spotted

Gerry McLees, head and shoulders sticking out of the passageway hatch leading down to the forward group of batteries. There didn't seem to be any problems in the compartment as far as he could tell.

When the bow rose so abruptly, de Medeiros thought that whatever the trouble was, it wasn't going to be so bad after all. The sub appeared to be on her way back to the surface.

Just then the dummy torpedo set up for a reload started to roll free. Loose in there with the *Squalus* now tilting so sharply, it would crush anyone in its path. Nichols, Torpedoman First Class Bill Fitzpatrick and a young seaman, Donny Persico, jumped for it and wrestled it back in place. Nichols finally threaded its nose ring with manila line and together the three men managed to lash down the wayward torpedo.

Some seawater mixed with air was sputtering out of the ventilation pipes, but it didn't amount to much. De Medeiros quickly shut the valves and the sprays of water stopped completely. By now, he could distinctly sense the backward slide down of the boat and realized that surfacing was out of the question.

He'd seen McLees in the forward battery. He couldn't remember where his other close pal, Lloyd Maness, was stationed for this dive. All he, like the others in the compartment, could do in the eerie silence was wait. And hope.

In the forward battery, as the *Squalus* struggled to rise, a coffeepot bounced across the pantry past one of the mess attendants. Feliciano Elvina. Elvina picked up the pot and tried to put it back on its stand, but it toppled over again. He finally placed it in a corner of the pantry deck. To his intense annoyance, water suddenly belched out of the faucet into the sink all over the dishrags he had squeezed dry a minute ago.

Muttering under his breath, Elvina stuck his head into the passageway to see what was going on. Everyone appeared to be yelling, but Elvina was no great shakes at English and he could not make out what they were saying. Then he spied the second mess attendant, his friend Basilio Galvan, back from finding out about the menu for the noon meal. Elvina looked at him in puzzlement. Galvan had been on submarines before and this was Elvina's first one. Galvan simply shrugged, however, and Elvina couldn't tell whether he was concerned. Galvan was both concerned and confused by the sudden turn of events, but as a veteran submariner in Elvina's eyes, he was determined not to show it. Finally Elvina just gave up. returned to the pantry and hunched down next to the coffeepot.

Allen Bryson, a machinist's mate, was on the forward battery phone when he heard the scream. Gerry McLees was about to close the passageway hatch over him when Bryson shouted out the news. McLees scrambled back up to see what was what.

Chief Electrician's Mate Lawrence Gainor had positioned himself at the aft end of the compartment to take voltmeter readings. He had yet to relay one of them to his recorder, a signalman named Ted Jacobs. But Gainor would have his hands full soon enough.

Sometimes a person's moment of truth comes so quickly that there is no chance to think about it. For Gainor, his twenty years of sub service came into instinctive play, triggered by whatever makes one man charge and another run, one man grapple with opportunity and another impotent.

At the first word of trouble, Gainor moved immediately to the watertight door between the forward battery and the control room, and with the help of Jacobs, he secured it. He could see the geysers of water spraying from the overhead network of pipes into the control room. Once the door was closed, he saw the water splattering against its eyeport. For all Gainor knew, the control room was flooded.

There was no time to dwell on it. As the forward battery lights began to flicker, he took another look at his voltmeters. They were discharging at a furious rate. Somewhere there was a bad short circuit.

He grabbed a flashlight and worked his way forward against the upward slant of the *Squalus* to the battery hatch. When he peered down into the well, he was greeted by a fearful sight. Solid bands of blue-white fire were leaping from battery to battery in eight-inch arcs. Stabbing through the darkness, they threw grotesque shadows against the sides on the inner hull. The heat was so intense that steam was pouring out of the battery cells and the rubber-compound insulation had begun to melt. As the boat continued her sickening drop, she was only seconds away from a gigantic explosion that would rip her apart even before she reached the bottom.

Without hesitation, Gainor lowered himself down there. The big batteries, six feet high, completely filled the space beneath the deck except for narrow center walk. Alone, squinting against the fiery bands dancing around him, he crouched on the walk and groped for the master disconnect switches. Finally he located the starboard switch and yanked it clear. Next he bent to his left for the port switch. A terrifying arc over it spluttered and flashed in his face. One brush against it would send him to a horrible death. Gainor was sure that he would be electrocuted before he could reach the switch. He tried anyway, and with a last desperate effort he jerked it free. The fierce arcs vanished.

Gainor stayed put for a minute, gathering himself. Then he quietly made his way up the ladder.

In the after battery, Lloyd Maness would face an equally daunting task. Like Gainor, Maness was preparing to call off voltmeter readings. He also never got to the first one. For both Maness and his recorder, Art Booth, the early stages of the dive were perfectly routine. Booth had penciled in the dive time on his notepad. Together, they waited for the meter indicator to stabilize after the transfer to battery power. They could hear executive officer Doyle issuing his familiar commands in the control room.

All at once, the same movement of air that Naquin had felt swept by them. Then they heard Kuney's stunned cry that the engine rooms were flooding. All hell broke loose in the after battery. The lights went out. In the dim glow of the emergency light, water was shooting every which way. Maness went right to his disaster station, the watertight door between the after battery and the control room. He stepped into the control room and got ready to swing the door shut.

As he did, Booth skipped past him.

Farther back in the after battery, Electrician's Mate First Class Jud Bland was manning the compartment battle phone. When he heard the incredible report come over it, he couldn't believe his ears. Then the water slammed into him. His initial thought was to close the valves in the overhead ventilation pipes. He wasn't quite sure where they were. After a dozen years with the surface fleet, not only was the *Squalus* his first sub, but he had not been on dive duty in the after battery before. As he felt for them in the gloom of the emergency lights, the *Squalus* lurched violently upward and sent him sprawling to his knees. By now he realized that she was long past the point where closing some valves would do any good. As the full impact of what was happening swept over him, Bland started toward the control room. Maness yelled at him to hurry.

Seaman Bill Boulton came on frantically behind Bland. One minute Boulton had been sitting at a mess table, idly staring into space, drying off after stowing gear topside. In the next, he was dumbfounded to see water streaming along the battery deck. For a moment, he could think only that the main-deck hatch above him had not been secured and he stood up reflexively to check it. Then he saw that the water around his feet was pouring in from the engine rooms. As he tried to puzzle this out, the sea rocketed in from pipes all over the compartment. And almost before he knew it, the upward pitch of the boat sent the water rolling back at him. It had already surged over the tops of his work shoes. Boulton splashed his way forward, more water springing suddenly at him in a terrifying crossfire. Dazed, Boulton stumbled blindly toward the control room. Then, all at once, he had passed Maness and fell into it.

At the far end of the after battery, Rob Washburn was still waiting for the pharmacist's mate, O'Hara, to give him aspirin for his cold when the water hit him. It shot out of the air blower over the medicine cabinet with explosive force, knocking Washburn to the deck on the port side of the compartment. He got back up just as the *Squalus* unexpectedly rose by her bow and was thrown headlong to the deck again. Once more, he managed to struggle up.

O'Hara was searching through his cabinet as the water gushed over his head, barely missing him. Then the bottles on the shelves started tumbling out. Instinctively, O'Hara tried to catch them. A moment later, he found himself sitting on the deck, water swirling at his waist. He flopped around and pushed himself up with both hands. He saw Washburn to his right and started to follow his erstwhile patient.

By this time, the slant of the *Squalus* was so steep that Washburn had to cling to the bunks lining the compartment as he worked himself forward hand over hand, O'Hara a few feet behind. Finally, he reached the control room. Lloyd Maness, holding the door, urged O'Hara on. At last, O'Hara also made it past him.

In the galley, Will Isaacs, the cook, waited impatiently for the *Squalus* to level off so he could switch his oven back on and get the meatballs going. A seaman, Alex Keegan, and a fireman second class, Roland Blanchard, were on mess duty helping Isaacs. When the dive began, Keegan had left to go to the crew's toilet across the passageway.

Isaacs and Blanchard never saw him again.

At the first klaxon alarm, Blanchard had started closing a valve in the hull ventilation line running through the galley. This was one of his regular dive assignments, and as had happened on previous plunges, he ran into difficulty trying to turn the stiff, new handwheel. There was a quick rush of escaping air and then the water followed, but there was so much pressure now that Blanchard couldn't budge the wheel at all.

After the sudden movement of air, Isaacs looked inquiringly into the passageway outside the galley. A solid stream of water smacked him in the face. He ducked away and glanced aft toward the forward engine room. The door to it was partially open and water was coursing through from the other side. Isaacs went immediately to the door and secured it.

Then he straightened up to look through the eyeport. The sight was awesome. A great cataract was thundering out of the air-induction outlet above the diesels. It had already buried them. Isaacs stood there, transfixed.

In the galley, Blanchard had given up trying to turn the handwheel and stepped into the passageway. When the *Squalus* tipped upward, all the water in the after battery came racing down the deck toward him. Blanchard waded forward fighting the current, arms flailing wildly to keep his balance. He had gotten about a third of the way through the compartment when he slipped. His head went under and he felt himself being carried back again. At the last second, his hand clutched a steel stanchion. He hung on to it and with savage frenzy, he pulled himself up. Kicking off from the stanchion, he lunged desperately for the nearest tier of bunks. He got to it and dragged himself from one tier to the next. The water wasn't as deep here, but it kept pouring down from the overhead pipes and the footing was miserable. Up head of him, he saw the door to the control room begin to close. He yelled out. Maness heard him and eased the door open again.

For Isaacs, time was fast running out. But, his face pressed against the eyeport, he seemed unable to tear himself away from the frightful sight in the forward engine room. He could not see any crewmen in there, just the thundering ocean. Then he became aware of the icy water lapping around his waist. Before he could move, it had almost reached his armpits. He frantically propelled himself away from the door, actually swimming, and barged right into one of the mess tables hidden by the rising surge. Isaacs went under, but he had a hand around a leg of the table bolted to the deck and he came up spewing salt water from his mouth. He kept going and Maness, holding the door open an instant longer, saw him. Isaacs floundered into the control room and dropped to his knees, gasping for breath.

Now Maness could delay no more. Indeed for agonizing seconds, it would appear that he had waited too long.

Twice he had paused before sealing off the control room, once for Blanchard, then for Isaacs. He peered into the blackness of the compartment. He thanked God that he couldn't see anybody else. To have closed the door in someone's pleading face would have been more than he could bear.

His task defied all odds. The door swung in from the after battery. It was oval and fitted into a steel frame that curved around the rest of the passageway. Normally, when the *Squalus* was on an even keel, it moved easily on its hinges. But now the ravaged sub was sagging by her stern at an angle of nearly fifty degrees. And Maness had to lift it toward him, almost as if it were a trap door. A trap door of solid steel, except for its eyeport, that weighed several hundred pounds.

He had to do it alone. There wasn't enough room for anybody to help him. Maness bent forward and pulled, the sea already spilling over the lip of the doorway. He strained harder, his feet braced against the sides of the door frame, beads of sweat full-blown on his forehead. The door began to swing up steadily, inch by inch. Then it stopped, neither moving up nor falling back.

Maness gritted his teeth. Summoning a last ferocious burst of strength, his arm and leg muscles quivering wildly, his shoulders threatening to pop their sockets, he heaved once more. And this time, the door shut.

On the other side was Sherman Shirley. He could only hope that there would still be a wedding, that Shirley was safely barricaded in the after torpedo room.

John Batick had made the wrong choice. Down in the well of the after battery instead of Gerry McLees, the hatch above him closed, he never had a chance.

A few moments later, in a swirl of trailing bubbles, the *Squalus* touched delicately on the North Atlantic floor, first her stern, then her bow. Inside, they hardly felt it. She had settled evenly on her keel, still slanting upward at an angle of about eleven degrees. Her emergency lights were out and she had no heat. She lay helpless in 243 feet of water. The temperature outside her hull was just above freezing.

In the control room, Chief Roy Campbell held a flashlight up to the eyeport of the door Maness had closed. An evil film of oily water rode against it on the other side. It was not quite eight-forty-five that morning. Less than five minutes had elapsed since the *Squalus* started her dive.

Up on the surface, it was as if she had never existed at all.

★ ★ ★ ★ ★

Navy ships raced to the scene of the lost *Squalus* alerted by the *Squalus*'s sister ship, the USS *Sculpin* that discovered the location of the sinking. Commander Charles B. Momsen, the leading expert on submarine survival and rescue, arrived at the scene aboard the USS *Falcon*. With them was the untested McCann rescue chamber, a modified diving bell designed by Momsen, which was lowered to the *Squalus*. All thirty-three survivors were rescued from the submarine. The *Squalus* was later raised, refitted, and recommissioned the USS *Sailfish* in February 1940. *Sailfish* would go on to serve twelve war patrols against Japan in World War II, sinking seven ships including the escort carrier *Chuyo,* and receive a Presidential Unit Citation.

Sound General Quarters, from *At Dawn We Slept*

GORDON W. PRANGE

> I fear that we have awakened a sleeping giant and instilled in him a terrible resolve.
>
> —Admiral Isoruku Yamamoto

December 7, 1941, is a date that will forever be etched into American memory. Japan's sneak attack on the American naval base at Pearl Harbor ended the long-standing policy of neutrality and America officially declared war against Japan the following day. By 1941, however, American neutrality was in name only. In August that year, President Roosevelt met with Prime Minister Winston Churchill and signed the Atlantic Charter declaring mutual support and envisioning a postwar world based on democratic values. American warships began escorting British convoys to Iceland as the U.S. Navy entered an undeclared war with German U-boats. In Asia, Roosevelt had backed the Nationalist Chinese government with money, weapons, and supplies to fight the invading Japanese army. Most important, the American government placed an embargo on metals and oil to Japan in an effort to force an end to Japan's war in China. The Japanese government, under the control of a war hawk army general Hideki Tojo, opted to strike out and seize the lands and resources they deemed rightfully theirs to create a Japanese empire. The only force in the Pacific capable of stopping them became the object of their attention—the United States Navy.

The mission of stopping the U.S. Navy from interfering with Japan's southern advance was left to Admiral Isoruku Yamamoto. A Harvard graduate, Yamamoto had served as a naval attaché in Washington and understood the might of American industry and became known for his opposition to any future war with the United States. In 1936, he became vice-minister for the Japanese Navy, a position in which he was targeted for assassination by ultra-loyalists for his antiwar views. By 1941, he was appointed Commander in Chief of the Japanese Navy and removed the political realm. Left with the task of formulating a war plan against the United States, Yamamoto knew the only chance of stopping the Pacific fleet would be a devastating blow on the first day of the war. His plan called for six fleet carriers and their escorts to sail undetected through the northern Pacific to within two hundred miles of Oahu and launch a devastating surprise raid against Pearl Harbor. The raid was planned to strike early on a Sunday morning, the time when most ships would be at anchor.

Gordon W. Prange took part in the American occupation of Japan following World War II where he was commissioned by Gen. Douglas MacArthur to write the official history of the war. He was one of the foremost experts on Pearl Harbor having interviewed many of the surviving participants from both sides. In the following chapter, Prange describes the opening moments of the Pearl Harbor attack from his most famous work, *At Dawn We Slept*.

★ ★ ★ ★ ★

Kimmel was still in his quarters dressing and awaiting confirmation of *Ward*'s report of the submarine sinking when Fuchida's first wave deployed a few miles north of Opana Station. At a point roughly opposite Haleiwa Field, Fuchida signaled for the general attack at 0750. Precisely one minute thereafter Murata called on his torpedomen for their strike. Northwest of Ewa the torpedo bombers split into two groups of eight planes each under Nagai and Matsumura and raced for the west side of Pearl Harbor. Another flight under Murata and Lieutenant Ichiro Kitajima, composed also of two groups but with twelve planes each, flew southeastward, then swung north and northwestward in a large arc over Hickam Field and headed directly for Battleship Row.

Each torpedo group attacked in formations of twos and threes. Every torpedo pilot had explicit instructions to close in on his target, even at the risk of his life. If his observer-bombardier thought he might miss, the pilot would make additional runs until quite sure of a hit. If, after several passes, the observer still could not get a good sighting, he was to use his judgment and choose another target.

Kimmel's telephone rang again. Murphy had called him back, this time to report that *Ward* had stopped a sampan hovering near the submarine action. Even as the duty officer spoke, Fuchida, now opposite Barber's Point, flashed to his horizontal bombers *Tsu, tsu, tsu*—much the same signal as his earlier *To, to, to,* but applicable only to his own group.

Takahashi's dive bombers had already swung into action. The sound of airplanes attracted the attention of Rear Admiral William Rhea Furlong, in command of Battle Forces Pacific, a formidable fleet of service vessels. Furlong was strolling along the quarterdeck of his flagship, the minelayer *Oglala,* awaiting his call to breakfast. *Oglala* was so ancient she seldom left dock, and the reaction of a seasoned sailor newly assigned to her was likely to be a half-incredulous, half-affectionate "What a tub!" This particular morning she happened to be in *Pennsylvania's* normal berth at Dock 1010, outboard the cruiser *Helena.* Furlong, who lived aboard the ship, was senior officer present afloat (SOPA) that morning.

Furlong paid little attention to the roar of engines until he saw a bomb drop. *What a stupid, careless pilot,* he said to himself, *not to have secured his releasing gear.* The missile exploded harmlessly in a shower of earth near the water's edge at the southwest end of Ford Island. As the pilot cut hard to port and sped up the channel, Furlong saw the red ball of the Rising Sun and reacted instantly. "Japanese! Man your stations!" he shouted. At his command *Oglala* flashed the alarm: "All ships in harbor sortie."

On *West Virginia* Ensign Roland S. Brooks saw what he thought to be an internal explosion on *California* and ordered Away Fire and Rescue Party! Actually the flame and smoke came from a burning hangar on Ford Island. His order brought hundreds of officers and men swarming topside, giving his ship a few precious seconds' grace and undoubtedly saving hundreds of lives.

At that instant, about 0755, Matsumura and Nagai led the third and fourth torpedo groups from *Hiryu* and *Soryu* respectively straight to the west side of Ford Island. In Matsumura's eagerness to confirm the vessels he dipped so low that his plane rustled the sugarcane and he felt "the warm air of an unending summer land." Within seconds a pair of torpedoes cut swift paths through the shallow water to the light cruiser *Raleigh* and the target ship *Utah.* This waste of priceless torpedoes infuriated Matsumura, who had specifically instructed his men to avoid *Utah.* But Lieutenant Tamotsu Nakajima, young and inexperienced, thought he saw one missile slam into her and followed suit. And very disgruntled he was later because he had not profited by his drill in the recognition of American ships. Listing heavily to port, *Utah* began to capsize.

Raleigh's officer of the deck called the antiaircraft men to their guns, assuming the air action to be "part of a routine air-raid drill." But just then, about 0755, a torpedo struck the cruiser at Frame 58, flooding the forward engine room and Nos. 1 and 2 firerooms. At once Seaman First Class Frank M. Berry ran for the ship's alarm, but it did not go off because "the electricity went the first thing."

The concussion awakened Ensign John R. Beardall, Jr., twenty-two-year-old son of the President's naval aide. He hurried to the quarter-deck in his red pajamas, and one of the first things he saw was "those big red balls . . . and it didn't take long to figure out what was going on." His antiaircraft battery went into action within five minutes because all of *Raleigh*'s 3-inch guns had their ammunition in the ready boxes. By 0805 *Raleigh* listed hard to port.

In spite of counterflooding, the list continued. Captain R. Bentham Simons immediately directed efforts to save his ship from capsizing. Meantime, at 0800 another torpedo had hurtled between *Raleigh* and *Detroit* about twenty-five yards from the latter's stern, to bury itself harmlessly in the mud.

In these crucial early moments Nagai flew across Ford Island, intent on hitting *Pennsylvania* in dry dock. But seeing that the mooring slip would check the torpedo, he loosed his missile at *Oglala*. As if to compensate the Japanese for having missed *Detroit,* the torpedo slid under *Oglala* and burst against the light cruiser *Helena,* crippling both ships in one blow. *Oglala*'s log described the result: "The force of the explosion lifted up fireroom floor plates and ruptured hull on port side." *Helena*'s log recorded: "At about 0757½, a series of three heavy explosions felt nearby. At about 0758, ship rocked by violent explosion on starboard side."

Incredibly, all this action took place while Murphy delivered his brief message to Kimmel. The duty officer was still speaking when a yeoman rushed into his office, shouting, "There's a message from the signal tower saying the Japanese are attacking Pearl Harbor and this is no drill." Murphy passed the shocking news to Kimmel. The admiral slammed down the receiver and dashed outside, buttoning his white uniform jacket as he ran.

Next door to Kimmel, the lawn of the Earles' new home commanded a clear view of Battleship Row across the harbor. Kimmel and Mrs. Earle stood transfixed as the planes flew over "circling in figure 8's, then bombing the ships, turning and dropping more bombs." They "could plainly see the rising suns on the wings and would have seen the pilot's faces had they leaned out." Mrs. Earle's sympathetic heart spilled over in grief and pity for the admiral as he watched "in utter disbelief and completely stunned," his stricken face "as white as the uniform he wore."

"I knew right away that something terrible was going on, that this was not a casual raid by just a few stray planes. The sky was full of the enemy," he said later. Gazing toward his beloved ships with bombers and fighters swooping over them like vampire bats, they saw "*Arizona* lift out of the water, then sink back down—way down." In those terrible moments neither uttered a word; the ghastly picture before them said everything.

History had already swept past Kimmel with the speed of a movie out of control, beyond human capability to see or comprehend. Any number of Americans saw Murata's flight as it lumbered in and peeled off to strike but assumed that local planes were practicing. Even when the first torpedoes began to fall, many observers reacted as did Lieutenant Lawrence Ruff, waiting for mass to begin aboard the hospital ship *Solace*: "Oh, oh, some fool pilot has gone wild."

One individual who grasped the situation quickly was Bicknell, who had a panoramic view from the lanai of his home above and behind Pearl Harbor. From the viewpoint of Japanese strategy, the attack made sense to him; nevertheless, the reality astounded him. "Well, naturally, when you are looking out of your window on a peaceful Sunday morning and see a battleship blow up under your eyes, you are pretty apt to be surprised." Suddenly he began "mumbling about these 'poinsettias and hibiscus'" much to his wife's perplexity. It had suddenly occurred to Bicknell that the Mori telephone call might have contained a code for certain types of ships.

If so, the code words merely confirmed what the Japanese already had learned. As they dropped their torpedoes that morning, Murata's men knew exactly what types of ship they would find in position. Murata waited eagerly for his observer's report. Would the new fins, perfected so late and adjusted so hurriedly, really work? "*Atarimashita!* ["It struck!"]" cried the observer. The triumphant cry echoed and reechoed as one after another the planes sent off their lone but mortal missiles. Elatedly Murata radioed his report: "Torpedoed enemy battleships. Serious damage inflicted."

This was the news that Japan's naval leaders awaited—the outcome of the all-important torpedo attack on Battleship Row. On that crucial mission hung the results of the entire operation. Genda's heart pounded with joy. *Now the attack will be a success,* he thought. Whatever fierce satisfaction Nagumo and Kusaka may have felt, they remained outwardly calm. They and their staff officers present on the bridge exchanged glances. A faint smile played over Nagumo's lips—the first time Genda had seen Nagumo smile since the task force left Hitokappu Bay.

One of the first torpedoes to strike *West Virginia* came from Matsumura on his second swipe at Battleship Row. "A huge waterspout splashed over the stack of the ship and then tumbled down like an exhausted geyser . . . immediately followed by another one. What a magnificent sight!" So impressed was Matsumura that he told his observer to photograph the scene. But the man misinterpreted the order and blazed away with his machine gun, wrecking the antenna of his own plane.

"By this time enemy aircraft fire had begun to come up very fiercely. Black bursts were spoiling the once beautiful sky," Matsumura recalled. "Even white bursts were seen mixed up among them." The white smoke came from harmless training shells as the Americans hurled everything imaginable at the Japanese while seamen smashed the locks of the ships' magazines. Now those magazines began to yield their deadly harvest, and Matsumura soared away, picked up a fighter escort, and headed for the rendezvous point.

Ensign Nathan F. Asher, on the bridge of the destroyer *Blue,* never understood how his men "got their ammunition from the magazines to the guns in the fast and swift manner that they did." A few of the crew had awakened with Sunday morning hangovers but later said "they had never sobered up so fast in their lives."

As luck would have it, *Vestal*'s officer of the deck was CWO Fred Hall, who the previous night had predicted a Japanese attack on Pearl Harbor. Hall immediately recognized the red disk under the bombers' wings and ordered Sound General Quarters! But the quartermaster, jaw at half-mast, stared at Hall as if he had lost his mind. "Goddamn it," howled the officer, "I said 'Sound General Quarters!' Those are Jap planes up there." And he himself pulled the signal at 0755. *Vestal* opened fire at 0805. A bomb struck her "at frame 110 port side" and "a second hit at frame 44 starboard side." Each bomb killed one man and wounded several others.

Oklahoma was moored port side at Berth F-5, outboard of *Maryland* in an exposed position. Goto closed in on his target. Suddenly the big ship loomed directly before him. "I was about twenty meters above the water," Goto said later, "when I released my torpedo. As my plane climbed up after the torpedo was off, I saw that I was even lower than the crow's nest of the great battleship. My observer reported a huge waterspout springing up from the ship's location. *'Atarimashita!'* he cried. The other two planes in my group . . . also attacked *Oklahoma.*"

Electrician's Mate First Class Irvin H. Thesman was ironing a pair of dungarees in the power shop when the public address system blared out: "Man your battle stations! This is no shit!" Although startled by such uninhibited language over the ship's PA, Thesman thought it just another drill. So he grabbed a bag of tools and a flashlight and dogtrotted to his station in the steering gear compartment.

Two hits in rapid succession had already torn into *Oklahoma*'s vitals. Boatswain Adolph M. Bothne found both the aircraft ammunition ready boxes and the fire and rescue chest locked. He picked up a hammer and a cold chisel from a gear locker. At that moment "a third torpedo hit in the middle of the ship, and the ship started to list noticeably. . . ." Bothne "had to walk uphill to go to the starboard side, and after they had the ready boxes open there and the ammunition out they had no air to load the guns, and one of the men said there was no fire locks on the guns."

Hastening toward his battle station in Turret No. 4 amidships, Gunner's Mate Second Class Edgar B. Beck decided there was no point in continuing on his way because "it was clear that we were going over." So he decided to concentrate on helping his buddies through the shell hoist, their only means of escape. He knew that when the ship capsized, the 14-inch shells, which weighed about 1,400 pounds, would break loose and crush to death anyone in their path.

Oklahoma's executive officer, Commander J. L. Kenworthy, was the senior officer aboard. He and the ship's first lieutenant, Lieutenant Commander W. H. Hobby, concluded "that the ship was fast becoming untenable and that an effort should be made to save as many men as possible." So Kenworthy ordered Abandon Ship and directed the men "to leave over the starboard side and to work and climb over the ship's side out onto the bottom as it rolled over."

Murata's strike on *West Virginia* and Goto's on *Oklahoma* came practically together. Now a torpedo swept right under *Vestal* and, in the words of Chief Boilermaker John Crawford, "blew the bottom out of *Arizona*." Major Alan Shapley, the tall, handsome commander of *Arizona*'s Marine detachment, was enjoying his breakfast when he felt "a terrific jar." Thinking one of the forty-foot boats must have dropped off the crane to the fantail, he ran topside to investigate. He vividly recalled some sailors standing at *Arizona*'s rail watching a flight of planes flash across the harbor. He heard one of the men remark, "This is the best goddamn drill the Army Air Force has ever put on!"

Captain Van Valkenburg and Damage Control Officer Lieutenant Commander Samuel G. Fuqua reached the deck about the same time, and the captain proceeded to the bridge. Fuqua directed Ensign H. D. Davidson to sound General Quarters. About that time the ship "took a bomb hit on the starboard side of the quarterdeck, just about abreast of No. 4 turret."

It was the torpedo strike which Kimmel and Mrs. Earle saw from Makalapa Heights. "I knew the ship had been hit hard," Kimmel said later, "because even then I could see it begin to list." He did not recall having summoned his car, but suddenly it appeared, braking to a screaming halt. His longtime driver, Machinist Mate First Class Edgar C. Nebel, was at the wheel. Kimmel dived into his car. As it roared off, Captain Freeland A. Daubin, commander of Submarine Squadron Four, jumped on the running board. The admiral and his hitchhiker reached headquarters at about 0805, just as *California* shuddered with her first torpedo, rapidly followed by another "port side at frame 110."

California, flagship of Pye's battle force, was moored singly in Berth F-3. This put her below the tanker *Neosho* to the southward on the edge of Ford Island in the direction of Pearl Harbor's outer channel and the sea. Train felt two distinct but rather dull thuds against the ship. These were the torpedoes crashing home. Immediately she began to list to port. By now guns blazed aboard *California.* But of all the battleships in Pearl Harbor that morning, she was least capable of absorbing punishment. In preparation for Monday's inspection several manhole covers had been removed and others loosened. When the two torpedoes struck, water poured into the fuel system, cutting off light and power. An alert ensign, Edgar M. Fain, directed prompt counter-flooding measures which saved the vessel from capsizing.

Up to this time the inboard battleships had escaped with little damage. Now Fuchida's horizontal bombers roared on the scene to strike them as well as the outboard craft. After giving his attack signal, Fuchida had dropped back from the lead position, the better to observe the action, yielding pride of place to his number two plane. The honor was well deserved, for this aircraft held Aso and Watanabe, the tireless bombing team which had made the initial breakthrough in high-level practice.

On the first run over the target, air turbulence prevented proper sighting, and only the number three plane released its missile. Throughout training this bombardier had experienced difficulty in timing. When Fuchida saw the bomb plunge ineffectually into the water, he assumed that the culprit had blundered and shook his fist at number three in a rage. The disappointed bombardier indicated by gestures that enemy fire had jarred his bomb loose. Fuchida felt remorseful for having jumped to conclusions but had no time to brood. His own plane now rocked as if hit by a giant club.

"Is everything all right?" he cried out.

"A few holes in the fuselage," his pilot replied reassuringly.

Two shocks thudded against *West Virginia*. By the time Commander R. H. Hillenkoetter, her executive officer, reached the quarterdeck, the ship had begun to list rapidly to port. Then came a "third heavy shock to port." Soon the top of Turret No. 3 caught fire. Another stunning explosion threw Hillenkoetter to the deck.

When the attack began, Captain Mervyn Bennion, *West Virginia*'s skipper, and her navigator, Lieutenant Commander T. T. Beattie, soon found communications disrupted, so they "went out on the starboard side of the bridge discussing what to do." Lieutenant Claude V. Rickets asked and received permission to counterflood, which he did with the able assistance of a boatswain's mate named Billingsley. This helped correct her list and kept her from capsizing.

As Kimmel dashed out of his car at headquarters, the explosion of bombs, the whine of bullets, the roar of planes, the belching guns of aroused defenders, the acrid smell of fire and smoke—all blended into a nerve-racking cacophony of chaos. Murata's bombardiers still dropped their torpedoes, while dive bombers pounced like hawks on nearby Hickam Field and Ford Island. Far above, high-level bombers rained their deadly missiles as fighters shuttled in and out, weaving together the fearful tapestry of destruction. Numb and stricken, Kimmel rushed into his office, his face a mask of bleak incomprehension as he tried to pull himself together amid the tumbling ruins of his world. He had neither time nor inclination for self-pity. "My main thought was the fate of my ships," he said, ". . . to see what had taken place and then strike back at the Japs."

Now his staff began to rally to his side. Smith found Kimmel, shocked but composed, watching the attack from the War Plans Office with Pye. He reminded them that they should not be together; a single blast could kill them both and leave the Fleet without a commander in chief. Pye moved to the other end of the building.

As Davis jumped out of his car, he observed a group of officers, enlisted men, and civilians standing around the headquarters, gaping into the sky. Conditions inside, in Davis's opinion, were not much better. The air officer immediately manned his telephone, trying to reach anyone, anywhere on Oahu, who could get the Navy's planes into the air to seek the source of the attacking aircraft.

Hurrying down the hall to his office, Layton ran into Captain Willard A. Kitts, Jr., Kimmel's gunnery officer. The captain proved his bigness of character by greeting Layton generously: "Here is the young man we should have listened to." Grimly just, McMorris said to Layton, "If it's any satisfaction to you, you were right and we were wrong." Layton could have done without such concrete vindication as the Japanese were providing. He plunged into a sea of intelligence reports, which constantly grew more and more complex and confusing. Like Davis, he tried to find the nest of these Japanese sea hawks shooting up the Pacific Fleet.

Murphy had already dispatched a message to CinCAF, CinCLANT, and CNO: "Enemy air raid, Pearl Harbor. This is not a drill." A few others followed. At 0812 Kimmel advised the entire Pacific Fleet and Stark: "Hostilities with Japan commenced with air raid on Pearl Harbor." Then at 0817 he instructed Patrol Wing Two: "Locate enemy force"—a succinct order easier to give than to accomplish.

The atmosphere in Kimmel's headquarters struck Curts as one of "no hysteria, but ordered dismay." The communications officer joined Kimmel and Smith as they, too, tried to determine from what direction the attacking planes had come. The three officers could not see the actual strikes, but speedy reports kept them abreast of the situation. The effectiveness of the Japanese operation astounded them. But even Davis assumed that the enemy had but one carrier or two at the most. At this time no one apparently recalled the Martin-Bellinger or Farthing reports, both of which had called the shots with almost uncanny accuracy.

Aboard the stricken *Oklahoma* about 150 men "perched along the blister ledge" at Bosun Bothne's direction. "Then the ship seemed to hesitate. . . ." At that moment the fourth torpedo struck. *Oklahoma* "bounced up, and when she settled down she turned over." Some of the men slid down the side into the water. Mrs. Earle still watched the grisly scene from in front of her home. "Then slowly, sickeningly, the *Oklahoma* began to roll over on her side, until, finally, only her bottom could be seen. It was awful, for great ships were dying before my eyes! Strangely enough, at first I didn't realize that men were dying too."

Thesman and his group in the steering gear compartment dodged to avoid being knocked senseless as lockers and spare parts tumbled down. At twenty-five, Thesman was the oldest in the group and felt responsible for his shipmates. Water began to trickle in through the ventilation system, and the sailors stuffed the ducts with mattresses, blankets, and anything else they could find.

At this time the entire Japanese force seemed to concentrate their particular fury on the hapless *Arizona* and *West Virginia*. Just after *Oklahoma* heeled over, *Arizona* trembled with an indescribably fearful explosion and concussion which seemed to suck the very life out of the air. It may have been the dedicated, crack bombardier Kanai who sent down the missile that hit beside the No. 2 turret and detonated in the forward magazine.

Almost 1,000 men perished in that frightful moment, including Admiral Kidd and Captain Van Valkenburgh. An ensign later told how the quartermaster had just reported to the captain a bomb hit "either by or on No. 2 turret." The next thing he knew, "the ship was sinking like an earthquake had struck it, and the bridge was in flames." Hastening forward after the first hit in a fruitless attempt to fight the fires, Fuqua met someone who informed him "that he observed a bomb go down the stack." This story has persisted; however, some survivors believe it incorrect, pointing out that the angle of the stack would have prevented it and that such a strike would have exploded in the boiler room, not the magazine. Fuqua, too, thought it improbable, but he did not intend to argue the point at that moment. Pausing only to order the forward magazine flooded, and finding that "all guns on the boat deck had ceased firing," he realized that "the ship was no longer in a fighting condition." He ordered Abandon Ship and set about rescuing the wounded.

Strangely enough, the explosion that destroyed *Arizona* saved *Vestal.* The concussion put out her fires as though a giant candlesnuffer had been clapped over her. It also sent tons of debris down on her decks—"Parts of the ship, legs, arms and heads of men—all sorts of bodies," even living men. The explosion flung overboard about 100 men from *Vestal,* among them her skipper, Commander Young. *Vestal*'s crew began to fish out of the water hideously burned refugees from *Arizona.* Aboard the repair ship each survivor received a shot of morphine, and shipmates hurried them to a hospital or to *Solace* as fast as possible.

About this time someone ordered Abandon Ship. Just as the first of the crew started to leave, a figure like some strange sea creature climbed out of the harbor and stood athwart the gangway. It was Young, oil dripping from his face and body, but none the worse for his dunking. "Where the hell do you think you're going?" he demanded of the officer of the deck.

"We're abandoning ship," the man replied.

"Get back aboard ship!" Young roared. "You don't abandon ship on me!" With that he and his remaining crewmen returned to their stations.

Debris from *Arizona* also covered *Tennessee* and accounted for more of her damage than the two Japanese bombs which hit her. The attackers continued to pound *Arizona,* which took a total of eight bombs in addition to the torpedoes. The ship became totally untenable at approximately 1032. Of her complement of 1,400, fewer than 200 survived the attack.

As though enraged because *West Virginia* seemingly refused to sink or capsize, Murata's torpedomen slammed more missiles into her. After she had taken six steel fish, Abe's flight of horizontal bombers dropped two bombs on her at 0808. A "large piece of shrapnel" struck Bennion in the stomach and mortally wounded him. Beattie sent for a pharmacist's mate, and Lieutenant Commander Doir C. Johnson hurried up with a big, well-built black mess attendant, Doris Miller. He had been the ship's heavyweight boxing champion, and Johnson thought he was just the man to help lift the captain out of danger.

The chief pharmacist's mate dressed Bennion's wound as best as he could. As smoke and flames engulfed the ship, Bennion ordered his subordinates to leave him where he was, the only order of his they ever disobeyed. He remained conscious, asking alert questions about the progress of the fight almost to the last. After he died, Johnson saw Miller, who was not supposed to handle anything deadlier than a swab, manning a machine gun, "blazing away as though he had fired one all his life." As he did so, his usually impassive face bore the deadly smile of a berserk Viking.

Thus far *Nevada* had escaped the fate of the other battleships, being in a less vulnerable position. At 0802 her machine guns "opened fire on torpedo planes approaching at port beam." This was Kitajima's group from *Kaga.* One of his planes fell to the battleship's fire "100 yards on port quarter. . . ." A second dropped shortly thereafter, but not before releasing his missile, which at 0803 tore a huge hole in the ship's port bow about frame 40 and flooded a number of compartments. This was the ship's "greatest structural casualty."

Nevada's skipper, Captain F. W. Scanland, was not on board, but Lieutenant Commander J. F. Thomas, USNR, senior officer present, took over promptly and efficiently. At 0805—just as Fuchida's high-level bombers appeared "on both bows"—*Nevada* began to list "slightly to port." The battleship's 5-inch and .50 caliber guns opened immediate fire. Within a minute "several bombs fell close aboard to port. . . ." Counter-flooding began two minutes later. Because burning fuel oil on the surface, ignited when *Arizona* received her first major strike, now threatened *Nevada,* "it was considered necessary to get under way to avoid further danger. . . ."

Tales of heroism far beyond the call of duty abounded on *Nevada,* as on every ship in Pearl Harbor. Twenty-one-year-old Ensign Joseph K. Taussig, Jr., whose admiral father had weaned him on the subject of a war with Japan, was officer of the deck. When General Quarters sounded at 0801, he acted as air defense officer and went at once to his battle station on the starboard antiaircraft director. Being the senior officer present in the AA battery, he "took charge and directed its fire" even after a missile passed completely through his thigh. Refusing all efforts to take him to a battle dressing station, he "insisted in continuing his control of the AA battery and the continuation of fire on enemy aircraft. . . ."

Although severely damaged, *Nevada* was still very much afloat and full of fight when Lieutenant Ruff scrambled up her side from *Solace*'s motor launch. He knew that, with the captain and other senior officers ashore, unusually heavy responsibilities would fall to him and to Thomas, who was belowdecks at his battle station. When Ruff got close enough to communicate, he suggested that Thomas run the ship's activities below while he, Ruff, would manage topside.

One by one Murata's torpedo bombers, having discharged their missiles, roared away, picked up a fighter escort and winged northward. They had lost five torpedo planes, all from *Kaga*. As always in dealing with contemporary battle reports, it is virtually impossible to determine exactly whom to credit with what specific kill. Indeed, American accounts were wildly at variance, as was only to be expected in view of the stunning surprise, the excitement of battle, and the billows of smoke rolling up from the burning ships. Moreover, the Americans were fighting, blind mad, and each man was eager to claim for his own outfit any aircraft he saw go down in flames.

When word reached Kimmel about the fate of his battleships, it wrung a groan of anguish from his lips. But much as the loss of his ships grieved him, what really tore his brave heart was the death and suffering of his men. These were not neat rows of statistics to Kimmel. In that day the United States Navy was a small, neighborly community where almost everyone knew everyone else. A man might enlist on one ship and stay with her until he retired twenty or thirty years later. Comradeship at Annapolis, service together, and family intermarriage bound the officers with ties none the less binding for being intangible. Kimmel knew thousands of men at Pearl Harbor by sight, hundreds by name, and scores as personal friends. All of them, from seasoned skippers to the greenest sailors, were his men, his responsibility.

Curts was standing beside Kimmel at the window when a spent bullet crashed through the glass. It struck the admiral on the chest, left a dark splotch on his white uniform, then dropped to the floor. Kimmel picked it up. It was a .50 caliber machine-gun bullet. Somehow the slug seemed symbolic. Much as Kimmel craved the chance to avenge this terrible day, in his heart he knew that the debacle spelled the end of his career as CinCUS. Kimmel was not given to dramatics. But such was the depth of his sorrow and despair that he murmured, more to himself than to Curts, "It would have been merciful had it killed me."

★ ★ ★ ★ ★

The Japanese attack on Pearl Harbor filled the American people with an outrage of hatred toward the Japanese and moral crusade to see the war through to the bitter end. Having totally underestimated the American character, Japan's leaders assumed when a war with Japan became too costly, the Americans would back down and seek a negotiated settlement. It can be said their opening move of the Pacific war ensured their eventual defeat as the Americans, and their Allies, would settle for nothing less than total victory.

The Galloping Ghost of the Java Coast

COM. WALTER G. WINSLOW

Some ships become legends through victory, others by defeat, and still others by the sheer courage of their captain and crew. Such was the case with the USS *Houston* (CA-30) who earned the nickname "Galloping Ghost of the Java Coast" during the first days of World War II. She was a Northampton class heavy cruiser launched on September 7, 1929, at Newport News, Virginia. Before the outbreak of war in 1941, the ship had already recorded an amazing history. In 1931, the *Houston* became flagship of the Asiatic Fleet. Later that year she steamed 600 miles up the Yangtze River to assist in rescue work during a devastating flood in the Yangtze River Valley. When Japan acted aggressively against Shanghai in 1932, the *Houston* was called upon to deliver Marines to China to help stabilize the situation.

President Franklin D. Roosevelt embarked on the ship for the first time in 1934. His 12,000-mile presidential cruise to Haiti, the Virgin Islands, Puerto Rico, Columbia, and Hawaii helped earn the *Houston* her nickname "the Rambler." FDR sailed with the *Houston* again in 1935, 1938, and 1939, his most notable trip being a fishing expedition to the Galapagos and other Pacific islands, which included an elaborate "King Neptune" ceremony when the ship crossed the Equator.

In March 1941, the *Houston* returned to the Asiatic, where she became the flagship for Admiral Thomas C. Hart, Commander in Chief of the U.S. Asiatic Fleet. In January 1942, the *Houston* and the rest of the Allied fleet were united as a multinational American-British-Dutch-Australian (ABDA) force, originally under the command of Admiral Thomas Hart, USN. An ABDA Combined Striking Force was under the command of Rear Admiral Kerel Doorman of the Royal Netherlands Navy.

In February, the Japanese sent an invasion force to capture Java escorted by a strong task force of heavy warships. On February 27, the ABDA fleet caught up with the Japanese fleet for the first major surface battle of the Pacific War, the Battle of the Java Sea. In an eight-hour engagement, the Japanese inflicted a devastating defeat against the ABDA ships, sinking or fatally crippling the Dutch cruisers *H.M. de Ruyter* and *H.M. Java*, and three destroyers. Although the *Houston* was hit twice by Japanese eight-inch shells, she and the Australian light cruiser HMAS *Perth* both survived the fierce battle.

On February 28, the *Houston* and the *Perth* proceeded to the port of Batavia in western Java, and partially refueled before attempting to pass through Sunda Strait that night in an effort to reach the safer waters of the Indian Ocean. As they approached the entrance to the strait near midnight, they unexpectedly encountered a Japanese covering force of nearly one dozen destroyers, three cruisers, and numerous torpedo boats and minesweepers that were protecting the invasion fleet. In the ensuing Battle of Sunda Strait, the *Houston* and *Perth* both aggressively fired at the attacking Japanese ships at close range, but, outnumbered and outgunned, they were no match for the enemy forces that completely surrounded them.

Commander Walter G. Winslow served aboard the *Houston* and recounts the ship's actions beginning several weeks prior to the Battle of Java Sea.

★ ★ ★ ★ ★

I stood on the quarterdeck contemplating the restful green of Java Coast as it fell slowly behind us. Many times before I had found solace in its beauty, but this night it seemed only a mass of coconut and banana palms that had lost all meaning. I was too tired and too preoccupied with pondering the question that raced through the mind of every man aboard, "Would we get through Sunda Strait?"

There were many aboard who felt that, like a cat, the *Houston* had expended eight of its nine lives and that this one last request of fate would be too much. Jap cruiser planes had shadowed us all day and it was certain that our movements were no mystery to the enemy forces closing in on Java. Furthermore, it was most logical to conclude that Jap submarines were stationed throughout the length of Sundra Strait to intercept and destroy ships attempting escape into the Indian Ocean.

Actually there wasn't any breathing space for optimism, we were trapped, but there had been other days when the odds were stacked heavily in the Japs' favor and we had somehow managed to battle through. Maybe it was because I had the Naval Aviator's philosophical outlook and maybe it was because I was just a plain damn fool, but I couldn't quite bring myself to believe that the *Houston* had run her course. It was with this feeling of shaky confidence that I turned and headed for my stateroom. I had just been relieved as Officer-of-the-Deck and the prospect of a few hours rest was most appealing.

The wardroom and the interior of the ship, through which I walked, was dark, for the heavy metal battle ports were bolted shut and lights were not permitted within the darkened ship. Only the eerie blue beams of a few battle lights close to the deck served to guide my feet. I felt my way through the narrow companionway and snapped on my flashlight briefly to seek out the coaming of my stateroom door. As I stepped into the cubicle that was my room, I took a brief look around and switched off the light. There had been no change, everything lay as it had for the last two and a half months. There had been only one addition in all that time. It was Gus, my silent friend, the beautiful Bali head I had purchased six weeks before in Soerabaja.

Gus sat on the desk top lending his polished wooden expression to the cramped atmosphere of my stateroom. In the darkness I felt his presence as though he were a living thing. "We'll get through, won't we, Gus?" I found myself saying. And although I couldn't see him, I thought he nodded slowly.

I slipped out of my shoes and placed them at the base of the chair by my desk, along with my tin hat and life jacket, where I could reach them quickly in an emergency. Then I rolled into my bunk and let my exhausted body sink into its luxury. The bunk was truly a luxury, for the few men who were permitted to relax lay on the steel decks by their battle stations. I, being an aviator with only the battered shell of our last airplane left aboard, was permitted to take what rest I could get in my room.

Although there had been little sleep for any of us during the past four days, I found myself lying there in the sticky tropic heat of my room fretfully tossing and trying for sleep that would not come.

The constant hum of blowers thrusting air into the bowels of the ship, the *Houston*'s gentle rolling as she moved through a quartering sea, and the occasional groaning of her steel plates combined to bring into my mind the mad merry-go-round of events that had plagued the ship during the past few weeks.

Twenty-four days had elapsed since that terrifying day in the Flores Sea, yet here it was haunting me again as it would for the rest of my life.

My mind pictured the squadrons of Jap bombers as they attacked time and again from every conceivable direction. After the first run they remained at altitudes far beyond the range of our anti-aircraft guns, for they had learned respect on that first run when one of their planes was blasted from the sky and several others were obviously hit and badly shaken. But that first salvo almost finished the *Houston*. It was a perfect straddle, and the force of those big bombs seemed as though a giant hand had taken the ship, lifted her bodily from the water, and tossed her yards away from her original course. There had been no personnel casualties that time but our main anti-aircraft director had been wrenched from its track, rendering it useless, and we were taking water aboard from sprung plates in the hull.

That day the crew had only the steady barrage from the anti-aircraft guns and Captain Rooks' clever handling of the ship to thank for keeping them from the realms of Davy Jones. But there was one horrible period during the afternoon when the Nips almost got us for keeps. A five-hundred pound bomb, and a stray at that, hit us squarely amidships aft. Some utterly stupid Jap bombardier failed to release with the rest of his squadron and Captain Rooks could make no allowances for such as him. The salvo fell harmlessly off the port quarter but the stray crashed through two platforms of the main mast before it exploded on the deck just forward of number three turret. Hunks of shrapnel tore through the turret's thin armor as though it were paper, igniting powder bags in the hoists. In one blazing instant all hands in the turret and in the handling rooms below were dead. Where the bomb spent its force, a gaping hole was blown in the deck below which waited the after repair party. They were wiped out almost to a man. It was a hellish battle which ended with forty-eight of our shipmates killed and another fifty seriously burned or wounded.

I strove desperately to rid myself of the picture of that blazing turret—the bodies of the dead sprawled grotesquely in pools of blood and the bewildered wounded staggering forward for medical aid—but I was forced to see it through. Once again I heard the banging of hammers, hammers that pounded throughout the long night as tired men worked steadily building coffins for forty-eight shipmates lying in little groups on the fantail. We put into Chilatjap the following day, that stinking fever-ridden little port on the South Coast of Java. Here we sadly unloaded our wounded and prepared to bury our dead. It seemed that in the hum of the blowers I detected strains of the Death March—the same mournful tune that the band played as we carried our comrades through the heat of those sunburned, dusty streets of Chilatjap. I saw again the brown poker-faced natives dressed in sarongs, quietly watching us as we buried our dead in the little Dutch cemetery that looked out over the sea. I wondered what those slim brown men thought of all this.

The scene shifted. It was only four days ago that we steamed through the mine fields protecting the beautiful port of Soerabaja. Air raid sirens whined throughout the city and our lookouts reported bombers in the distant sky. Large warehouses along the docks were on fire and a burning merchantman lay on its side vomiting dense black smoke and orange flame. The enemy had come and left his calling card. We anchored in the stream not far from the smoldering docks where we watched Netherlands East Indian Soldiers extinguish the fires.

Six times during the next two days we experienced air raids. Anchored there in the stream we were as helpless as ducks in a rain barrel. Why our gun crews didn't collapse is a tribute to their sheer guts and brawn. They stood by their guns unflinchingly in the hot sun, pouring shell after shell into the sky while the rest of us sought what shelter is available in the bull's-eye of a target.

Time and again bombs falling with the deep-throated *swoosh* of a giant bullwhip exploded around us, spewing water and shrapnel over our decks. Docks less than a hundred yards away were demolished and a Dutch hospital ship was hit, yet the *Houston,* nicknamed "the Galloping Ghost of the Java Coast" because the Japs had reported her sunk on so many similar occasions, still rode defiantly at anchor.

When the siren's bailful wailing sounded the "all clear," members of the *Houston*'s band came from their battle stations to the quarter deck where we squatted to hear them play swing tunes. God bless the American sailor, you can't beat him.

Like Scrooge the ghosts of the past continued to move into my little room. I saw us in the late afternoon of February 26, standing out of Soerabaja for the last time. Admiral Doorman of the Netherlands Navy was in command of our small striking force. His flagship, the light cruiser *De Ruyter,* was in the lead, followed by another Netherlands light cruiser, the *Java.* Next in line came the British heavy cruiser *Exeter* of *Graf Spee* fame, followed by the crippled *Houston.* Last in the line of cruisers was the Australian light cruiser *Perth.* Ten allied destroyers made up the remainder of our force. Slowly we steamed past the ruined docks where small groups of old men, women, and children had assembled to wave tearful goodbyes to their men who would not return.

Our force was small and hurriedly assembled. We had never worked together before, but now we had one common purpose which every man knew it was his duty to carry through. We were to do our utmost to break up an enemy task force that was bearing down on Java, even though it meant the loss of every ship and man among us. In us lay the last hope of the Netherlands East Indies.

All night long we searched for the enemy convoy but they seemed to have vanished from previously reported positions. We were still at battle stations the next afternoon when at 1415 reports from air reconnaissance indicated that the enemy was south of Bowen Island, and heading south. The two forces were less than fifty miles apart. A hurried but deadly serious conference of officers followed in the wardroom. Commander Maher, our gunnery officer, explained that our mission was to sink or disperse the protecting enemy fleet units and then destroy the convoy. My heart pounded with excitement for the battle later to be known as the Java Sea Battle was only a matter of minutes away. Were the sands of time running out for the *Houston* and all of us who manned her? At that moment I would have given my soul to have known.

In the darkness of my room the Japs came again just as though I were standing on the bridge . . . a forest of masts rapidly developing into ships that climbed in increasing numbers over the horizon . . . those dead ahead, ten destroyers divided into two columns and each led by a four stack light cruiser. Behind them and off our starboard bow came four light cruisers followed by two heavies. The odds weigh heavily against us for we are outnumbered and outgunned.

The Japs open fire first! Sheets of copper colored flame lick out along their battle line and black smoke momentarily masks them from view. My heart pounds violently and cold sweat drenches my body as I realize that the first salvo is on its way. Somehow those big shells all seem aimed at me. I wonder why our guns don't open up, but as the Jap shells fall harmlessly a thousand yards short I realize that the range is yet too great. The battle from which there will be no retreat has begun.

At twenty-eight thousand yards the *Exeter* opens fire, followed by the *Houston*. The sound of our guns bellowing defiance is terrific, the gun blast tears my steel helmet from my head and sends it rolling on the deck.

The range closes rapidly and soon all cruisers are in on the fight. Salvos of shells splash in the water ever closer to us. Now one falls close to starboard followed by another close to port. This is an ominous indicator that the Japs have at last found the range. We stand tensely awaiting the next salvo, and it comes with a wild screaming of shells that fall all around us. It's a straddle, but not a hit is registered. Four more salvos in succession straddle the *Houston,* and the lack of a hit gives us confidence. The *Perth,* 900 yards astern of us, is straddled eight times in a row, yet she too steams on unscathed. Our luck is holding out.

Shells from our guns are observed bursting close to the last Jap heavy cruiser. We have her range and suddenly one of our eight-inch bricks strikes home. There is an explosion aboard her. Black smoke and debris fly into the air and a fire breaks out forward of her bridge. We draw blood first as she turns out of the battle line, making dense smoke. Commander Maher, directing the fire of our guns from his station high in the foretop, reports our success to the Captain over the phone. A lusty cheer goes up from the crew as the word spreads over the ship.

Three enemy cruisers are concentrating their fire on *Exeter.* We shift targets to give her relief, but it is not long after this that *Exeter* shells find their mark and a light cruiser turns out of the Jap line, smoking and on fire. Despite the loss of two cruisers, the intensity of Jap fire does not seem to diminish. The *Houston* is hit twice. One shell rips through the bow just aft of the port anchor windlass, passes down through several decks and out the side just above the water line without exploding. The other shell, hitting aft, barely grazes the side and ruptures a small oil tank. It too fails to explode.

Up to this point the luck of our forces had held up well, but now there is a rapid turn of events as the *Exeter* is hit by a Jap shell which does not explode, but rips into her forward fireroom and severs a main steam line. This reduces her speed to seven knots. In an attempt to save the *Exeter,* whose loss of speed makes her an easy target, we all make smoke to cover her withdrawal. The Japs, aware that something has gone wrong, are quick to press home an advantage, and their destroyers, under heavy support fire from the cruisers, race in to deliver a torpedo attack.

The water seems alive with torpedoes. Lookouts report them approaching and Captain Rooks maneuvers the ship to present as small a target as possible. At this moment a Netherlands East Indies destroyer, the *Kortner,* trying to change stations, is hit amidships by a torpedo intended for the *Houston.* There is a violent explosion and a great fountain of water rises a hundred feet above her, obscuring all but small portions of her bow and stern. When the watery fountain settles back into the sea it becomes apparent that the little green and grey destroyer has broken in half and turned over. Only the bow and stern sections of her jackknifed keel stick above the water. A few men scramble desperately to her barnacled bottom, and her twin screws in their last propulsive effort turn slowly over in the air. In less than two minutes she has disappeared beneath the sea. No one can stand by to give the few survivors a helping hand for her fate can be ours at any instant.

It is nearing sundown. The surface of the sea is covered with clouds of black smoke, which makes it difficult to spot the enemy. It is discovered that Jap cruisers are closing in upon us, and our destroyers are ordered to attack with torpedoes in order to divert them and give us time to reform. Although no hits are reported, the effect of the attack is gratifying for the Japs turn away. At this point the engagement is broken off. The daylight battle has ended with no decisive results; however, there is still the convoy, which we will attempt to surprise under the cover of night.

We check our losses. The *Koertner* and H.M.S. *Electra* have been sunk. The crippled *Exeter* has retired to Soerabaja, escorted by the American destroyers, who have expended their torpedoes and are running low on fuel. The *Houston, Perth, De Ruyter,* and *Java* are still in the fight, but showing the jarring effects of continuous gunfire. Only two destroyers remain with us, H.M.S. *Jupiter* and H.M.S. *Encounter.*

The *Houston* had fired 303 rounds of ammunition per turret, and only fifty rounds per gun remain. The loss of number three turret had been a great handicap, but there are no complaints for the *Houston* has done well. The Chief Engineer reports that his force is on the verge of complete exhaustion and that there have been more than seventy cases of heat exhaustion in the fire rooms during the afternoon's battle. We are in poor fighting condition, but there is plenty more to be done.

During the semi-darkness of twilight we steam on a course away from the enemy in order to lead any of their units which might have us under observation into believing that we are in retreat. When darkness descends we turn and head back.

Shortly after this H.M.S. *Jupiter,* covering our port flank, explodes mysteriously and vanishes in a brief but brilliant burst of flame. We are dumbfounded, for the enemy is not to be seen yet we race on puzzling over her fate and blindly seeking the transports.

An hour passes with nothing intervening to interrupt our search, and then high in the sky above us a flare bursts, shattering the darkness. Night has suddenly become day and we are illuminated like targets in a shooting gallery. We are helpless to defend ourselves, for we have no such thing as radar, and the plane merely circles outside our range of vision to drop another flare after the first one burns itself out, following it with another and still another.

We cannot know for sure, but certainly it is logical to assume that the enemy is closing in for the kill. Blinded by the flares we wait through tense minutes for the blow to come.

On the ship men speak in hushed tones as though their very words will give our position away to the enemy. Only the rush of water as our bow knifes through the sea at thirty knots, and the continuous roaring of blowers from the vicinity of the quarterdeck, are audible. Death stands by, ready to strike. No one talks of it although all thoughts dwell upon it.

The fourth flare bursts, burns, and then slowly falls into the sea. We are enveloped in darkness again. No attack has come and as time passes it becomes evident that the plane has gone away. How wonderful is the darkness, yet how terrifying to realize that the enemy is aware of our every move and merely biding his time like a cat playing with a mouse.

The moon has come up to assist in our search for the convoy. It has been almost an hour since the last flare, and nothing has happened to indicate that the enemy has us under observation. During this period Ensign Stivers has relieved me as officer of the deck. I climb up on the forward anti-aircraft director platform and sprawl out to catch a bit of rest before the inevitable shooting begins. I hardly close my eyes before there comes the sound of whistles and shouting men. I am back on my feet in a hurry and look over the side. The water is dotted with groups of men yelling in some strange tongue which I cannot understand. H.M.S. *Encounter* is ordered to remain behind to rescue them.

Now we are four, three light cruisers and one heavy. We plow on through the eerie darkness. Suddenly out of nowhere six flares appear in the water along our line of ships. They resemble those round smoke pots that burn alongside road constructions with a yellow flame. What exactly are they, and how did they get there? Are they some form of mine, or is their purpose to mark our path for the enemy? No one dares to guess. Either eventuality is bad enough.

As fast as we leave one group astern, another group bobs up alongside. We cannot account for them, and this oriental deviltry is as bewildering as it is confusing. None of us has ever seen such a phenomenon before. We continue to move away from them, but other groups of floating flares appear.

The uncertainty of what is to follow is nerve wracking. We look back and there, marking our track on the oily surface of the sea, are zig-zag lines of flares which rock and burn like ghoulish jack-o-lanterns. We leave them on the far horizon and no more appear. We are again in welcome darkness.

At approximately 2230, lookouts report two large unidentified ships to port, range 12,000 yards. There are no friendly ships within hundreds of miles of us, therefore these are the enemy. The *Houston* opens up with two main battery salvos, the results of which are not determined, and the Japs reply with two of their own which throw water over the forecastle. With this exchange of fire the Japs disappear in the darkness and we make no effort to chase them, for we need all of our ammunition to sink transports.

There is no relaxing now. We are in the area where anything can happen. Hundreds of eyes peer into the night seeking the convoy, as we realize that the end of our mission is approaching.

During the night the order of ships in column has been shifted. The *De Ruyter* still maintained the lead, but behind her comes the *Houston,* followed by the *Java* and *Perth* in that order.

A half hour passes without incident, and then with the swiftness of a lightning bolt a tremendous explosion rocks the *Java* 900 yards astern of the *Houston.* Mounting flames envelop her amidships and spread rapidly aft. She loses speed and drops out of the column to lie dead in the water, where sheets of uncontrolled flame consume her.

Torpedo wakes are observed in the water, although we can find no enemy to fight back. The *De Ruyter* changes course sharply to the right, and the *Houston* is just about to follow when an explosion similar to the one that doomed the *Java* is heard aboard the *De Ruyter.* Crackling flames shoot high above her bridge, quickly enveloping the entire ship.

Captain Rooks, in a masterpiece of seamanship and quick thinking, maneuvers the *Houston* to avoid torpedoes that slip past us ten feet on either side. Then joined by the *Perth,* we race away from the stricken ships and the insidious enemy that no one can see. How horrible it is to leave our allies, but we are powerless to assist them. Now that Admiral Doorman has gone down with his blazing flagship, the Captain of the *Perth* takes command, for he is senior to Captain Rooks, and we follow the *Perth* as he sets a course for Batavia.

What an infernal night, and how lucky we are to escape. It seems almost miraculous when the sun comes up on the next morning, February 28, for there have been many times during the past fifteen hours when I would have sworn we would never see it.

The *Houston* was a wreck. Concussions from the eight-inch guns had played merry hell with the ship's interior. Every desk on the ship had its drawers torn out and the contents spewn over the deck. In lockers, clothes were torn from their hangers and pitched in muddled heaps. Pictures, radios, books, and everything of a like nature were jolted from their normal places and dashed on the deck.

The Admiral's cabin was a deplorable sight. At one time it had been President Roosevelt's cabin, but no one could have recognized it now as such. Clocks lay broken on the deck, furniture was overturned, mirrors were cracked, charts were ripped from the bulkhead, and large pieces of soundproofing that had come loose from the bulkheads and overhead were thick in the rubble on the deck.

The ship itself had suffered considerably. Plates already weakened by near hits in previous bombing attacks were now badly sprung and leaking. The glass windows on the bridge were shattered. Fire hose strung along the passageways were leaking and minor floods made it sloppy underfoot.

The *Houston* was wounded and practically out of ammunition, but there was still fight left in her, plenty of it.

These events accompanied by many others played upon my mind in the minutest detail, until at last my senses became numb and I relaxed in sleep.

It was nearly 2400 when, *Clang! Clang! Clang! Clang!,* the nerve shattering "General Alarm" burst through my wonderful cocoon of sleep and brought me upright on both feet. Through two and a half months of war that gong, calling all hands to battle stations, had rung in deadly earnest. It meant only one thing, "Danger"—man your battle station and get ready to fight. So thoroughly had the lessons of war been taught as to the sharp, heartless clanging of that gong that I found myself in my shoes before I was even awake.

Clang! Clang! Clang! Clang! The sound echoed along the steel bulkheads of the ship's deserted interior. I wondered what kind of deviltry we were mixed up in now, and somehow I felt depressed. I grabbed my tin hat as I left the room and was putting it on my head when a salvo from the main battery roared out overhead, knocking me against the bulkhead. We were desperately short of those eight-inch bricks and I knew that the boys weren't wasting them on mirages. I flashed my light to assist me in passing through the deserted wardroom and into the passageway at the other end, where a group of stretcher-bearers and corpsmen were assembled. I asked them but they didn't seem to know what we had run into. I left them and climbed the ladder leading to the bridge.

As I climbed there was more firing from the main battery, and now the five-inch guns were taking up the argument. I realized that it was getting to be one hell of a battle and I started running. On the communication deck where the one-point-one's were getting into action, I passed their gun crews working swiftly, mechanically in the darkness without a hitch, as their guns pumped out shell after shell. Momentarily I caught a glimpse of tracers hustling out into the night. They were beautiful.

Before I reached the bridge every gun on the ship was in action. The noise they made was magnificent. The *Houston* was throwing knockout punches. How reassuring it was to hear, at measured intervals, the blinding crash of the main battery, the sharp rapid crack of the five-inch guns, the steady methodic *pom, pom, pom, pom,* of the one-point-one's; and above all that, from their platforms high in the foremast and in the mainmast, came the continuous sweeping volleys of fifty-caliber machine guns which had been put there as anti-aircraft weapons, but which now suddenly found themselves engaging enemy surface targets.

As I stepped on the bridge the *Houston* became enveloped in the blinding glare of searchlights. Behind the lights I could barely discern the outlines of Jap destroyers. They had come in close to illuminate for their heavy units which fired at us from the darkness. Battling desperately for existence the *Houston*'s guns trained on the lights, and as fast as they were turned on, just as fast were they blasted out.

Although the bridge was the *Houston*'s nerve center, I was unable to find out what we were up against. This was mainly because the tempo of the battle was so great and every man stationed there so vitally concerned with his immediate duty that I was reluctant to butt in at such a time and ask a question that had little relative meaning. What we had actually run into was later estimated to be sixty fully loaded transports, twenty destroyers, and six cruisers. We were in the middle of this mass of ships before either side was aware of the other's presence.

Suddenly surrounded by ships, the *Perth* and *Houston* immediately opened fire and turned sharply to starboard in an effort to break free. However, the fury of the Japs was not to be denied and the *Perth* was mortally wounded by torpedoes. Lying dead in the water she continued to fire with everything she had until Jap shells blasted her to bits and she sank.

When Captain Rooks realized that the *Perth* was finished he turned the *Houston* back into the heart of the Jap convoy, determined in the face of no escape to sell the *Houston* dearly.

At close range the *Houston* pounded the Jap transports with everything she had, and at the same time fought off the destroyers that were attacking with torpedoes and shellfire. Jap cruisers remained in the background, throwing salvo after salvo aboard and around us. The *Houston* was taking terrible punishment. A torpedo penetrated our after engine room, where it exploded, killing every man there and reducing our speed to fifteen knots.

Thick smoke and hot steam venting on the gun deck from the after engine room temporarily drove men from their guns but they came back and stayed there in spite of it. Power went out of the shell hoists which stopped the flow of five-inch shells to the guns, from the almost empty magazines. Men attempted to go below and bring shells up by hand, but debris and fires from numerous hits blocked their way. In spite of this they continued to fire, using star shells which were stowed in the ready ammunition boxes by the guns.

Number Two turret, smashed by a direct hit, blew up, sending wild flames flashing up over the bridge. The heat, so intense that it drove everyone out of the conning tower, temporarily disrupted communications to the other parts of the ship. The fire was soon extinguished, but when the sprinklers flooded the magazine our last remaining supply of eight-inch ammunition was ruined, which meant that the *Houston* was now without a main battery.

Numerous fires were breaking out all over the ship and it became increasingly difficult for the men to cope with them. Another torpedo plowed into the *Houston* somewhere forward of the quarterdeck. The force of the explosion made the ship tremble beneath us, and I realized then that we were done for.

Slowly we listed to starboard as the grand old ship gradually lost steerageway and stopped. The few guns still in commission continued to fire, although it was obvious that the end was near. It must have torn at the Captain's heart, but his voice was strong as he summoned the bugler and ordered him to sound "Abandon Ship."

When I heard the words "Abandon Ship" I did not wait to go down the ladder which already had a capacity crowd, with men waiting; instead I jumped over the railing to the deck below. That was probably a fortunate move, for just as I jumped a shell burst on the bridge, killing several men. I trotted out on the port catapult tower where the battered and unflyable hulk of our last airplane spread its useless wings in the darkness. It contained a rubber boat and a bottle of brandy, both of which I figured would come in handy, but I was not alone in this, for five people were there ahead of me.

Despite the fact that we were still the target for continuous shells and the ship was slowly sinking beneath us, there was no confusion. Men went quietly and quickly about the job of abandoning ship. Fear was nowhere apparent, due possibly to the fact that the one thing we feared most throughout the short space of the war had happened.

Captain Rooks had come down off the bridge and was saying goodbye to several of his officers and men outside his cabin, when a Jap shell exploded in a one-point-one gun mount, sending a piece of the breach crashing into his chest. Captain Rooks, beloved by officers and men, died in their arms.

When Buda, the Captain's Chinese cook, learned that the captain had been killed, he refused to leave the ship. He simply sat cross-legged outside the Captain's cabin, rocking back and forth and moaning "Captain dead, *Houston* dead, Buda die too." He went down with the ship.

During this time I made my way to the quarterdeck. Dead men lay sprawled on the deck, but there was no time to find out who they were. Men from my division were busily engaged in the starboard hangar in an effort to bring out a seaplane pontoon and two wing-tip floats that we had filled with food and water in preparation for just such a time. If we could get them into the water and assemble them as we had so designed, they would make a fine floating structure around which we could gather and work from.

I hurried to the base of the catapult tower where I worked rapidly to release the lifelines in order that we could get the floats over the side and into the water. I uncoupled one line and was working on the second when a torpedo struck directly below us. I heard no explosion, but the deck buckled and jumped under me and I found myself suddenly engulfed in a deluge of fuel oil and saltwater.

Up until that moment I must have been too fascinated with the unreality of the situation to truly think about it and become frightened, but when this sudden torrent of fuel oil and water poured over me, all I could think of was fire. It was the most helpless sensation I ever had experienced in my life. Somehow I hadn't figured on getting hit or killed, but now I was gripped with the sudden fear of blazing fuel oil on my person and covering the surface of the sea. I was panicked, for I could figure no escape from it. The same thought must have been in the minds of the others, for we all raced from the starboard side to the shelter of the port hangar. No sooner had we cleared the quarterdeck than a salvo of shells plowed through it, exploding deep below decks.

Events were moving fast, and the *Houston* in her death throes was about to go down. There was only one idea left in my mind, and that was to join the others who were going over the side in increasing numbers. Quickly I made my way to the port side and climbed down the cargo nets that were hanging there. When I reached the water's edge I dropped off into the warm Java Sea. When my head came above the surface I was aware that in the darkness I was surrounded by many men, all swimming for their lives. Frantic screams for help from the wounded and drowning mixed with the shouts of others attempting to make contact with shipmates. The sea was an oily battleground of men pitted against the terrors of death. Desperately I swam to get beyond reach of the sinking ship's suction. As much as I loved the *Houston* I had no desire to join her in a watery grave.

A few hundred yards away I turned, gasping for breath, to watch the death of my ship. She lay well over to starboard. Jap destroyers had come in close and illuminated her with searchlights as they raked her decks with machine-gun fire. Many men struggled in the water near the ship, others clung desperately to heavily loaded life rafts, and then to my horror, I realized that the Japs were coldly and deliberately firing on the men in the water. The concussions of shells bursting in the midst of swimming men sent shock waves through the water that slammed against my body with an evil force, making me wince with pain. Men closer to the exploding shells were killed by this concussion alone.

Dazed, unable to believe that all this was real, I floated there, watching as though bewitched. The end had come. By the glare of Japanese searchlights I saw the *Houston* roll slowly over to starboard, and then, with her yardarms almost dipping into the sea, she paused momentarily. Perhaps I only imagined it, but it seemed as though a sudden breeze picked up the Stars and Stripes still firmly two blocked on the mainmast, and waved them in one last defiant gesture. Then with a tired shudder she vanished beneath the Java Sea.

The magnificent *Houston* and most of my shipmates were gone, but in the oily sea around me lay evidence of the carnage wrought by their last battle. Hundreds of Jap soldiers and sailors struggled amidst the flotsam of their sunken ships; and as I watched them drown or swim for their lives, I smiled grimly and repeated over and over, "Well done, *Houston!*"

★ ★ ★ ★ ★

Only 368 survived the battle and the sinking of the U.S.S. *Houston* of a crew of over 1,000. Japanese patrol boats machine-gunned survivors while they were in the water and many were swept into oblivion by the strong currents of the Sundra Straits. The survivors who were spared by the Japanese were sent to Burma to work as slave laborers until the end of the war. Many of the prisoners died of malnutrition and disease. Captain Rooks received posthumously the Medal of Honor for this extraordinary heroism. USS *Houston* was awarded the Presidential Unit Citation and two battle stars.

Midway, from *How They Won the War in the Pacific*

EDWIN P. HOYT

> They had no right to win, yet they did, and in doing so they changed the course of a war. More than that they added a new name—Midway—to that small list that inspires men by example . . . Like marathon, The Armada, The Marne. Even against the greatest of odds, there is something in human spirit—a magic blend of skill, faith and valor—that can lift men from certain defeat to incredible victory.
>
> —Walter Lord

The names of great sea battles ring out through the ages: Salamis, Trafalgar, Tsushima, Jutland, each a moment in history when the fate of nations were decided. For the United States, the most decisive battle occurred in early June 1942 around the island of Midway, deep in the central Pacific. It was a time when the United States and the Allied powers were still reeling from the Japanese onslaught during the first six months of the war. In a breathtaking offensive, Japan had virtually paralyzed the American fleet at Pearl Harbor in December and seized control of the Dutch East Indies, Burma, Malaya, Singapore, Hong Kong, and the Philippines. Japan's strategy was clear: create a defensive zone of islands throughout the Pacific and bring the United States Navy into a decisive battle where it would be destroyed. The Americans, still at war with Germany, would realize that attempting to attack Japan through this vast defensive network would be too costly to bear, and seek a diplomatic settlement giving Japan free reign to finish the war in China and create a Japanese empire.

To make matters even more difficult, in 1942 the war in the Pacific was being fought on a shoestring of men and materials as Allied efforts were focused on defeating Germany. President Roosevelt needed a victory against Japan to boost the morale of the American people. On April 18, the carrier *Hornet*, accompanied by *Enterprise*, sailed to within six-hundred miles of Japan and launched eighteen Army B-25's under the command of Lt. Col. James H. Doolittle in a surprise raid against Tokyo. The attack was a huge embarrassment to the Japanese Navy, and its leader Admiral Isoruku Yamamoto, the man who had engineered the Pearl Harbor raid. It became clear that Midway must be taken to complete the outer defenses of Japan, and lure the American fleet into a decisive battle.

The ace in the American sleeve, however, was the success of Allied intelligence at breaking the Japanese codes. American naval intelligence had been able to read parts of Japan's JN-25 naval codes for some time. It was Commander Joseph J. Rochefort of the U.S. Navy's Combat Intelligence Unit at Hawaii that had predicted the Japanese attempt to piece Port Moresby leading to the battle of the Coral Sea that forced the Japanese to withdraw. He now predicted a new offensive that he estimated would target the island of Midway.

With only three carriers available to defend the United States, Admiral Nimitz made the crucial decision to commit them to battle. Knowing in advance where his enemy would strike gave them a chance to ambush the Japanese fleet and strike a mortal blow. Facing them was the heart of the Japanese Navy, and the carriers that had wreaked havoc on the Pacific Fleet six months earlier on December 7. Edwin P. Hoyt describes the battle from his book *How They Won the War in the Pacific: Nimitz and His Admirals*.

★ ★ ★ ★ ★

May 5-June 30, 1942

One day early in May Lieutenant Commander Edwin T. Layton, Pacific Fleet intelligence officer, came into Admiral Nimitz's office to present the admiral with a detailed analysis he had worked up with Lieutenant Commander Rochefort, showing the probable intentions of the Japanese, based on intercepted Japanese naval radio dispatches. Thanks to Rochefort's partial breakdown of the Japanese naval code, the intelligence men were able to read enough of the material to gain important clues.

Nimitz took up Layton's report with his senior staff. What Draemel and Pye had feared from the beginning seemed to be materializing: a Japanese move into the Western and Northern Pacific.

The analysis was imperfect, and there was room for doubt. The Japanese had used a code name for the place they planned to invest, and Nimitz was not absolutely certain this was Midway. He made a test. In the clear he sent a message which indicated that Midway was short of water. A few hours later the Japanese indicated that the place they would attack was short of water.

By May 16 Nimitz was certain that unless the Japanese were using massive radio deception for some reason he could not understand, they were planning a major offensive in the Central or North Pacific. Specifically he feared the attack against Midway, and a raid on Oahu, around the first week in June.

What was to be done? The striking force must be used. That force now was down to three carriers, one of them injured. Perhaps the carriers could be assisted by a battleship covering force—but the prewar battleships were very slow, and although Admiral Pye was a brave and intelligent officer, these battleships would need very strong protection from light ships if it was worthwhile at all to move them out from the west coast.

The problem was to get Halsey into Pearl, and out again, with his two sound carriers, and to bring the *Yorktown* back and get her repaired in time.

King, perhaps sensing that if the forces at Pearl Harbor were lost he would have nothing else for west coast protection, decided against the use of the battleships in the coming struggle. Layton was queried and queried again, and he said he would stake his reputation on the accuracy of his reports. So Nimitz decided to lay it out in one piece—to make the supreme effort, hazarding the American forces, as Pye had been unwilling to do in the Wake confrontation.

On May 18 Nimitz held a final planning conference. He decided then to reinforce Midway with a part of a raider battalion, station four submarines off the islands, use Midway to stage Army bombers, use a dozen PBYs for searching, and employ Task Force 16 plus the *Yorktown,* if it could be repaired in time. He would also send out a North Pacific force, under Admiral Theobald, to move to an Alaskan rendezvous.

Admiral Yamamoto, the commander in chief of the Japanese combined fleet, proposed to take Midway, occupy the Aleutians, and raid Oahu. But through the efforts of Rochefort and his associates, the Americans had a very good idea of what the Japanese planned to do—and when and where.

The seven old battleships were to sail east to the Pacific coast. Task Force 16, arriving at Pearl Harbor about May 26, would be turned around in two days and sent to Midway by June 1. Task Force 17 would arrive at Pearl Harbor on May 28, and if the *Yorktown* could be repaired there in four days, it would be done. That was the key to the whole defense, for *Saratoga,* at San Diego, could not be ready for sea until June 5, and *Wasp,* headed for the Pacific, could not arrive in time.

In mid-May, estimating the enemy courses of action, Nimitz and his staff erred slightly in assessing Admiral Yamamoto's strategy. He wrote:

> The enemy knows our building program—and that in time—our forces will be sufficiently strong to take the offensive. He further knows our defenses are inadequate now—but gradually being strengthened. Hence, from the time factor alone, such operation should be conducted at the earliest possible time. While he is "extended," he is able to assemble a considerable force—as most of the occupied territory is unable to make any real effort. He knows that Australia is being heavily reinforced from the United States and would undoubtedly desire to cut that supply line. But he may also consider midway to be just another WAKE and ALASKA undefended. Regardless of our ideas of his strategic possibilities, the purpose here is to discuss immediate possibilities.

Japanese Admiral Isoroku Yamamoto had become so worried about the increasing activity of the American fleet in the south that he proposed an action that should destroy that fleet. His worries were based on what Halsey, Fletcher, Brown, and Fitch had accomplished in their raids, and on Yamamoto's knowledge of the United States industrial potential. He had opposed war against the United States, in the first place, because he knew that potential, and was only too well aware of Japan's slender resources in steel and oil. While the rest of the Empire, and much of the naval high command, basked in the happy glory of success, Yamamoto warned that unless he could knock out the American fleet there was going to be trouble. Within two years, he said, the balance of naval power would shift to the United States unless the American fleet could be put out of action in 1942.

Yamamoto proposed, then, to occupy Midway Island, and also the Aleutians, and thus pose the double-barreled threat to the United States of enemy forces in their very back yard. He suggested that such occupation, along with the destruction of the American fleet, would make the government of the United States negotiate a peace that would leave Japan free to expand in China and the waters of the Pacific Ocean.

One of the deciding factors in persuading the naval general staff to Yamamoto's view was the Doolittle Tokyo Raid in April. The General Staff agreed to a four point plan for 1942: June—capture Midway, Adak, and Kiska; July—invade New Caledonia and Fiji; July—stage carrier strikes on Australia; August—send the combined fleet to strike Johnston and the Hawaiian Islands.

Perhaps it was just as well that the real intentions of Yamamoto and his men were unknown, and that the Japanese striking power was underestimated. The Japanese were bringing to Midway four carriers, two battleships, three cruisers, fourteen destroyers, and five oilers in the striking force. To cover the actual occupation of Midway they would have two battleships, nine cruisers, one light carrier, eleven destroyers, and various other ships. To screen the transports would come another eleven destroyers, plus seaplane carriers, minesweepers, and a dozen transports in the train. Then there was the main body, with three more battleships, a light carrier and two seaplane carriers, a cruiser, and thirteen more destroyers, which could either accompany the Aleutian invasion force or the Midway force, or attack the American fleet.

As for intentions, certainly Admiral Yamamoto wanted to occupy Midway. Having done so, and having created a Japanese air base there, he proposed to challenge the remnants of the American fleet and destroy them, thus making the Pacific Ocean into a Japanese lake.

Radio intelligence indicated that the Japanese left Saipan on May 26 for Midway. Having set the wheels in motion, Nimitz's task was to sit, wait, and take advantage of opportunity.

Nimitz received a serious blow that day. Admiral Halsey brought Task Force 16 into port. One look at Halsey, and Nimitz knew that his favorite fighting commander could not be available for Midway. The strain of the past few months, plus personal family problems of the most serious nature, had affected Halsey's nerves, and he was suffering from skin eruptions that made sleep impossible and kept him in constant pain. It was off to the hospital for Halsey, and then came the problem of choosing a substitute for him.

At this time, several basic changes were in the offing. Vice Admiral Wilson Brown had fallen ill while on the Pacific coast, and had said something about feeling that he needed a rest. He was now recovered. His statement, however, gave Admirals Jacobs and King the chance they wanted, to remove him for a younger man, and they assigned him to the First Naval District; in essence, as far as the war was concerned, this amounted to deportation to Siberia. Admiral Draemel was severely shaken by events of the past few months and his constant vigil in the nights; also, he was not thinking along Nimitz's lines and was not effective as chief of staff. Draemel, then, was to replace Brown as commander of the Amphibious Force of the Pacific Fleet, still just a potential unit, for the most part. Both men took the change in good part, as admirals almost always did. Brown was disappointed and said as much to Nimitz, who wrote him a very friendly letter assuring the older admiral that he, Nimitz, had nothing to do with the change. It was true, strictly speaking, because Nimitz had abjured the responsibility, and thrown it back on Washington.

For a new chief of staff, Nimitz chose Rear Admiral Raymond Spruance, who had proved himself in his forays with Halsey as an aggressive, fighting admiral, and more, in the sessions on the folding chairs in Nimitz's office, as a shrewd and trained strategist.

Spruance was a small, trim man whose passion for exercise exceeded even that of Nimitz; it was said that Spruance like nothing better than a ten-mile walk to spruce himself up for the day. He was a Baltimore boy, a few years younger than Nimitz, and had graduated from the Naval Academy in the class of 1901. His record at the Academy had been good: he stood twenty-sixth in a class of 209 graduates. He was two years behind Nimitz, a year behind Ghormley, Fletcher, Towers, Draemel, and Fitch. Spruance was distinguished at the Academy for his studies in electrical engineering, but later he spent six years at the Naval War College, five of them as a member of the staff, which meant that he was more than an apt student of naval tactics and strategy. He was not an airman, but he had a strong respect for the principal weapon at the fleet's disposal in this coming fight. "The carrier," Spruance said, "is a highly mobile, extremely vulnerable airfield from which you can operate short range aircraft and do much more accurate bombing than long range bombers from land airbases can do."

After considering the possible commanders who could move quickly into action, and recalling Halsey's words of high praise for Spruance, Nimitz chose Spruance to lead the Halsey task force into battle. Nimitz was not totally pleased with the actions of his commanders in Task Force 17, at least not at that moment. On May 27 Task Force 17 entered port, and Admiral Fletcher came to headquarters to report himself to Nimitz. There were some searching questions about Fletcher's activities in the past three months in the South Pacific. King might be one to judge in anger, but never Nimitz, and gently he asked Fletcher to explain why his force had been so ineffectual. Fletcher retired to his flagship, then, and wrote a long explanatory letter about his activities.

Nimitz read, and on May 29 he made his decisions and wrote King a letter which indicated the state of affairs at Pearl Harbor on the eve of the Midway battle.

Dear King,

I have finally had an opportunity to discuss with Fletcher during a three day stay in port, his operations in the Coral Sea area, and to clear up what appeared to be a lack of aggressive tactics of his force. I also discussed with him the opportunities for using light forces in night attacks following the aerial attacks from his carriers in early May.

Both these matters have been cleared up to my entire satisfaction, and, I hope, will be to yours. . . .

The long delay and apparent lack of aggressive tactics can be charged partly to lack of sufficiently reliable combat intelligence upon which to base operations, to the necessity for replenishment of fuel and provisions, and to the replacement of defective leak proof tanks in fighter planes.

I hope and believe that . . . you will agree with me that Fletcher did a fine job and exercised superior judgment in his recent cruise in the Coral Sea. He is an excellent seagoing, fighting naval officer, and I wish to retain him as a task force commander in the future.

Nimitz noted that Halsey was sick, but thought it was only a temporary indisposition.

He is in the best of spirits, full of vim and vigor, and anxious to get going again. But he does need a short period of rest. He is neither ill nor on the sick list.

Fletcher with Task Force 17 will leave on the forenoon of May 30 to join Spruance and to take charge of the two task forces which contains three carriers. I have not yet separated Task Force 16 into two task forces, each with a carrier, but expect to do so after these operations are over. At this time it is essential that our organization be stabilized as much as possible.

The *Yorktown* was docked yesterday for inspection and repair of a minor leak. When she leaves tomorrow, 30 May, she will have a full complement of planes and will be in all respects ready to give a good account of herself.

We are very actively preparing to greet our expected visitors with the kind of reception they deserve, and we will do the best we can with what we have. We are thankful for the many contributions now coming in from the army.

To offset the bad news about Halsey, there was good news about *Yorktown*. Although Nimitz had underestimated the damage so as not to worry King, the carrier really was not too badly hurt, and could be put in service by May 29, if drydocked to patch oil leaks and reinforced internally. Some 1,400 men poured into her and worked for two days and nights, doing a reconstruction job that Admiral Fitch had estimated would take three months. (Fitch, by the way, backed Fletcher's actions in the South Pacific all the way. Later, Admiral J. J. Clark was to write that *Lexington* could have been saved if only Fletcher had sent off planes he had on deck, which could have intercepted the Japanese attack on the other carrier. Clark, who had once been executive officer of the *Yorktown,* was critical of Fletcher and Captain Elliott Buckmaster. Fitch's comment: "He was not there.")

On May 28 Admiral Spruance left Pearl Harbor with Task Force 16, which consisted of the carriers *Enterprise* and *Hornet,* with six cruisers and nine destroyers. Two days later Admiral Fletcher came out in the reconstituted *Yorktown* with two cruisers and six destroyers. Nimitz had shown his faith in Fletcher by putting him in charge of the operation.

"You will be governed by the principle of calculated risk," Nimitz wrote in his orders to the two commanders, "which you will interpret to mean the avoidance of exposure of your force to attack by superior enemy forces without good prospect of inflicting . . . greater damage on the enemy."

Nimitz had suggested that they move to a point northeast of Midway, where they could flank the Japanese as they came in from the northwest. Spruance and Fletcher agreed. Spruance arrived in the area, about two hundred miles northeast of Midway, on the morning of June 1; Fletcher arrived the next afternoon. Both forces had fueled before meeting, and were probably as ready as they would ever be for action.

They were very careful. Spruance learned that the radio operators on *Enterprise* had picked up a high-frequency TBS (talk between ships) message from Pearl Harbor to the inshore patrol just off the islands. It was a freak—TBS was not supposed to extend more than a few miles—but it spooked Spruance so that he ordered his task force to keep off the TBS unless absolutely necessary. And he gave the pilots grave warning: he would not use the radio to bring back any carrier planes which might get lost while on a mission. Even his message to task force was transmitted by signalmen, not by radio or TBS.

As the Americans converged and began to search and wait, the Japanese moved steadily down on them. Vice Admiral Chuichi Nagumo was moving from the northwest, with a force built around the four carriers *Soryu, Hiryu, Kaga,* and *Akagi.* Three hundred miles behind was Admiral Yamamoto's main force. The second carrier striking force, and the Attu and Kiska invasion forces, all under Vice Admiral Boshiro Hosogaya, had split off and were coming near the Aleutians from the southwest. Vice Admiral Shiru Takasu led a screening force that would split off and follow the invasion force about five hundred miles behind. And finally, up from Saipan in the southwest came the transports and the minesweepers, and the heavy cruiser from Guam, and from Japan itself the main body of the landing force that would invade Midway and make it part of the Japanese Empire.

The Japanese submarines were to set up two picket lines, about halfway between Hawaii and Midway, for it was the Japanese idea that the American fleet was sitting in Pearl Harbor and would have to be drawn out. The Midway invasion was expected to draw out the Americans, so the striking force that included Admiral Nagumo's four carriers could be alerted by the submarine pickets, make a few calculations, and then polish off the American carriers once and for all as they steamed up into the trap.

The Americans were lucky. The Japanese submarines arrived late on station, and the American task forces were already past them, on their way to Midway. The Japanese had provided for seaplane reconnaissance of Pearl Harbor on May 30. The flying boats were to meet Japanese submarines off French Frigate Shoals, refuel, and carry out their mission. But when the submarines arrived there, they found two American seaplane tenders at anchor, and two American flying boats also there. So the Japanese canceled their plans for a look, which would have warned them that only one American carrier was in harbor. They might even have seen Fletcher's force move out, heading toward the Midway atoll.

At 0904 on June 3 a Midway search plane came upon part of the Japanese minesweeping group, coming up from the southwest, and reported two cargo ships sighted five hundred miles out. Twenty minutes later another patrol plane reported six ships, again coming up from the southwest, seven hundred miles out. Later another contact was made with eleven ships.

That afternoon nine B-17s from Midway flew out to intercept the "eleven-ship" force. They dropped bombs but did not hit anything because they came in at extremely high altitude.

At dawn on Thursday, June 4, Admiral Nagumo's four carriers launched 36 horizontal bombers, 36 dive bombers, and 36 fighters against Midway, and brought the second wave of the same type of planes up on deck to ready for another strike. This time, however, the multipurpose horizontal bombers were armed with torpedoes, in case ship targets should appear.

As the Japanese carrier planes flew toward Midway, sixteen B-17s took off to attack the transports which were bringing the invaders from the west. At 0545 in the morning an American patrol bomber caught sight of two enemy carriers. All the planes at Midway that could fly took off, and the torpedo bombers, Army B-26's and Marine dive bombers headed for the carriers. The twenty-seven fighters were kept over Midway for protection.

The assorted bombers went in against heavy antiaircraft fire and zooming Japanese fighters. The B-26's hit nothing, and two of the four were shot down. The TBF's hit nothing, and five of the six were splashed.

The Marine dive bomber pilots were inexperienced; instead of dive-bombing they came in to glide-bomb. Twelve were shot down, and they hit nothing. The B-17's, diverted to the carriers, came in at twenty thousand feet and hit nothing. The Japanese antiaircraft guns and the Zero pilots could not reach them, so they lost no planes.

The Japanese carrier planes, meanwhile, slashed across Midway and began bombing and strafing, taking care to save the runways they thought they would be using in a few days.

In the Japanese carrier force, Admiral Nagumo surveyed the situation before him. The Americans still had air power at Midway, which ought to be knocked out. He had no reports of surface shipping anywhere around. So the admiral ordered the bombers of *Akagi* and *Kaga* back down to the hangar decks where the torpedoes would be removed and changed for bombs.

The Japanese were to sight the Americans just before 0730 that morning, but even then the identification was confused and it was an hour later before Admiral Nagumo learned that there were big ships in the area, and concluded, without immediate confirmation that there must be a carrier in the bunch.

The Americans, moving cautiously with their far smaller force, were in action already. Early in the morning, Admiral Fletcher had launched a dawn security search to the north, looking for the Japanese they knew to be in the area, because of the sighting before 0600 of the carrier planes, and the sighting of two of the carriers a few minutes later.

"Two carriers and battleships bearing 320, distance 180, course 135, speed 24," came the message from the flying boat.

When Admiral Spruance was informed, he turned on a course to intercept and raised the speed of Task Force 16 to twenty-five knots. Fletcher instructed Spruance to attack the enemy carriers when they were definitely located.

Miles Browning, the slender, caustic chief of staff of Task Force 16, whose services Spruance had secured from the ailing Halsey, suggested that the timing of the first attack on the Japanese be made as soon as possible. That way, said Browning, there was a good chance of catching the Japanese with their decks foul with newly landed planes that were unready for action.

Spruance's plan had been to launch at 0900, when he estimated that they would be around 100 miles from the enemy. Since the American torpedo bombers had a range of only 175 miles, that distance seemed safe for recovery of the TBDs. But Spruance was quick to see Browning's point, and he undertook the calculated risk. He launched without actual location of the enemy, hoping he knew their position, which he estimated to be about 155 miles away, bearing 239.

Captain Murray in the *Enterprise* and Captain Marc Mitscher in the *Hornet* were ordered to turn south, into the wind, and begin launching, just after 0700.

First the combat air patrol went off and began circling the formation. Next went the dive bombers, some armed with 500-pound and some with 1,000-pound bombs. The torpedo planes took off, followed by fighters which were to escort the slow torpedo bombers to the target and protect them.

At this point the inexperience of the Americans influenced the course of events. About twenty minutes before the last planes were launched, the presence of the American ships was apparently discovered by a Japanese search plane. That would account for the turn of the Japanese carriers off the course on which they had been spotted earlier.

Spruance then ordered the dive bombers from *Enterprise* to go ahead of the torpedo planes and fighters, and hit the carriers. This decision put an end to the coordinated attack that had been planned, but Spruance was more interested in surprise.

Task Force 17 was operating independently, and launching its planes as well. But as the planes began to search the expected area, they did not find the Japanese, who had changed course.

First to find the enemy were the planes of Torpedo Squadron 8, which had flown off *Hornet*. In the morning confusion, the *Enterprise* fighters accompanied the *Hornet* torpedo bombers instead of their own, and then lost touch even with these bombers. So Torpedo 8 suddenly found itself in sight of the enemy, with no protection.

Lieutenant Commander John C. Waldron, the leader of Torpedo 8, finally saw the Japanese as he was running low on fuel. He reported the contact, and asked permission to withdraw and refuel before attacking. But Spruance and Browning, aboard the flagship, knew the importance of surprise in a carrier battle. The reply was negative. "Attack at once," was the order.[12]

Without fighter protection, low on fuel, knowing how the deck was stacked against him, Waldron headed in. The weather was good. The visibility was excellent. The whole approach was made at low altitude, in complete view of the Japanese—and their deadly Zero fighter planes.

---

[12]This report is contrary to the legend of Waldron's heroic sacrifice. It is, however, documental.

The squadron was in two divisions. First came four two-plane sections, then two more two-plane sections and one three-plane section. Lieutenant Commander Waldron headed for the southern-most of the carriers, until he saw the mushrooms of the antiaircraft fire, then he turned to the central carrier. When they were about sixteen thousand yards out, the Zeros came down onto the deck and the slaughter began.

Ensign G. H. Gay, a Naval Reserve officer, was flying one of those TBDs, in the last section of the second division. As Gay moved toward the target he heard an anguished voice from his gunner. He had been hit. Gay went on in, dropped his torpedo at eight hundred yards, and it missed, like all the other torpedoes of Torpedo 8. He pulled up over the bow of the carrier and turned sharply into her wake, but then a Zero dived down and an explosive shell carried away his left rudder control. A bullet struck him in the left arm, and a fragment hit him in the left hand, He took the plane down, made a crash landing, but the right wing carried away and the plane began to sink. He had no time to rescue his radioman before the plane went down, leaving the ensign treading water.

The rubber boat in its bag had floated clear, and so had a black cushion from the bomber compartment. Gay inflated his life jacket, grabbed the boat bag and held it, and covered his head with the black cushion, so the Japanese would not see him. Several Zeros zoomed low, but he was not observed.

Ensign Gay then had a ringside seat at the arena where the *Kaga,* the *Akagi,* and the *Soryu* were performing.

At first it was quiet except for the landing of Zeros on the carriers. He noted, with the interest of a professional, how the other fellows did it, coming in on long approaches, from straight astern, with long intervals between planes. And then the action began.

Hornet's dive bombers had found nothing, and went empty-handed to their carrier when they ran low on gas. *Enterprise*'s torpedo planes found the Japanese at about 0930, but their attack was more successful than that of Torpedo 8 only in that four of the fourteen TBDs managed to get back to their carrier. There were no hits.

But the very ineptness of the American attack worked in its favor this day, for the Japanese grew careless, and their fighter cover was pulled down low above the sea by the chase for the lumbering torpedo bombers.

As the TBDs flamed into the sea, *Enterprise*'s dive bombers were searching for the enemy. They did not find the Japanese where they expected them, but an accommodating Japanese destroyer led them to the carrier force, and they sighted the enemy at 1005.

The torpedo bombers had accomplished two other useful feats in their sacrifice: they had caused the carriers to maneuver constantly during this critical period, and their brave gestures against the impossible odds they faced had given the Japanese a certain contempt for the American weapons, if a definite respect for American willingness to die. The Japanese had watched the B-17s come in like little specks in the stratosphere and drop their hopeless bombs. They had watched the clumsy tactics of the ill-trained Marine bombers, and the misses of the B-26s, too. Suddenly, however, down screamed the dive bombers of the *Enterprise.* Ensign Gay, who was watching from his wet ringside seat, said that most of them did not even seem to be using their dive flaps, for they came in at very high speed, dropped their bombs, pulled out just above the water, and sped away.

Kaga and *Akagi* were just getting ready to launch their planes for a strike, when the bombers began scoring hits. In a moment Gay saw flames arising from the flight decks, and billowing black clouds of smoke dirtied the blue sky.

Soon *Akagi* was a wreck, and Admiral Nagumo transferred his flag to the cruiser *Nagara*. Then the *Yorktown* dive bombers found the carriers, and attacked *Soryu*. The torpedo planes suffered the fate of the squadrons of the *Hornet* and the *Enterprise*; only two of a dozen returned to the *Yorktown*; but the dive bombers started several fires on *Soryu,* and not one dive bomber from *Yorktown* was even damaged, so thorough was the confusion of the Japanese.

Spruance was elated with the performance of *Enterprise* and *Yorktown,* but much less pleased with that of the men of *Hornet*. He wanted that fourth carrier, and had *Hornet*'s planes done their job, *Hiryu* might have been found that morning. Instead, *Hiryu*'s planes found *Yorktown* at 1205, and the dive bombers put three holes in her, stopping her, starting fires, and damaging the flight deck. In two hours the damage was partly repaired. *Yorktown* could operate her planes, and make nineteen knots. But a few minutes after she launched her second strike, *Hiryu*'s torpedo bombers came in and put two torpedoes into the carrier, jamming the left rudder and giving her a list that soon stood at 23 degrees. Admiral Fletcher moved his flag to the cruiser *Astoria*. Soon Captain Buckmaster ordered the *Yorktown* abandoned (for which he was later criticized severely by some of Young Turks, especially the fighting admiral J. J. Clark).

But in turn, the planes of *Enterprise* had found the *Hiryu* by 1700 that afternoon, and sped in to attack. Four dive bombers scored hits on this fourth carrier, and soon she was dead in the water. "*Hornet* and *Enterprise* groups now attacking fourth carrier located by your search planes," was the message Admiral Spruance sent to Fletcher, who was in overall command still. "*Hornet* about twenty miles east of me. Have you any instructions for future operations?"

Fletcher replied: "Negative. Will conform to your movements." Thus a gallant Admiral Fletcher, knowing the battle was virtually won, turned tactical command, and the chance for glory, into the hands of his subordinate, because Spruance's primary weapons—the carriers—were intact and ready to fight while Fletcher's own major weapon was out of action. He detached the two cruisers from the task force and sent them to Spruance. He would keep the destroyers, and attempt to salvage the *Yorktown*.

After the first attack on *Yorktown* her planes began landing on the *Hornet* and the *Enterprise,* and served, in fact, as replacements for the many that had been lost in the day's action. Some of these were lost to enemy action, many to force landings when their fuel ran out. After recovering all the aircraft from the attack on *Hiryu,* Spruance headed east, away from the enemy. He knew that out to the west was the enemy, a powerful force, more powerful than his own, perhaps. Here is the way Spruance spoke of his decision immediately after the battle:

> After recovering our air groups following their second attack, Task Force 16 stood to the eastward, southward and back to the westward during the night. I did not feel justified in risking a night encounter with possibly superior enemy forces, but on the other hand, I did not want to be too far away from Midway the next morning. I wished to have a position from which either to follow up retreating enemy forces or break up a landing attack on Midway. At this time the possibility of the enemy having a fifth CV [fleet carrier] somewhere in the area, possibly with his Occupation Force or else to the northwestward, still existed.

In fact, Admiral Yamamoto wanted a surface engagement. He believed there was only one American carrier and that it was out of action. When Admiral Nagumo began to withdraw, Yamamoto relieved him and put Vice Admiral Kondo in charge of the striking force. Kondo moved toward Midway to make a night bombardment, but later that mission was canceled and the Japanese retired to the northwest.

At daybreak Task Force 16 was moving west at fifteen knots. The weather was very bad. The submarine *Tambor* made the first report of the Japanese, sighted ninety miles west of Midway. Early that morning, trying to avoid the *Tambor,* the Japanese cruisers *Mikuma* and *Mogami* collided, and then headed slowly away from the action toward the repair station at Truk.

Spruance was looking for the enemy. As the weather cleared, he learned that one group was west of Midway and the other group was northwest. He chose the northwest group to chase; it contained, he understood, the crippled carrier and two battleships, one damaged. All he found that day were two small ships, apparently destroyers. The planes took a night landing, and one crashed in the water astern of *Enterprise,* because of the pilot's unfamiliarity with the technique. The crew was saved, and all other planes made it aboard the two carriers, although sometimes landing on the wrong one.

That second night Spruance headed west. "I figured the enemy DDs [destroyers] would report our attack and that he might either get the protection of bad weather ahead or else change course to the westward to head for Japan and to throw us off."

Next morning the search planes found two groups of Japanese ships southwest of the task force, about forty miles apart. They had found *Mogami* and *Mikuma,* and dive bombers sank *Mikuma* that day and damaged *Mogami* so badly that it took one year to repair her when she reached Truk.

Identification by the pilots was so faulty that they believed *Mikuma* was a battleship. But what difference? The victory was completely glorious. The reason, Spruance indicated, was the uncertainty of American knowledge about the dimensions of these Japanese ships. Before nightfall he questioned the pilots of two photographic planes, and came to the conclusion that the sunk ship was a cruiser of the *Mogami* class (a pretty good guess). "She was definitely larger than the other cruiser accompanying her," Spruance said. (*Mogami*'s bow had been torn off in the collision with *Mikuma,* and that was the reason for the wrong conclusion in her case.) Meanwhile, on Saturday, June 6, a Japanese submarine torpedoed the *Yorktown,* sinking her and the destroyer *Hammann,* which was alongside, taking away some of the glory.

Admiral Yamamoto, still hoping to salvage some shred of victory from his inglorious defeat, attempted to lure Spruance into the range of the shore-based Japanese aircraft at Wake Island. By the end of the day, Spruance's force was running low on fuel, and he also felt that he had pushed his luck about as far as was sensible. The Japanese shore-based planes had a range of six hundred miles from Wake, and he was determined to stay outside the seven-hundred-mile circle. He sent back destroyers, and found himself with only four, not enough to screen his carriers against the Japanese submarines known to be in the area. So Spruance turned east, and the battle of Midway came to a close.

At Pearl Harbor, Nimitz and his officers had been waiting eagerly for the bits of news as they came in. On June 4 Nimitz said, "It may be the greatest sea battle since Jutland." If the outcome was as unfavorable to the Japanese as he hoped, it might end their expansion in the Pacific. Nimitz was worried, however, because the total destruction of Torpedo 8 symbolized what had happened to the American fleet that day: the United States had lost a large percentage of highly trained pilots who would be hard to replace. (The Japanese, of course, had lost far more, the pilots and aircrews of nearly every plane of the four carriers. The bite of Midway would be felt by the Japanese naval air force throughout the rest of the war.) On the second day, Nimitz issued a conservative communiqué about the victory. The staff was jubilant, terming the battle a major defeat for the enemy.

"This was a great day for the American Navy," said the Gray Book of the Commander in Chief of the Pacific Fleet that day. The Cincpac gray book was the unofficial war diary—very secret and sometimes more informative as to attitudes at Pearl Harbor than any other documents to come out of the war. The nation was not to know the Navy's real role in that battle for a considerable length of time. At Midway, Army B-17 bombers had the first crack at the Japanese—and did not score *a single hit,* yet that failure did not keep the Army Air Corps from claiming it had won the battle of Midway. Nimitz was constrained by security to forbear from reply—the Japanese would have liked nothing better than to know precisely what had happened to them at Midway and what American dispositions and losses had been. Secretary Knox was aware of the facts and concerned about them, as he indicated to Nimitz, at the same time sending out a new public relations officer, perhaps rather pointedly.

> Confidentially [the Secretary wrote], there is a great deal of feeling here and, I understand, also in the Fleet, on account of the obvious attempt of the Army Air Corps to play up their part in the Midway battle. It is most unfortunate that they have this disposition and I have a memorandum on my desk together with a copy of the Honolulu paper which contains a statement by General Arnold which I propose to discuss with Secretary Stimson at the first opportunity. He feels as strongly as I do about anything likely to produce friction between the two services and I feel sure that he will take the necessary measures to prevent this sort of thing happening again. . . .

This incident was the occasion for deep-seated resentment of the Army by Navy airmen during the Pacific war.

Knox did what he could. He was, in private life, publisher of the *Chicago Daily News,* and he arranged to have war correspondent Robert J. Casey write a series of articles explaining the facts of Midway. But by and large the Army had the first publicity, and many people went through the war believing the B-17s had smashed the Japanese navy.

That navy was not smashed, but the power of its air force was very definitely curtailed, with the sinking of four of her carriers (*Kaga, Akagi, Soryu,* and *Hiryu*) and the loss of 250 planes and more than two thousand men.

Having sunk four carriers and a Japanese cruiser and destroyed an invasion before it ever got started, Spruance's reaction was typical and terse. In writing to Nimitz, he was primarily interested in what had been learned.

> The operations during this period have been most interesting and instructive. We must, I think, improve our identification of types from the air . . . . Another point is that emphasis should be placed on continued tracking of enemy forces by shorebased planes whenever conditions permit. It would have been of great assistance if the damaged CV [fleet carrier] had been tracked down on Friday . . . . For use against CVs, particularly those caught with planes on deck, our present bombs are perfect. For use against tough ships with armored decks, we must have an armor piercing 1000 lb bomb. Against such targets I would use about half of each. The present type works terrible destruction on the unarmored portion of the ship, but it does not disable except after many more hits than should be necessary. We have a 1600 lb AP bomb now, but to use it our present dive bombers have to reduce their gas carried, which is not a satisfactory solution.

Regarding Fletcher, Spruance was most generous.

> I cannot close . . . without expressing my admiration for the part that Fletcher in the *Yorktown* played in this campaign. We had a fine and smoothly working coordination between the two Task Forces before the fighting commenced. When the battle started, the *Yorktown*'s attack and the information her planes furnished were of vital importance to our success, which for some time was hanging in the balance. The *Yorktown* happened to be between the *Hornet* and *Enterprise* and the enemy's fourth and still functioning carrier, so she took his blows.
>
> Halsey's splendid staff have made my job easy. I appreciate more than I can tell you the fact that you had sufficient confidence in me to let me take this fine Task Force to sea during this critical period. It has been a pleasure to have such a well-trained fighting force to throw against the enemy.

The reason for the letter was that Spruance had been ordered to move north in the vicinity of the Aleutians, meet with Fitch and the *Saratoga* group, and then go after the enemy again. This was just what Yamamoto wanted, and he was attempting to lay a trap for Spruance, going so far as to make a plain-language radio broadcast that was supposed to come from a disabled battleship—bait for the Americans. But since Nimitz had begun to suspect the existence of a trap and ordered Spruance back to Pearl Harbor, the effort came to nothing.

In a way, the Midway battle had been a "makey-learn cruise" of the first order, for two commanders had learned a great deal about carrier operations. Admiral Marc Mitscher came home in the *Hornet* with a number of ideas. America needed something to compete with the Japanese Zero fighter, he said. American fighters should have the same fuel capacity as the planes they escorted. Radio silence had been broken on the fighter director circuit. Again, he added a plea for IFF equipment, along with other advice. In his official report, Spruance added that ships unsupported by fighters are easy prey to carrier air attack, which seemed obvious, and that a carrier air group which had suffered heavy losses in action should go ashore to train and receive replacements—meaning the supply of replacement air groups, which was not nearly so obvious.

When the action report of the Battle of Midway—some three inches of single-spaced typed paper, with diagrams and photos—was completed, Nimitz studied it and made some comments for the eyes of Admiral King, matters of gravest importance to the future of naval operations in the war.

He advocated the procurement of B-17s and B-24s for the Navy, as better planes than the PBYs for continuous tracking under conditions where enemy air is present.

He noted how ineffectual high-altitude horizontal bombing had proved, and recommended that island and coastal base planes be torpedo bombers and dive bombers.

He recommended the supply of the Marines with Army-type planes for use from shore bases, instead of the carrier-type planes with their built-in limitations.

He noted the lack of coordination of dive-bombing and torpedo-plane attacks, which cost most of the American torpedo planes. He also noted that the TBD planes in use "are fatally inadequate for their purpose. The loss of the brave men who unhesitatingly went to their death in them is grievous." He asked for long-range carrier fighters to protect the better TBFs.

Nimitz agreed with Mitscher and Spruance about the superiority in speed, maneuverability, and climb of the Zero. "These characteristics must be improved," he said, "but not at the cost of reducing our *present overall superiority* that in the battle of Midway enabled our carrier fighter squadrons to shoot down about 3 Zero fighters for each of our own lost."

Since in most engagements the American fighters were outnumbered, he suggested the increase in the number of fighters in each carrier from eighteen to twenty-seven. He endorsed Spruance's view on the need for replacement air groups.

Nimitz called for sharper, more thorough air training, better, quicker launching and attack, better tracking of enemy formations, and superfrequency voice sets for voice communication. He called attention to improved communications, improved gunnery ("Some crews have been in enough battles to consider themselves seasoned veterans"), better aircraft torpedoes with larger warheads designed for high-speed drops, and the thousand-pound armor-piercing bomb.

At the Battle of the Coral Sea, King had been critical of Fletcher for not using cruisers and destroyers in night attacks against the Japanese, and the Commander in Chief reiterated that criticism of the Midway action. Nimitz had to be prepared to explain. At the same time, he was preparing for his next meeting with King in San Francisco, watching the Aleutian situation, where the Japanese had landed and occupied two islands, and preparing for offensive action that was coming later in the South Pacific.

On June 29 Nimitz decided to send Task Force 11, Task Force 18, and the Second Marine Division to the South Pacific, where they would report to Ghormley. Fletcher was in charge of the force. Cincpac's plans section was ready with an estimate for an offensive in the Bismarck-Solomons area.

Then Nimitz took off, in the big flying boat, accompanied by Flag Secretary Commander Preston Mercer and Assistant War Plans Officer Captain Lynde McCormick, for Alameda air station. Just before 0900 on June 30 the big plane moved down over San Francisco Bay and prepared to land on the water. Swooping in, she moved low, and as she landed, struck an unnoticed telegraph pole floating in the bay, with such force that the bottom was slashed and the plane nosed over. Immediately, the shocked officers in the greeting contingent ashore sent the launch out for rescue. Nimitz carefully picked himself up, in the upside-down plane, and clambered out a hatchway.

"I'm all right," he shouted to Mercer, "but for God's sake save that briefcase." (The briefcase contained the three-inch report of the Battle of Midway.)

The copilot, Lt. Thomas M. Roscoe of Oakland, was killed in the crash, and several of the other survivors were injured. When the launch reached them, Nimitz climbed in with the others, and then stood up.

"Sit down, you" bellowed the coxswain.

Nimitz obeyed. A few moments later the sailor recognized his Pacific Fleet commander, and was horrified. He tried to apologize.

"Stick to your guns, sailor," Nimitz said. "You were quite right."

At the air station, all the survivors were rushed to the hospital for checkup. Nimitz, who hated hospitals and confinement, struggled free shortly and made his way home to Berkeley, where Mrs. Nimitz was spending the war, and found a change of clothes. Mercer, who was as sopping wet as the rest of them, had to put on a loud checked summer suit he had bought in San Diego before the war, and appear in that rig, much to his chagrin, when he met Commander in Chief King.

Among the exhibits for discussion at the meetings in Vice Admiral D. W. Bagley's office in the federal building was a discussion of the role of the battleship by Admiral Pye.

Pye suggested that the Japanese loss of five carriers in recent weeks had changed the situation so that the battleships might be used for the first time in the war. Still, Pye recognized that

> the war to date, both here and in Europe, has proven without doubt that even battleships are more vulnerable to torpedoes and bombs than had been previously estimated. This increased vulnerability has been due in large part to higher explosive charges than were considered probable heretofore, and in a large part also to the increased number of hits made by the greatly increased use of the torpedo plane, and by the increased proportion of dive bombers.

Battleships, then said Pye, should be employed only where their fire power could be used against ship or shore defense with enemy air and submarine defenses neutralized, or at least anticipated, and the losses discounted.

Specifically, Pye considered and discarded the use of battleships against Kiska or Attu in the Aleutians, unless Nimitz proposed to recapture these islands, with the battleships providing support.

In the Central Pacific, battleships might be useful against Wake—if accompanied by at least one carrier, Pye said.

If the Japanese tried to invade Australia, Pye saw the battleships as useful—"any and all possible naval strength would be of value." But unless logistics could be improved, the operation of Task Force One (the battleships) would be impracticable for any extended period.

In minor amphibious operations, cruiser and carrier support seemed to him enough. When the Japanese hold on important islands was threatened, and the Japanese main fleet might come out, then the battleships should be used to engage the Japanese main fleet.

But most practically, the old battleships could be used to prevent invasion of Midway or the Hawaiian Islands.

For a battleship man, this acceptance of limitations seemed very progressive, but Pye was always progressive. King agreed with just about everything Pye said, and they discussed the continuing need for development of tactics for large forces.

At this meeting, Nimitz and King, and the other officers who were present—going in and out to give information on specific subjects—were vitally concerned with the coming offensive to be launched in the South Pacific. Looking ahead, King suggested that the future would mean movement to Truk, then Guam, then Saipan.

Rear Admiral Richmond Kelly Turner, the planner whose eye had always been on amphibious operations, had been selected to supervise the landings on Guadalcanal island, and now Nimitz was ready to send him to Melbourne to discuss the whole operation with Ghormley and General MacArthur. The problem involved some change in the line of Cincpac-CincSoWesPac responsibility, because the Solomons fell within MacArthur's area, but this would be a Navy show.

Turner sat in on the discussions for a time. Nimitz wanted a promotion for Fletcher to vice admiral, and King agreed: he had accepted Nimitz's appraisal of Fletcher's actions at Coral Sea. Nimitz also wanted the authority to appoint task force commanders regardless of seniority, an authority he did not then have. They discussed other aspects of the coming operation for a time, and then Turner withdrew. Nimitz and King talked about Alaska and then about personnel. Mitscher's name came up, and Nimitz spoke highly of him. (King and the others had not always spoken so highly of Mitscher.) Halsey was still sick, and if he did not come back, Nimitz said, he wanted Aubrey Fitch to become the senior air flag officer of the fleet. Several officers of the Pacific Fleet had been indiscreetly involved in a leak to the press on the breaking of the Japanese naval code, and their fates were discussed.

Nimitz broke from the seriousness for a moment to report that he had rented a small house on Oahu for the rest and rehabilitation of senior officers. (It came to be called Prostate Rest.) Then they got down to the tiresome but vital business of logistics for the expanding naval operations in the South Pacific. They talked about medical storehouses, a fleet anchorage in New Caledonia, and the effective life of a submarine captain. (A captain could be expected to hold up for three or four full patrols—about a year—before needing a prolonged rest.)

Nimitz asked for more tankers, and this request was discussed in full. The problem as always these days, was balancing the absolute needs of the Pacific Fleet against the growing demands of the war in Europe.

★ ★ ★ ★ ★

The loss of four Japanese carriers at Midway was the turning point in the Pacific war. From that point on the United States, having blunted the sharpest edge of the Imperial Japanese Navy, would take the initiative. In August the Navy and Marines would move against the Japanese held island of Guadalcanal in the first major counteroffensive of the war. It would begin a campaign of attrition that would become the death knell for the Japanese Navy.

First Blood, from *The Men of the Gambier Bay*

EDWIN P. HOYT

The USS *Gambier Bay* and the small fleet of "Taffy 3" are synonymous in the Navy with courage. On October 25, 1944, the small group of escort carriers and destroyers was responsible for providing air cover supporting the invasion of Leyte off the island of Samar. The American invasion of Leyte was the beginning of the end for Japan's military rulers. If the Philippines were liberated by the United States, no hope for Japan would remain. Having already lost what remained of their carrier aviation forces in the Battle of the Philippine Sea four months earlier, Vice Admiral Ozawa would use his few remaining carriers as decoys to draw the American fleet away from Leyte. Two powerful surface groups would then sail into the central Philippines to annihilate the invasion transports in Leyte Gulf.

The southern Japanese force was commanded by Rear Admiral Nishimura and would advance through the Surigao Strait south of Leyte. The northern force under Vice Admiral Kurita would come down the San Bernadino Strait past the coast of Samar to strike the American fleet from the northeast. Kurita's force included the super-battleships *Musashi* and *Yamato*, three other battleships, a dozen cruisers and their escorts—a stunning group of naval firepower.

The American fleets were divided between Admiral William F. Halsey's Third Fleet and Admiral Thomas C. Kinkaid's Seventh Fleet. Following air attacks on the Kurita's center force on October 24, sinking the battleship *Musashi,* Admiral William F. Halsey moved his Third Fleet northwards to destroy Ozawa's carriers. Through a miscommunication between Halsey's Third Fleet and Kinkaid's Seventh, the San Bernadino Strait was left undefended. Kurita's fleet had been seen on a reverse course at

3:00 that afternoon, but two hours later the enemy ships turned southwards once more toward Leyte.

That night Vice Admiral Kinkaid's Seventh Fleet defended the southern approaches to Leyte in the battle of Surigao Strait, annihilating the Japanese southern force. At dawn however, Kinkaid received the astounding report that the Seventh Fleet's escort carriers had been surprised by the Japanese main force off Samar and were under heavy attack. Kurita's center force had achieved its mission and penetrated the San Bernadino Straits heading for Leyte Gulf. All that stood between them and the American transports was the small group of escort carriers and destroyers of "Taffy Three." Edwin P. Hoyt describes the courage of these sailors as they faced some of the mightiest warships of the Japanese Navy from his book *The Men of the Gambier Bay*.

★ ★ ★ ★ ★

When they saw what the ship faced, the three pilots on the catwalk rushed to their staterooms and found their life preservers, their guns, knives, canteens and other survival gear that they had chosen for emergency. They hurried to the ready room. It was empty but the blackboard had a message from Commander Huxtable:

"Bisbee, take charge. Weatherholt, Gallagher, and Pyzdrowski, fly off with torpedoes when ready." The four extra TBMs were still on the hangar deck, where the crews were loading and arming torpedoes. Bisbee came in, saw the message, ran to the hangar deck and came back. they would have to launch individually, as the planes came up in the elevator. Bisbee turned to the others, "Gallagher, you go first. Weatherholt, you team up with him if you can. Pyzdrowski, you go third. Don't wait for me. I'll wait for the last plane."

The time was 7:05. It was just twenty minutes since the sighting of the enemy had been confirmed and the *Gambier Bay* had gone to General Quarters.

Lieutenant Bisbee grabbed Pyzdrowski's arm. "Pyz," he said, "Give me the combination to your locker. We need a drink around here." Suddenly Pyzdrowski realized that he was about to take off, and that most of these pilots in the ready room, and Lt. Vereen Bell, would be stuck to ride the ship to whatever destiny she might have. He recited the combination to his liquor locker twice to Bisbee, and then followed Gallagher and Weatherholt up to the flight deck. Bisbee, Vereen Bell, John Holland, Joe

Phipps, Ernie Courtney, Leo Zeola, John Tetx, Joe McCabae, Owen Wheeler and Tuffy Barrows would not be launched. There were no planes. So if they needed a drink to conceal their disappointment, they were welcome to it. Bisbee took off for the Pyzdrowski stateroom, and the three pilots with places moved toward the flight deck. The passed the upper first aid station, and Pyzdrowski saw Dr. Wayne Stewart, the flight surgeon, setting up his surgical shop. It reminded him of what he had read of the old days in sailing ships, when the surgeons got ready their saw and burning irons, and strewed sawdust on the deck to soak up the blood that would flow.

Almost at the moment the pilots reached the flight deck, Gallagher's TBM came up the elevator, with its torpedo in place. Gallagher and his air crewmen leaped aboard. Immediately the plane was rolled to the catapult to be yoked for launching. The plane captain ran along behind, yelling and waving his hands. "It's go no gas. It's got to be gassed. Wait." It was 7:08. As the airedales hesitated, a voice came over the TBS from Bendix, the command ship:

"All carriers launch all aircraft."

The captain signaled. Launch. Gallagher nodded and waved his hand. He knew by that time that he had only forty-five gallons of gas in the TBM, perhaps enough to keep him flying for five minutes after takeoff. He also had a one-ton torpedo that should be delivered. As soon as the torpedo bomber was airborne, Gallagher turned left and headed for the first big ship he saw.

The next plane up the elevator was Bob Weatherholt's TBM. There had been no forgetting with this one, it was loaded already with a full tank of gas. Weatherholt got into the plane calmly, smoking a cigarette, and just before the catapult operated, he flicked it over the side, grinned and took off.

The third plane came up, loaded with gas and a torpedo. Jerry Fauls the gunner, Bob Jensen, the radioman, and Pyzdrowski shook hands, stepped up to the TBM, and took their places. The plane was taxied to the catapult. Pyzdrowski's eyes were glued to the deck-edge controller who watched the catapult light console. He used his fingers to signal the catapult launch officer the status of the catapult charge and the instructions of the bridge. The clenched fist meant hold. One finger up meant get ready. Two fingers up meant clear to fire. The controller's fist was clenched as the plane was hooked up. then he raised one finger and Pyzdrowski turned to face the launch officer. He waited. And he waited. And he waited.

It was 7:30. For fifteen minutes a squall had lain between the ships of Taffy 3 and Admiral Kurita's force, and only a few salvo splashes had come in, remarkably near *White Plains* and *Fanshaw Bay* given the circumstances and the absence of Japanese spotter planes. Admiral Sprague used this respite to ask Admiral Kinkaid down south if he might move the whole protective carrier force toward the safety of the battleship fleet. The answer was no. So Admiral Sprague knew that the escort carriers were regarded as expendable. If they had to be sacrificed to save the main body of Kinkaid's fleet, then that was hot it was going to be. They could maneuver east or west, but they could not head south to safety. Whether or not they could have achieved safety was questionable anyhow. The small carriers had been operating for many weeks without dockyard attention and seventeen knots was regarded as a good speed for them. *Yamato*, the Japanese superbattleship, had a flank speed almost twice that of the Kaiser carriers.

The controller held one finger up waiting on the bridge command. Pyzdrowski could not understand it. "She's charged. Let 'er go," he shouted. He looked at Commander Borries and called to him. "Let me go." Borries pointed silently to the ensign atop the ship's mast. The captain had headed downwind to try to escape the enemy. One Japanese cruiser was moving around the northeast flank of the carriers, and salvos were beginning to fall close. The Japanese radar was not nearly so advanced as the American, so Admiral Kurita's gunners relied on old device: their various salvoes were color-coded so that the gunners could correct their aim. A green series of splashes would be followed by a red series, then yellow. And each series came closer to *Fanshaw Bay*, *White Plains*, and *Gambier Bay*. The cruiser was coming at thirty knots, and soon would have a square shot at the *Gambier Bay*. The salvoes increased in concentration.

Captain Vieweg was busily "chasing salvoes." On the principle that lightning does not strike twice in the same place, as soon as one salvo of shells plunked into the water, the captain turned in that direction. Then came another salvo and he turned again. As Weatherholt was launched salvoes straddled the ship. It was 7:25. The range was close enough now that Admiral Sprague ordered the carriers to "open fire with the pea shooters," and in a moment the five-inch gun on the fantail began shooting.

Pyzdrowski got the "cut" signal. He shut off the engine of the TBM, jumped out and ran for the bridge. "What's the matter?" he shouted. "The catapult is charged." Commander Borries held up his first "Wait." Pyzdrowski ran back to the plane and ordered Fauls and Jensen out. He intended to fly this one himself, along. The signal was to hold up. He jumped out and again ran to the bridge, calling to Borries. "We can take off without wind." It was true. While the ship was in harbor at Espiritu Santo, the torpedo bombers had been fitted with new twin-barrel

Honeywell carburetors which were promised to increase engine efficiency. Carrier doctrine, however, said you must not take off except into the wind, and with salvoes falling all around the ship. Commander Borries was not about to argue with the captain.

"Sure, sure," he said to Pyzdrowski, and then he pointed at the catapult. The TBM was just then being shot off, pilotless. It took off beautifully, just as Pyzdrowski had said it would.

It climbed for a moment, then flipped over on its left side and went into the water. The last plane had left the *Gamier Bay*. It as 7:50 A.M.

Lieutenant Stewart, in charge of the first eight fighters that had left *Gambier Bay* before dawn, was totally unaware of what was happening in the beginning. His mission was to support the groups troops on Leyte with strafing, bombing, and rocket attacks. This activity consumed a large amount of fuel, and so about 7:30 he was considering a return to the *Gambier Bay* for fuel. When he called the air controller, he learned that the Japanese had arrived in force off Samar, and that his carrier was under attack and could not land any planes. The same was true of all the other carries of Taffy 1, 2, and 3: they were running from destruction and their planes had to take care of themselves. The alternative was Tacloban airfield, which was in worse shape on the 25 than it had been the day before when Zeola landed there. The night's rain had made a sticky mess of the dirt runway. But what else was there to do? By the time Stewart brought his flight of eight over Tacloban, a hundred planes were orbiting. They came from the sixteen escort carriers of Admiral Sprague's command and from Halsey's fleet carriers offshore; and they shared a common plight: they had no place else to go. The first fighter in the pattern made a pass over the field, then came into land. His gear caught in the mud, and the plane nosed over in the middle of the runway, blocking it. The next plane, desperate, landed in the sand on the seaward side of the runway. He bumped down and bounced along but he was down safe and so was his plane, and that was what counted. Thereafter, planes began landing on sand and runway every few seconds. Some nosed over. Some came in hard, and the landing gear crumbled beneath them. Some caught fire, but the planes continued to land. Hundreds of soldiers appeared to help pull and drag planes off the runways and the clear spots, so more planes could land. The Tacloban field was like a giant beehive, with the worker bees coming to carry off the injured to make room for more to land.

After Commander Huxtable had the order from the flagship to "attack" he left his six fellow torpedo pilots toward the enemy. As long as the planes were under 1,000 feet they could see the Japanese ships below, but to make an attack they had to gain altitude and come down through the clouds. The weather was so bad, however, that it seemed unlikely a high altitude attack could be successful, and the flagship had ordered immediate action. Below he could see the four cruisers and four battleships in the gloom; at least that is what he thought he saw. Without doubt he could also see the American destroyers and destroyer escorts running in to make torpedo attacks on the big Japanese ships to stop the punishment of the escort carriers.

Huxtable did not even know what loads the other TBMs were carrying. His own plane had only ammunition for the guns, but at least, he said to himself, he could give the enemy a scare. So he headed down in a shallow dive on the starboard side of the line of cruisers. He could see the red balls of anti-aircraft tracer coming up as he dived at 190 knots. Huxtable came in to about 2,500 yards. The anti-aircraft fire was growing more intense, and he pulled up in a wide circle. The Japanese kept shooting with five-inch shells, and he flew through the smoke of the bursts, they were so close.

Not knowing what Admiral Kinkaid had said to Admiral Sprague that morning, Huxtable volunteered the information to Bendix that the best course for the carrier force was due south. There was no comment.

Lieutenant Bassett was right behind Commander Huxtable when they took off from the carrier. As Huxtable dove for the cruisers, Bassett was on his wing; Huxtable took the second ship in the column and Bassett peeled off to attack the lead ship, a *Mogami*-class cruiser. Bassett had two bombs. As he dropped the first at 2,000 feet the anti-aircraft fire became intense, and the TBM was hit and began to shudder. Immediately he dropped the second bomb and pulled out of the thirty-five-degree dive at 1,000 feet and turned into the clouds ahead of the cruiser. So he did not see the results of his bombing, but he heard no explosions and was included to believe that his two 500-pound bombs had not been fused, and that they did not explode even if they struck the target. Just then, he did not much care; his mind was totally occupied with the shuddering TBM. How badly was it damaged? He climbed to 8,000 feet on instruments, deep in the clouds. When he emerged his crewmen could check the damage to the tail. The starboard horizontal stabilizer had been hit from below and a hole ten inches wide had been blown in the bottom side, with the shell emerging to make a hole 18 inches wide at the top. When Bassett pulled back the stick he felt a binding, but that was all. The instruments responded properly. The question was how much structural damage had been suffered, and could the plane fly to a landing place? Radioman

Houlihan found apiece of shrapnel in his compartment and a hole in the port window. But that was all the damage. Bassett flew toward Tacloban field, but when he got there so many planes were stacked up in the sky that the field was accepting emergency landings only. He circled for an hour; meanwhile the others of his group came up, and he joined them to land at Dulag airfield shortly after 11 A.M.

Ensign Crocker had also joined up with Commander Huxtable. His plane, like Huxtable's, had no bomb load, so the commander told Crocker to hang back and not go in on the first pass. But Crocker felt he had to so something, so he flew in low alongside the cruiser to divert their anti-aircraft fire. The Japanese five-inch guns fired on him, and one burst came so close it knocked out his instruments and his radio. He saw a TBM smoking, and tried to lead it to Tacloban. It was apparent, however, that the TBM was not going to make it, and in a few seconds it nosed down, and landed in the water about a mile ahead of the American ships, nosed over, and soon sank. Crocker saw the three crewmen get out. He dropped several dye markers and a float light. Then he made another pass and dropped his seat boat pack to the men in the water. He then circled, waiting for another plane to come along to join up with, but none came. He made an attack on the Japanese destroyers at the edge of the formation then, firing his guns and rockets. In the turret, gunner Charlie Westbrook fired his single .50 caliber gun. The Japanese anti-aircraft gunners were good shots; they put a 20-mm shell into his port wing and engine, but there was no loss of power. When Crocker ran out of ammunition on this third run, he headed for Dulag to land. When he came in, and was taxiing off the strip a fighter ran into the TBM and damaged the propeller.

Ensign Shroyer had also joined Commander Huxtable. When Huxtable attacked the cruisers, Shroyer went after one of the battleship. He had two 500-pound bombs, but on his first run he strafed only because the cloud cover restricted the visibility so badly as he attacked. He came out of the attack at 2,000 feet right over the cruisers, and for a moment the air all around him was filled with anti-aircraft bursts. But he dived for the deck and escaped. He climbed then to 10,000 feet and attacked a *Tone*-class cruiser, following a dozen FM-2s that were strafing. He dropped his two bombs, and they hit the fantail of the cruiser. He did not see that, but Lieutenant Lischer, piloting one of the fighters, and Lt. Paul Garrison, a *Kitkun Bay* pilot, both saw the bombs hit. Half an hour later Shroyer flew over the cruiser and saw it was dead in the water. He headed for the escort carriers, but was ordered to Tacloban. There he was diverted to Dulag and landed.

Lieutenant Gallagher had taken off with that first plane of the TBM group that were loaded with torpedoes. Knowing that his gas supply was severely limited he headed straight for the enemy ships and dropped his torpedo against a cruiser. No one saw the results, but in a moment Gallagher joined up with commander Huxtable, seeking instructions. His plant had been hit in the attack, and the engine was smoking. Huxtable told him to head for the beach, and Gallagher obeyed and turned.

The engine sputtered and died. Gallagher headed for the water and landed. His was the plane that Crocker saw go into the water. The three men got out, into a rubber boat, and waved. Crocker flew off, and no one else reported them. They were never seen again.

Lieutenant Weatherholt had taken off just behind Gallagher, but fortunately his plane had been gassed. He circled the *Gambier Bay*, waiting for Pyzdrowski and Bisbee, but they did not come. After half an hour of circling, Weatherholt went off to find other planes to join for an attack. He found one other torpedo plane, and went in with that plane to attack a battleship. They attacked from the two sides of the bow. The other plane dropped first and the battleship turned toward the torpedo and then straightened out. Weatherholt dropped and sped for the deck to avoid the anti-aircraft fire. He did not see any hits.

Lieutenant Roby was one of the first to rush from the ready room to the flight deck when the captain called on the pilots to man all planes, as the Japanese fleet approached. Roby launched at 6:55, circled and joined six of the carrier's other fighters. They climbed toward the Japanese fleet. Twenty minutes after taking off, they saw Japanese destroyers below, and dived down to strafe. Roby made three runs. He got separated from the other VC-10 fighters and joined another group to make more passes. Again he was separated and joined a third group. By 8:00 his guns were empty, but he continued to make dry runs on cruisers to harry them and draw fire. Just before 10:00 he flew to Tacloban, circled for nearly an hour, and then landed.

Ensign Bennett, flying a TBM, got separated from Huxtable in the clouds and joined up with one VC-10 fighter. Together they attacked the Japanese cruisers. The fighter went in first on a cruiser and they TBM followed. Bennett had no bomb load nor any rockets. He strafed with the wing guns and his gunner and radioman strafed. They came out and saw the battleships and attacked. Bennett did not believe his attacks did any damage, but they did divert anti-aircraft fire from other attacking planes. He headed for the beach hoping to find some bombs, but was diverted to the carrier *Manila Bay*, and landed on the flight deck at 10 o'clock.

Lt. (jg) Joe McGraw was one of the escorts for Huxtable's little group of torpedo planes. He made eleven strafing runs on a *Fuso*-class battleship. He saw one Japanese cruiser listing and apparently badly damaged. He also saw one escort carrier dropping far behind the others and smoking badly. He did not know it was the *Gambier Bay*.

Lieutenant Phillips was with a group of VC-10 fighter that attacked the destroyer disposition. On his first strafing run all but on eof his guns jammed. He kept on attacking with that one gun, until it ceased firing. Then he went to Tacloban. Ensign Wallace and Lieutenant Hunting both joined attack groups that went in to strafe either battleships or cruisers. They attacked until their ammunition was gone, and then they went to Tacloban.

Ensign Osterkorn, in a TBM, did not find any planes of VC-10 when he took off from the carrier. He headed for the enemy fleet and attacked alone. As he came out of the run, he saw a group of fighters and joined up on them for his second attack. He dropped his two bombs on a cruiser but saw no results. Then he went to Tacloban and as diverted to Dulag.

Lieutenant Seitz made eight or nine runs on cruisers and destroyers, and before he left the battle area he saw one Japanese cruiser and two destroyers dead in the water.

Lieutenant Ellwood made repeated runs on the cruisers to help the bombers unload without being smothered in anti-aircraft fire. His guns gave him trouble and finally quit altogether, whereupon he made dummy runs. He saw one bomb hit the bow of a cruiser and apparently knock out the forward turret. When he was down to forty gallons of gas he turned toward Tacloban.

Lieutenant Dugan's experience was almost the same, although he concentrated on the destroyers. The results, as with the others, were impossible to ascertain from the air, and of course, in the melee, with planes from all the eighteen carriers involved in the action, it was impossible to tell whose attacks produced results. Ensign Shroyer's hit on the after section of a cruiser was an exception. That ship may have been the *Chokai* or it may have been the *Chikuma*, although the Japanese believed the tremendous explosion aft on that ship was caused by a torpedo. No matter, the Japanese accounts credited the American planes with an effective effort on a whole. The cruiser *Suzuya* was badly damaged. *Tone* was damaged and her captain was badly wounded by strafing fighters. It would have been poetic justice had the fighter been one of VC-10's, for *Tone* was the cruiser that attacked the *Gambier Bay* most effectively that day. *Chikuma, Haguro* and *Chokai,* proud cruisers, were all damaged by air attackers. Several of the cruisers sank on their way back to safety later in the day. Not all this damage was done by the aviators, of course. For another battle story was being told that morning on the surface, by the destroyers and destroyer escorts.

As Admiral Kurita's force swooped down that morning all that stood between the carriers and disaster were the little ships of the destroyer screen. They turned like foxes to fight, and just before seven o'clock they came under fire from the Japanese ships. They began to attack. The destroyer *Johnston* went in first with torpedoes, fired and ducked into a rain squall. Destroyers *Hoel* and *Heermann* and the destroyer escort *Roberts* followed. *Johnston* kept nipping at the heels of the Japanese until she was sunk. *Hoel* went in, attacked, scored hits on Japanese ships and came under heavy fire. She, too, was sunk. *Heermann* also went into action. The men of the *Gambier Bay* knew the *Heermann* well. Indeed, Lt. Bucky Dahlen was aboard her that day, with his air crewmen.

Two air space crewmen had been assigned to a repair party, and Lieutenant Dahlen, who had volunteered to help, was sent to the gunnery officer to spot Japanese planes. When no Japanese planes appeared, he returned to the bridge to ask Commander Hathaway for another assignment. He arrived at the same moment as a Japanese shell, which killed him and three others. Captain Hathaway was not at that moment on the bridge, having gone to the fire control tower where he could see better. Captain Hathaway survived, and so did his ship, but Bucky Dahlen's second lease on life had lasted less than twenty-four hours.

The destroyers and the destroyer escorts most certainly saved the carriers that day, or most of them. The cost was the loss of *Johnston* and *Hoel* and *Samuel B. Roberts*, and the carriers did not remain unhurt. But the fact that half of them were not destroyed was attributable to the fierce attack from air and sea that the Japanese encountered off Samar.

The first carrier to be hit was *Kalinin Bay*. At 7:10, when Captain Vieweg first started chasing salvoes, *Kalinin Bay* took the first of fifteen shells. *White Plains*, with salvoes falling around her and obscuring her from view, was not hit at all. *Kitkun Bay* was straddled and straddled again, but never hit. *St. Lo*, the starboard ship in the second line of carriers, was also nearly hit half a dozen times, but she was saved for another fate. (She was hit by a kamikaze plane later in the day with such force that the fires could not be put out and she sank.) But the principal honor as a sacrificial victim that day belonged to the *Gambier Bay*. When Admiral Sprague began maneuvering to try to put water between his force and the enemy, the change of course put the *Gambier Bay* at the end of the line, nearest the enemy.

The course change came at 8 o'clock. Ten minutes later the Japanese drew first blood from the *Gambier Bay.* A shell struck the after end of the flight deck on the starboard side, starting fires on the flight deck and down on the hangar deck. Several men were killed or wounded. In damage control, Seaman DiSipio was sent to fight fire, but the fires were so many that he gave up, and instead began carrying wounded men down to flight surgeon Stewart's aid station. It was 8:11.

★ ★ ★ ★ ★

The actions of Taffy 3 with help from Taffy 2 aircraft sank two enemy cruisers and inflicted other damage on the vastly superior Japanese fleet, which miraculously, withdrew from battle just after 9:00 A.M. Taffy 3 came under kamikaze attacks later that morning that sank the escort carrier USS *St. Lo.* Halsey's strikes on the Japanese northern force on October 25 managed to sink Ozawa's flagship *Zuikaku* and two light carriers, crippling the third. Nimitz would order Halsey's Task Force 34 to return to Samar but by then it was too late to take part in the actions of Taffy 3.

Hell Below, from *Take Her Deep!*

ADM. I. J. GALANTIN

> Out of the depths I have cried unto Thee, O Lord. Lord, hear my voice . . .
>
> —Psalm 130

Some of the greatest legends in the American Navy come from the submariners. After the attack on Pearl Harbor, it was the submarines that were in place to strike the first blows against the Japanese Navy. They would become the Achilles heel of the enemy merchant marine and a mortal threat to any Japanese warship that crossed their path. During the Second World War the Silent Service destroyed over 1,300 enemy ships, cutting vital supply lines, denying reinforcement of ground forces, and sinking enemy warships. They would also perform special operations taking supplies to guerilla forces in the Philippines, rescuing key personnel and American citizens from capture, and life guarding downed airmen including a future U.S. President George H.W. Bush by USS *Finback* in September 1944.

These victories were not without the loss of American submarines and men. Fifty-two submarines were lost during the war with the lives of over 3,500 sailors. In some cases, a boat and her crew simply disappeared for causes unknown. As the Japanese took major losses from submarine attacks, they invested more ships and technological efforts to anti-submarine defenses. The cat and mouse game of attack and evasion became more and more deadly. Captain Ignatius J. Galantin and his crew aboard the USS *Halibut* survived one of the most devastating attacks on an American submarine during World War II. In the following chapter, "Hell Below," Galantin narrates the experience as his submarine comes under attack in the Luzon Straight in November 1944 from his book *Take Her Deep!*

★ ★ ★ ★ ★

During the night of November 13 we observed an unusual amount of Japanese air activity, enough to force us down for a brief period. Clearly the area was being swept for some important traffic. Diving in Bashi Channel at dawn we patrolled along the most probable shipping route. It was a beautiful Pacific day, a blue, almost cloudless sky embracing the deeper blue of the sea whose moderate swells had only an occasional whitecap. Visibility was excellent.

Just before noon we heard the pinging of distant sonar. Speeding up and heading for the contact thus disclosed, we soon made out the tops of a northbound convoy. It was a group of at least four ships, one large modern freighter and three smaller ones. On our side of the convoy were four small escorts; there were probably others out of sight on the far side. To get close enough for an attack we had to use high, submerged speed, a noisy six knots, with only occasional brief looks through the scope. As we closed, the freighters were seen to be in two columns, zigzagging frequently. The track angle for our torpedoes was good, and the gyro angles small, but we would have to fire at long range or not at all. The torpedo run of 3,100 yards was the best we could get. Unfortunately, the three minutes it would take the fish to reach the target would give it time to zig at least once more.

At 1320 we fired four torpedoes at the largest ship. I was glad to see that a freighter in the far column overlapped our target. We swung rapidly to the right with full rudder to bring our stern tubes to bear. During the turn I kept an eye on the escorts; their sonars were pinging rhythmically and they gave no sign of being alerted. Jim busied himself with the new setup on the TDC, and Chief Quartermaster O'Brien, with stopwatch in hand, marked the time of torpedo run. "Mark! They should be there!" But there was no explosion until two more minutes had passed.

I swung the periscope quickly from the escorts to the freighter in the far column. She was making black smoke and dropping astern. The sound of another torpedo explosion came through the water and, soon after, a strange, loud, fast buzzing noise unlike any we'd heard before.

Men in the crew's mess reported they heard this sound pass over us four times, approaching from starboard which was the direction of the escorts as well as the direction our fish had been fired. Men in the forward part of the boat thought it crossed over us three times.

Woodrow Burgess was our new yeoman and telephone talker. "Ask them what it sounds like," I told him.

It was variously described. To Ship's Cook 2c Thomas it was high speed screws; to Chief Griffen it was a torpedo; to Chief Terry an airplane flying low. To me in the conning tower the sound came as a fast, low-pitched buzzing, increasing in loudness and then decreasing for an estimated total of forty seconds. I heard it only once. I had no impression that it circled our ship, but men both forward and aft were positive it did.

As the sound faded a heavy explosion, similar to a depth charge, occurred close to port. I was puzzled by the strange noise and fearful of a new antisubmarine weapon. "Take her deep! Use negative and full speed!"

Whatever we heard, it could not be one of our torpedoes running erratic. It was too improbable to suppose that six minutes after being fired it would seek us out, pass over us several times, then explode close aboard. Neither would its turning circle permit it to pass overhead more than once.

Four more heavy explosions lit up the DCI. They detonated close to starboard but above us as we leveled off at 325 feet. They did not have the characteristic "click-brr-roomp-woosh" of depth charges.

For seventeen minutes we ran quietly, trying to slink away. Two escorts could be heard overhead, one on either quarter, their sonar echoes bouncing off our hull. All seemed to be going well. We had been in this situation many times and I felt no special concern. We were rigged for depth charge and I took my usual seat on the deck at the top of the ladder from control.

Suddenly all hell broke loose. Simultaneous with the tremendous concussion of a depth charge close by, I saw the cork lining of the hull crack and yield, pushed inboard by the deformation of the hull. The radar transceiver and the periscope hoist motors were knocked askew. Glass shattered and gauges broke. The sonar went dead. It was time to abandon the conning tower.

Pulling the lower hatch shut behind us and pounding its dogs, or latches, firmly into place, we were now all locked within the ship's main pressure hull. There were eighty of us, but we were split into small groups in the eight separate compartments of our ship. Each group was sealed from the next by the heavy watertight doors which had been slammed shut when rigging for depth charge.

When the depth charge explosion wrecked the conning tower, the light bulb which illuminated the TDC had popped out. Jim Conant grabbed it in instinctive reaction and somehow scrambled down the ladder without breaking it. He stood now in the control room tenderly cupping the bulb in his hand, as though the safety of our ship depended on that fragile glass globe.

For two minutes all seemed calm, save for the sharp probing of the Japs' active sonar beams now bouncing off our hull at a quicker pace. A few hundred feet overhead, Japanese sonar operators watched intently on their oscilloscopes the greenish blob which denoted our presence, or listened carefully to the sharp, metallic echoes which our hull returned. The rapidity of the pinging clearly indicated they had solid contact on us, were not in doubt as to our position and movement. We had survived many depth chargings in the past, and had no doubt we would do so again, but it was clear this was a more professional ASW performance than any we'd experienced in the past. Surely the near miss that had driven us from the conning tower was a lucky shot that could not be repeated in the complex problem of space and motion that stood between us and our enemy. Its solution would bring both triumph and disaster, one to the hunter, the other to the hunted. Would our pursuers gauge properly our course, our speed, our depth, the sinking time of depth charges? On our part, we had no weapons with which to attack or ward off our enemy. In a close-in engagement with shallow-draft, maneuverable ships our torpedoes were useless. If we were forced to the surface we'd have only the fire of our modest gun armament to divide against the more nimble surface craft. Here, deep under the ocean, lay our best protection; but would we choose the best depth, turn at the proper time, speed up or slow down at the right moment? These were not discrete thoughts racing through my mind, but this was the aggregate of intuition and reason that now guided us.

Suddenly several close depth charges, very loud, shook *Halibut* violently. These came so nearly together that it was not possible to count them accurately. I was standing in the control room, one hand gripping the ladder to the conning tower, watching the depth gauges over Jack Hinchey's shoulder, when I saw for my first and only time a phenomenon other skippers had reported. I saw, or rather had the sensation of, a greenish glow in the room, much as a lightning flash will illumine a dark night. Did I see it or did I imagine it? It was like "seeing stars" after a violent blow to the head. Was I merely stunned or frightened? But there was no time for speculation. It was 13:46:24 by Tokyo time, forty-six minutes and twenty-four seconds after one o'clock in the afternoon, civilian time. That was the moment at which our control room clock, our master, daily timekeeper, stopped. When we got back to Pearl, one of ComSubPac's scientists would offer the dubious explanation that the bluish-green flash was caused by sound waves of a frequency so high that they approached the speed of light.

The tremendously loud explosions, the disintegration of familiar equipment around us, the vibrations of the ship as if she was a giant fish trying to shake off a hook, had stunned and frightened me momentarily. Was this the way it would end?

No one spoke or uttered a sound. No one seemed hurt. Jack leaned over the shoulders of his bow and stern planesmen, Vogel and Sturgeon, as all three grimly concentrated on holding our depth.

We were below our safe operating depth when the depth charges exploded. The enormous concussion had driven *Halibut* 100 feet deeper. We were now at 420 feet. The explosions just a few feet over the forward battery compartment had forced us down as though a giant hand was pushing a toy boat underwater. But better down than up. Explosions beneath us would have blown us toward the surface and, if we could not keep from broaching, our presence on the surface would have drawn a storm of enemy gunfire.

Chalfant on the hydraulic manifold, Allison on the air manifold, Emmett on the trim manifold stood silently awaiting instructions. Their grips on a familiar valve wheel or lever gave them reassurance. Chief Roberson looked around the room, appraising everyone, ready to help where needed.

I broke the silence. "Jack, can you hold her?"

"I could use more speed, captain," Jack was as calm and casual as if this was a routine, morning dive to get a BT trace.

The high speed we had used to get within torpedo range of the convoy had consumed much of our battery capacity, and there were several hours of daylight before we dared surface. The submariner's instinctive hoarding of his battery, his miserly expenditure of amperes—the very life blood of his ship when submerged—made us jealous of every amp expended. As long as we could hold our depth or inch upwards it was better not to increase our r.p.m.

"You're doing fine. Try to ease up to three-fifty."

I was cool and confident once more. We'd received no more depth charges. Our sonars were out of order, but we could hear no screw noises overhead.

All around us was a shambles. There was much minor damage; everything that had been loose was displaced and thrown about. Most glass was shattered. Oil and water fittings leaked. The master gyro was knocked out. Personnel seemed stunned, but went about their tasks quietly as if this was just another damage control drill.

Guy manned the sound-powered phone which linked us to all compartments. He received their damage reports and gave instructions. In every compartment men struggled to control damage and stop leaks. By the action and attitude of our ship I knew we had no catastrophic fracture of the hull. We would be on our way to the bottom by now if that were true.

Suddenly word came over the phone: "Chlorine gas in the forward battery!" The dread report, most serious of all the problems we faced, hit me with chilling effect which I did my best to hide. We would have to handle it as only one more of the difficulties we were struggling with. We were still drawing power from the forward battery, and the boat was not getting noticeably heavy forward. There could not be a major rupture of the hull. The best we could do now was to keep the deadly gas confined to the sealed-off officers' country. Stationed in that compartment when we had rigged for depth charge were Lieut. (jg) Ray Stewart, Ensign Bill Kidwell, and our two steward's mates, Strauther Wallace and John Phillips. Wallace was an experienced submariner, a big, burly, likeable man. Phillips was a neophyte sailor, much younger, slighter, and more articulate. They were the only black men in our crew.

Even before Guy could give them orders to secure the compartment and evacuate, the handle on the heavy watertight door which led to officers' country began to revolve. Pulling open the door, Ray and Bill leaped into the control room and slammed the door shut behind them. They had ordered Wallace and Phillips to go forward to the torpedo room and to seal that door behind them.

"Chlorine gas" was not a casualty that could be rehearsed realistically. None of us had been exposed to it. The navy had not developed a harmless, substitute gas with the same odor to use in drills. We had only described it, warned of its danger, and specified how to secure the battery compartment where it generated.

The young officers were flushed and agitated, but fully in control of themselves. In the room full of men grimly concentrating on their jobs, Ray waited for me to have time for his report. Bill braced himself against the housing of the master gyro. His shirt was wet with perspiration, and his face showed bewilderment at all that he was experiencing on his first war patrol.

Guy recalled that Bill's father had visited our ship during overhaul in San Francisco. At lunch that day Mr. Kidwell had said of Bill's forthcoming duty, "Submarine duty would be a good experience for a young man."

Guy looked at Bill and said in his calm, laconic, deadpan fashion, "Good experience for a young man."

It was the perfect remark to break the tension. I grinned along with everyone else.

From Ray's report I gathered that the tremendous concussion of the depth charge barrage, which sounded to him like a thousand sledgehammers pounding the hull, had thrown all four men off their feet. They were showered with cork from the lining of our hull, with paint flakes, and with dust from the ventilation piping. Fittings from bulkheads and deck were broken loose, and light bulbs were shattered. The books of the wardroom library spilled from their cupboard on the forward bulkhead. Drawers and lockers in officers' and chiefs' quarters were flung open, and loose items strewn about. China and glassware in the officers' pantry were smashed. There was a sharp, hissing sound, as if water under pressure was squirting through a crack. A strange, pungent odor filled the room. To two junior officers the combination was convincing evidence that the battery compartment beneath the wardroom deck was filling with deadly chlorine gas. Somehow saltwater must be reaching the sulphuric acid electrolyte of the main storage batteries. With no means to control this, the battery ventilation ducts were sealed and the compartment abandoned.

Running silent was no longer a major concern. The enemy knew where we were. We could do nothing about the banging and rattling from topside damage, and the noisy squealing coming from propeller shafts and screws. In the control room Jack worked with his bow and stern planesmen, trying to ease our ship gradually up to 350 feet. Complicating Jack's problem was the fact that our regular depth gauges were bent or shattered. He had to rely on small sea pressure gauges and convert their "pounds per square inch" to "feet" of submergence. The reading of 176 on a sea pressure gauge meant that we were at a depth of 400 feet.

Orders to the main power switchboard in the maneuvering room went by telephone. Should there be trouble there, we needed to know at once. Under the savage pounding of our hull and the intense shocks given any equipment mounted on the hull, it seemed a miracle that we had no fire in the main control cubicle or in the batteries.

Chief Braun and his two main power controllermen, electrician's mates Arthur Grisanti and David Else, were locked in the confined, sweltering maneuvering room. Braun was a strong character, a tough-minded, practical sailor who could be counted on to "tell it like it is."

In reply to a question he said, "Mr. Goolyotto, it's OK back here. Both batteries read OK. We can give you what you want."

What we wanted was a few more r.p.m. Vogel had his bow planes on hard rise but we hung at 400 feet.

"Guy, tell Braun to build up ten turns slowly, but to watch his voltage carefully."

There was no compass heading for quartermaster 2c Henderson to steer by. "Just leave the rudder amidships," I ordered.

The course we made good was of little concern. We were in the deep ocean, well offshore, in no danger of running aground. We could no longer hear anything overhead. There was no need to twist and turn. It was just as well to hold a steady course and not make Jack's job even more difficult.

We were still not sure what really had happened in the forward battery compartment. By now I knew we could not be taking serious amounts of water, but what had caused the gas? What were conditions in the battery well?

Chief Roberson had been thinking hard. He read the gauge on the forward bulkhead of the control room, which measured the pressure in the officers' quarters and the battery compartment under them. The air pressure was 52 pounds per square inch!

If the pressure hull was ruptured, the pressure in the compartment would be the same as the sea's. At our depth the pressure gauge would then read 176 pounds per square inch. Besides, if the compartment was flooding from sea we could not hold our depth; we would be heading for the bottom four miles below.

There could be only one explanation for the sudden rise in the air pressure of the battery compartment. No. 1 air bank was located in the forward battery well, its heavy, steel bottles secured to the pressure hull to either side of the battery. These interconnected flasks stored air compressed to 2,500 pounds per square inch, which we used to blow main ballast tanks when surfacing. Each night we topped them off with our air compressors as religiously as we recharged our batteries. Somehow the air pressure in the bank must be released.

In time we would learn that the violent explosions over and around our ship had deformed the hull and caused the copper piping leading from the air bank to pull out of its silver soldered joints. Released into the volume of the whole compartment, the air from the flasks raised the compartment pressure to 52 pounds per square inch.

Forward of the control room, watertight doors were hinged so that they swung aft to close; those abaft the control room were opposite. This meant that the compartment pressure acting on the door leading aft to the control room made it impossible to open. Conversely, the pressure on the door giving access to the forward torpedo room was restrained only by the strength of the dogs which held that door's rubber gasket firmly against its knife edge. It was essential that we know whether we indeed had chlorine gas to cope with. There was only one way to find out. The forward torpedo room would have to ease up gradually on their door and sniff carefully for gas.

Since his battle station was the forward torpedo room, Ensign Alexander was senior man in the compartment. Guy got him on the phone and explained what we wanted done. "Caution him to be very careful, Guy. There's lots of pressure on that door."

I waited grimly. If it really is chlorine, I thought, we'll keep it confined in the forward battery compartment until we can surface and ventilate.

The control room was unnaturally quiet. The bow and stern planes had not been put out of commission; we could still operate them in "power." The only sound was the occasional click of their control switches as Vogel and Sturgeon worked to hold us at 350 feet.

Braun reported no problem with main power. He was drawing normal current from the forward battery; it could not have serious damage. A fire there would be devastating. Jack now had good depth control, so we took off the extra turns we had used. Every amp was important.

Jim Conant became aware of the light bulb in his hands. Firecontrolman 2c Silvio Gardella, who took care of the TDC, was standing beside him. "Here, Gardella, you take it," said Jim sheepishly. Then he shambled to the radio room where Chief Lawrence and radioman Joe Janus were trying to protect the badly damaged sets from the water dripping from the flooded antenna trunk.

Guy spoke into his phone, "Control, aye aye." As he listened his face was expressionless as always, his only sign of more than usual emotion being the nodding of his close-cropped head.

"Are you sure?" A pause. "He does?" Then, "That's good." Guy never used three words if two would do.

In his flat, matter-of-fact tones, almost as if passing chit-chat, Guy reported. "Alex says he doesn't smell chlorine. He had Soulis check it, and he agrees." (Chief Torpedoman Jim Soulis was the senior enlisted man in the compartment.) "It smells funny, but they don't know what it is. The door is secured again."

As long as the forward battery compartment retained its high pressure our ship would remain divided in two parts and we could not assist our men struggling with the damage in the forward torpedo room. With 52 pounds per square inch acting on it, the control room door was sealed as firmly as if it were welded shut.

I felt older. I realized I really *was* "the Old Man," the skipper my men were counting on to make the right decisions. But I was confident, too. Eight years of submarine duty and many emergencies had prepared me for this. For more than a year *Halibut* had responded to every demand I placed on her, escaped every attack made on her. Now she had survived the most violent, most accurate blows the enemy could deliver. With every second that passed, I was more certain that we could handle our problems.

I ordered the doors abaft the control room to be put "on the latch," and sent Joe Galligan aft to learn first-hand what problems we had. Men could now move from room to room to assist in the inspections and repairs required.

The first step in lowering the pressure in the forward battery compartment was to let it expand into the torpedo room. Torpedoman Ed Bertheau slowly backed off the door locking mechanism until high-pressure air whistled through the crack under the rubber gasket. Finally the pressure in the two rooms equalized at 28 pounds.

Now able to enter the battery compartment, Alex and Soulis made a quick inspection. They found many cracked cell tops and all ventilation ducts disconnected, but a battery that still functioned despite the leakage of electrolyte. A later, more detailed inspection would disclose that 10 cells of the total of 126 were completely dry, and that many others were cracked and leaking.

The source of the strange odor was clear. Everything loose had been flung about. Glass bottles and containers in the chiefs' and officers' bunkrooms had been shattered or spilled. The contents of the wardroom pantry and its refrigerator were on the deck. The combined, indefinable odor of sweat, shaving lotion, hair tonic, shoe polish, medicine, vinegar, salad oil, coffee, food and sulphuric acid had meant to our men that the emergency we had so often drilled to handle—Chlorine Gas in the Forward Battery!—was at hand.

I was reassured by the more complete reports now being telephoned from forward, but our shipmates were still separated from us by a heavy steel door which the cumulative pressure of 28 pounds per square inch bound shut. Somehow we would have to equalize the pressure on both sides of the door. There was no provision for this in the design of the ship, no interconnecting pipe or valve we could open. The bulkhead flapper valves in the ventilation supply and exhaust lines were themselves held fast shut by the same pressure.

I discussed possibilities with Guy, Jack, and Chief Roberson, but it was Chalfant who came up with the solution. From its manifold in the control room, the trim line ran to the variable (trimming) tanks in the forward room. By sacrificing its normal use and removing valve bonnets, we could interconnect the two rooms and thus bleed the pressure into the control room. From there we could release it into the rest of the boat.

Jack had a good trim and said he could do without the trim line if we didn't move too many men back and forth.

As soon as we'd instructed Alex what to do, Emmett proceeded to unbolt the heavy, corresponding flange on his manifold. In the pump room below us, motor mac Warren Easterling monitored the trim pump and the maze of other vital auxiliaries. He had so many leaks from sea, distorted pipes, and misaligned shafts that he called for help. Chief Roberson jumped down the hatch for a quick look, then sent for Paul Eurich to give Easterling a hand.

As the valve bonnets were loosened, the foul-smelling air from forward began to whistle past the flanges. The volume of air we had to release through a four-inch pipe would make this a long, noisy process.

Meanwhile, in the heat and pressure to which they were exposed, our men in the forward room were working to exhaustion. The room had been particularly hard hit. The skids on which the 2,000-pound torpedoes were strapped had jumped one foot under the violent down-thrust given the boat. The deck plates were dislodged and men were thrown into the bilges. Sea valves had spun open, admitting much water. Tank tops and hull contours that had been level or smooth were wrinkled and deformed. Numerous bolts on manholes and flanges were sheared or bent. A steady stream of water came from the breach of the signal ejector, and water dripped from the forward escape trunk. It was flooded and useless. With all the excess weight we'd gained forward, no wonder we'd had trouble working our way up.

Gene Oakey, an intelligent, very likeable, powerful young fireman, was a member of the torpedo reload crew. When the enormous shock and deafening explosion hit, he was knocked into the bilge. He was convinced that he was going through the bottom of the boat. He would swear to me that as he grasped wildly for support he saw in the after corner of the room, in a brilliant white light, the figure of the Madonna with outstretched arms. To this day he remains convinced he was not hallucinating.

Chief Soulis and his gang reacted instantly to the chaos in their space. They closed valves, tightened hatch dogs, took up on loose bolts, cleared away loose gear, and searched for damage. While most struggled to control damage, other men took turns rotating our sonar heads by hand power. The sonar receivers and amplifiers still worked, but the training motors had been knocked out and their shafts bent. The slow, straining rotation of the sonar domes by hand gave a sketchy audio picture of activity on the surface. It seemed strangely quiet and ominous.

Were our hunters lying low, waiting for some false move on our part? We were certainly making enough noise with our squealing shafts, singing propellers, topside banging, and internal racket to announce our location and invite more barrages of depth charges.

But they didn't come. I reasoned that, desperately short of shipping as they were, the Japanese had instructed their ASW commanders not to leave a convoy unguarded, prey to another submarine of a wolf pack, while they worked over one that was in no position to harm their flock. Whatever the reason for their lack of persistence, the knockout punch was not delivered. We crawled away battered and bleeding, victims of only a long knockdown count. Every minute we were left unmolested, painfully climbing back to 300 feet, struggling to control and repair damage, our chances of escaping, of surviving to fight again another day, increased greatly.

The process of bleeding down the excess pressure from the two forward compartments into the rest of the ship continued. Finally the pressure that had been 52 pounds in the forward battery, then 28 in both forward compartments, became 12 when released throughout the entire ship. When the pressure on both sides of the control room's forward door was equalized, we opened it and sent men forward to assist those isolated and exhausted in the torpedo room.

A careful catalog of damage would be made later, but under the direction of their chief petty officers, all hands were inspecting, testing, or repairing the machinery and equipment they were responsible for. It was a subdued, continuous, all-hands evolution as we gradually eased toward the surface.

Cautiously we eased up on the dogs of the conning tower hatch. When no water appeared, we threw open the hatch and re-entered the conning tower. It was dry, but a shambles of distorted hull, misaligned or wrecked equipment, broken glass, shattered cork insulation. Both periscope hoist mechanisms were out of line, but we were able to raise the scopes. No. 2, the slender attack scope, was useless, its interior optics damaged. No. 1 was barely usable, internally dirty and foggy, but three hours after the last depth charges exploded, its objective lens pierced the surface. With Quartermaster Henderson leaning on the handles to help me push the damaged periscope around, a look around showed all clear.

It was 1645; the sun was still high, and it would be two and a half hours before it would be dark enough to surface. We needed all that time.

We desperately wanted our SJ radar, not only to alert us to enemy forces, but to help locate our own subs in the vicinity. Our radio transmitters and receivers were knocked out. If we could get the radar back in operation it would serve both as I.F.F.[13] and as a communication link to our sister subs. Ray Welley was crouched on the conning tower deck, his wiring diagrams, tools, and instruction books spread out around him. Ignoring the wreckage and confusion about him, he went through his meticulous check-off procedure, isolating faults. Never one to waste words, not naturally an optimist, he promised nothing except, "I'll do my best, captain." That was good enough for me.

★ ★ ★ ★ ★

The USS *Halibut* received a Presidential Unit Citation for the actions taken on her final war patrol. The damage sustained during the attack could not be repaired, and she was decommissioned in July 1945. Galantin would retire from the navy an admiral in 1970.

[13]Identification, Friend or Foe—an electronic device that received coded, high-frequency radiations, which identified friendly forces.

The Capture of *U-505*

RADM. DAN V. GALLERY

> Enemy Submarines are to be called U-Boats. The term Submarine is to be reserved for Allied under water vessels. U-Boats are those dastardly villains who sink our ships, while Submarines are those gallant and noble craft which sink theirs.
>
> —Winston Churchill

The war in the Atlantic was the longest and most crucial campaign of World War II. It was because of German U-boats that the United States had entered the First World War after the opening of unrestricted submarine warfare around the British Isles. In September 1939, Europe was again at war. The United States remained neutral, yet supplied much of the Allied needs for food and war materials. President Roosevelt carefully edged the United States closer to war when Congress modified the Neutrality Act in November 1939, allowing belligerent nations to purchase weapons on a "cash and carry" basis. American warships carried out "neutrality patrols" in the North Atlantic tracking movements of German ships.

In 1940, a 300-mile neutral zone extended from American shores. In March 1941, Congress passed the Lend-Lease Act, which empowered the president to provide economic and military support to countries whose defense was vital to the United States. As American warships began escorting allied convoys to and from Iceland with the signing of the Atlantic Charter that August, the U.S. Navy entered an undeclared war with the German Kriegsmarine. On October 31, 1941, while escorting convoy HX-156, the American destroyer USS *Reuben James* was torpedoed and sunk with the loss of 115 of 160 crewmen, including all of her officers.

Japan's attack on Pearl Harbor on December 7, 1941, brought Germany into the war against the United States four days later when Hitler declared war in support of Japan. The war in the Atlantic began in a devastating fashion in January when a small fleet of U-boats arrived off the east coast, sinking over 600 ships by the end of August in what German Admiral Donitz called Operation Drumbeat. What followed was a decisive counter attack by the U.S. Navy that included advancements in technology to help track and locate enemy submarines. Using the Allies Ultra code breaking and radio signals intelligence, losses of German submarines began to rise as convoy battles raged along the sea-lanes to Europe. Advancements in ship borne radar and radio intercept tracking, forward firing "hedge hog" depth charge launchers, and the introduction of long-range bomber aircraft armed with surface scanning radar helped turned the tide against German submarines. By May 1943, German wolfpacks had been withdrawn from the North Atlantic due to crippling losses. The hunters had become the hunted.

The heart of the Allied success was their code breaking and radio tracking intelligence that allowed convoys to avoid enemy submarines. Commander Kenneth A. Knowles, led the U.S. Navy's F-21 "Atlantic Section" Tracking Room. In conjunction with his British counterpart, Commander Rodger Winn of the Royal Navy, they were able to begin taking offensive action to hunt down and destroy the U-boats. Hunter-killer groups were formed to seek out and destroy submarines based on the intelligence provided by the Allied tracking rooms. This resulted in the first capture of an enemy man of warship by the U.S. Navy since the war of 1812 when the *U-505* was tracked and located near Cape Verde Islands in May 1944. A task group consisting of the escort carrier *Guadalcanal* and five destroyer escorts, was sent to intercept. Before sailing the group commander, Captain Daniel V. Gallery, requested information on the enemy submarines that would be necessary to attempt boarding a U-boat if it could be brought to the surface. He devised a plan of attack and his sailors rehearsed boarding exercises. In the following selection, Gallery describes the action of June 4, 1944, when his hunter-killer group finally tracked down *U-505* off French West Africa.

★ ★ ★ ★ ★

That morning at breakfast, my orderly brought me the ship's Plan of the Day. This is a routine mimeographed sheet, drawn up the day before, setting forth the operations we *think* we will conduct the next day and containing various official announcements of interest to all hands. I noted one item somewhat wryly. It was a list of names entitled, "Final Crew For Captured U-boat."

We had been revising our original boarding party almost daily for the past three weeks to get the best qualified people for a prize crew. We had plenty of eager volunteers for this duty who had never seen a submarine, except the *U-515*, but we wanted men who had some knowledge we might put to use, men who knew something about diesel engines, storage batteries, or had served in submarines. But now, right after this notice that we had finally made up our minds was posted on all bulletin boards, we were abandoning the hunt. There might be some caustic comments about this in the bunk room that night. "Ah well," I thought, "maybe we will have better luck on the trip back to Norfolk." But in view of what happened within a few hours, this plan of the day caused my crew to credit me with an infallible crystal ball from then on.

Incidentally, we did find one man on the ship who had served in a U.S. submarine and who immediately became our submarine "expert." He had been a yeoman on an S-boat, and could tell us anything we wanted to know about the paper work or filing system on a submarine!

Right after attending Mass that morning on the hangar deck, I was up on the bridge, seated in the skipper's chair overlooking the flight deck. It was a beautiful, clear day, with a light breeze and medium sea. We had only two fighter planes aloft maintaining a token patrol, because we figured our only possible target was out of range far astern of us. I was still fuming over the "fact" that we had let him get away from us.

Suddenly, at 1110, the squawk box on the bridge blared forth, "Frenchy to Bluejay—I have a possible sound contact!" (Frenchy was the U.S.S. *Chatelain* Commander Dudley Knox. I was Bluejay.)

This was nothing to get excited about yet. We had been getting possible sound contacts for the past month on whales, layers of cold water, and other natural phenomena in the sea. But you always treat a "possible" as the McCoy until you find out otherwise.

"Left full rudder," I said. "Engines ahead full speed." Then grabbing the mike of the "Talk Between Ships" radio, I broadcast, "Bluejay to Dagwood—take two DE's and assist Frenchy. I'll maneuver to keep clear."

This told the screen commander (Commander F. S. Hall) that it was his party from here on. An aircraft carrier right smack at the scene of a sound contact is like an old lady in the middle of a bar room brawl. She has no business there, can contribute little to the work at hand, and should get the hell out of there leaving elbow room for those who have a job to do. As we gained sea room to the west, I banged off a couple of turkeys to lend a hand if they were needed, but warned the pilots, "Use no big stuff if the sub surfaces—chase the crew overboard with 50 calibre fire."

As we veered off to the west, *Pillsbury* and *Jenks* raced over to help *Chatelain* which had picked up her contact so close aboard that she ran smack over it before she could make up her mind what it was. She now announced, "Contact evaluated as sub—am starting attack," and wheeling around under full rudder, she maneuvered into firing position again. She made a complete circle pinging away on her contact, straightened out and fired a salvo of twenty hedgehogs, which arched up in the air and splashed into the water like a huge handful of rocks one hundred yards ahead where the sonar was pinpointing the as yet unseen sub. All eyes locked on the spot and we ticked off each second after the splashes. When the count reached ten, we knew there would be no explosion and began to doubt that *Chatelain*'s contact was really a sub.

Pillsbury and *Jenks* were now prowling warily within hailing distance of the *Chatelain* and probing the contact with their sonar. If this *was* a sub and if *Chatelain* missed again, they would pounce on it and plaster it themselves.

Suddenly our two fighter planes circling over the spot like hawks, opened up with their machine guns, blasted a few bursts of 50 calibre into the water about one hundred yards from where the hedgehogs hit and yelled over the radio, "Sighted sub—destroyers head for spot where we are shooting!"

The *Chatelain* heeled over again under full rudder and headed for the bullet splashes where the pilots saw the dim shape of the completely submerged sub—trying to go deeper. At 1121, 11 minutes after the first sonar echo, *Chatelain* fired a spread of twelve six hundred pound depth charges all set to explode shallow.

From the carrier a few seconds later, we saw the ocean boil astern of the *Chatelain* and felt it quake as a dozen geysers spouted into the air from the underwater explosions. As the great white plumes were subsiding, Ensign Cadle in one of the circling "Wildcats" shouted, "You've struck oil Frenchy, sub is surfacing!"

At 1121[frac12] on June 4, 1944, one hundred fifty miles west of Cape Blanco, French West Africa, the *U-505* heaved itself up from the depths and broke surface seven hundred yards from the *Chatelain*—white water pouring off its rusty black sides. Our quarry was at bay.

When a cornered sub first breaks surface, you can never be sure whether he came up to abandon ship and scuttle or to fire a spread of torpedoes and try to take some of our ships to the bottom with him. "Pillsbury," *Jenks* and *Chatelain* cut loose with all the guns they had, and for about two minutes, 50 calibre slugs and 20 and 40 mm. explosive bullets hammered into the conning tower and tore up the ocean around it. Our fighter planes sent streams of hot metal ricochetting across her decks. Fortunately, all the three-inch stuff we fired missed, as did a torpedo fired by *Chatelain* when she thought the sub was swinging around to bring her own torpedo tubes to bear.

As the sub ran in a tight circle to the right, small crouching figures popped out of the conning tower and plunged overboard. While these men were leaping for their lives amid our hail of bullets, I broadcast to the Task Group, "I want to capture that bastard, if possible."

After about fifty or so men had gone overboard, Commander Hall, at 1126, ordered, "Cease firing"—and the ancient cry, "Away all boarding parties," boomed out over modern loudspeakers for the first time since 1815. The *Pillsbury*'s party, led by Lieutenant (jg) Albert David, had already scrambled into their motor whale boat and the boat plopped into the water and took off after the sub, which was still circling to the right at five or six knots. As that tiny whale boat took off after the circling black monster, I wouldn't have blamed those men in the boat for hoping that maybe they wouldn't catch her. The Nantucket sleighride they might get if they did overhaul her would top anything in Moby Dick! But cutting inside the circle the gallant band in the boat drew up alongside the runaway U-boat and leaped from the plunging whale boat to the heaving, slippery deck. As the first one hit the deck with the whaleboat's bow line, it looked for all the world like a cowboy roping a wild horse. I grabbed the TBS and broadcast, "Heigho Silver—ride'm cowboy!"—not a very salty exhortation but readily understood by all hands.

On deck was a dead man lying face down with his head alongside the open conning tower hatch, the only man killed on either side in this action. He was Hans Fisher, one of the plank owners of the *U-505* who had been aboard since commissioning. David and his boys now had a wild bull by the tail and couldn't let go. They were in charge of the topside of this submarine, but God only knew who was down below or what nefarious work they were doing. Somebody had to go below and find out.

No one in that boarding party had ever set foot on a submarine of any kind before—to say nothing of a runaway German sub. Anyone who ventured down that conning tower hatch might be greeted by a blast of gunfire from below! Even if abandoned, the ship might blow up or sink at any moment. That sewerlike opening in the bridge leading down under the seas looked like a one way street to Davy Jones's locker for everyone in the boarding party.

Lieutenant David, Arthur K. Knispel and Stanley E. Wdowiak, jammed all these ideas into unused corners of their minds and plunged down the hatch (David told me later that on the way down he found out exactly how Jonah felt on his way down into the belly of the whale).

They hit the floor plates at the bottom of the ladder ready to fight it out with anyone left aboard. But the enemy had fled for their lives and were now all in the water watching the death struggle of their stricken boat. My boys were all alone on board a runaway enemy ship with machinery humming all around them, surrounded by a bewildering array of pipes, valves, levers, and instruments with German labels on them. They felt the throbbing of the screws still driving the ship ahead and heard an ominous gurgle of water coming in somewhere nearby. This was a new version of the "Flying Dutchman," even more eerie than the old sailing ship with all sails drawing and not a soul on board.

But the submarine was all theirs. All theirs, that is, if they didn't touch the wrong valve or lever in the semi-darkness of the emergency lights and blow up or sink the boat. David yelled up to the boys on deck to tumble down and lend a hand while he, Knispel and Wdowiak ran forward for the radio room to get the code books. They smashed open a couple of lockers, found the books and immediately passed them up on deck, so we would have something to show for our efforts in case we still lost the boat.

Some readers, knowing that all naval code books have lead covers to make them sink, will ask why didn't the Germans throw these code books overboard? But why throw a code book overboard from a submarine which you are abandoning in over a thousand fathoms of water, thinking she will be on the bottom in another couple of minutes? *Nothing* had gone overboard except the crew and we now had in our possession one U-boat, complete with spare parts and all charts, codes and operating instructions from Admiral Doenitz. It would be the greatest intelligence windfall of the war, if David could keep her afloat.

It seemed doubtful that he could, because the sub was now in practically neutral buoyancy, was riding about ten degrees down by the stern and was settling deeper all the time.

One of the first to plunge down the hatch in response to David's call from below was Zenon B. Lukosius. As soon as Luke hit the floor plates he heard running water. Heading for the sound he ducked around behind the main periscope well and found a stream of water six inches in diameter gushing into the bilges from an open sea chest. By the grace of God the cover for this chest had not fallen down into the bilges where we wouldn't have been able to find it, but was lying on the floor plates. Luke grabbed it, slapped it back in place, set up on the butterfly nuts and checked the inrush of water. By this time the boat was threatening to up-end like the *U-515* any minute. If she had, she would have taken the whole boarding party with her. Luke got his little chore done just in the nick of time. Another minute might have been too late.

Luke told me later that while he was jamming that cover back in place, he was too busy to be scared. But when he tore his Mae West life jacket on a sharp projection in the conning tower, that really shook him—because he didn't know how to swim.

The sub was now so low in the water that the swells breaking across the nearly submerged U-boat were beginning to wash down the conning tower hatch. David ordered the man left on deck to close the hatch while he and his men continued their work below. The main electric motors were still running and driving the sub in a circle at about six knots.

Meantime, I had reversed course, got back to the scene of action and sent over a whale boat with Commander Earl Trosino and a group of our "experts" in it. They arrived aboard the sub literally "with a bang." A swell picked up their boat and deposited it bodily on the deck of the sub, breaking the boat's back and spilling the occupants on deck unceremoniously. This blow from above caused some concern even to David and his stout-hearted lads below, who at this time were engaged in ripping electric wires off things which they thought were demolition charges.

When Trosino and his crew scrambled up to the bridge, they couldn't get the conning tower hatch open. It was stuck as if fastened from the inside, a partial vacuum inside the boat holding it down so the boys couldn't budge it. The circling U-boat was constantly passing Germans in their rubber boats and Mae Wests, so Trosino's boys grabbed one, hauled him aboard and asked him how to open the hatch. The German showed them a little valve which let air into the pressure hull, equalizing the pressures inside and out and enabled them to get the hatch open.

"Thanks Bud," said Trosino, and shoved him overboard again.

Trosino then scrambled down the hatch and took over command from David in the same spot where Oberleutnant Meyer had assumed command after Cszhech ran out on him. No other U-boat ever had so many changes of command under fantastically improbable circumstances!

I cannot speak too highly of the job that Trosino did in keeping that sub afloat. He too had never been aboard a submarine before. But he had spent most of his life at sea as a chief engineer in Sun Oil tankers. He is the kind of an engineer who can walk into any marine plant, whether it is installed in the *Queen Mary* or a German U-boat, take a quick look around the engine room and be ready to put the blast on any dumb cluck who touches the wrong valve at the wrong time.

He spent the next couple of hours fighting to keep the sub's head above water. It was touch and go whether he would succeed or not and they had to keep that conning tower hatch closed. A lot of the time Trosino was down in the bilges under the floor plates tracing out pipelines. Had the sub taken a sudden lurch and up-ended herself, as it was quite probable she would—Earl wouldn't have had any chance whatever to get out. I recommended him for a Navy Cross when we got back to Norfolk. All he got was a Legion of Merit. He did this job in the wrong ocean! But that Legion of Merit is worth more than some of the Navy Crosses they were handing out in the Pacific at this time.

Trosino got the right valves closed and didn't open any of the hundreds of wrong ones. While he was doing this, Gunner Burr went through the boat looking for demolition charges. Our intelligence reports told us we would find fourteen five-pound TNT charges placed against the hull, several in each compartment. We had no information on their exact location or how the firing mechanism worked. Gunner Burr found and disarmed thirteen while Trosino was bilge diving. They found the fourteenth in Bermuda three weeks later! The Germans had been so sure when they abandoned ship that this sub was on the way to the bottom within minutes, that they hadn't set the firing devices! This information is worth only a raised eyebrow now, but when Burr, Trosino, David and their boys were aboard that first day, the knowledge that there was an unlocated demolition charge raised the hackles along all their spines.

Shortly after Trosino got aboard, the *Pillsbury* came alongside to pass salvage pumps over and take the sub in tow. Her skipper didn't allow for the fact that submarines have large flippers sticking out from the bow under water on both sides. The sub's port bow flipper cut a long underwater slice in the *Pillsbury*'s thin plates as she came alongside, flooding two main compartments and making it necessary for the DE to back off and fight to keep herself afloat.

Trosino reported that as long as the sub had headway, she rode about ten degrees down by the stern. But when he slowed her down, she lost the lift of her stern diving planes, settled to a steeper angle and submerged the conning tower hatch. The *Pillsbury* reported a DE couldn't do the towing job, so I headed over to take her in tow myself. As we drew near, Trosino pulled the switches and stopped the sub.

Working fast, we laid our stern practically alongside the nose of the sub, threw over a heaving line with a messenger line and an inch-and-a-quarter wire towline bent on. As the lads on the heaving, slippery deck of the sub were struggling to secure the towline, with four loaded bow torpedo tubes of the submarine practically nuzzling my after end, I said a fervent prayer. "Dear Lord, I've got a bunch of inquisitive lads nosing around below in that sub—please don't let any of them monkey with the firing switch!"

When the tow line was secured, we eased ahead, took a strain, and got underway again with the U.S. colors proudly flying over the swastika on a boat hook planted in a voice tube on the *U-505*'s bridge. As we gathered speed the stern came up and they could open the hatch again. I cracked off an urgent top secret dispatch to CinCLant and Cominch, "Request immediate assistance to tow captured submarine *U-505*." That dispatch really shook the staff duty officers back home. At first they didn't believe it and demanded a recheck on the decoding—but lost no time getting necessary action underway in the improbable event that it was true.

It soon became apparent that although we had our bronco roped, she wasn't broken to the halter yet. She sheared way out on our starboard quarter and rode out there listing to starboard and stretching the tow line as taut as a banjo string. Her rudder was jammed hard right. But I couldn't do anything about that now—I had four planes in the air that were getting low on gas.

So, hauling our non-cooperative prize behind us, we swung into the wind and landed our planes. With that sub dragging its heels back there I could only make about six knots so the pilots didn't have much wind across the deck for landing. But everyone seems to rise to the occasion at a time like this and they made it look easy—so easy, in fact, that I launched a couple more. Our speed and maneuverability was seriously restricted by the tow, making us a sitting target for any other sub that came along, so I figured we *had* to keep our planes aloft.

Meantime, the *Pillsbury* had been wallowing astern of us, struggling to stay afloat. She now flashed a message that two main compartments, including one engine room were flooded to the water line, but she hoped to get underway again in a couple of hours on one screw. I detached the "Pope" to stand by her, the other three DE's formed a screen around us and we dragged our prize off at six knots. Next day knowing that the *Pillsbury*'s skipper would be worried about a board of investigation when he got home I sent him the following signal: "This is for your files regarding damage done to your ship this cruise. This damage was done executing my orders and I assume responsibility." Commander Casselman of the *Pillsbury* still thinks I'm a nice guy.

Now I was in real trouble on fuel. One thing was for sure, I didn't have enough left to make Casablanca with that U-boat in tow. I was bashful about sending an official dispatch admitting I had made the unpardonable blunder of stretching my fuel supply too far. If I had stopped to think about it, I would have realized that at this point I could have admitted almost anything, including membership in the communist party, and no one would have given it a second thought. Finally, I swallowed my pride and sent a dispatch suggesting I head for the nearest friendly port, Dakar. CinCLant promptly vetoed this and said, "Further orders coming soon."

Sunset was approaching so we now battened the sub down for the night and brought our boarding parties back to the ship. Trosino informed me he thought she would stay afloat. He also reported that he thought the after torpedo room was flooded but couldn't be sure because the water tight door was dogged shut and he didn't want to open it for fear of flooding the boat. He also said there was what looked to him like a booby trap on the main dog. He had been so busy over there he hadn't noticed that the rudder was jammed but said he could get it amidships for me next morning.

Shortly after sunset the *Flaherty* announced she had a disappearing radar blip and *Chatelain* chimed in with a "Possible sound contact." The only thing I could do was pray and stick on a few extra turns to get the hell out of that area quicker. I must have put on too many because at midnight the tow line snapped and we spent the rest of the night circling the sub under a full moon and rousing our two-and-one-quarter-inch wire up on deck to put over in the morning.

During the night we got orders from CinCLant to take our prize to Bermuda. (Dakar was full of spies and if we had gone in there, news of the capture would have reached Germany before our anchor's splash subsided.) Admiral Ingersoll diverted the fleet tug *Abnaki* from an east bound convoy to take over the towing job and also the oiler *Kennebeck* to refuel the task group.

Next morning we got the big tow wire rigged and when Trosino came back from the sub he reported he had put the rudder amidships, using the electric controller in the conning tower. But as we gained headway again, it became apparent that the rudder hadn't moved at all. The electric rudder *indicator* in the conning tower had come back amidships, but the rudder was still hard right. We would have to get into the after torpedo room and hook up the hand steering gear to move it.

I had been itching to get aboard that craft myself and the booby trap on the torpedo room door gave me the excuse I wanted. I was an ordnance post-graduate and knew as much about fuses and circuitry as any one on board, so I had designated myself as officer-in-charge of booby traps in the capture plans. Trosino and I took along four helpers and went over to investigate.

As we drew alongside the heaving U-boat, riding with its bow out of water, the stern clear under, and seas breaking over the conning tower hatch, I wasn't so sure I had any business being there. After we had scrambled up on the bridge and I could see that we had to close the conning tower hatch behind us after we went down to keep the seas from coming in after us, I could think of a dozen more important things I should have been doing at this time . . . this trip wasn't really necessary! But the skipper can't back out when he has gone that far. Down the hatch we went, this being the first time *I* had ever been on a submarine. Trosino was a veteran by now, so he led the way aft. The battery was practically flat and the lights burned very dimly. The boat was way down by the stern and wallowing heavily. The air stunk. That trip through the control room, diesel engine room, and after motor room, seemed endless. As we went further and further aft, I suddenly remembered that one way of correcting trim in a sub was to have men move to the high end of the boat, and here were four of us trooping aft to the heavy end of a boat that was teetering on a knife edge! But we had passed the point of no return on this junket when we went down the hatch. You do your best to look calm, cool, and collected, and to tell yourself, "You can't live forever anyway."

At the after bulkhead of the motor room, Trosino put his flashlight on an open fuse box and said, "There she is Cap'n." There were a dozen exposed fuses in the box and many wires leading in and out. The cover of the box opened downward and was lying across the main dog of the watertight door to the torpedo room. To move the dog you had to close the cover of the fuse box. This had the makings of a booby trap and closing the cover *might* complete a circuit that would blow us all up.

But I didn't think so. This was an improbable place for a booby trap—the Germans obviously hadn't expected us to board their ship, so why set booby traps? It looked to me as if that cover had been jarred open accidentally after the door was dogged shut. A close scrutiny of the wiring and circuits revealed nothing suspicious.

You can't hem and haw over a question like this very long when you are twenty-five feet under water in a wallowing submarine, and one nice thing about fiddling with booby traps is that you find out right away, after you have sprung one, whether your calculations were right or not. I eased the cover shut and nothing happened.

Now for the door. Three of us braced our backs against it so we could get it closed again if water started squirting out, and we moved the main dog carefully till we had just cracked the hatch. No water. We swung the door open and scrambled aft to the hand steering gear. In half a minute we had it hooked up and moved the rudder back amidships. As we gave the wheel its final spin, I said, "Let's get the hell out of here." There being no objections—out we went, everybody trying his best to walk up that long slanted passageway nonchalantly. The salt fresh air smelt mighty sweet as we clambered out into the sunlight on the bridge.

While we were below, my lads on deck had been busy with a paint brush. In big red letters across the face of the conning tower they had emblazoned the name "Can Do Junior." My crew always called the "Guadalcanal" the "Can Do." Everyone in the task group has referred to the *U-505* ever since, as "Junior."

The sub towed properly now and we proceeded at eight knots for our rendezvous with the *Abnaki*. On June 9, 1944, we turned our tow over to *Abnaki* and refueled the task group from the *Kennebeck*. Then we formed a screen around the *Abnaki* and "Junior" and headed for Bermuda, 2,500 miles away.

Ever since we opened that booby trap, Earl Trosino had been after me to let him start the sub's diesels and bring her in triumphantly under her own power. I wish now I had let him do it. But at the time I was afraid that if we got fancy and tried to start the engines somebody might open the wrong valve and sink the boat. I hereby apologize to Trosino and his brave lads for underestimating them. I'm sure after all the other improbable things they did, they would have brought her in with colors flying.

Trosino did one thing that some of my submariner friends still seem skeptical about when I tell it. At the end of the second day, there wasn't enough juice left in the sub's battery to run a bilge pump. By this time Earl had figured out how to pump out the after ballast tanks and bring the boat up to an even keel, *if* he had power to run the pump. But I wouldn't let him start the diesels so he couldn't charge the battery in the usual way. (Note: Each of the sub's main shafts has a diesel engine on one end, the propellor on the other, and an electric armature in the middle. When you charge the battery, the diesels turn the propellers and the armature as well, which then acts as a generator and puts juice back in the battery. When cruising submerged you unclutch the diesels and your storage battery supplies juice to turn the armature and propel the ship.)

Trosino figured out how to set the switches so the armature would generate juice if something turned it. Then he disconnected the clutches joining the heavy diesel engines to the propeller shafts and asked me to tow at ten to twelve knots that night. I did, and dragging the sub through the water at this speed with the big diesels disconnected made the propellers windmill in the water. This made the main shafts turn and the armatures had no way of knowing that they weren't being turned in the usual manner. They obediently made juice and recharged the battery. Next morning Earl was able to run a ballast pump and bring the boat up to full surface trim.

By this time we had all prisoners from the sub aboard the "Guadalcanal"—fifty-nine out of a crew of sixty. Oberleutnant Harald Lange was badly wounded and I went down to see him in sick bay. Because of his wounds he hadn't seen our people get aboard his boat and he thought his order to scuttle her had been carried out. He wouldn't believe we had her in tow until I sent over to the sub and got a picture of his family off his cabin desk. This convinced him, and he said over and over again, "I will be punished for this." I tried to cheer him up by pointing out that Germany was losing the war and that a new regime would replace the Nazis. He kept shaking his head and saying, "No matter what happens, I will be punished."

Maybe he was right. I have had some letters from Lange since the war, and reading between the lines I can see that he may be blamed for things which were not his fault. So far as I know, no legal action has been taken against him by the German government, but perhaps other former U-boat skippers exclude him from organizations to which he should be welcome. If so, this is a grave injustice, in my opinion.

Lange was the victim of circumstances. He did exactly what several hundred other U-boat skippers did when they thought the end was at hand and surfaced to give their crew a last chance to survive the war before scuttling their boats. Perhaps a dozen or more of these boats could have been captured if we had been prepared to send off boarding parties. I still think I could have towed the *U-515* home if I had exercised proper foresight before she surfaced. Kretschmer, the greatest ace of them all, was captured with most of his crew, and his U-boat lay helpless on the surface with two British destroyers close aboard for much longer than it took us to get aboard the *U-505*.

I am told that various false stories have circulated in Germany that the *U-505* surrendered. She did not surrender any more than several hundred other German subs that did the same thing surrendered. If there is any discrimination against her crew in Germany now, it is wrong. In my opinion, the man responsible for her capture was Czech. That crew should have been broken up and spread around among a dozen U-boats as soon as she came in from the cruise on which Czech ratted on his men by committing suicide. Lange inherited an impossible situation. He and his men, like most other U-boat sailors, were conscientious men who did their duty, were worthy opponents who almost beat us in a fair fight, and should be treated as such now.

On June 19, 1944, we escorted the *Abnaki* and *U-505* into Bermuda with the traditional broom hoisted at our main truck. A delegation of experts from Washington swarmed aboard the sub and we turned our fifty-nine prisoners over to the Commandant of the Naval Operating Base, Bermuda. They were imprisoned there in a special camp all by themselves till the war was over, when they were returned to Germany.

Some people, waxing enthusiastic about this capture, say that the ability to read German naval codes from then on shortened the war by several months. I doubt this. The invasion of Normandy began two days after we got the *U-505*, and once the U.S. Army got ashore in France, the duration of the war was in their hands, so long as the Navy kept them and the Air Force supplied with the stuff they needed. The Navy could still prolong or even lose the war by losing control of the seas, but it couldn't do much to speed up the tempo of operations ashore. The capture did save seamen's lives by providing complete technical data on German subs and new developments, such as the acoustic torpedo.

The big thing we got out of it was the ability to read the German naval codes. We got the current code books, the cipher machine, and hundreds of dispatches with the code version on one side and German translation on the other. Like all military services, the German Navy changed their code about every two weeks, so enemy cryptographers wouldn't be constantly working on the same system. But the key to the routine changes was in the code books. We read the operational traffic between U-boat headquarters and the submarines at sea for the rest of the war. Reception committees which we were able to arrange as a result of this eavesdropping may have had something to do with the sinking of nearly three hundred U-boats in the next eleven months.

This brings me to what I think is the most remarkable part of this whole improbable episode. It was very important to prevent knowledge of this capture from reaching Germany. If it had, the Germans would have heaved all the old code books overboard, changed their whole system, and issued brand new ones, which are always kept ready for issue in just such an emergency. While towing the sub to Bermuda we carefully explained this to all hands in the task group and directed them to tell *no one,* but no one, what had happened on this cruise.

We had about three thousand young lads in that task group, all of whom had seen the whole thing happen and who came back from that cruise just bursting with the best story of their lives. But they knew they shouldn't tell it. I am very proud indeed of the fact that the Germans never found out we had this U-boat till the war was over. The boys *did* keep their mouths shut.

I think this speaks very highly indeed for the devotion to duty and sense of responsibility of the average young American wearing bell-bottom trousers. When I read the headlines these days about atomic secrets leaking from high level sources and important government officials popping off with top secret stuff just to get in the headlines, I feel even prouder of my lads in Task Group 22.3. As long as we continue to raise kids like those, the country will survive despite the bureaucrats and politicians.

While lecturing the boys on the importance of keeping the capture secret, I also laid down the law on souvenirs. I pointed out that there's no use having a souvenir unless you can show it around and brag about it and that regulations required all captured equipment to be sent to Office of Naval Intelligence in Washington. "So," I said, "If anyone has picked up a souvenir, turn it in to the exec's office tomorrow and no questions will be asked. But we will lower the boom on anyone found with souvenirs after tomorrow."

Next day the Exec's Office was inundated with the damnedest collection of stuff you've ever seen—Lugers, flashlights, cameras, officers' caps, German cigarettes, etc., etc. It was incredible that while struggling to keep a sinking U-boat afloat, the men whose lives were in danger could find time to accumulate all that junk.

I knew that the boys would all rather have turned in their right arms than these souvenirs. So, in accordance with the regulations, we tagged the souvenirs with the names of the "owners" and told the boys that (according to the book) at the end of the war the Office of Naval Intelligence would return them. Most of us, including me, were naive enough to believe this! But nobody ever saw their souvenirs again. After peace broke out the Washington bureaucrats absconded with them.

Checking back on this capture now, it seems that the *U-505* and my task group simply had a rendezvous set up for us in the book of destiny and that there was no avoiding it. The *U-505* was never where I thought she was until the moment she popped up almost under foot. I was searching the wrong areas all the time, except that last night when my planes must have missed her by inches once, and by seconds another time.

Plotting my own track that night and the courses flown by my planes against the track given by the *U-505*'s war diary, it is apparent that we should have spotted him about ten o'clock. One of my planes passed within six miles of him when he was surfaced recharging his battery. My radar operator should have picked up a faint blip on his scope but he didn't. By the same token, the sub's Naxos operator should have picked up our plane's radar, but *he* didn't, although apparently he had picked up every other airplane within miles of him for the past two weeks. Two hours later, and only five minutes after the sub finished recharging and submerged, another one of my planes passed smack over the spot where he had just gone down.

I suppose I can say that at any rate, I was right in my decision to turn back and search that area again. But I was right *for the wrong reason.* I had turned back because I was certain we had made contact with him the night before. Actually, he had not been in our search area at any time the night before, and our contacts had been phonies.

So it is apparent now that this whole business hinged on the fallible workings of two men's minds—mine and Lange's. Working on false premises, both of us made decisions which combined to bring out an extremely improbable result. Had either of us decided to do things just a little bit differently from what we did, the result would not have come about.

What causes such things as this to happen? I don't know of any way to explain it except to say, "Maybe our daily morning prayer had something to do with it."

It's no good to say it was all a matter of chance. If it had been, I should have made at least one "correct" decision instead of the series of wrong ones I did make, and one correct decision would have upset the apple cart completely.

Naturally the advance planning that we did on this thing belongs on the credit side of the ledger. So also does the venture into night flying, although in the final analysis the only real affect it had on this operation was to hold us in the area for one more night. Had we found the *U-505* at night, there would have been no possibility of capture—that boarding idea was improbable enough in broad daylight, it was impossible at night.

This whole operation is an example of the fact that a military commander controls events only up to a certain point. He can anticipate certain things, perhaps even set the stage for them to happen, and can be ready to cash in on them if they do happen. But whether they will happen or not depends on many things over which he has no control. One is what goes on in the other commander's mind and another is what goes on in his own. Both of these mental processes are subject to influence from above, or by Divine sufferance, from below. I am not trying to say that we have no control over our destiny on this earth. But I do say that in many things we control it only up to a certain point. Beyond that point nebulous things which occur inside men's brains decide the issue. In this particular instance, I speak from firsthand experience when I say the stuff that ran through my mind for a week or so was all wrong, but the final result was very good. . . .

The only moral I can see to all this is to plan your operations carefully, get the best advice you can from experts, fix it so that if certain things happen, you will not be caught flat-footed, and then, rely on the motto we have stamped on all our pennies—"In God We Trust."

★ ★ ★ ★ ★

Lieutenant Albert Leroy David would receive the Medal of Honor for leading the boarding party that captured *U-505*. The real treasure recovered from *U-505* that could not be disclosed at the time of Gallery's writing, were two M4 Enigmas, and examples of a new secret German acoustic homing torpedo. Captain Gallery would retire from the Navy a rear admiral. *U-505* was saved from becoming a target ship after the war by the Gallery's brother, Father John Gallery, who inspired the people of Chicago to move *U-505* to the Museum of Science and Industry where it remains today, the only Type IX-C boat still in existence.

Kamikazes, from *The Battle of Okinawa*

GEORGE FEIFER

To blossom today, then scatter;
Life is so like a delicate flower.
How can one expect the fragrance to last forever?
—Admiral Takajiro Onishi, father of the kamikazes

Living, to be overwhelmed with the immeasurable blessings of Imperial goodness. Dead, to become one of the country's Guarding Deities and as such to receive unique honors in the temple.
—A choice put to Japanese pilots

When I fly the skies
What a splendid place to be buried
The top of a cloud would be.
—A kamikaze volunteer before setting out on his mission

The Chinese emperor Kublai Khan sent an invasion fleet to seize the islands of Japan in 1281. Without warning, a typhoon arose and destroyed most of the ships as they approached shore, forcing the others to turn back. The Japanese considered their salvation an act of the gods and called the event Kamikaze, which translates "divine wind." In 1944 an American fleet was fighting its way toward Japan. Having suffered major defeats as the Japanese retreated across the Pacific, their situation grew desperate. Japan had never been invaded or even defeated in a war. The home islands were sacred in Japanese eyes, as was their emperor whom they considered a living god. No sacrifice would be too great to ensure the safety of their homeland.

Self-sacrifice was already a key virtue of Japanese culture. Ritualistic suicide was the only honorable way for a defeated warrior to die. Surrender to the Japanese soldier was unthinkable. The ancient Japanese code of the warrior, Bushido, taught the maxim of death before dishonor and loyalty above all. As the Allies fought their way across the Pacific they encountered this fanatical Japanese resistance. By 1944, however, most of the Japanese Navy had been destroyed, her armies defeated or bypassed on Pacific islands. In the air, Japan's finest pilots who began the war were dead or wounded, and their remaining aircraft heavily outnumbered and outclassed by new American fighters. In June the United States had taken Saipan putting the Japanese home islands in range of the new B-29 Superfortress heavy bomber. The way was being paved for an eventual invasion of Japan itself. Japan needed a new miracle to save itself.

Vice Admiral Takijiro Onishi, of the Japanese Navy's First Air Fleet would provide that miracle. Based in Manila, his mission was to assist Japanese warships to stop any invasion of the Philippines. With only a handful of aircraft under his command, Onishi organized the first "Special Attack Corps" of pilots who would seek out enemy ships and fly their bomb laden aircraft directly into them. The Kamikaze was reborn in an all out effort to save Japan. They would become the most feared, and one of the most effective weapons of the Pacific war. Author George Feifer illustrates the history of the Japanese Kamikazes from his book *The Battle for Okinawa*.

★ ★ ★ ★ ★

In the end, the primary objective of *Yamato*'s last mission was to scatter the defenses against an air assault on the American invasion fleet. The great battleship had been chosen both as the best decoy for luring away the greatest number of enemy interceptors and as the stoutest target for withstanding their attacks for the longest possible time—giving Japanese planes a turn against the American fleet. Some nine hundred aircraft took part in that offensive of April 6 and 7.

Launched from a ring of airfields on the mainland, Formosa, and occupied Shanghai, the effort was mounted in weak coordination—the best the Japanese High Command could manage—with Operation Heaven Number One. Wave upon wave of Japanese planes sank three destroyers, two ammunition ships, one LST, and one minesweeper, as well as damaging a light carrier, eleven destroyers, two destroyer escorts, and eight other craft off and near Okinawa. On the April 7 of *Yamato*'s sinking, more strikes hit a battleship, carrier, destroyer, destroyer escort, and one other vessel.

That use of Japanese aircraft defied logical explanation. While American dive-bombers were having their way with the Imperial Navy's greatest prize, her appeals for air cover went unanswered. A mere two hundred miles away, however, the nine hundred Japanese planes were swarming over the very ships that had launched the *Yamato*-hunting Hellcats, Helldivers, and Avengers. Just after the veteran carrier *Hancock*'s first such launch, a Zero slipped through her screen of battleships, cruisers, and destroyers in one Task Force 58 battle group and headed straight for her starboard bow. It dropped a bomb on her flight deck, then put a twenty-foot hole there by crashing farther aft. Seventy-two men were killed and eighty-two wounded by explosions that set fire to her hangar deck and twenty parked planes.

That Zero was suicidal, like more than a third of the planes dispatched on April 6 and 7 and roughly the same proportion throughout the Okinawan campaign. Altogether, the Japanese would mount just under nine hundred air raids on the island and the American fleet, by far the war's greatest effort. Compared to five thousand to six thousand sorties by conventional dive-bombers and torpedo planes—that is, by pilots who didn't intend to crash—nineteen hundred were flown by kamikazes. (That's the American tally; official Japanese records document the loss of 2,944 kamikaze planes.) It was those "special" missions that prompted the greatest American consternation and fear, and not only because they caused some 80 percent of the damage to the fleet. Kamikazes greatly increased tension—even from the extreme pitch of ordinary air attacks—because every sailor on every ship was convinced they were aiming for him. A British historian saw the kamikazes reintroducing an element of personal threat that "had been absent from naval warfare since the days of boarding and hand-to-hand fighting."

The April 6 attack was the first massive one on American ships at Okinawa, but individual Japanese planes and small groups had been dogging them even before L-day. Kamikazes crashed a battleship, two destroyers, and a destroyer-minesweeper on March 27, when the fleet was bombarding the island and taking Kerama Retto, the cluster of little islands the Americans had wisely seized before L-day. A landing craft was hit the next day. On March 31, carrier-based American fighters "splashed" two planes attacking the heavy cruiser *Indianapolis*—flagship of Admiral Spruance, commander of the 5th Fleet—and antiaircraft fire from the nearby *New*

Mexico downed a third. But a fourth managed to scrape a wing against the cruiser before careening into the sea. Its bomb crashed through several decks on the port side and exploded in an oil bunker, killing nine men and wounding twenty.

Half of the more than seven hundred planes that attacked the fleet on L-day itself were kamikazes. Before dawn that morning, two explosions in quick succession awoke the Marines still fitfully sleeping below decks on *Hinsdale,* flagship of a troop transport division. Frightened passengers frantically dressed in pitch darkness, the ship having lost electrical power immediately. One Marine managed to control his trembling hand enough to light a cigarette on the third try. After ten infinitely long minutes, an order was shouted down the hatches for all hands to proceed to their abandon-ship stations.

The predawn grayness had hidden the plane from straining look-outs and its low altitude over the water had allowed it to evade radar, so no one aboard the ship, or the three dozen others in her squadron, saw the attacker visually or electronically until the last moment. The plane itself was also unusual. Most that crashed intentionally were obsolete models that had been stripped of usable instruments, loaded with explosives, and fueled for a one-way trip. The pilot of this first-line Tony fighter may have decided on his own not to return from his mission.

But in other respects, *Hinsdale*'s trial was much like that of scores of ships sunk or severely damaged in that unfathomable way. The Tony crashed into her port side amidships at the waterline. Flames shot high enough to severely burn men on the bridge some fifty feet above. More of the sixteen killed and thirty-nine wounded were in the engine room, into which the plane telescoped. The living passengers, "strung tight as violin strings," abandoned ship.

Twenty-four sailors and Marines on an LST participating in the fake landing in the far south joined the L-day dead. The regular Japanese submarine force was too weakened to pose much threat; the surface fleet could muster only enough strength for the last effort by *Yamato* and her screen; the scattered Okinawan shelters of most suicide submarines and suicide boats would be captured before their craft could get under way. It was left to the kamikaze pilots to do almost all the sinking and killing, and they would keep at it throughout the campaign; the Navy's ordeal was only beginning.

That twenty-two ships were hit and eleven sunk in the attack of April 6–7 was particularly dismaying to Americans because carrier strikes on mainland airfields on the morning of the sixth were thought to have destroyed virtually all Japanese planes able to reach the fleet from there. That would not be the campaign's last expression of American optimism stiffened with poor intelligence of Japanese camouflage, dispersal, and digging—in this case, of vast systems of underground hangars, tunnels, and barracks being completed at many mainland installations.

Crews of American ships also tried to convince themselves that the Japanese had "shot their bolt" with their kamikaze attacks; only isolated bases could still get a few craft into the air. "Christ, we must have knocked out every plane they had left on those home islands!" a lieutenant in a carrier's recreation room assured fellow players in a pinochle game. But late the same afternoon, the radar screen of the destroyer *Leutze* revealed dozens of bogeys some ninety miles west and closing at two hundred knots, their pilots pleased to be attacking out of twilight's blinding setting sun.

The first lookouts spotted the formation thirteen minutes later. Pandemonium reigned on and above *Leutze* and *Newcomb,* a sister destroyer that joined the antiaircraft firing with her every gun but couldn't stop one plane from crashing into her aft stack and another from hitting her amidships with a large torpedo or bomb that demolished her vital parts. As *Newcomb*'s stores of ammunition and petroleum products fed her fierce blaze, a third plane hit her forward stack, spraying enough additional aviation fuel over decks and sailors to send flames hundreds of feet into the air. Gallantly going to her aid, *Leutze* was crashed by a fourth plane among the dozens that were shot down or missed on their own.

The two destroyers' fire-control crews fought the damage in searing heat. Sailors struggled to shore up bulkheads, secure steam lines, extinguish fires in magazines. Some were burned to death trying to fight flames and reach trapped fellow crew members, while *Newcomb*'s surgeon operated through the night in her wardroom, surrounded by destruction and carnage. Forty-seven were killed or missing, fifty-eight wounded—but both scorched wrecks were eventually towed to Kerama Retto and saved, whereas even more intense attacks sank *Bush,* with a loss of thirty-five killed and missing and twenty-one wounded.

No fewer than forty to fifty planes attacked *Bush* that afternoon. One crashed between her stacks, allowing its bomb to explode in an engine room; another hit her port side, starting a fierce fire that killed all the wounded who'd been taken to the wardroom. Casualties on *Calhoun,* a fourth destroyer that had to be abandoned and eventually sunk by American guns, were seven of twenty-six officers killed and eighty-seven of 307 men. *Calhoun* had fought off eleven raids before dawn that morning, five in the space of fifteen minutes. Two previous kamikaze crashes that afternoon damaged her so severely that the last one, by a pilot who persisted although his plane was ablaze, made little difference. Of the nine more destroyers hit that day, one was sunk, two had to be scrapped, and three went unrepaired until after the war.

The Japanese goal was to cut off American supplies and naval support so their Army could better deal with the enemy ashore. That was wishful thinking: Even with sufficient supplies of planes and aviation fuel, the hot kamikazes—Divine Wind—wouldn't have melted Operation Iceberg, as the Americans had code-named the Okinawan invasion. But they did cause the American Navy by far its greatest terror and torment of the war. Nothing of the kind had ever been mounted by one force or endured by another.

> The feeling of utter helplessness that wraps around you when you are aboard a ship crippled by enemy action [hit us] . . . on Easter morning. . . . We had been warned to be ready for such a possibility but when it happened, it was startling, unbelievable and more than a little fearsome.
>
> —Herbert Shultz, a combat correspondent

The knowledge that pilots were intent on killing themselves in order to kill others was terrifying in itself. The act was "incomprehensible" and "inhuman" to many American sailors, who wondered whether the Japanese who were resolved to blow themselves to bits were religious fanatics or simply drunk or drugged. To the fighting men, nothing did more to confirm their enemy's singularly sinister nature. "The whole idea is eerie," one lieutenant told another on the carrier *Belleau Wood*. "I just can't figure out how anybody can just commit suicide without feeling anything. It's against human nature."

"It doesn't matter to those Nips," his fellow officer answered. "They don't think the same way we do." An American admiral who observed kamikazes plunging at Okinawa waxed more theoretical: "I doubt if there is anyone who can depict with complete clarity our mixed emotions as we watched a man about to die in order that he might destroy us in the process. There was a hypnotic fascination to a sight so alien to our Western philosophy."

In fact, the kamikaze phenomenon wasn't *quite* so alien to Western practice, if not philosophy. Occasional German pilots had used suicide attacks against Allied planes, although their superiors never organized a special force of them. American and British leaders, Winston Churchill and Douglas MacArthur among them, ordered some of their commanding officers never to surrender in certain circumstances. In addition, Britain as well as Italy and Germany had very small units manning "special attack" weapons, chiefly small boats and planes that made some nearly suicidal missions. American pilots of obsolete torpedo planes in the Battle of Midway knew they'd probably be killed or gravely wounded attacking the Japanese carriers, and reprieves were few in some instances: Eight of eight from the carrier *Hornet* were downed, ten of fourteen from *Enterprise,* and ten of twelve from *Yorktown.* The brave squadrons that lost every one of their planes came close to being kamikazes in some ways, and the crews knew the odds when they took off.

Every nation cherishes its tales of wounded heroes who know they'll probably die charging the enemy but remain determined to do their utmost to stop him. "Give me liberty or give me death" might be seen as the philosophical and emotional underpinning of the American Navy's experiments with near-suicidal submersibles during the War of Independence and the Confederate Navy's similar interest during the Civil War. And a kind of suicidal desperation prompted Pickett's Charge. The Alamo, so elevated in the folklore celebrating American bravery, had something in common with Japanese resolution. Perhaps because everything Japanese seemed sinister or demented, it occurred to few Americans—even those who'd loved *They Died with Their Boots On,* an extremely popular Hollywood tale on the eve of Pearl Harbor—that their own myths sanctified warriors' sacrificial deaths. Many more Americans might have been eager to die for honor and country, or at least applaud those who did, if their nation had ever faced the shock of total national defeat now confronting the Japanese. For the kamikaze movement can't be understood without taking into account Japan's unwillingness to accept the enormity of the prospect looming before her. In a similar situation, self-sacrificing American pilots might have been acclaimed as heroes.

> The special attack operations were truly impossible to bear in terms of our natural human feelings but Japan having been put in an impossible position, those unreasonable measures were all that was left to us.
>
> —Emperor Hirohito, a year after the end of the war

The kamikaze institution was founded—as much as any single event can qualify for that distinction in a country with a long tradition of honorable self-sacrifice—six months earlier, when a rear admiral commanding an air flotilla in the Philippines deliberately crashed a dive-bomber on an American carrier. That fine officer was known for his Western attitudes—understandably so, because he'd begun his naval training with the Royal Navy after an English public school education. However, he despaired over the Imperial Navy's defeats and the decimation of his squadrons. His pilots, replacements for a great corps of aces shot down or lost in sunken Japanese carriers, were so ill trained that a third of them flying out from Japan never reached the Philippines.

The admiral believed two dozen lucky ones could stem the entire American advance by sinking its big carriers—not an absurd idea, especially after the whole Japanese advance had been stopped largely by the loss of the Imperial Navy's four carriers at Midway. It would be simplistic to call him the usual "Japanese fanatic" for his own dive onto USS *Franklin* in October 1944. In any case, he posthumously won a gifted ally. Although his crash, a deliberate violation of orders, horrified most Japanese staff officers almost as much as it did *Franklin*'s crew, Takajiro Onishi, a high-ranking admiral who arrived from Tokyo days later to assume command of all naval aircraft in the Philippines, was moved. Onishi had earlier encouraged pilots to perform just such crashes as a last resort. Now he, who had the bluntness of warriors utterly dedicated to purpose and corresponding contempt for compromising politicians, launched a campaign to make them a regular practice.[14]

Onishi's intention shocked much of the naval brass, who much more approved of the man he had relieved in Manila, a skilled professional who would fight to the death in suitable equipment but saw no value in needlessly sacrificing his precious pilots. "When you can show me how to bring the men back from special attacks, I'll listen," Onishi's more prudent predecessor had told his raised-in-England colleague when he arrived to replace him. But the resourceful, fearless Onishi quickly organized a small volunteer force resolved to put the major enemy carriers out of action for a week. That was the first organized use of suicide missions in the Pacific War, although there had been isolated attacks before, some by damaged planes, a few premeditated. Even though Onishi's initial mission hit two carriers, and later ones also achieved some striking successes, the Imperial High Command did not approve the special attack philosophy until the enemy fleet was massing for L-day—partly because air attacks had sunk only one ship and damaged a dozen-odd others off Iwo Jima. But now Onishi had the satisfaction of seeing his once highly controversial approach incorporated into the defense plan, then elevated to an essential

[14]Although *kamikaze* acquired quick notoriety in the West, the proper name was *shimpu*, a different reading of the same characters with a more dignified, solemn ring, more befitting the pilots' heroic undertaking. Like *harakiri, kamikaze* later became vulgar in Japan: a moniker for assorted daredevils, from taxi drivers to breakneck skiers, as Ivan Morris pointed out.

plank, as the highest Army as well as Navy officers convinced themselves that this last resort would change the course of the war.

In that view, what happened on Okinawa itself wouldn't much matter. In fact, many in the High Command now saw Ushijima's task as no more than delaying the enemy so that as many enemy warships and supply vessels as possible could be finished offshore. Ivan Morris, perhaps the most careful student of Japanese attitudes toward sacrifice, would call the kamikaze operations "the principal manifestation of the country's will to resist . . . during Japan's death throes." The Battle of Okinawa, Morris would write, "more and more assumed the character of a culminating suicidal explosion."

Onishi, who was given overall charge of mass kamikaze attacks against the fleet at Okinawa, represented certain profoundly Japanese qualities—which, however, included some that all peoples would be proud of. It was no accident that the dynamic maverick, who despised talk as a substitute for action, was Japan's leading naval aviator and chosen collaborator of the best naval brains—or that he'd helped Admiral Yamamoto, the "Japanese Nelson," plan his Pearl Harbor attack. The model of personal courage was an impressive combination of traditional selfless virtues and mastery of technological advances. Many of his most idealistic junior officers adored him.

Most of the "treasures of the nation," as he called the kamikaze pilots, would have been any nation's treasures. A majority were in their early twenties—university students until their recent call-up. More had studied the humanities than the natural sciences or engineering. Still gripped by poetry, they filled their last thoughts with symbols of beauty. One volunteer saw his commitment in the images of an eighteenth-century nationalist writer's verse: "What is the spirit of Yamato's ancient land? / It is like wild cherry blossoms, / Radiant in the rising sun." Just as those blossoms scattered without regret after dispersing their short-lived radiance, the young hero explained, "so must we be prepared to die for Yamato without regret."

As Morris pointed out, most kamikaze pilots, far from the "fierce, superstitious, jingoistic fanatics" foreigners usually imagined, were in the upper ranks of university students in intelligence, sensitivity, and culture, including Western culture. As the Okinawan garrison was being bludgeoned toward its inevitable defeat, driven superiors pressed a small but growing number of young pilots and trainees to join "volunteer" suicide units. Nevertheless, superior officers who actually selected pilots for the flights were likely to have more genuine volunteers than they could accommodate.

Straight to the end of the war, many units had twice as many eager candidates as planes. Most were driven less by a desire to kill than by their wish to perform a lofty deed that would win admiration at their bases and a place among the country's heroes at the Yasukuni Shrine. Most of all, they wanted to sacrifice themselves for a cause more noble than personal advancement. Part of that cause was protecting their families and sacred Japan from foreign intrusion, especially since most truly believed their cherished nation and people would be forever destroyed unless they gave their utmost, including the utmost self-denial. On top of the great debt almost all Japanese youth felt to their parents for having conceived and raised them, many of the young heroes' final poems, diary entries, and letters to their families so abounded in love and desire for virtue—if also in ignorance of their beloved country's Asian and Pacific atrocities—as to seem nearer the limit of human goodness than evil.

Dearest Parents,

Words cannot express my gratitude to you. It is my hope that this last act of striking a blow at the enemy will serve to repay in small measure the wonderful things you have done for me. . . . I shall be satisfied if my final effort serves as recompense for the heritage bequeathed by our ancestors. . . .

My dear parents . . . I shall be leaving this earth [tomorrow morning] forever. Your immense love for me fills my entire being down to my last hair. And that is what makes this so hard to accept: the idea that with the disappearance of my body, this tenderness will also vanish. But I am impelled by my duty. I sincerely beg you to forgive me for not having been able to fulfill all my family obligations. . . .

My greatest regret in this life is the failure to call you "chichiue" [revered father]. I regret not having given any demonstration of the true respect which I have always had for you. During my final plunge, although you will not hear it, you may be sure I will be saying "chichiue" to you and thinking of all you've done for me.

The world in which I lived was too full of discord. As a community of rational human beings, it should have been better composed. Lacking a single great conductor, everyone let loose with his own sound, creating dissonance where there should have been melody and harmony.

We're going to die. . . . I will fight for my country or for my personal honor, but never for the Navy, which I hate! . . . It is dominated exclusively by a clique of Naval Academy officers. [Another pilot called the Navy a "beast!" but willingly died for his honor and country.]

This is my last day. The destiny of our homeland hinges on the decisive battle in the seas to the south, where I shall fall like a blossom from a radiant cherry tree. . . . I am grateful from the depths of my heart to the parents who

> reared me with their constant prayers and tender love. And I am grateful as well to my squadron leader and superior officers, who have looked after me as if I were their own son and given me such careful training.
>
> The Japanese way of life is indeed beautiful and I'm proud of it, as I'm proud of Japanese history and mythology, which reflect the purity of our ancestors. . . . And the living embodiment of all wonderful things from our past is the Imperial Family, which is also the crystallization of the splendor and beauty of Japan and its people. It is an honor to be able to give my life in defense of these beautiful and lofty things.

Letter after letter expressed gratitude for the chance to repay parents and the nation. Nor did the volunteers stop valuing their own lives during their final days. Air raids on their bases, where some lived in miserable conditions despite their honored status, multiplied throughout the Okinawan campaign, terrifying even some of the pilots scheduled to die on the morrow. Yet many were indeed radiant that following morning when they made their sacrifice.

Of course there were exceptions. Not all the thousands of kamikaze pilots were the studious, considerate, idealistic souls their parents would remember as their best, kindest sons. Scores spent their final hours drunk on sake rather than on lofty thoughts. Others made the gesture less from heroism than calculation: Since everyone was going to die in the war anyway, better to die a pilot, with its rewards—perhaps including a warship to one's credit. Amid the laughter and song, some wept with fear, regret, or frustration for having to sacrifice themselves to a hopeless cause when they'd only begun to live. At least one strafed his command post before flying off toward the enemy fleet. A larger number masked their resentment—but they were a small minority. Most young men experienced joy and elation when chosen for the honor—and impatience, bitterness, or self-hatred when rejected. Some burst into tears and cried unashamedly when not permitted to join comrades on their final missions. Onishi promised the Divine Wind would be ushered in by the "purity" of the youth he loved, and there it was, in the hearts of highly educated, lovingly raised young men, trembling with desire to attain the highest patriotic virtue.

But if most kamikaze pilots were far from the moronic or drugged robots imagined by the blue jackets on the strained targeted ships—in fact, distinctly better educated and more refined than almost all the Americans who degraded them—the stark ignorance of the culture from which the movement grew doesn't invalidate the sailors' and infantrymen's gut reaction that their enemy was in some way "nuts." A former kamikaze pilot—the sole survivor of his group of twenty-one officers—argued in 1989 that "this so-called suicide mentality" was hardly specific to the Japanese. "The spirit of self-sacrifice exists in all countries among all peoples, particularly among the young who are innocent and free of cynicism when they are in a wartime, life-or-death situation."

Yes, in a way—as argued too several pages earlier. Still, the larger truth is that the kamikaze phenomenon as practiced in 1945 could not have taken place elsewhere.

The American infantrymen who threw themselves on Japanese hand grenades in order to save their buddies were expressing an impulsive, unthinking surge of camaraderie, not an intentional desire to kill themselves. The Alamo's defenders didn't intend to die, except, perhaps, when it was too late for another choice. Jimmy Doolittle's pilots knew it would take luck to land in China after bombing Tokyo from the carrier *Hornet* in April 1942, but they had at least a hope and a chance. Those rare exceptions were no more the counterparts of kamikaze pilots than the swashbuckling Onishi was a naval officer like heroic naval officers elsewhere.[15]

An uneducated American footslogger on Okinawa summed up the difference as tellingly as any historian or sociologist, revisionist or otherwise: "Our infantrymen landed on Pacific islands knowing they might die but hoping they wouldn't. Kamikaze men knew the outcome in advance."

Perhaps defeat was more shameful to Japanese. Perhaps their long tradition of fighting to the death against impossible odds explained the existence of an organized, mass force for such military waste. The country's equally long veneration of mythical young heroes whose destruction guarantees society's survival also surely played a role. (Ivan Morris noted that it was almost a prerequisite of Japanese tales that their young heroes died achieving their lofty aims—or failing to.) Whatever the practice's origin and however realistic its initial purpose—stopping the enemy's onslaught by sinking his carriers—it swelled into an escape to mystical salvation, in

[15]Commanding ever fiercer loyalty for his courage and boldness, the dashing but kindly looking Onishi would become an object of an intense cult by passionate junior officers until—and after—Japan's surrender prompted his agonizing, eighteen-hour suicide. He's reported to have said, "There will probably not be anyone, even in a hundred years, to justify what I've done," but his remorse came only after the inconceivable surrender. His every action having been based on that "impossibility," it could now seem he'd sent thousands of young men to a useless death—but not a meaningless one, as they'd had the joy of dying beautifully for a cause they believed to be just.

which sense it *was* characteristically Japanese. The mainland slogan about a hundred million *gyokusai,* the jewel shattered into myriad pieces, was now much more insistent than when General Ushijima's glum predecessor on Okinawa had cited it a year earlier. "Better we all die."

By now, young Japanese were dying in a panoply of special attack weapons, including crash boats, human mines, and human torpedoes. Simplified midget submarines designed in 1943 by three young naval officers failed to achieve significant results at Okinawa. It was chiefly their hidden pens, carved out of cliffs, that had been captured in Kerama Retto and the Okinawan north, where Americans gaped at the little boats in which men were prepared to head out on a one-way trip toward a selected ship. A few did manage to score in nearby waters, their targets never knowing what hit them. Sailors on ships loaded with munitions, dynamite, and aviation fuel needed no second order from their captains to "shoot at anything larger than a cigarette butt" that moved in the water at night.

The most important of such weapons was the *ohka* (exploding cherry bomb), an aerial cousin of the midget submarines conceived in disappointment that even the very small percentage of kamikazes that managed to hit home often failed to sink American ships because their impact speed was too slow. Promising to crash half a ton of high explosives at six hundred miles an hour, the 1944 *ohka* touted by Radio Tokyo as a guarantee of American defeat was essentially a rocket-powered bomb released by a converted bomber. It had just enough fuel for a short, sharp dive, just enough wing area for slight maneuvering on the way down, and just enough cockpit space for a man to squeeze into—for it too was manned, like a German V1 rocket with a pilot.

Americans called that weapon *baka* ("idiot bomb" or "screwball"), as if in search of comic relief from the apprehension it generated. Pilots and antiaircraft gunners found the speedy rockets almost impossible to hit once they were launched. But their weight made their mother planes sitting ducks for American interceptors. In their raids, too, *ohka* kamikazes maintained their gratitude for the chance to die honorably. The crew of one mother plane reported that its *ohka* pilot, a twenty-two-year-old lieutenant, slept peacefully as they approached the target on April 12—but that was the only mother plane in a squadron of eight that managed to return to its base.

One hundred eighteen of the 185 planes used in *ohka* attacks would be destroyed, at a cost of 438 Japanese airmen. On one occasion, sixteen of sixteen Betty mother planes dispatched toward American carriers were shot down in ten minutes, despite a fighter escort of fifty-five planes (many of which developed mechanical trouble before the force approached its target). Still, improved versions, including a final one with an engine adapted from a German jet, were designed and produced right up to the end of the war for use against the fleet that would take part in the invasion of the mainland.

The kamikaze pilots embodied the peculiarly Japanese attitudes of the time even more than the engineers who designed so many special attack weapons. Many prized their death for its own rewards, almost as if it were more important than its purpose. Although the call was for "death simultaneously with a mortal blow to the enemy," the former was often the chief objective, which helps explain why the net results of the raids were pitifully disproportionate to their enormous expenditure of equipment and first-rate men. The human waste was the greater folly: Months or years of pilot training were squandered on the single, usually futile charge in the flying coffins. Yet Imperial General Headquarters became so convinced of salvation by suicide attacks that it issued an order implying that all armed forces should employ that "lunacy," in the later assessment of the commander of an air flotilla that dispatched them from the mainland.

> That proved the High Command, utterly confused by a succession of defeats, had lost all wisdom . . . and degenerated to the point of indulging in wild gambling. The order was nothing less than a national death sentence. Like every military order, it was issued in the name of the Emperor and therefore not open to question or criticism, no matter how outrageous.

The young heroes had been girded by the long history of Japanese literature that elevates death as "the only pure and thus fitting end to the perfection of youth," in Ian Buruma's summary. Perhaps their longing was less for death than for what Buruma called "a supremely sensual state of unconsciousness" remembered from early childhood, when Japanese boys were powerfully indulged by their mothers. Whatever the cause, the greater the likelihood of defeat, "the more certain it was that the Japanese would fight to the death in battle or kill themselves following defeat," as a former kamikaze pilot put it in 1989. The impossible odds at Okinawa enhanced rather than diminished the romance with exquisite death. The more obvious the futility, the more noble the sacrifice.

That would be far from universally true in the 32nd Army on land. Many of its more educated reserve officers, responsible for their men's lives as well as their own, would be caught between the military code's absolute requirement to be ready to die and humanistic feelings much intensified by their men's suffering. Besides, dispatch on suicide missions on Okinawa was usually not an honor but a punishment, meted out to men in bad favor—who were often just such liberal officers. But there were far fewer complications for young kamikaze pilots. "If I go away to sea, I shall return a brine-soaked corpse," pledged the old anthem that often ended the pretakeoff ceremonies. Gunning their engines, the youth were as enticed by self-destruction as destruction of the enemy.

Although assurances that *Yamato damashii* would triumph in the end continued sounding, many pilots, by now often barely trained, appeared to believe it no more than that their sacrifice would help alter the course of the war. Too bright and skeptical to swallow the promises or to respond to military fanfares, they'd pleaded for their opportunity to die because their objective was as much gesture as military tactic—like much of Japanese thinking as a whole. It was as important, perhaps more important, to express utter sincerity in a just cause, no matter how hopeless—or precisely *because* it was hopeless—as to damage the enemy's gargantuan navy. Tale after folktale about young heroes dying for doomed causes had taught that life's meaning couldn't be realized by calculating military advantage any more than by anything else attainable through mere reason. The ultimate goal was higher, purer.

The last letters also reflected a fervent desire to surmount petty, earthly interests. Attaining the longed-for spiritual victory over material comforts probably accounted for much of the young men's joy on the eve of their final flights. Such victory often required a "Zen-like suppression of reason and personal feelings, a blind devotion to direct action, and an infinite capacity for hardship and pain." Takajiro Onishi called the lucky men "already gods without earthly desires." Many penned their letters in eager anticipation for their "splendid" death, "as sudden and clean as the shattering of crystal." With "no remorse whatever," they truly "never felt better."

> We were bubbling with eagerness. . . . I thought of my age, nineteen, and of the saying "To die while people still lament your death; to die while you are pure and fresh; this is truly *bushido*."
>
> Yes, I was following the way of the samurai. My eyes were shining as I stepped on board [my plane] once more. I remembered with pleasure [a fellow officer] quoting from a poem and telling me I would "fall as purely as the cherry blossom" I now held.
>
> Defeated but unconquered, men of the 65th Fighter Squadron were born separately but die together.
>
> Warmest greetings [to a brother]. I hope you are all well. As for me, duty calls more and more. What a fine reward determination is. It gives one peace of mind. After all, the body is only an attachment of the spirit.

> I know that no purpose can any longer be served by my death but I remain proud of piloting a suicide plane and it is in this state of mind that I die. . . . Tomorrow a man in love with liberty will leave this world. I may have given you the impression of being disillusioned but at the bottom of my heart I am happy to die.

> Dear Parents:
> Please congratulate me. I have been given a splendid opportunity to die. . . . How I appreciate this chance to die like a man!

Looming military defeat *increased* the appeal of a death that demonstrated denial of self-interest and even community advantage. Belief counted more than reason, the purity of the motive more than the result. The ability to defy rationality and logic was itself a triumph, which was surely why many young pilots felt disgust and disgrace when they crashed without dying—and why others were plunged into depression when their missions were aborted; in their own words, they felt "deprived" of death. The disappointment of one group that returned to its base alive because bad weather near Okinawa had concealed the targeted ships became acute when it learned another had nevertheless pursued the attack that day, its pilots accomplishing nothing apart from their sublimely noble deaths.

> If in doubt whether to live or die, it is always better to die.
>
> —A saying repeated to kamikaze pilots and other Japanese warriors

> Once a Japanese man decides to do something, he carries it out to the bitter end, and at all costs.
>
> —A father-mentor to his son in a contemporary comic book for boys called *I Am a Kamikaze*

Many kamikaze pilots, even knowing they couldn't seriously damage the American fleet, hoped their demonstration of sublime dedication might shock the spiritually inferior enemy into defeat. Actually, however, it prompted the reverse reaction, reinforcing Americans' conviction that the demented Japanese had to be prostrated utterly. In the end, the supreme self-sacrifice of the suicide missions was also an expression of supreme selfishness. Yes, the pilots achieved their self-denying feats by heroically suppressing their own feelings, but they also ignored or discounted the feelings of others. To hell with the larger consequences of proving their utter purity—such as their enemies' frightened loathing of Japan.

Even if the men of the 10th Army and 5th Fleet had known that what attracted many kamikazes was less killing others than dying well themselves, precious few would have been interested. So much stark evidence of "degenerate" thirst for blood at such "inhuman" cost nipped any desire—slight to begin with among most Americans—to probe deeper into the unfathomable Oriental mentality. The cost ineffectiveness of kamikaze operations also comforted few Americans. Well after the campaign, the Navy would reveal that thirty-three ships had been sunk, well over half by kamikazes, and 368 ships and craft damaged, more than fifty seriously. (As with calculations of the bombing damage to Japanese cities, various reports give different casualty and damage figures. These are probably accurate to within a ship or two.)

Carriers also lost 539 planes—but the Japanese cost was staggering. On some days, up to 90 percent of the planes delivering mass attacks, conventional and kamikaze together, were destroyed—a total of 7,830 for the three months of the Okinawan campaign. The kill ratio of the kamikazes alone was naturally far higher, and most of the tiny percentage that managed to crash on ships instead of into the sea did so on superstructures, causing relatively superficial damage. Huge as the attack of April 6–7 was, the fleet comprised more ships than the nine hundred Japanese planes—and none larger than a destroyer was sunk that day or later. Some four thousand treasures of the nation died for that strategically minor wounding off Okinawa, most of them less than twenty-one years old.

But what mattered to American crews was their own hell, not the enemy's irrationality. When their ships weren't under attack, their life was tolerable, at least by Pacific War standards. There was often far too much rain and too little usable water: Tense watches at General Quarters under deluges in April and May were followed by days and nights of blistering heat that turned ships into furnaces. The sun was so strong by mid-May that a careless touch of a plane parked on a flight deck could cause a burn, and the stifling heat intensified the rashes, diarrhea, and outbreaks of boils in the overcrowded quarters. Still, most crews had dry clothes, relatively clean beds, and three squares on most days—unimaginable luxuries to combat infantrymen.

During the air attacks, however, supreme terror gripped. There was also fear of suicide boats and rumors of Japanese swimmers attaching charges to ships' bottoms, which prompted the posting of guards with submachine guns around the deck and men packing carbines or .45s when they went topside. "At night, anything that moved got riddled," Fred Poppe would remember. "Any sound, any sight including whitecaps—we were plain scared. And when one guy opened up, everybody fired at everything. So there were lots of ricochets and accidents." Transfer to a larger

LST on the opposite coast, near Naha, did nothing to lessen Poppe's fear. "Kamikazes just poured at us, again and again. It scared the shit out of us, far more than on L-day. We'd get warnings about half an hour before they appeared, and the waiting was scary too, the knowing what was coming when those pilots' one wish in the world was to kill you."

The Japanese called their April 6–7 operation Floating Chrysanthemum Number One. In addition to almost daily missions of one to twenty planes, they would stage nine more such mass attacks at weekly intervals, each launched from a variety of airfields and lasting from two to five days. The ten Floating Chrysanthemums provided "shows" awe-inspiring enough to momentarily divert combat troops on land from their anxieties. The spectacle of an armada firing ten thousand guns faster than seemed possible at swarms of attackers was mesmerizing. Norris Buchter spent L-day night on a slope several hundred yards from the beach where he'd come ashore. The sky above the invasion fleet riding in the darkness offshore was so full of tracer shells from the thousand-odd ships' antiaircraft fire that it glowed like coals. "It was like a hundred July Fourths together. What a terribly magnificent carnival!" William Marshall ran to the top of a coral hill on a night later in April to see two sections of a severed destroyer emanating an eerie glow as they drifted apart, burning fiercely. When both sections sank, a "gigantic" explosion sent shock waves up through the hill and a blinding light flashed "as though several suns had detonated" into the night. When a kamikaze hit an ammunition ship a few evenings earlier, John Grove blinked at "a huge multicolored fan of fire and shells" on the horizon. The macabre sight was also "magnificent, except that I knew it had to mean the death of maybe hundreds of Americans."

Medical Corpsman Joseph Bangert, the wise-guy son of John D. Rockefeller's driver, was "on the throne"—a hole in the Okinawan ground—one May evening when he saw two kamikazes attack *New Mexico.* One of the battleship's five-inch shells exploded directly under the first plane, lifting it just clear of her mastheads, but the plane's bomb detonated in a stack, turning it into a giant blowtorch. The second plane, also hit several times, held on and crashed into the gun deck. "That wagon took off like a shot," Bangert remembered in amazement. "I guess to avoid other strikes. I couldn't believe a big ship could move that fast." (Although fifty-four were killed or missing and 119 wounded, *New Mexico* wasn't listed among the badly damaged ships because she was able to continue fighting.)

Dick Whitaker watched "the daily and nightly spectacle" when his company was pulled back for rest and replenishment on high ground, from which both the Pacific Ocean and East China Sea, where ships still extended to the horizon, were sometimes visible. "During the day, the ships threw up so much ack-ack that daylight almost disappeared in a million black puffs. During night attacks, the concentration of fire made a kind of twilight—incredible. So much fire would have seemed truly impossible if you didn't see it."

When Navy construction units nicknamed the Seabees landed soon after the combat troops to begin bulldozing roads for American traffic, they erected a large movie screen on top of a hill. Betty Grable vehicles were favorites, some repeated so often that the audience said the lines along with the actors. But the alternate show of suicide pilots diving on frantic ships, also visible from there, sometimes beat the competition.

Although American troops would best remember the night attacks that floodlit the sky, the Japanese usually timed their flights to arrive at twilight, when their planes were most difficult to see. Whitaker noticed independently that twilight was the hour of the most awesome shows. It seemed to him inconceivable that a single attacking plane could penetrate a sky solid with smoke from antiaircraft bursts long enough to reach its target. He watched in amazement as some managed the feat, then crashed into an oily fireball of their bombs, their fuel, and themselves.

Ordinarily, he felt little sympathy for swab jockeys. At least they had good chow and could take a shower at night. (He didn't know how rare showers actually were; most ships had to maintain severe water rationing.) They could jump into a clean sack—while he and his platoon slept, or couldn't sleep, in a hole in the ground "soaked to the skin, freezing our asses off and without the protection of a ship or anything else." But when kamikazes struck, Whitaker felt pity for the crews. Sailors had no foxholes. They couldn't dig in during their moments, or hours, of terror. Infantrymen nearer the shore who saw the wreckage of ships blown to bits—sometimes with a dozen or so sailors' bodies—were even more aware of the price being paid at sea.

The same extravaganza prompted very different reactions in 32nd Army spectators. For the beleaguered defenders, the first reward was a brief suspension of the shelling of their positions while the attention of the American fleet turned skyward. Many Japanese who profited from that blessed break felt guilty toward the young heroes who provided it. Still, the temporary cessation of the enemy's barrages enabled them to relax and enjoy some brief moments "watching the Ryogoku." (Tokyo's Ryogoku district held a captivating fireworks display every year.)

A single master switch seemed to turn on the sirens[16] and searchlights of the American ships, "a brilliant show in itself." Then the Japanese planes approached with their metallic roar. Picked up by the searchlights, they became the targets of "millions of antiaircraft bullets and shells . . . a panorama of incomparably gorgeous display." Another Japanese soldier remembered the American fleet's nonessential lights going out "in a blink" when the kamikazes approached, "and the blazing stream of antiaircraft fire gushing upward with a terrifying explosion. Then we'd catch a glimpse of [a plane] hurtling down from the sky like a pebble lit up in the beam of a searchlight . . . or sometimes wrapped in its own flame."

The ships' rapid-fire pompoms awed Japanese soldiers. They threw up tens of thousands of rounds to crisscross the lower sky like some cosmic fireworks display beneath explosions of higher-caliber automatic shells, beneath, in turn, bursts of flak that blanketed the upper sky. The transfixed soldiers prayed the planes would stay up until they could crash into the targets at which they were aiming with such stunning bravery. When they succeeded, joy surged through the otherwise tormented watchers before they dashed back to cover, often in tears of gratitude.

Soon the quick ventures from the caves to watch the spectacle acquired a more formal description: "To go worshipping the Special Attack Forces."

> Come evening, the mountain rumbles. A thunderous sound can be heard in the cave—from which we leap out, shouting, "Yea! Our Tokkoki [special attack] planes have come!" We go up the mountain and see . . . that the clouds over the sea are red. The enemy fleet is firing its antiaircraft guns, all of them. Tens of thousands of tracers crisscross like a fountain, turning the sky fiery above the ships. . . . Shining like a single grain of rice, our Tokko braves this barrage. The minute we catch sight of it, it hurtles toward the water in flames . . . or goes straight for an enemy ship, releasing a gigantic pillar of fire. . . . The sound of the firing, like the beating of a colossal drum, suddenly stops. . . . Some of us go down on our knees and worship toward the sea, worship the Tokko. "Well done! Thank you!"

[16]Hearing the sirens one day, Kenjiro Matsuki, the star of Japan's first professional baseball team, reckoned he had half an hour of safety and left his cave for a nearby well, planning to wash his face for the first time in over a month. But for some reason, perhaps because that particular kamikaze attack didn't materialize, the ships quickly turned their searchlights off and resumed their bombarding. A shell landed so close to Matsuki that fragments hissed like hot pokers when they splashed into the well—into which he too jumped for protection. Rushing back to his shelter, he swore never again to take such a risk.

Inside the caves, maniacally exaggerated reports of the success of the air attacks provided additional exaltation. Masahide Ota and other messengers from 32nd Army headquarters at Shuri Castle distributed uplifting news about kamikaze victories, mainly in the form of a one-sheet newspaper. "Our brave eagles" sank twenty-one enemy ships, it reported on April 7. Two days later, thirty were supposedly sunk and eighteen crippled; on April 13, nineteen sent down. "Our Air Force continues attacking . . . with fierce intensity," the paper added.

> Since April 12, our results include, as far as we could determine:
> Sunk: Carriers—1, Cruisers—2, Cruiser or Transport ship—1,
> Destroyer—1, Transport ship—1
> Damaged: Battleships—1.

The arrival of such misinformation filled the caves with loud cheers. The tiny newspapers went from hand to hand, surrounded by soldiers who bent over them to read the great tidings for themselves. Few doubted that the (virtually nonexistent) Japanese submarine fleet was in the process of strangling the land enemy by destroying his overextended supply lines. Soon, their wonderfully successful Air Force would turn to helping them on land.

By the campaign's end, it would be claimed that kamikazes sank forty-nine carriers, battleships, and cruisers. But although the actual total in those categories was zero, the logic that the Americans couldn't continue to lose ships as they reportedly were lifted the dejection caused by the Japanese retreats on land and the wretchedness of cave existence. Cheeks shone with optimism in the darkness. Shigemi Furukawa, a former high school teacher, later saw that as part of "a curious battlefield psychology [in which] we took whatever 'information' fed our wishful thinking for certain fact, no matter how often we were disappointed."

The wishful thinking extended to some of the highest commanders. Staff officers of Vice Admiral Matome Ugaki, commander of the 5th Air Fleet based on the home island of Kyushu, spoke of huge enemy losses after each Floating Chrysanthemum. The admiral thought it "almost certain" that special attack forces of the first one, on April 6–7, destroyed four American carriers. "In the light of so many reports of crashes on enemy carriers," he noted in his diary on April 11, "there can't be many undamaged ones still operating." Evidently Ugaki—who would himself take off in a plane and disappear, an almost certain suicide, after the Emperor's call for surrender in August—was genuinely convinced the American Navy would soon be "finished off."

Crashes on the carriers did force a few to suspend operations. The damage and losses were terrible in comparison to what the American Navy had suffered anywhere previously in World War II. But no carrier was put permanently out of action, let alone sunk, during the entire Okinawan campaign. On the second day of the Sixth Floating Chrysanthemum, a kamikaze suddenly dived from some low clouds toward *Bunker Hill,* one of the carriers whose planes had disposed of *Yamato* five weeks earlier. The Zeke hit the flight deck, setting parked planes alight in a huge conflagration. Just as its bomb penetrated the deck, a Judy dived almost vertically and did the same, its bomb also exploding below. In moments, three decks were ablaze almost the full length of the ship, the inferno fed by more parked planes and aviation fuel in hangar and working spaces. Three hundred ninety-three of her crew were killed and missing and another 264 were wounded, but *Bunker Hill* survived.

Three days later, in the interval between the Sixth and Seventh Floating Chrysanthemums, fighter-interceptors and antiaircraft guns shot down twenty-five of the twenty-six planes attacking *Enterprise,* but the approach of the twenty-sixth made throats go dry on the carrier.

> All the batteries were firing: the 5-inch guns, the 40mm and the 20mm, even the rifles. The Japanese aircraft dived through a rain of steel. It had been hit in several places and seemed to be trailing a banner of flame and smoke but it came on, clearly visible, hardly moving, the line of its wings as straight as a sword.
>
> The deck was deserted; every man, with the exception of the gunners, was lying flat on his face. Flaming and roaring, the fireball passed in front of the "island" superstructure and crashed with a terrible impact just behind the forward lift. The entire vessel was shaken, some forty yards of the flight deck folded up like a banana skin.

The worst damage came from a bomb exploding deep in a lower deck. Fourteen men were killed, sixty-eight wounded. The "Big *E*" had been hit twice before, most recently by two planes within an hour. This time she had to retire for major repairs in a navy yard, not to return to sea—like *Bunker Hill*—until after the war.

Royal Navy carriers consistently suffered less damage when hit. Five of them formed the core of a British fleet that, together with surface-support and supply and service vessels, was designated Task Force 57. Its appendage to Iceberg a fortnight before L-day had been less than an example of heartwarming Anglo-American cooperation. After catastrophic losses early in the war, senior British officers were keen to return to the Indian Ocean, where their former possessions in Burma, Malaya, and Indonesia awaited liberation from the Japanese. Suspicious of the old colonial interest, however, their American counterparts strove to keep the Royal Navy out of the Pacific anywhere west of Hawaii or, failing that, to relegate it to sideshows. They wanted John Bull to share the glory of Japan's final defeat even less than they wanted American resources drained to supply British ships. In the end, however, the political leaders surmounted the military-strategic rivalries. Churchill offered Roosevelt the British fleet for Pacific island campaigns rather than for any Indian Ocean operation, and the president quickly accepted.

But although American staffs then turned characteristically generous with supplies, some high-ranking officers continued nudging the Royal Navy as far aside as possible in order to "forestall any possible postwar British claim that they had delivered even the least part of the final blows which demolished the remains of Japanese seapower," as an English historian would see it. Nevertheless, the British worked unsparingly to make Task Force 57 a balanced, self-supporting force.

Its main assignment was to neutralize Sakishima Shota, a small archipelago of islands between Formosa and Okinawa. TF 57 repeatedly bombed and shelled those islands, some of which had important military airfields repaired by sedulous Japanese soldiers and native workers after every strike. The fleet's peripheral location, some three hundred miles southwest of Okinawa, guaranteed it would have little chance for publicity and every chance of being attacked from enemy airfields on the Chinese mainland as well as nearby Formosa, where many Japanese pilots were more experienced and skilled than the mainland's young graduates of crash courses. Beginning on L-day, when they acted as a decoy to divert attention from the vastly larger American force off the landing beaches, the British ships served as a shield across the approaches to the battle site from Formosa and China. But although they were occasionally the principal raid targets, naval design rooted in national attitudes kept their damage relatively minor and casualties relatively few. Working in an atmosphere of determination to avoid World War I's catastrophic casualties, British naval architects had given their carriers flight decks of three inches of armor plating instead of teakwood.

American designers disliked armored flight decks because their weight reduced stability and striking power. TF 57's five carriers together provided only 244 planes, slightly more than half the number on American carriers of equivalent size. (Their steel decks also made the crews' quarters even more like infernos after weeks under the fierce sun.) They were also slower, less maneuverable, and less protected by antiaircraft armament than their American counterparts. Still, their better damage control proved crucial for withstanding kamikaze attacks. All five carriers were hit at least once, often with spectacular impact. But the same aircraft that often penetrated wooden American decks and exploded into havoc below usually "crumpled up like a scrambled egg," in an American observer's simile, against British steel. "When a kamikaze hits a U.S. carrier, it's six months' repair in Pearl [Harbor]," observed another American. "In a Limey carrier, it's 'Sweepers, man your brooms.' "

Although it was never quite that easy for the Limeys, virtuoso pilots whose crashes would have put an equivalent American carrier out of action for months merely slowed the British quarry for several hours or reduced their rate of launching planes. When a Zeke with a five-hundred-pound bomb crashed on *Indefatigable*'s flight deck from an almost vertical dive, the blast killed eight ratings but left only a three-inch dent in the heavy steel. Even some multiple fires caused by several nearly simultaneous crashes were extinguished within a quarter of an hour. The chunks of the smashed Japanese planes—and of their pilots, in the form of skull splinters or a single finger stuck to a bulkhead—were pushed over the side, together with the incinerated British ones that had been parked on the flight deck, mostly American-made Avengers, Hellcats, and Corsairs. The carriers were fully operational again.

At one point, TF 57 set a Royal Navy record since Nelson and the era of sail: thirty-two continuous days at sea. Throughout them, they diverted a share of the Japanese planes from the vastly larger American fleet, and every diverted kamikaze was a blessing to TF 58. When senior American officers counted their own casualties, their coolness toward the "Forgotten Fleet," as a chronicler later dubbed it, inched toward respect and even a little affection.

Of the seventy-eight hundred Japanese planes lost, thousands were piloted by youths with barely enough training to get them into the air and attempt the quick dive they prayed would crown their deaths with the additional glory of a hit. Thousands crashed into the sea without coming close to their targets. As is so much in war, it was a matter of chance. Men on unluckier ships became deeply impressed with their attackers' patience and cunning—and with reason: Some were skilled pilots. The experts dived "with the velocity of a comet" for their targets' vulnerable parts, such as carrier elevators, and chose the most vulnerable moments, during plane launching and recovery, when quick maneuvering was extremely difficult. Captains had learned, as one put it, that it was "fatal" to hold a steady course during an attack.

Artful Japanese timing also delivered carrier pilots waiting to take off in their own planes into a special chamber of hell: Strapped into their cockpit seats, they saw kamikazes approaching and every sailor, except gun crews, racing for cover. Ships could rarely tell whether approaching aircraft were conventional or kamikaze until almost the last moment, when the dives began. When two or more kamikazes dived in a coordinated attack from varying points at varying angles, they much increased the chances of a successful crash no matter how brilliant the maneuvers to avoid them.

Apprehension on the ships increased even further because the crews could also rarely tell until that last moment whether the planes coming in were piloted by experts or novices. Looking up at five-hundred-pound bombs strapped to bellies or extra fuel tanks under each wing, they tried to guess. Even an almost empty plane could be lethal. In one case a wheel bounced off a kamikaze and decapitated a gunner, who had been firing furiously until the moment of the crash he was desperately hoping to prevent. Near misses too could cause significant damage. Another kamikaze totally disabled its target ship by hitting the water hard and close enough to flood both boiler and engine compartments.

> Get the destroyers. Without their radar warning of our approach, we will enjoy great success.
>
> —Admiral Matome Ugaki, commander of the 5th Air Fleet

> Although your historian himself has been under kamikaze attack and witnessed the hideous forms of death and torture inflicted by that weapon, words fail him to do justice to the sailors on the radar picket stations.
>
> —Samuel Eliot Morison, naval historian

Attacks against the capital ships naturally attracted the most attention, but the tin cans and other attendant vessels suffered proportionately more. Human resources are almost always more strained on smaller naval ships, and many of those in particular were intentionally stationed directly in harm's way: "sitting ducks of Okinawa," as one observer called them.[17]

To protect the main body of the fleet, the Americans established a ring of sixteen early-warning radar picket stations in the most probable approaches of the attacking planes, ranging out to about seventy-five miles from Okinawa. (That was in addition to Task Force 58's own picket group and to some seventy-five American planes always orbiting in concentric circles above the island and the picket ships during daylight. Those carrier-based combat air patrols shot down hundreds of easy pickings but also risked flak from their own side's ships with daredevil courage during the thick of the Floating Chrysanthemums.) Destroyers and destroyer escorts did most of that dangerous picketing in slow-speed circles, although minelayers, smaller gunboats, and landing craft were soon added in the effort to increase antiaircraft firepower against the swarms of attackers.

Since many shaky pilots were unable to keep their rickety planes aloft long enough to reach the choicer targets of the carriers and transports, those unarmored little craft took a disproportionate share of the dives. Although kamikazes badly damaged thirteen American carriers, ten battleships, and five cruisers off Okinawa, only smaller ships, with their skimpier antiaircraft armament, went down: a dozen between late March and the end of June, in addition to three sunk by conventional air attacks. Naval historian Samuel Eliot Morison concluded that destroyer crews living in daily and nightly terror of them were probably under greater stress for a longer period than had previously been experienced by any seamen serving in a surface fleet.

> Men on radar picket station, to survive, not only had to strike down the flaming terror of the kamikaze, roaring out of the blue like the thunderbolts that Zeus hurled at bad actors in days of old; they were under constant strain and unusual discomfort. In order to supply 650-pound steam pressure to build up full speed rapidly in a destroyer, its super-heaters, built only for intermittent use, had to be lighted for three and four days' running. For days and even nights on end, the crew had to stand general quarters and the ship kept "buttoned up." Men had to keep in condition for the instant reaction and split-second timing necessary to riddle a plane bent on a crashing death. Sleep became the rarest commodity and choicest luxury, like water to a shipwrecked mariner.

[17]Merchant ships manned by civilian crews were also fat targets. One Liberty ship struggling to off-load was attacked by seventy-two kamikazes. The hospital ship *Comfort* was also hit, although probably in error, by a plane in flames and out of control. Six nurses were among the twenty-eight killed.

That drew a greater distinction between kamikaze and conventional attacks than most Japanese themselves would have made. Many veteran pilots considered too valuable for the former flew strikes that were suicidal in all but name; they wore no parachutes and didn't expect to return. By the sixth week, the demarcation between suicide missions and ordinary ones was increasingly blurred. "They were all human bullets," Denis and Peggy Warner argued, "whether they chose to die in kamikaze aerial attacks, in banzai charges, in *ohkas,* or on small boats loaded with explosives." And although most of the less publicized Japanese infantry was not specifically suicidal, its night attacks, especially by units that had been reduced to near inoperative, were almost the same. Very few of Ushijima's eighty thousand regular troops expected to return to Japan, nor did the twenty thousand to thirty thousand Okinawans conscripted in the Home Guard expect to live, though a far larger percentage of them wanted to.

Besides, chroniclers understandably overwhelmed by the shipboard terror had little notion of the suffering on Okinawa itself. It is probably true that "never in the annals of our glorious naval history have naval forces done so much with so little against such odds for so long a period," as the commander of the radar pickets claimed. But the land battle was harder, and many Japanese units did a lot more with a lot less against incomparably greater odds for a longer period. Americans on ships hit by kamikazes had only a brief taste of the experience of Japanese soldiers on the island, who for months faced an almost constant rain of bullets, shells, and bombs.

Still, the ordeal of the radar picket vessels was indeed unprecedented in many ways. On and on went the kamikaze attacks, bringing dread to sailors who didn't want to believe the "crazy Japs" had more planes left after so many had been shot down. But they had thousands left—never mind their condition—and the grim drama with the spectacular sights and unequaled intensity played again and again: the pilots' half-hypnotic last minutes in their planes, the tension on the ships below, the guns with the glowing barrels, the sky red with tracers and "almost literally black" with bursts of antiaircraft shells, the sea churned up by spray from the shorts, the crew members' rush to toilets to cool feet seared by their decks. The absence of relief from shooting down any part of an attacking force, because it was always the last plane that scored; the hope that no crash would come amidships to make the ship go dead in the water and become a sitting duck; the gun crews' unflinching fire as planes did hit, engulfing them in flames. The jettisoning of anchors, torpedoes, guns, and all other possible weight to try to save listing vessels; damage-control crews operating as bucket brigades when all power was lost and the fire hoses were useless; burned survivors struggling to stay afloat in a sludge of sea, oil, and blood around crippled and sinking hulks—into which new bombs fell. Knots of sailors using their last energy for an excited burst of swimming toward rescue vessels and dying of exhaustion, other knots drowned by big seas, crushed by the hulls of sister ships come to help, or wriggling from their life jackets and letting themselves slide under, even though possible rescue was near, because they could stand no more agony . . .

The destroyer *Laffey*'s picket station during the Third Floating Chrysanthemum was on a straight line between Kyushu and Okinawa. Enemy planes filled her radar screen—up to fifty closing bogeys at one point—from first light of April 16. During one eighty-minute period, at least twenty-two planes dived at her from all points of the compass. Her decks were repeatedly strafed. One bomb scored a near miss; four others hit. One kamikaze splashed almost alongside; six others crashed home. (Eight hit another tin can on another day.) Ton for gross ton, the attack was probably more intense than even *Yamato* had experienced, and *Laffey*'s trial, until being taken in tow by a sister ship, lasted almost as long. Despite the explosions, flames, and casualties—thirty-one missing and killed, seventy-two wounded—no gun was abandoned, although only four of her 20-millimeters were operable when the Japanese broke off.

Those small-caliber guns proved little use in stopping a determined pilot. Even direct hits by the larger ones often failed to do that. One of the most remarkable scenes of the whole remarkable tableau was of Japanese planes lurching forward on their collision courses even when repeatedly hit and in flames—even when their pilots were riddled and parts of the planes had broken off and spun into the sea. No amount of fire from a ship under attack ensured her safety until the attacker, or swarm of them, fell into the sea. The strain from that enemy bravery added further to the anxiety. A Japanese writer's recent claim that "the sight of a single Japanese plane raised terror in the hearts of men on the enemy vessels" conveyed an essential truth.

The desperation of nearly all combatants to take out the enemy in battle had an added edge when nothing but shooting down the relentless planes *in time* and *far enough away* could save the targeted ships from fierce damage. (Such furious firing of course led to even more mistakes than usual when masses of young men were operating an immense assemblage of complex guns. "I saw something today which made my blood run cold, something I shan't soon forget!" said an officer on a landing ship medium on April 6, during the First Floating Chrysanthemum. American gunners had shot down a Hellcat—a blunder that would be repeated regularly in the frenzy of defense.) When a ship's power was knocked out, as often happened, gun crews operated their guns manually—work so arduous that healthy young men with adrenaline pumping could keep it up for only two minutes. Nothing better illustrated the old Asian proverb about dying twice when one knows one is about to die.

Permanent General Quarters would have exhausted the crews beyond ability to function reasonably. With hundreds of extra duties to keep the ships as ready and as free of inflammable materials as possible, steaming day and night under the usual normal high-condition watches was depleting enough. On top of that, nerves were "exposed and quivering like wires stripped of insulation," in the image of one sober chronicler.

Despite fire- and damage-control skills honed in repeated encounters, the new repair berths in Kerama Retto swelled with gutted ships and hulks. The final toll of naval casualties over the course of the campaign would be 4,907 killed or missing and 4,824 wounded, far more than in any previous battle of the war, including one-sided Pearl Harbor, where fewer than half that number died. (It was extremely rare for the number of deaths to exceed the number of wounded, as here: testimony to the infernos ignited by the crashes.) Nearly 20 percent of the Navy's total casualties in the Pacific, Atlantic, and all smaller seas throughout the war were inflicted off Okinawa.

Only forty-five kamikazes would participate in the Tenth Floating Chrysanthemum on June 21–22, down from the First's 355. On average, the eight in between involved progressively fewer planes but without proportionate relief of strain in the fleet. And those Japanese numbers decreased partly because officers on the home islands had already begun husbanding for the struggle there, for which they'd be able to muster ten thousand or more planes for kamikaze use. When B-29s joined TF 58's carrier strikers bombing mainland fields in mid-April, many Japanese planes were transferred from the Navy to Operation *Ketsu* (last resort) under overall command of the Imperial Army. The honor of its chiefs—who also controlled the government—unconditionally required a final battle on the mainland, whatever the odds, even if (or precisely because) there was no hope of winning. The specter of ultimate defeat increased rather than diminished the commitment to special attacks. "I see the war situation becoming more desperate," a squadron leader wrote in his cockpit moments before following five of his pilots in their final dives at Okinawa. "All Japanese must become soldiers and die for the Emperor."

★ ★ ★ ★ ★

The devastation caused by the fanatical resistance on Okinawa, and by the kamikaze attacks, was a central factor in President Truman's decision to use atomic weapons against Japan in August 1945. Their use brought an early end to the war and avoided a Soviet invasion of Japan or the planned Allied invasion of Kyushu set for November. American planners estimated well over a million U.S. casualties to capture central Japan if the invasion had gone forward.

In the Water: Gulf of Maine, from *Due to Enemy Action*

STEPHEN PULEO

I never had a son, but if I did, I would want him to have the same integrity and dedication to the truth as Paul Lawton.

—Bernard Cavalcante, Senior Archivist,
U.S. Naval Historical Center

The names of famous ships lost to enemy action during World War II are well-known to Americans, each ship offering a remembrance of great battles and noble sacrifice. Such ships as the USS *Arizona*, the *Yorktown*, *Gambier Bay*, *Wahoo*, and many others will never be forgotten. Yet not every action of the war would be fought in decisive battles or by famous ships. Even as the strategic victory over Germany and Japan was achieved by late 1944, bitter fighting continued. Men continued to die on faraway battlefields, in prison camps, and on the high seas—even a stone's throw from our home shores within hours of the end of the war in Europe.

Such was the fate of *Eagle 56*, a small, antiquated corvette built in 1919, relegated by 1945 to minor training duties and patrolling the Gulf of Maine. April 23, 1945, she was towing targets for Navy dive bombers just off the coast near Portland. Lurking nearby was *U-853* commanded by a young Lieutenant Helmut Frömsdorf, foolishly eager to achieve a victory for his boat and crew before the war's end. The German torpedo devastated the small American craft, killing forty-nine of her sixty-two officers and men. Knowledge of the *U-853*'s location was only known by a handful of officers in the Navy's top secret tracking room. Even though the survivors reported seeing a U-Boat surface after the attack, the explosion of *Eagle 56* was attributed by the Navy as an accident due to a boiler explosion. The mystery was sealed a few days later when *U-853* paid for its captain's indiscretion when it was sunk with all hands by USS *Atherton* and USS *Moberly* south of New London, Connecticut, May 6, 1945.

Author Stephen Puelo recently published the Story of *Eagle 56* in his book *Due to Enemy Action*. Diver and historian Paul Lawton had come across the story of *Eagle 56* from two brothers whose father had been killed in the sinking. It became clear to Lawton the official version of the ship's loss and the memories of the survivors did not match. Lawton spent years researching the event and sent his findings to the senior archivist at the Naval Historical Center, Bernard "Cal" Cavalcante. The final pieces of the story were put into place by Cavalcante who knew of previously classified documents that proved *U-853* had been tracked by Navy intelligence into the Gulf of Maine. Puelo records the story of the attack and the quest over fifty years later to have the Navy change their findings on the loss of the ship. The following chapter describes the moment *U-853*'s torpedo struck the American corvette.

★ ★ ★ ★ ★

April 23, 1945
In the water, Gulf of Maine
12:15–12:40 p.m.

The *U-853*'s torpedo detonated under the *Eagle 56*'s starboard side amidships, blowing the subchaser out of the water, breaking her keel, tearing her in half, and unleashing a geyser of water that shot one to two hundred feet skyward. The blast killed forty-nine men in all: five of the ship's six officers, including Commander James Early, plus forty-four members of her crew. John Scagnelli was the only *Eagle 56* officer to survive, and the only crewman to escape from the forward section of the ship. Johnny Breeze, Harold Petersen, Oscar Davis, and nine others from the stern half of the ship jumped into the freezing North Atlantic water and held on long enough to be rescued. Along with Scagnelli, they would become known as "The Lucky Thirteen."

Scagnelli's good friend, Jack Laubach, left his beloved Ginny a widow; Laubach and Early, the *Eagle*'s skipper, were last seen on the bridge. Ivar Westerlund, who arrived from Brockton, Massachusetts, in time to board the *Eagle* just before it left port, went down with the ship, leaving Phyllis a widow and their four children fatherless. Harold Glenn, who had kissed his wife, Esta, good-bye on the front steps of their apartment that morning, perished in the attack. Fredrick "Mike" Michelsen, who relieved Petersen on the engine room watch, also died in the explosion, leaving his pregnant wife, Pauline, behind.

Immediately after the blast the *PE-56*'s stern section began sinking quickly, although as many as two dozen men in the aft compartments were able to struggle topside, scramble up the pitching deck, and jump into the freezing water before the stern disappeared below the whitecaps about seven minutes after the torpedo struck. The severed bow portion of the ship also settled quickly amidships, pitched on her side, her tapered stern rising high in the air, perpendicular to the water, her exposed anchors and the large painted number "56" visible to the crew members who had abandoned ship. The bow section remained afloat for approximately fifteen minutes before it, too, sank beneath the choppy waves and went to the bottom.

All personnel on the bridge, including Early and the other officers, and virtually all the men belowdecks in the bow section—including those in the Chief Petty Officer (CPO) quarters, radio shack, wardrooms, officers' quarters, galley, and forward crew compartment—were killed and went down with the wreck. Only Engineering Officer Scagnelli escaped from the bow section. When Scagnelli was asked later if he could account for the loss of all the officers and crewmen on the bridge and in the chart house, he testified: "Their doors may have been closed and when the explosion occurred that may have slammed them tight. They have two doors, one on the starboard side and one on the aft port side. The port was dogged [locked]." Scagnelli was then asked whether he believed that most of the men in their living compartments were likely trapped in the ship's hull after the explosion. "Yes, sir," he said, "the explosion rendered a great many of them unconscious . . . As I came through [making his escape] I didn't hear any yelling or screaming or calling for help." Years later, naval historian Paul Lawton would write: "Many of the *PE-56* officers and crewmen were thrown against bulkheads and rendered unconscious by the explosion, becoming entrapped belowdecks, as their only means of escape became flooded, taking many men, still alive, down to the cold, dark, crushing depths of the North Atlantic, where they suffered agonizing deaths, entombed within the wreckage."

The tremendous explosion was witnessed by Cape Elizabeth's Casco Bay Magnetic Loop Receiving station, approximately five miles away, and by the Portland Harbor Entrance Control Post (HECP) at Fort Williams, about nine miles away. Reinforcing just how close the *Eagle* was to home, Portland residents reported hearing the roar of the blast, and some who lived in the city's highest hill sections saw the waterspout that erupted when the *Eagle* broke in half. The USS *Selfridge*, USS *Nantucket*, USS *Woolsey*, and several other nearby vessels all witnessed the blast, sounded their General Quarters, and headed for the scene to begin rescue operations. *Selfridge* Commanding Officer J.A. Boyd (USN), whose ship was seven miles away, reported later that he witnessed "a white column of smoke and vapor about 100 feet high . . . [it] appeared larger than from a depth charge [that the *Eagle 56* carried], persisted for at least 20 seconds, and had the appearance of an external, rather than an internal underwater explosion . . . The explosion was heavy, the ship broke in two immediately . . ." Lieutenant Guy V. Emro (U.S. Coast Guard), commanding officer aboard the *Nantucket*, which was only two and a half miles away from the *PE-56* when she exploded, later recounted: "The immense amount of water in the air I judged to be about 250 to 300 feet high. . . . The explosion must have come from without [outside the ship's hull], due to the immense amount of water and parts of the ship lifted in the air. I have witnessed a boiler blow-out, but that explosion could be compared in no way to the power displayed in this one . . ."

As the rescue ships raced to the scene, their commanders and crews knew they were racing against time: God only knew how many *Eagle 56* crew members had survived the terrible explosion, but any sailor could figure out that they would not live long immersed in the icy water.

And there was another worry for these men to consider. It was true that they were just a few miles from the U.S. shoreline, most of them engaged in routine maneuvers on an overcast April day as the end of the war neared. Yet, they had to reconcile the reassurance of that reality against the foreboding unease they felt about the likely cause of the *PE-56* explosion—an enemy torpedo—and the obvious question *that* conclusion begged: Was the U-boat that fired the torpedo still lurking out there?

John Scagnelli could barely see. Darkness and blood obscured his vision as he stumbled, dazed, along the narrow corridor, groping his way and praying that the only ladder that led topside was still intact. The explosion had lifted Scagnelli off his bunk and flung him like a rag doll, headfirst into the bulkhead in his cabin, opening a deep gash in his scalp that now bled profusely. He had remained conscious after the collision with the bulkhead, which most likely saved his life. When he opened his stateroom door, the passageway had been pitch black, almost ghostly. Scagnelli heard no screams or shouts or running feet; the only sound was hissing steam escaping from broken pipes outside his stateroom. It was as though he were the only man on the ship. Scagnelli knew something terrible had happened—he first thought a mine or torpedo had rocked the *Eagle*—and he knew his only chance for survival was to get off of the ship. But where were the others?

His prayers, not the last he would utter on this day, were answered when he found the ladder and clambered topside, where he saw water spilling into the starboard passageway. The only way off the ship would be through the portside passageway, but to his horror, he saw that his exit was blocked by a metal food locker, six feet tall and nearly four feet wide, that had slid from its spot when the ship began to list, and wedged itself into the passageway. Scagnelli, standing six-foot-two himself, attempted to muscle the locker, but it wouldn't budge. Water poured in from the starboard side, and Scagnelli knew time was running out. He searched frantically for a way off the ship. Then he noticed the twenty-inch space between the top of the food locker and the ceiling of the passageway. He took a running jump and hooked his arms across the top of the food locker, hoisting his big frame off the floor, struggling to scrabble up the front of the smooth metal container, knowing time was short, feeling the ship listing more, hearing water rushing in faster. He flopped the upper half of his body across the top of the food locker, squeezed first his head and wide shoulders and then his torso and legs through the crawl space, and dropped on the other side of the locker into knee-high water on the open main deck. With a shock, he realized the explosion had broken the *Eagle 56* in half.

Immediately, he saw heads bobbing in the water a distance away, the first men he had seen since the explosion, too distant to have come from where he had been. They must have been in the *Eagle*'s aft, or stern, section—and where the hell *was* the stern? Scagnelli couldn't see it. He plunged into the freezing water and pushed off, swimming as hard as he could in the direction of his shipmates, trying to get as far from the ship as quickly as possible before it sank and its swirling downdraft sucked him under with it. Moments later, a safe distance away, he stopped swimming and started treading water. He looked back and saw the front of the bow section rise out of the waves and point heavenward, almost majestically, her white "*56*" in stark relief against her gray hull and the gray water and gray sky that filled Scagnelli's field of vision.

Then the *Eagle 56*'s broken bow section, from where he had barely escaped, seemed to shudder once . . . then once more . . . before plunging downward and disappearing beneath the surface, taking every man except a dazed Lt. John Scagnelli to the bottom with her.

The *U-853*'s torpedo tore into the *Eagle 56* fourteen minutes after Fred Michelsen relieved Harold Petersen on the engine-room watch, its rocking blast killing Michelsen instantly. Petersen, who moments earlier had headed aft to splash cold water on his sweaty face, was about to reach into his footlocker when the explosion flung him headfirst into an upright locker and dislodged a bunk that slammed into Petersen's back.

He regained his composure and made his way to the next compartment, the mess hall, first to the starboard ladder, only to find the explosion had blown it from its hinges. The portside ladder was loose, but usable, and as Petersen approached it, he bumped into his friend, mess cook Robert Coleman.

"I can't swim, Pete," Coleman said.

"Bob, we have to get off this ship!" Petersen replied.

They had started up the ladder when Petersen heard loud moaning. He jumped off the ladder, searched frantically, and spotted an injured Fireman 1st Class Leonard "Leo" Surowiec lying amid some debris. Petersen hoisted him up, dragged his motionless body to the ladder, pulled him halfway toward topside, but Surowiec slipped from his hands. "I lost him," Petersen would say later, "and there was no time to go back down and get him."

Petersen reached the top deck and stood next to Coleman, the stern section of the ship sinking fast, the water ankle-deep.

"I can't swim, I just can't," Coleman shouted again.

"We have to go!" Petersen screamed, grabbing Coleman's arm. "Right now, or we're going under!"

They jumped into the freezing water together, and Coleman disappeared immediately. Petersen searched frantically, but knew he had to get away from the doomed *Eagle*, whose stern section sunk beneath the waves within seven minutes. "Bob never came up; I never saw him again," he would remember nearly sixty years later. "There was supposed to be a swimming test to get into the Navy. I never knew why he couldn't swim."

Petersen swam for his life, barely escaping the pull of the *Eagle*'s broken stern section. He headed for a floating fifty-gallon drum that was already supporting two other crew members. As he approached, he saw one man, his arms "nearly frozen stiff" from the bitterly cold water, lose his grip on the barrel and slip silently beneath the surface. Petersen wrapped his own arms around the barrel and saw bobbing heads around *Eagle* crew members treading water, trying desperately to hang on. He also spotted several floating pieces of wood shoring that had broken loose when the *Eagle* exploded. He left the barrel, collected as many pieces of wood as he could, and shoved them in the direction of his shipmates. Then he grabbed two more, for himself and Bill Thompson, who had been hanging onto the barrel.

"Take these, they're easier to hold onto," Petersen shouted.

"Pete," Thompson said, "I can't make it. I'm too tired. I'm too cold."

Growing numb himself, Petersen searched the horizon and saw a plume of black smoke—a rescue ship!—still in the distance but closing fast. He shook Thompson. "See that smoke?" he shouted. "See it? That's our rescue. Hang on—just hang on a few more minutes and it'll be here." Thompson nodded slightly, though Petersen saw that his lethargic shipmate's eyes had begun to glaze.

Petersen *willed* the rescue ship to move faster. Thompson was on the brink of giving up, with Petersen clutching him and hugging the shoring at the same time. For years after the sinking, Petersen would find it difficult to shake the guilt of failing to save the lives of two men—Surowiec and Coleman—within moments of the explosion; men he had touched, who were *in his grasp*.

Petersen vowed he wouldn't lose a third.

The explosion slammed Johnny Breeze to the deck and literally blew him out of one of his shoes. The pipe he had been filling with tobacco clattered across the floor. He and Oscar Davis, in the stern half of the ship, scrambled up, reached the escape ladder in the forward crew's quarters, and headed topside. Johnny Luttrell was ahead of them on the ladder, moving too slowly for Breeze, who cupped his hand on Luttrell's backside and hoisted him five rungs upward.

With Davis on his heels, Breeze stepped through the doorway of the after deckhouse onto the fantail of the ship, already tilted upward at a 20-degree angle and growing steeper, since this half of the *Eagle* was sinking from amidships. Breeze and Davis were in ankle-deep water, figuring out what to do next, when Davis grabbed his friend, pointed off the port quarter, and said, "Look, Breezy, there's a sub." Breeze looked quickly, saw the sub's black conning tower, but "didn't stop long enough to take a second look . . . we had to get off the ship and away from it before it went under and took us with it."

By now, the fantail was pitched at such a steep angle that Breeze and Davis were forced to crawl up the deck on their hands and knees, but quickly, as water was beginning to swirl onto the ship. Breeze reached as far as the depth-charge rack on the starboard side and was removing his remaining shoe when he looked over the side and saw a twelve-foot-long four-by-four length of shoring floating in the water. He forgot the sub, forgot *everything*, and concentrated on the piece of timber that he believed could save his life. Barefoot now, he jumped into the 38-degree water, Davis behind him, and latched onto the shoring. Immediately, Breeze spotted the lifeless body of his friend, Fireman 1st Class Norris Jones, floating toward him. "Jonesy" had been working in the fire (boiler) room at the time of the explosion, and, like every man in the scorching confines of the boiler room, had worked stripped to the waist. Breeze had to push Jones's body away from the shoring, and as he did, he saw that his friend had a terrible wound on his back, "a huge bump, a gnarled knot . . . the back was broken, you could tell. When the torpedo hit, he was probably thrown against something." Breeze would note emphatically later that Jones had no burns or scald marks on his upper torso, wounds which would surely have been visible had a boiler explosion shattered the *Eagle 56*.

Luttrell and Davis joined Breeze on the piece of shoring and they kicked frantically away from the sinking stern-half of the ship, which had all but disappeared beneath the waves. Breeze looked to his right and saw Lt. John Scagnelli swimming toward them. When the muscular Scagnelli grabbed onto the twelve-foot piece of shoring, his weight pulled all four men under briefly; the others popped up quickly, but Breeze couldn't get his head above the waves and he felt himself drowning, unable to breathe, but clinging to the wood for dear life. Mercifully, he felt Johnny Luttrell clamp his hand around the back of his neck and yank him to the surface. But would the shoring hold four men? Breeze wasn't sure it mattered anyway. He thought they were all going to perish from exposure. He saw heads bobbing in the water around him—later he said one man counted twenty-five in all—and saw men slip beneath the waves and never resurface.

Across from him on the four-by-four, Davis, for the second time in minutes, spotted a vessel. This time, it wasn't a German U-boat, but a rescue ship steaming toward them. "Look, Breeze, there's a ship," Davis said almost matter-of-factly.

Breeze didn't believe the ship would arrive in time. His body was numb from the cold; he couldn't feel *anything* unless he moved. He was a cocky twenty-two-year-old kid who liked to think he could do just about anything, but humble enough now to know he was in big trouble.

The *Eagle 56* was gone, both halves of her now deep beneath the surface, her bow section entombing as many as thirty sailors trapped inside. As many as two dozen escaped from the stern, but several of them had already died in the water, unable to cling any longer to the small chunks of debris that floated amid the choppy waves. The debris was the only evidence that the *Eagle* had ever been there. "The ship had two life rafts, located amidships . . . that were supposed to have automatically released and floated free in the event the ship went down," wrote Paul Lawton. "The life rafts did not deploy, however, and the few survivors, none of who [sic] were wearing warm clothing, foul-weather gear, or life jackets, struggled in the chilling waters to keep from drowning, clinging to any wreckage that remained afloat, including wood shoring timbers, oil drums, and milk cans which had floated free of the wreck."

As the rescue ships steamed toward Scagnelli, Petersen, Breeze, Davis, Luttrell, Thompson, and the rest, they were racing against time. The *Eagle 56* survivors immersed in freezing water were in danger of dying from hypothermia, the subnormal temperature within the central body. Skin and external tissue cools very quickly, and within ten to fifteen minutes, the temperature of the heart and brain begins to drop. When the body's core temperature—normal at 98.6 degrees Fahrenheit—drops below 97 degrees, shivering usually occurs and motor functions are reduced. At 92 to 95 degrees—moderate hypothermia—serious complications develop, including muscle rigidity that erases manual dexterity. Victims appear dazed, their speech slurred, shivering becomes violent and uncontrollable, amnesia can occur, and behavior becomes irrational. Hypothermia victims have been known to engage in "paradoxical undressing"—taking off clothing, unaware that they are cold. Lethargy, depression, and an "I don't care" attitude grip the victim. Severe hypothermia occurs when the body temperature drops to 92 degrees or below. Shivering occurs in waves, but then ceases because the heat output from burning glycogen in the muscles is not sufficient to counteract the continually dropping core temperature; the body shuts down on shivering to conserve glucose. The pupils dilate, the pulse rate decreases, and at 90 degrees, the body tries to move into hibernation, shutting down all peripheral blood flow and reducing breathing rate and heart rate. At about 85 degrees, the body enters a state of "metabolic icebox" in which the victim appears dead and is still alive. Death usually results when the body's temperature plunges to between 75 and 80 degrees; cardiac and respiratory failures occur as breathing becomes erratic and very shallow, cardiac arrhythmias develop, and any sudden shock may set off ventricular fibrillation, stopping the heart permanently.

Water temperature is only one factor in determining cold-water survival. Others include body size, fat, and activity within the water. Large people cool slower than small people. Fat people cool slower than thin people. By swimming or treading water, a person will cool about 35 percent faster than if remaining still. In water temperatures below 40 degrees, exhaustion and unconsciousness occur in fifteen to thirty minutes, and the expected survival time is as little as thirty minutes, and as long as ninety minutes at the outside.

As the *Selfridge*, the *Nantucket*, and the other rescue ships approached the scene, almost all of the freezing *Eagle 56* survivors were on the verge of moderate hypothermia. Every minute would count in the rescue, and the margin of error would be close to zero.

Clutching the same piece of shoring, John Scagnelli and Johnny Breeze, their bodies numb from the cold water, were engaging in the same activity, though neither would know it for years: each was praying. Scagnelli, who could no longer feel the scalp injury or anything else, struck a bargain with God: "Let me get out of this and I promise to devote my life to helping others." Breeze prayed, too, and for the first time in his life "actually believed someone could hear me . . . that someone was listening." After a few moments of begging God to spare him, Breeze realized he was being selfish. "It hit me that there were sixty-one other guys on the ship, and who the hell was I to just pray for me?" he recalled later. "I started to pray for them, and the good Lord saw fit to spare me."

Clinging to another piece of timber, an exhausted Harold "Pete" Petersen, who had spent his time in the water assisting his shipmates, felt the numbness consume his body "from bottom to top." Yet he refused to focus on his own plight. Instead, he continued to talk to Bill Thompson, imploring him not to give up, and by boosting Thompson he strengthened his own resolve. As the smoke plumes from the rescue ships grew closer, Petersen knew he couldn't hang on much longer, but he also knew that if *he* slipped under the water, Thompson would die, too.

★ ★ ★ ★ ★

In May 2001, Chief of Naval Operations Adm. Vern Clarke concurred with the findings of the research done by Lawton and Cavalcenate, and forwarded the report to the Secretary of the Navy, Gordon R. England. The Navy reclassified the loss of *Eagle 56* as a combat loss and recommended that Purple Hearts be awarded to its 49 dead and 12 survivors. This occurred in June 2001, at a special ceremony aboard the museum ship USS *Salem* in Quincy, Massachusetts, when the Navy awarded the Purple Heart to the three survivors and next of kin of those lost.

USS *Consolation*, from *Quiet Heroes*

COM. FRANCES OMORI

The United States Navy Nurse Corps was formally established by the Congress in 1908. Women had worked as nurses aboard Navy ships and in Navy hospitals for a hundred years previously as volunteers. During the American Civil War, Catholic Sisters of the Holy Cross served in Navy facilities and on board the pioneer hospital ship *Red Rover* in the Mississippi River area. During the 1898 Spanish-American War, the Navy employed a modest number of female contract nurses in its hospitals ashore and sent trained male nurses to sea on the hospital ship *Solace*. In World War I several ocean liners were converted by the Allies to serve as temporary hospital ships.

The first dedicated hospital ship built for the Navy, the USS *Relief*, went into commission in 1920 creating the first permanent duties for women at sea. The ships would prove an invaluable asset allowing the essential medical aid for battlefield casualties as near as possible to the front, saving thousands of lives. Frances Omori, a Commander in the U.S. Navy, wrote the acclaimed *Quiet Heroes* about the Navy nurses in the Korean War. The following chapter describes life aboard the USS *Consolation* as they receive Marine Corps casualties from the desperate fighting in the nearby mountains of the Korean battlefields.

★ ★ ★ ★ ★

I was an infantry platoon leader, Fox company, Second Battalion. We landed in the afternoon of 15 September 1950 near Inchon and advanced toward Seoul.

> I was wounded in the neck and should on the afternoon of 19 September 1950 and evacuated back to Inchon to a field hospital. The next day we were taken to the *Consolation* in the harbor in Inchon.
>
> I was on the *Consolation* for about four days. The nurses I remember tended to the sick and wounded in a most professional manner. We all thought very highly of them. They made time to just sit and chat . . . tell a few jokes. They were so selfless and caring that we knew we had the best of care. Our nurses were our rock to lean on.
>
> —Maj. Robert Maiden, USMC (Ret)

Departing from San Francisco, California, in July 1950, the *Consolation* was a ship of firsts. She was the first hospital ship to:

- Arrive in Korean waters,
- Include a women medical officer (doctor) on her staff,
- Use an electroencephalograph (brain wave tracing) machine at sea,
- Install and use a blood bank as standard equipment,
- Mount a helicopter flight deck on the ship,
- Receive casualties from battlefield via helicopter.

The *Consolation* furnished medical support for United Nations Forces and had the capacity to provide medical and surgical care for 786 bed patients.

They Came to Serve

Capt. Helen Louise Brooks, Nurse Corps, U.S. Navy (Ret), celebrated her eight-first birthday in 1999.

> From as far back as I can remember, I said I was going to be a navy nurse. I didn't know at that time if the navy had nurses.
>
> I completed St. John's Hospital School of Nursing, worked for a while, then joined the navy in 1944. I served until 1946 and then went into the inactive naval reserve.
>
> I graduated from Boston University, then went to Yale where I earned by degree in nursing education. In 1950, I volunteered to go back into the navy [because] they desperately needed help in Korea.
>
> It took about three weeks to get to the ship.

Comdr. Marion Barbara Hire, Nurse Corps, U.S. Navy (Ret), grew up about forty miles from Fargo, North Dakota.

I graduated from the Saint Francis School of Nursing and joined the navy in 1943. There was a war; it was the thing to do.

Haire served from July 1943 until July 1946 when she joined the inactive navy reserves and then was recalled to active duty in July 1950. On 30 August 1950, Haire, Brooks and five other nurses received orders to the *Consolation*. They reported to the Federal building in San Francisco on 14 September 1950, flew from Alameda Naval Air Base on 19 September 1950. This began their journey to the Far East to meet their ship. Haire recounts this trip in her journal.

We left Barbers Point on a DC-4 about 1400 [2:00 PM] . . . an oil leak was discovered on one wing. We returned to have it fixed . . . nothing serious, but rather unsetting [We] thought of the eleven nurses lost off Kwajalein the day before.

Finally they arrived in Tokyo at Haneda Airport.

After the usual delay, they got us all in a rickety old bus [and] we set out for Yokosuka about forty miles [away].

Once at Yokosuka, they were taken to a deserted building. The nurses were urgently needed aboard ship, so they would be flown to Sasebo. The other officers who arrived with them would take the train. The nurses arrived at Tachikawa Air Base, but the army was not expecting them. They were put up for the night and told that details would be worked out in the morning. One of Haire's bags was lost, so she and Brooks pulled together some nighclothes. It was cold that night. They woke at five the next morning to continue on to Sasebo.

We were sent to the terminal to await our plane . . . regulations required everyone flying in an army plane wear parachutes . . . our [slacks] were in our footlockers. After a great deal of discussion, a major waived the rule.

The six nurses were packed into a C-46 with troops in full combat gear. When they finally arrived at Ashiya, another army base, again the army didn't know what to do with the women.

Finally the army decided the quickest way to get the nurses to Sasebo was by train. After a few stops, the doors opened and the officers they had parted from three days prior in Yokosuka got on the train. The officers made the trip just as fast to this point as the nurses who had flown. When they reached Sasebo, they found themselves in another holding pattern. Haire explains:

> . . . two weeks after we arrived, we were told that we were to go to Itazuki . . . [then] flown to Kimpo, near Inchon.
>
> A few hours before we were to leave, we got word that the ship was on its way back to Yokosuka. We took the train to Itazuki, spent the night. . . . Next day in the rain, [we] took off by air for Haneda airport. We spent the next two nights and a day in Tokyo lodged at a women's hotel.
>
> On the afternoon of the second day we took the train to Yokosuka and as we drew into the station I saw our great white ship! It was Friday the thirteenth and after our weary wanderings, she looked like home. We were ready to begin our life at sea.

Finally on 18 October 1950, Brooks, Haire and the five other nurses were settled on board. The *Consolation* headed for Wonsan, on the east coast of Korea.

Comdr. Fred Ewing Smith, Medical Service Corps, U.S. Nary (Ret), served as a first class hospital corpsman during the Korean War.

> I was born and raised in Louisiana. Patriotism, I think, was an important part of our lives. World War II was a popular war, if there is such a thing, and we felt we needed to do something for our country. All the guys in my high school . . . joined the service after graduation. . . . I think in those days, people talked more if you didn't go.
>
> So I went to the navy recruiting office and said, "Here I am." I was too skinny. The (recruiter) told me to go home and to eat a lot of bananas and drink water. When I went back, I was sick of bananas. They weighed me and I weighed enough, so I got in. . . . I got orders to the *Consolation* right after the war broke out.

Lt. Floy Mangold (Christopher), Navy Nurse Corps, U.S. Navy (Ret), was stationed at Patuxant River Naval Air Base when she got her orders.

> When we received our orders, we were thrilled and excited. We would go home for about two weeks, then we'd go to California to meet the ship.
>
> I went home to Oklahoma, then flew on to San Francisco. Most of the [older] nurses had served in World War II. I was one of the youngest nurses. We were too young and naïve to be scared. We worked very hard. I mean we worked night and day around the clock because the wounded just kept coming.

From September 1950 to September 1952, the *Consolation* rendered service to key battles, including the invasion of Inchon and the evacuation of Hungnam. During this period 12,000 patients were admitted to the hospital. About 17,000 were treated as outpatients. Many patients were women and children who were casualties of war.

Patients Arrive

On 19 October 1950, the *Consolation* arrived in Korean waters. Then Comdr. Fred Smith describes their arrival into Pusan.

> We pulled into Pusan. The patients on stretchers were waiting for us. I understood some were wounded a week or so earlier. Their bandages were only changed one or twice. There were just too many of them and not enough people or supplies.
>
> So the first night we got about 300 patients. They arrived until about two or three o'clock in the morning. They were lined up on the pier at Pusan. We were using the litter hoists to get the patients onboard. We dropped a hook down to the pier. Those on the pier would hook the stretcher on. It would be brought up to the level of the ship. Then it would be swung on board.
>
> There was a triage officer and nurses right there. They'd look at the patients and tell us which ward to take them to. From then on, it was busy . . . very exciting . . . and pretty tiring as I remember it.

Haire and some of the nurses had a chance to see Pusan. Haire described what she saw:

> We inspected the main street of Pusan . . . there was very little to see, just filth and squalor. Living conditions seem worse than in Japan. The children are cute though. Some of the women dress in curious empire-style dress: an extremely high waistline and a full skirt to mid calf. Sometimes the skirt is separate from the top. Others wear very full pantaloons with a band round the ankle. I don't know how they manage to look so good in them; much better than we [did] in our slacks.
>
> A few of the older men wore their curious white costumes. Though gray would be a better word. A few native articles, mostly brass, were for sale but the prices were exorbitant [and] have tripled since the ship was here last. My corpsmen tell me that beer costs a dollar a can on the black market.

Lt. Comdr. Marie Dalton (Thomas), navy Nurse Corps, U.S. Navy (Ret), gave her impressions of Korea:

> The first thing you noticed was the smell of the honey pots. And of course, they made kimchee [fermented cabbage]. The didn't diaper their children; [the children] just went in the fields. So of course you'd get those odors.

The marines landed at Wonson and met little or no opposition. On 27 October 1950, the *Consolation* was anchored in Area George, Berth 101, Wonsan Harbor, Korea. Land mines were the main concern. Commander Haire wrote in her journal:

> The area which is supposedly swept of mines is marked with flags. There are a number of mine sweepers . . . other ships we passed—the *Missouri*, the *Eldorado*, the *Toledo* and several others.
>
> Just before noon the patients began to arrive. I had ten by 1500 (3:00 PM). Only two were battle casualties. Both marines with shrapnel wounds. It was satisfying to be busy.

Still in Wonsan Harbor, the patients continued to arrive. On 28 October 1950, 141 patients were admitted in addition to the 202 already on board. In a journal entry, Commander Haire described the patients arriving.

> The ward is filling fast and we are kept busy. At 2000 [8:00 PM] we went out to watch patients being brought aboard. A destroyer converted into a transport came along side. Ambulatory patients are brought aboard in a chair swung over the side. Litter patients are brought on with a hoist: four lines are fastened to the litter, one on each corner and then the hoist and the pulley brings them up. It's quite a sight. Everyone quiet and efficient until all the patients are transferred, and then the sailors from either ship start kidding each other.

Commander Smith remembers the feverish pace.

> We got the most serious cases. A lot of abdominal and head wounds. We had great surgeons. The laboratories, the x-rays, and the ORs worked at a frantic pace. The nurses were trying to get the patients cleaned up and comfortable.
>
> We always tried our best to have the best food we could get for them. The kitchen was going all the time. It was teamwork . . . really great to see it happen.

Captain Brooks was a surgical nurse. The operating rooms were definitely kept busy.

> We had three operating rooms and at least two operating tables in each room. Sometimes things would be done outside on the stretchers. The patients were brought down according to severity.

We really didn't have a triage. We sort of did the triage outside the operating rooms. It worked. We just didn't have the space.

I remember one smallpox case. I had never seen smallpox before. It was a sight to behold. He was completely covered, including in[side] his mouth and down his throat.

We had a good number of the Korean marines. They were very good patients . . . very stoic people. Many had belly wounds, gun shot wounds or shrapnel. We also had prisoners of war.

The relaxed atmosphere was short lived. According to Commander Haire's journal, more patients arrived on 2 November 1950.

A large influx of marines this afternoon, most of them from a group that [was] ambushed about six miles from Wonsan this morning. All was chaos; it just isn't possible to get everything done. One kid had a bad abdominal would. They came in unshaven, dirty, exhausted, looking about forty years old. And most of them are still in their teens. I could just sit down and cry for them, if I had the time.

The food situation is a mess. No pun intended. But they think it is wonderful and only complain that it is hard to start eating after having been on c-rations so long.

3 November 1950. This was the worst day yet . . . It is just killing me not to be able to do what one ought for these kids, but there isn't time. Oh well, guess I will go to the movies and [try to] forget my troubles.

4 November 1950. I live from one crisis to another, and it is 3:30 PM before I know it. I go off duty utterly exhausted both physically and mentally. Both a duty and evacuation party is going out tomorrow and so we must brace ourselves for a fresh onslaught of casualties.

7 November 1950. What a night! I never stopped running, except for fifteen minutes for dinner. We had ten to nineteen admissions on C-4 alone. It seems that some sixty Americans met up with a large group of North Koreans and these were the survivors. Things couldn't have been any worse. They came in a steady steam . . . In shock or next to it. Bloody, dirty and all the rest . . . these fellows just don't complain. Although two were critical and two serious, we didn't lose them.

9 November 1950. The doctors told one of my boys [patient], aged twenty, that he would have to lose his right arm. He was running a high temp, so I tried to combine a few words of comfort with an alcohol run. But if there is a formula that covers such situations, I haven't found it . . . I feel that I failed miserably.

10 November 1950. Today I hit the jackpot, five letters. Now I can understand why even the fellows I met just casually used to beg for letters. Mail becomes so terribly important.

We are running out of supplies and we leave to go back to Yokosuka. We will be in the states by 19 December 1950 and be in Norfolk by 29 December 1950.

18 December 1950. It is below zero on deck. . . . Was out on deck twice to watch the firing which was so loud during the movie that the ship shuddered with it. Star shells, flares, tracers. I am learning a new vocabulary.

23 December 1950. We four nurses on C-3 and C-4 are making Christmas stockings for the boys. It seemed a better idea than giving money. We are making them out of crinoline and stitching them with red yarn . . . filling them with shorts, skivvy shirts, candy, gum, cookies, and cigarettes.

26 December 1950. Morale is very high. We left Pusan at noon. The sun shining brightly and the weather mild.

28 December 1950. Arrived in Yokosuka about 4:00 PM [1600]. After dinner we got into our blues the first time in two months. Went over to the club and were swept into a party that a task force was throwing.

29 December 1950. The experts think that Yokosuka will be bombed and are making plans accordingly.

After spending time in Japan for rest and rehabilitation, the *Consolation* reported back to Pusan in January 1951. On 2 February 1951 she remained in Pusan with 648 patients on board. By March 1951 the *Consolation* was headed back to Yokosuka. Commander Haire wrote in her journal.

9 March 1951. Marie Dalton is coming aboard for duty. It seems amazing, but I hope she will be happy.

Lt. Comdr. Marie Dalton (Thomas), Nurse Corps. USN (Ret) was born into a navy family.

I had five cousins who were in the navy during World War II. My grandfather was a World War I navy veteran.

As a nurse, I felt that it was important to take care of the wounded. That's why I joined the navy. I was at Naval Hospital Yokosuka from September 1950 until March 1951.

In March 1951, I got orders to the *Consolation* to replace one of the nurses who got seasick. I packed my seabag and my footlocker. The *Consolation* was in port in Yokosuka, so I got in a small boat and went to where she was tied up. She just pulled away from the pier. At first they were not going to let me on. they were in the process of deploying. I had papers in hand. Waving them, I explained I had orders to board. They finally let me onboard.

In April 1951, the navy's *All Hands Magazine* reported:

More than 25,000 patients have been treated on board *Consolation* . . . during approximately seven months in the Korean theater . . . establishing a record for hospital ships . . .

. . . (Better than) ninety-eight percent of all wounded UN fighters treated on board have recovered.

Dubbed by the GIs as the "Galloping Ghost of the Korean Coast" because of her eerie night view . . .

. . . [W]on . . . her Battle Efficiency Pennant . . . [took] aboard nearly 2,000 wounded at Pusan . . . [at] Inchon, *Consolation* handled over 1,000 cases . . . [at] Wonsan . . . treated nearly 1,500 and at Hungnam . . . treated a record-breaking 2,000.

In October 1951, Sgt. John L. Fenwick, USMCR (Ret), was cared for aboard the *Consolation.*

I was wounded for the third time ten days before I was rotated home. I was hit by a North Korean machine gun on 5 October 1951.

Three bullets hit my ammo belt. These were the worst gunshot wounds. They struck me in my left flank involving the iliac crest, three vertebras, destroyed the sacro-iliac joint, severed an artery. I had an exit wound in my lower back the size of a fist.

Platoon corpsman William Snowden saved my life. He dragged me to safety. I was hit by two more bullets in my left upper arm. He was hit twice in his right shoulder. Despite his painful wounds, he dragged me to a safe place and administered to my wounds.

Medevaced to the field hospital, "Easy Med." Was operated on by Lt. Comdr. Phil Cerack. He removed eighteen inches of small intestine. He used a total of 837 sutures during surgery.

After all the surgical tubes were removed, I was flown to the *Consolation.*

When I arrived there, I thought I was in heaven. Large bunks with clean sheets and navy nurses. My nurse was a lieutenant commander, a World War II veteran. She was wonderful.

She asked me if I would like some ice cream. I couldn't believe it when she asked me what flavor I wanted. I grabbed her hand and kissed it. I said, "You nurses really are angels of mercy." Then I lost it. I cried like a baby slobbering all over her hand. It was hard to believe after a year of suffering deprivations. We were near starvation. There was so much pain and suffering. And now there was something as great as this. This nurse took care of me. It was hard to believe it was true.

Helicopter Deck

According to an excerpt from the 1953 ship's cruise book, the *Consolation* was selected as the experimental hospital ship. It was fitted with a helicopter landing deck. Having a helicopter deck could expedite transportation of the wounded to hospital facilities. In May 1951, the *Consolation* headed back home to California. On the way, Commander Haire received good news and then, as the *Consolation* gets closer to California, Commander Haire reports that the excitement mounts.

28 May 1951. I am getting my back longevity pay.

Approximately $280, which will see me home.

5 June 1951. Our last day out. Tonight we can see the lights of California along the shore and we expect to dock about 2:00 PM tomorrow. Have been picking up radio programs all day; same old commercials. The patients are all excited.

6 June 1951. This was the day. From noon on we lined the rails but the ship was not docked until almost 4:00 PM. There was a navy band. Top brass with brief speeches and crowds of friends and relatives. Very exciting, but hard to realize we are really back in the states.

A sixty-by-sixty-foot landing platform was constructed at the U.S. Naval Shipyard in Long Beach, California. Work was completed on 16 August 1951. The *Consolation* returned to the Korean Theater to resume her mission of medical support.

Prior to the helicopter landing platform, patients were brought alongside in small boats called LCVPs or LCMs (landing craft). The *Consolation*'s electric winch would drop its wire slings into the boats, which would hoist the stretcher (litter) or chair-borne patients aboard. During the typhoon season in the Far East, this operation could be extremely hazardous.

With the helicopter deck in place, the marine helicopters flew their missions of mercy when all small craft at sea were prohibited. A September 1952 article in the *Leatherneck* explained the process.

> Day and night the *Consolation*'s radio shack picks up messages. Some of them sound like this: "Hospital ship *Consolation*, this is Charlie Three. I have one walking wounded and two litter cases. One is a serious head injury. Will arrive at your ship in approximately three minutes."

> Within seconds this message reaches the Officer of the Deck on the bridge. "Flight Quarters" is sounded . . . on the PA system throughout the ship. The chief of medicine is notified. He alerts the neurosurgeon.
>
> The helicopter comes in. Hovers over the deck and lands. Before the rotor blades have coasted to a stop, the chock-men have secured the plane in position. The doctor and litter bearers are disembarking the patients. The ambulatory are guided to the hospital spaces. The litters are carried up the ramp to an emergency treatment room for examination and disposition. Total time from shore to ship and treatment, less than five minutes.
>
> Capt. John W. McElroy, USN, skipper of the *Consolation*, has been on hand at most landings to observe and study operations. The *Consolation* has demonstrated . . . that helicopter flights from the fighting front to a hospital ship are . . . the most practical and fastest method of handling battle casualties.

The 1953 *Consolation Cruise Book* provided a synopsis of the *Consolation*'s service during the Korean War. In late March 1952, when battle action increased on the Korean western front, the *Consolation* was ordered to Inchon Harbor to furnish medical support to the troops. Soon after her arrival the flow of patients began. By boat and helicopter they came. Battle casualties were admitted and received within minutes of being wounded.

The *Consolation* maintained a daily patient census of 400 plus for ten weeks. In June 1952, she was ordered home. During this period, she underwent overhaul and maintenance.

On the morning of 8 September 1952, the *Consolation* left her berth at Long Beach, California. She was on her way back to Korea. Her mission was again to aid the men wounded in the Korean hostilities.

The *Consolation* arrived in Inchon Harbor as another big Communist offensive was underway. During the first four days, the doctors, nurses and corpsmen worked around the clock. They got as little as eight hours sleep during a four-day period. In a twenty-four-hour period, as many as sixty-two helicopters landed on her fantail.

After serving for ten months on her third trip to Korea, the *Consolation* was ordered back to the States. All hands felt proud to have contributed to the United Nationals effort. During this ten-month stay overseas, the *Consolation* cared for 3,635 United Nationals troops and civilians. Since the outbreak of the Korean War in June 1950, the *Consolation* served thirty-one months in Far Eastern waters. She cared for a grant total of 18,433 patients. On average, seventy-six percent of their hospital beds were regularly used at this time.

I was wounded the night of 23 December 1952. I was treated at a field hospital and then taken to the *Consolation* on Christmas Day 1952. My wounds consisted of mortar fragments in the hand, arm, neck and in my eye, which was destroyed.

Our platoon corpsman gave me immediate care. When we returned to our MLR [main line of resistance], he put me on a helicopter to the field hospital. The corpsman gave me and the other wounded excellent care in a calm and gentle manner.

At the field hospital I was having trouble breathing. So I was given a tracheotomy. I was transferred to the *Consolation.*

Since I had a lot of congestion it was necessary to apply suction to keep the tracheotomy tube open. The nurses and corpsmen on the *Consolation* were always busy with patients in the ward. They kept an eye on me. All I had to do was raise my hand. They would come and clean out the tube. Although it was a rather unpleasant job, they did it cheerfully. They did everything they could to make me comfortable.

After about a week on the *Consolation*, one of the nurses brought in a Polaroid camera. She took my picture so I could send it to my parents. When I got home they told me how much that picture meant to them.

When it was time for me to leave the *Consolation* for Yokosuka, I got a set of recycled dungarees. I said my good-byes to the nurses and the corpsmen. One of the nurses gave me a set of her lieutenant junior grade bars. I guess she thought I might get a better seat on the plane if they knew I was an officer. It was very thoughtful of her.

Although that was almost fifty years ago I will never forget the excellent medical care I received from the nurses, doctors, and corpsmen of the U.S. Navy. I wish I could recall the names of those who cared for me [but] I will never forget their cheerful faces and how they helped me get over some rough times.

—1st. Lt. William Gilwee, USMCR (Ret)

★ ★ ★ ★ ★

During the Korean war three hospital ships, the USS *Consolation*, *Repose*, and *Haven*, would serve the wounded Marines before they were transported to the Naval hospital in Yokosuka, Japan. The nurses and doctors of the Navy would make a lifetime impression on the men under their care.

Nine Dragons, from *Brown Water, Black Berets*

THOMAS J. CUTLER

> It had become a place of darkness. But there was in it one river especially, a mighty big river, that you could see on the map, resembling an immense snake uncoiled, with its head in the sea, its body at rest curving afar over a vast country, and its tail lost in the depths of the land.
>
> —Joseph Conrad, *Heart of Darkness*

The Mekong Delta of southern Vietnam is a vast region of fertile ground and waterways that supplies much of the country's needs for rice. It is also home to about half the population of southern Vietnam. During the Vietnam War it was a region of vital importance to the South Vietnamese government, hotly contested by the communist insurgent guerillas who controlled much of the area. The most dangerous area in the region was the "Rung Sat" or "killer jungle" in Vietnamese. It covered an area of approximately 400 square miles of dense jungle, canals, and tributaries between the Thi Vi River to the east and Soi Rap River to the west. During the rainy season, 80 percent of the Rung Sat was underwater. It was a huge region of terrain that bordered the main shipping channel to Saigon, and it was a major base of operations for the Viet Cong and their North Vietnamese allies.

In 1965 the United States raised the ante from advising the South Vietnamese to combat role against communist insurgents. The U.S. Navy at the time had no river patrol craft and no operational program for riverine warfare. In good American tradition, one was improvised in the form of "MacLeod's Navy," a small group of antiquated landing craft (LCPL) and men assigned to patrol and interdict communist movements in the

Rung Sat zone and to develop river warfare tactics. The mission came under the command of Lieutenant Kenneth Logan MacLeod III, a determined and creative officer who would pave the way for the future of the Brown Water Navy in Vietnam. In the following chapter, Thomas J. Cutler, a veteran of the riverine warfare in Vietnam, describes an early patrol into the Rung Sat with the "River Rats" from his highly regarded book, *Brown Water, Black Berets*.

★ ★ ★ ★ ★

In the Tibetan Plateau of Central Asia, melting snow sends rivulets coursing downward over ancient rocks in a relentless quest for the sea. These rivulets merge to become streams cascading through pathways defined by gravity, their adolescent voices gathering in chorus to penetrate the silence of the land, until at last they reach the stage of maturity that Western man calls a river. In Tibet the people call this river Dza-Chu, the Water of the Rocks.

Dza-Chu, the world's eleventh longest river, changes its name several times along the 2,600-mile journey to the sea. As it races through the forbidding gorges of China's Yunnan Province it becomes Lan-Ts'ang Chiang, or Turbulent River. Then it flows more placidly into the northern reaches of Indochina and continues southward, becoming Mae Nam Khong to the Thais, Me Nam Khong to the Laotians, and Mekongk to the Cambodians. As the great river flows past Phnom Penh, the capital city of Cambodia, it fans out; by the time it crosses into South Vietnam, it has created one of the largest river deltas in the world. Westerners refer to the entire river, from Tibet to Vietnam, as the Mekong, and this massive delta as the Mekong Delta.

The main river branches into four separate rivers as it crosses South Vietnam's foot: from north to south, the My Tho, Ham Luong, Co Chien, and Hau Giang. The Americans frequently called the southernmost of these by its French name: the Bassac River. The Vietnamese call the entire complex Cuu Long Giang—the River of Nine Dragons—symbolizing the many mouths that yawn into the South China Sea. In reality, there are only eight, but to the Vietnamese eight is an unlucky number, so they choose to count nine for good fortune.

The delta itself is an alluvial plain that constitutes about one-fourth of the total land area that was South Vietnam. It is an area rich in rice, and about half of the population of South Vietnam resided there. Little wonder that the Mekong Delta was vitally important to the South Vietnamese government and that the Viet Cong exerted some of their most intense efforts there. An embassy official said, "That's where the Viet Cong have their heart, their greatest strength, control, and influence."

In 1965 the delta had only one major hard-surface road, Route 4, running from Saigon to Ca Mau. Nearly all travel and commerce depended upon the network of rivers, streams, and canals that crisscrossed the area. In light of the growing commitment of American combat forces, U.S. strategists resurrected the Bucklew Report and took a serious look at introducing U.S. Navy patrol craft into the waterways of the delta to interdict the infiltration routes out of Cambodia and to wrest some of the control away from the Viet Cong forces there. There were only two obstacles: the U.S. Navy had no river patrol craft to speak of, and no corporate knowledge of riverine warfare.

MacLeod's Navy

Two small boys sat across from one another on the cracked sidewalk, a cookie tin between them forming the arena. Each carefully lowered his matchbox into the tin while the other Vietnamese boys around them chattered excitedly. As the two slowly opened the boxes, long hairlike antennae emerged from each, waving in the oppressive Saigon air.

Lieutenant Kenneth Logan MacLeod III, USN, watched a large cricket emerge from each matchbox. They stood facing each other from opposite corners of the cookie tin, one black and the other a chocolate brown. MacLeod could hear chirps as he peered over the heads of the shouting and laughing boys into the miniature coliseum. One boy took a toothpick with bits of hair attached to the end and waved it in front of his cricket; an instant later the two insects were grappling in a fury of bites and kicks. The boys cheered wildly, and one of them jumped up so quickly his head nearly caught MacLeod on the chin.

In less than a minute the combat was over, with the brown cricket the victor. One of the boys turned to leave, but when he saw MacLeod hovering he stopped and grinned, revealing more spaces than teeth. "Hey, Joe," he said. "Black one VC, huh?"

"Let's hope so," MacLeod said and turned to continue down the tree-lined boulevard. He passed the Continental Palace Hotel, with its ever-present contingent of multinational reporters and various uniformed Americans scattered across the terrace. As he turned onto Duong Tu Do (Freedom Street—formerly the Rue Catinat in the days of French colonialism), he watched a young Vietnamese girl sail past on her Vespa motorscooter, the rear flap of her traditional *ao-dai* dress tied to the back fender to keep it from tangling in the cycle's machinery. The white flap billowed out behind like the mainsail on an ancient square-rigger, but the noisy engine coughed out a stream of blue smoke in adamant testimony to the twentieth century. Vespas, Lambrettas, and *xich-los* (bicycle-powered two-seater taxis) were everywhere. MacLeod smirked, remembering that he'd heard or read that the reason the Viet Cong had never taken Saigon was because they realized it would be impossible to fight their way through the traffic. He weaved in and out among the throngs of Vietnamese and foreigners that seemed to have been poured into Tu Do Street in equal numbers. In 1965 the many nightclubs that would later make Tu Do Street famous to American GIs had not yet emerged. There were many dressmaker's shops where the smart shopper could purchase a custom-made silk gown for about eight U.S. dollars.

Minutes later, MacLeod was in a small shop trying to adjust his eyes to the darkness. An old woman with protruding cheekbones and coal-black teeth emerged from behind a curtain. When she saw him, she bowed slightly and vanished again behind the curtain, emerging a few seconds later with a bundle of brightly colored cloth draped over one arm. Shuffling over to MacLeod, she unfolded one of her creations for him to inspect. The diffused light from the street caught the colors of a beautifully tailored American flag.

"You like?" the woman said.

"I like," he said, and she smiled proudly, the blackened teeth glistening as she nodded.

MacLeod watched her carefully wrap the two flags and wondered how she could sew with such gnarled old hands. He paid her the previously agreed-on price and then handed her some extra piasters, which brought forth a torrent of thanks accentuated by deep bowing. MacLeod, embarrassed, quickly left the shop.

As he stood in the bright afternoon sunshine trying to decide on the best route back to his boats, he muttered, "Not exactly my idea of Betsy Ross."

The two thirty-six-foot-long LCPLs eased away from the Navy repair-facility dock at the foot of Saigon's Cuong De Street, the shark's teeth on their bows flashing menacingly in the fading evening sunlight. The American flags flapping from the masts of the boats moving down the river in tandem were already beginning to show the wear of several weeks' worth of nightly patrols.

The lead boat's coxswain, Boatswain's Mate Third Class Rick Chapman, looked back over his shoulder at the lieutenant standing near the starboard gunwale amidships. "Mr. MacLeod," he said.

The lieutenant turned toward Chapman, a Swisher Sweet cigar clenched between his teeth.

"Steinberger says we're the only boats on the rivers flying the U.S. flag. Is that right?" Chapman asked.

"Probably," MacLeod answered with a puff of smoke.

The boats droned along the Saigon waterfront. Red tiled roofs and lush green trees seemed to fill all the spaces between the multistoried white hotels and government buildings. Music drifted across the water from the Majestic Hotel.

MacLeod thought about what Chapman had asked. As far as he knew, they were the only boats on river patrol in Vietnam under the Stars and Stripes. U.S. craft had been patrolling the coastline for several months on Market Time, but MacLeod was certain that his two boats were the first on the rivers. Some weeks before, back in August, MacLeod, who had been conducting a feasibility study for using amphibious LCPLs as coastal patrol craft, had suddenly been assigned a new mission. Rear Admiral Ward, then CHNAVADVGRU, had directed that Market Time be expanded into the rivers of the Mekong Delta and the Rung Sat Special Zone, where the Viet Cong seemed particularly strong. MacLeod was told to start patrolling the river network south of Saigon with his LCPLs and to develop tactics for these patrols. Rumors were circulating that a new Navy patrol craft, specially designed for river patrol, would arrive in Vietnam by the beginning of next year.

MacLeod had been promised the best LCPLs that could be found in the Pacific Fleet. What arrived were four dilapidated relics, two of which had to be sent to Subic Bay for major overhaul, while the other two needed many hours of mechanical and hull repair by MacLeod's team of talented and enthusiastic sailors. They stripped off years of accumulated paint, reinforced rust-thinned areas, repaired the tired old diesels, and mounted a veritable arsenal of weapons. They got what they could through legitimate supply sources; the rest was obtained by "MacLeod's Midnight Marine Supply Company," as they liked to call themselves. Through patience and creativity they markedly reduced the engine noise by incorporating some discarded French mufflers into the LCPL exhaust system. They added searchlights by adapting a battery of tank headlights and some automobile spotlights. When they were finished, the LCPLs didn't look much like their former selves: pedestal-mounted .50-caliber machine guns stood prominently fore and aft, .30-calibers protruded amidships, a tall thin mast was mounted amidships with a circular white radome at its peak, and shark's teeth and eyes were painted on the bows.

MacLeod's sailors were a swashbuckling group of young warriors. The second-in-command, Lieutenant (j.g.) Hal Graber, USNR, had quit medical school in order to join the Navy. Petty Officer Chapman had served in the Junk Force as an advisor and found his subsequent stateside tour dull, so he terminated it early by volunteering to go back to Vietnam. They were all proud of their new role and were playing it to the hilt. They called themselves "MacLeod's Navy" in a reference to the then-popular *McHale's Navy* television series about a World War II PT-boat skipper and his unorthodox but always triumphant crew.

On this October evening, a war correspondent from the *Arizona Republic,* Paul Dean, had joined "MacLeod's Navy" for a patrol in hopes of getting a story. Tall and rugged, he quickly hit it off with the "River Rats" (another sobriquet adopted by the LCPL sailors).

As the two-boat patrol left Saigon behind, Dean followed MacLeod into the tiny cabin just forward of the coxswain's flat. It was stifling down there, out of the breeze. MacLeod pulled out a chart and began walking a pair of dividers across the paper in a southerly direction.

"Where are we headed?" Dean asked.

"Into the Rung Sat," MacLeod answered.

"Is that the place they call 'Forest of Assassins'?"

"That's the one." MacLeod pulled off his green fatigue cap, revealing a closely cropped crew cut, and wiped the sweat off his forehead with his fingertips. "That place has always been a no-man's-land for anybody but pirates and outlaws. Now the Viet Cong have taken it over as a training and staging area. They've got a hospital and a munitions company somewhere in there and supply depots all over the place. Until we came along they had uncontested control of practically the whole area."

"What's it like in there? I mean what is there about the area that makes it such a great hideout?"

"It's a goddamned maze! Nothing but rivers and streams and canals all laced together through thick forests of mangrove. Half of it's swamp; the rest is islands, lots of them. There are no roads to speak of. The Vietnamese Army's got enough sense not even to think about going in there, so they turned it over to the VNN, but they haven't got the assets to set up any kind of meaningful deterrence."

Dean reflected for a moment and then asked, "So where do you and your LCPLs come in? What do you hope to accomplish with only two boats?"

MacLeod picked up the chart from the table in front of him. "Our stated mission is basically experimental, to see if we can disrupt some of Charlie's movements in the area. If we're successful on a small scale, then the Navy will come in here and in the Mekong Delta in a big way and clean out this infestation." He rapped the backs of his fingers against the chart as he spoke. "In reality, I think we've upset Mr. Charles a lot more than was originally expected. He doesn't know when or where we're going to turn up. I never tell anybody where we're going each night so there's no chance of a leak. We just appear in different places at different times and give these bastards a big headache." He pointed to several places on the chart where grease pencils had left black crosses. "Here's where we've caught him with his pajamas down already." He pointed to several other marks on the chart. "And here's where he's tried to hit us. I have no doubt that we're high on his list of priorities."

"So you think there's a real need for the U.S. Navy to get involved in river patrol?" Dean asked.

"Definitely. The VC are in control of a lot of the Mekong Delta, and they use the rivers and canals there for infiltration of supplies from Cambodia. They practically own the Rung Sat. And the shipping channel into Saigon is along the Long Tau River, and that runs right through the Rung Sat! MACV is real worried that Charlie's going to be able to sink a large ship there and really screw up traffic. A lot of Vietnam's economy and the war effort depend upon keeping that channel open. I don't think there's any question that the Navy's coming in here. The need is obvious, and the coastal patrols have broken the ice for using Navy craft in an operational role. We're just the first in what I'm sure will be a major involvement."

Both men left the cabin and emerged on deck. Saigon was a soft glow of diffused light off their port quarter, and the palms along the riverbank to the west were silhouetted against the orange remnants of the sun.

"That's Nha Be just ahead," MacLeod said to Dean. "Last friendly outpost before the Rung Sat. Time to suit up."

All around the craft, crew members were donning helmets and flak jackets. There were nine men in the crew: MacLeod, a coxswain, an engineer, four gunners to man the machine guns, and two ammunition-handlers. Four of the crew were Vietnamese; the others were American.

A few minutes later they had left Nha Be behind. Ahead, the river looked black and forbidding. MacLeod turned on the radar. Crew members removed canvas covers from the machine guns, and the boat's running lights were extinguished. MacLeod spoke into the radio handset, and LCPL-2 began closing up the distance. Her running lights too blinked off.

Dean leaned close to MacLeod to be heard above the engines. "What now?" he asked.

"We head deeper into the forest and we watch for curfew violators," came the reply.

The boats continued. The glow from the west vanished, and soon they were swallowed completely by the darkness. An occasional flicker from the dense vegetation was the only light except for the dials on Chapman's instrument panel and the pale glow reaching out of the radar screen's hood whenever MacLeod's face was not pressed into it.

MacLeod's hoarse voice suddenly broke the silence that had set in when they entered the Rung Sat: "I think we've got a live one . . . dead ahead. Back it off, Chapman."

When the engines throttled back, the bow settled into the river. Dean sensed movement about him as crew members took up their stations. He could hear the metallic sounds of guns being loaded.

"Light 'em up," MacLeod said, and a searchlight that seemed brighter than the sun severed the darkness ahead.

A tiny sampan, no more than fifteen feet long, with a minute dinghy in tow was illuminated in the harsh white glare of the searchlight. Several figures that had apparently been sleeping on the low cabin roof jumped up and raised their hands high.

Chief Warrant Officer Tham, one of the VNN members of LCPL-1's crew, called out across the water, telling the sampan to come alongside for inspection. Its occupants didn't respond immediately, so Tham fired a .45-caliber round into the air from his pistol. The shot sounded like a thunderclap in the still air, and the sampan immediately began coming their way.

LCPL-2 hovered astern, careful to remain in the darkness behind the searchlights while LCPL-1's crew searched the sampan.

Dean noticed that the air exposed in the light of the searchlight beams was filling with flying insects that looked like snow in a blizzard. He dabbed quickly at a drop of perspiration tickling his cheek, not sure that it wasn't one of the flying creatures.

Because the search revealed only fishing lines and rusty bait cans, the sampan was released after its occupants received a lecture from Chief Warrant Officer Tham regarding curfews. Tham had also confiscated their identification papers and would turn them in for further investigation by local authorities.

During the next several hours the River Rats stopped about a dozen sampans without finding anything of interest. Each time, the crew's tension would build and then collapse as the danger came and went. The routine took its toll, and some of the crew dozed between confrontations.

Trying to ward off sleep, MacLeod, Chapman, and Dean took up the ritual of mid-watch sailors everywhere, swapping sea stories and tales of their lives. At one point they discovered that all three had been born in January. They wondered what the horoscope was for Capricorns that night.

The hours wore on. The boats reached the point where the Soi Rap River empties into the South China Sea, and they turned east briefly, then north into the Dong Tranh River. The radar showed the river gradually narrowing as they continued northward. MacLeod explained to Dean that the Dong Tranh eventually merged with the Long Tau, the main shipping channel, but got pretty tight before that point. He said that the banks of the Long Tau had been defoliated by chemicals to make it hard for the enemy to operate there; but their present stretch of river had not been defoliated, and they could be pretty certain that they would be "rubbing elbows" with Charlie as they got in deeper.

At 0515 it was still pitch dark when three moving contacts appeared on radar farther upriver. The engine sound climbed from a monotonous growl to a businesslike roar. Crew members awakened and moved to their stations, their anticipation climbing again.

As they closed in, MacLeod called to Gunner's Mate Second Class Ray Steinberger on the twin fifties up forward: "Get ready on the lights." A pair of spotlights had been mounted with the machine guns to permit easy training of the lights and illumination for the guns. "Okay, hit 'em with the lights," MacLeod said.

Steinberger complied, and a glare assaulted everyone's eyes. Dean could make out several startled faces aboard the three motorized sampans before them. Several seconds passed. Then, in a lightning-quick move, one of the men in the sampans whipped out a rifle and fired it without hesitation at the lights. The River Rats had their cue. Gunfire exploded from LCPL-1. Red and white tracers raced across the water, and answering bullets danced across the deck of the LCPL.

Dean watched as MacLeod, ignoring the rounds about him, calmly inserted a 40-mm round into his grenade launcher and fired it at the lead sampan. An instant later, the target disintegrated before their eyes, splinters raining into the river in every direction.

Out of the mangroves on the shore behind LCPL-1, automatic weapons fire announced the presence of more enemy as the remaining two sampans raced for cover. Lieutenant (j.g.) Graber's LCPL-2 opened up on the mangroves. One of LCPL-1's crew nearly fired on LCPL-2 in the confusion, but MacLeod alertly averted his mistake, redirecting the fire to the shore position. Within seconds all enemy firing had been silenced. The two sampans, taking advantage of their shallower drafts, disappeared into the swamp.

MacLeod quickly assessed his damage. The boats had suffered no major casualties, and the only injuries to the crew consisted of a few skinned knuckles and Dean's brush with death as a tracer round passed so close that its heat burned his elbow.

The River Rats pounded one another's backs in exultation; all seemed to be talking at once. MacLeod went into the cabin and emerged a moment later to pass around a box of Dutch Masters, which he called his victory cigars.

Seven hours later, MacLeod's Navy arrived back at Saigon tired but happy. They cleaned weapons, checked engine oil, and did all the other chores that took precedence over sleep.

After an hour, MacLeod, Dean, and Chapman had one more task to complete. Digging up the previous day's newspaper, they turned to the horoscope section and read the entry for Capricorn: "Today should be a time to relax. Tonight will bring much activity."

Ken MacLeod's service on this and many other similar patrols did not go unrecognized. On 15 April 1966 he was presented with the Bronze Star with Combat "V" and the following citation from the Secretary of the Navy:

> For meritorious service from 1 September to 4 November 1965 while serving with friendly foreign forces engaged in armed conflict against the enemy in Viet Nam. As commander of two LCPL river patrol boats attached to Rung Sat Special Zone, Viet Nam, Lieutenant MacLeod participated in over twenty combat night operations in which he came under enemy fire. His exceptional initiative and aggressive action were prime factors in significantly reducing the freedom of movement of the enemy. Although subjected to sniper fire and mining, Lieutenant MacLeod continually ignored the dangers and relentlessly carried out his mission of seeking out and destroying the enemy. His courage, sense of responsibility and dedication to duty were in keeping with the highest traditions of the United States Naval Service.

But this was not the only recognition that MacLeod (and others like him) received. The day after the award ceremony an article appeared in the San Diego papers describing what MacLeod had done to earn the Bronze Star. A few days later he received a letter:

> Congratulations on your decoration for cowardly heroism in Viet-Nam. The U.S. Christian Crusaders are doing a wonderful job massacring the people and devastating their people with no bombers to bomb back and no warships to fight the mightiest navy in the world.
>
> Killing unarmed people on unarmed fishing junks should be worth the Congressional medal. Fighting a country that can not fight back—must be fun.

★ ★ ★ ★ ★

Ken MacLeod finished his Vietnam combat tour and returned to Coronado, California where he helped evaluate the Navy's new river patrol boat (PBR) design later used with the SEALS and retired from the Navy in 1970. That same year the United States transferred the last of its river patrol force boats to the South Vietnamese government marking the end of the Brown Water Navy. The *Stars and Stripes* would report: "In the four years since its inception, the Brown Water Navy fought thousands of brief but bloody battles for control of large water-bound areas of Vietnam's rice bowl and of major enemy supply routes from Cambodia. Names like 'Blood Creek,' 'Coral Bend,' and 'Rocket Alley,' were etched into the lore of the struggle for Vietnam's crucial inland waterways as the Brown Water Navy patrolled border rivers, delta canals and the shipping lanes to Saigon that run through the Rung Sat special zone."

The Ballad of Whitey Mack, from *Blind Man's Bluff*

SHERRY SONTAG AND CHRISTOPHER DREW

> To the Soviets, American submariners were more than an enemy; they were ever present pests. To other Americans, they were simply the anonymous men of the Silent Service.
>
> —Sherry Sontag

One fact stood out after the end of World War II—the submarine had come of age. It had proven to be a decisive weapon against the empire of Japan. German U-boats had brought Great Britain close to the brink of defeat in 1942 before the Allies regained control of the Atlantic. Submarines would play a definitive role in the Cold War between the United States and the Soviet Union as part of a "strategic triad" of nuclear deterrence based on long-range bombers, nuclear missiles, and submarines. A technological arms race with the Soviets became the central feature of the Cold War. The addition of nuclear propulsion for submarines enabled them to stay at sea for as long as necessary. The ability to launch missiles while submerged meant nuclear weapons could be placed within a few hundred miles of an enemy shore, giving them no time to react if war came.

Admiral Hyman G. Rickover oversaw the construction of America's first nuclear submarine, the USS *Nautilus* commissioned in 1954. She was the first submarine to navigate under the North Pole, an incredibly dangerous mission even today. The Soviets were the first to launch a ballistic missile from a submarine. The USS *Triton* would make the first submerged circumnavigation of the earth in 1960. That same year the American Polaris missile program became operational, allowing the submarines to launch missiles with a range of 1,400 miles. A new class of boat was commissioned in 1967 with the fast attack USS *Sturgeon*, whose mission was to stalk enemy submarines and gather intelligence. American fast attack boats gave the United States a precious defense against Soviet missile submarines in the event of war.

Much of what American submarines accomplished during the Cold War remained secret. In 1999, however, journalists Sherry Sontag, Christopher Drew, and Annette Lawrence Drew published *Blind Man's Bluff* describing some of the US Navy's amazing submarine missions to gather intelligence of Soviet missile tests, monitor enemy harbors, and track enemy submarines. In the following chapter they describe the mission of Captain Chester M. "Whitey" Mack and the USS *Lapon* as they trailed the first Soviet Yankee Class ballistic missile submarine in enemy waters in 1969.

★ ★ ★ ★ ★

Commander Chester M. Mack, 6'6" maverick known as "Whitey," after his pure blond pate, looked through his periscope out onto the Barents Sea. He was here in search of a new and lethal soviet ballistic missile submarine that NATO had dubbed, without mirth, the "Yankee."

It was March 1969, and in one terrifying technological leap, the Soviets had finally come out with a nuclear-powered missile sub with a design that seemed borrowed from Polaris and that might be capable of striking the White House or the Pentagon from more than 1,000 miles offshore. It was Mack's job to learn more about it.

Mack had driven his sub straight through the Barents, the zealously guarded training area for the Northern Fleet, the Soviet Navy's most advanced and powerful. He was traveling with the arrogance of somebody who knew he was at the helm of one of the Navy's newest subs, a Sturgeon-class attack boat armed with the latest sonar and eavesdropping equipment. He was also traveling with a lot more luck than most, because in this game of hit and miss, he had just found what he was looking for.

There in front of his scope was a Yankee, 429 feet long, 39 feet across, weighing in a 9,600 tons. Mack sidled *Lapon* up to within 300 yards and stared.

"Holy Christ, that son-of-a-bitch looks like a Mattel model," he blurted out. The submarine was indeed a Polaris look-alike, from the shape of its hull down to its sail-mounted diving planes. The image was broadcast down in the crew's mess on a television wired to the periscope—what submariners called "periviz." Lack, Mack would even air reruns, the sight was that striking.

Mack hooked a Hasselblad single-lens reflex camera onto the periscope and held down the shutter. The film advanced on a motorized drive as *Lapon* moved slowly forward, Mack lifting her scope out of the water for only seven seconds at a time in an effort to avoid detection. With each peek of the periscope, he grabbed a few photos, each time capturing another small portion of the massive boat. It would take seven of the photos pasted together to show the entire Yankee.

During the years the first Yankees were under construction, U.S. intelligence had collected little more than fuzzy images captured by spy satellites showing the Soviets were preparing to mass-produce the new weapon. But over the last year, as the Yankees ventured out on sea trials, U.S. surveillance subs had been moving in for a closer look at this nuclear monster decorated with sixteen doors hiding sixteen portable missile silos. The Yankee seemed a huge advance over the other ballistic-missile subs the Soviets had put to sea, the diesel-powered Zulus and Golfs and the first nuclear-powered missile boats, the Hotels. None of those boats had inspired the same fear the Yankee inspired now. The earlier subs were loud and easy for SOSUS and sonar to spot. Now the U.S. sub force was faced with a crucial question: Did the Yankee mimic more than Polaris's shape? Was it possible that, just six years after the Cuban Missile Crisis, the Soviets were positioned to launch a first strike with little or no warning? If the subs were as silent and deadly as they seemed, then, at the very least, the Soviets would have matched the United States in creating a second-strike capability, a way to punch back if all their land missiles and bombers were destroyed.

Captain James Bradley knew his spy program had already produced a lot of critical information about the development of soviet subs and missiles. Photographing the sunken Golf had been a technological coup. But the Golfs posed little threat compared to the Yankees, and nothing was more important now than learning how to find these new subs, how to destroy them.

Photos of a Yankee did only so much good. The U.S. Navy and its NATO allies needed to see these boats in action, see just where they carried their missiles, needed to collect sound signatures to ensure that the subs could never pass SOSUS listening nets unheard, and so that surveillance subs and sonar buoys dropped by P-3 Orion sub-hunter planes could recognize the threat as it passed.

Someone had to get close to a Yankee in action, and he would have to stay close enough for long enough to give the United States ammunition to counter the new threat. For this, almost any risks were warranted.

As pumped up as Mack was from his photographic feat, he knew that the real star of the sub force would be the man who accomplished a long trail. Other commanders knew it too, and even the loss of *Scorpion* was not enough to kill the fighter-jock bravado that the new mission was sparking within the ranks. But Mack was feeling quite proprietary about the Yankees now, and he was certain he could be the guy to get in close and stay there. He was sure of that even though nobody else had been able to. Mack had that kind of an ego.

In fact, everything about this thirty-seven-year-old commander was big. His towering, 240-pound frame didn't quite fit through *Lapon*'s low hatches and narrow passageways, and he was almost always bent over in the control room, littered overhead with a maze of piping and wire. Submarines were just too small to contain Whitey Mack. He was a larger-than-life renegade, much like the heroes in the novels he devoured by the basketful. He saw himself as the hero I a story he was writing as he went along, a story ruled by his own tactics and sometimes by his own rules.

He had never attended the naval Academy. Instead, he was recruited into officer's Candidate School by a brash ROTC XO at Pennsylvania State University who bragged that he won his wife in a poker game. Mack himself was the son of a Pennsylvania coal miner, and he held up this lack of official polish as a badge of honor. Mack labeled himself a "smart-ass kind of guy," and he faced down his superiors with piercing blue eyes and a brand of brass that had nothing to do with epaulet stars. With wry irony, he sported a homemade pair of Russian dolphins alongside his standard American dolphins—the emblem of the U.S. submarine fleet—and he liked nothing better than to rush about his submarine shouting obscenities in Russian.

"A faint heart never fucked a pig." That was *Lapon*'s motto and it had been ever since Mack's first voyage on the sub when he used the phrase to announce his decision to follow a new soviet sub close to her territorial waters. (The line was recorded on a continuous tape running in *Lapon*'s control room.) Although, when the subject came up once in front of an admiral, Mack delicately altered the phrase to "A faint heart never won a fair maiden."

Mack had plunged into command of *Lapon* in late 1967, first by horse-trading with other commanders for the men he believed would create an all-star crew, then by installing all manner of experimental, and often unauthorized, equipment on his submarine. He alternately inspired and mercilessly drove his men. He alternately impressed and badgered senior admirals, until he was allowed to skip the usual months of U.S.-based shakedown training and head straight into the action.

To a large degree, Mack was emblematic of his era. Throughout the sub force, captains who avoided risks were branded with nicknames such as "Charlie tuna" or "Chicken of the Sea." Still, Mack left his superiors—not to mention other commanders who prided themselves on their own daring—debating whether he was dangerously blurring the line between valor and recklessness. To be sure, those close-up photos of the Yankee were as valuable as any intelligence anyone had gotten lately, but Mack had also taken other immense risks for limited intelligence return.

Lapon had already been detected in the Barents once under Mack's watch. It may have been a glint of sunlight off her periscope, no one was sure, but suddenly the men in *Lapon*'s radio shack heard a Soviet pilot sending out an alert in Russian: "I see a submarine."

When *Lapon*'s officer of the deck pointed his periscope toward the sky, he saw a helicopter pilot who seemed to be looking right at him. "He's got the biggest fucking red mustache I ever saw!" the officer exclaimed.

"That's close enough," Mack said, breathless, as he raced from his personal quarters into the control room, still in his skivvies. "We better get the hell out of here." With that, he got his boat out of Dodge before the soviets had a chance to mount a full search.

Mack also had driven so close to two Soviet subs conducting approach and attack runs that *Lapon* ended up in the path of one of their torpedoes. Mack knew that, for an exercise like this, the Soviets were shooting duds. But he had no intention of proving his point by letting the torpedo hit. Instead, he sent the order to the engine room that kicked *Lapon* into high speed. Flying "balls to the wall," as submariners say, Mack outraced the weapon. (The incident occurred just after he had taken *Lapon* out searching for *Scorpion*, though well before anyone realized that a torpedo might have killed that boat.)

Two spooks on board, George T. "Tommy" Cox and Joseph "Jesse" James, were so shaken by the incident that when they later tried to grab a smoke in the radio room, neither man could steady himself long enough to light up. Cox wanted to be a country-western singer, had once taken first place at the Gene Hooper Country Western show Talent Contest in Caribou, Maine, and had worked his way through high school playing backup at a place called Cindy's Bar. After this trip on *Lapon*, he recorded a ballad called "Torpedo in the Water" on his first and only collection of submarine greatest hits, *Take Her Deep*. The song was an ode to a close call:

> There's a 400 pounder of TNT
> 'Bout to blow us to eternity.
> Gee, I hate to see a grown man cry,
> But goodness knows that I'm too young to die.
> Torpedo in the water, and it's closing fast.

From her encounter with the torpedo, *Lapon* carried back transcripts and photographs of the initial part of the test, as well as rolls of film filled with other soviet activities—all of it interesting, none of it crucial, none of it enough to make Whitey a star—*the* star—of the Atlantic Fleet.

Instead, it was another man who was so heralded, Kinnaird R. McKee, a lithe southern gentleman with bushy eyebrows and a showman's flair. He had set the standard for surveillance operations when he was on the USS *Dace* (SSN-607), and even though McKee's stellar command was nearly over by the time Mack photographed the Yankee in March 1969, he stood as an icon in the sub force. In 1967, McKee had not only photographed a soviet nuclear-powered ice-breaker as it was being towed, but he grabbed radioactive air samples that proved the ship had suffered a reactor accident. The next year, in one breathtaking mission, McKee collected the first close-up photographs and sound signatures of not one by two of the second generation of Soviet nuclear-powered subs: an attack sub and a cruise missile sub that NATO had named the "Victor" and the "Charlie." He had found one of the new subs in the waters off Novaya Zemlya, a large island between the Barents and Kara Seas that was one of the Soviet's main nuclear test areas.

Like Mack, McKee had been detected. Indeed, he had snapped a photograph of a Soviet crew member standing on the deck of one of the subs and pointing right at the *Dace*'s periscope just before the Soviets began to chase. McKee had to outrace a group of soviet surface patrols pinging wildly with active sonar. He finally managed his escape by driving *Dace* straight under the hazardous reaches of the Arctic ice. When it was safe to emerge, he continued his mission, locating the second new Soviet sub within a week.

"Gentlemen, the price of poker has just gone up in the Barents Sea," McKee announced on his return at a session with the Joint Chiefs of Staff and members of the Defense Department. With typical flair, he captured his audience with a briefing no less dramatic for his exclusion of the detection and his omission of the shot of the soviet crewman pointing at *Dace*. McKee's presentation and his slide show of other photographs shot through his scope went over so well that his immediate superiors never thought to criticize him for allowing his sub to be detected. Instead, for McKee, the mission was marred only by the fact that the Navy had refused to let him name the Soviet submarines he had found.

His manner, as much as anything was what separated McKee from the likes of Whitey Mack. McKee was everybody's idea of a hero. While Mack bullied his way through the system, McKee was one of those officers pegged early on for the fast track to the top. This was a man who courted his sweetheart, Betty Ann, by spinning her through a winter's night in a Jaguar convertible with the top down and then spun her about with a marriage proposal thirteen days later. On *Dace*, he courted the vigilance of his junior officers by promising cases of Dewar's scotch and Jack Daniels to any who helped him spot the new soviet subs. He won over admirals with the same flair, conjuring up such amazing tales of his exploits that the men who reigned over the U.S. submarine force never thought to question the risks he took.

Mack also had other competition in the Atlantic Fleet. There was Alfred L. Kelln, the commanding officer of the USS *Ray* (SSN-653), who had shot the very first pictures of a Yankee. Then there was Commander Guy H.B. Shaffer of the USS *Greenling* (SSN-614), who had slipped his sub directly beneath both a Charlie and a Yankee a few months before Mack spotted one. That gave *Greenling*'s crew a chance to record the noise levels and the harmonics that the soviet boats created in the water and the chance to film the hull and propeller, underwater through the periscope, with a new low-light television camera. Indeed, *Greenling* got so close to the underside of the Yankee that had the Soviets checked their fathometer, the ocean would have seemed very shallow, perhaps not more than 12 feet deep.

The job, known as "underhulling," was enormously dangerous. At any time, one of the soviet submarines could have moved to submerge right on top of *Greenling*, but the payoff was enormous as well. The United States had the first acoustic fingerprint of a Yankee submarine, and the sounds from *Greenling*'s tapes were quickly plugged into the SOSUS computers.

Now one question remained: Would the data collected by *Greenling* be enough the make the Yankees stand out as they moved into the open ocean din of fishing boats, marine life, and currents? Nobody would know that until somebody accomplished the longer trail through an actual deployment.

The race was on. Mack and the other commanders took their turns, steaming again out past 50 degrees north latitude, out of U.S. waters, and out of touch with fleet leaders back home, toward the Barents Sea and the Yankees' home ports.[18]

[18]Tightly coordinating their efforts with U.S. submariners, British subs sometimes helped fill in what had become a nearly seamless round-robin surveillance of the Soviet ports in the Barents. There were only a couple of British subs trained for the task, and they went near Soviet shores only during spring and fall, but those subs were dedicated to the spy mis-

Mack's chance came in September 1969. As *Lapon* pulled out of Norfolk, she was stocked with a mountain of eggs, meat, and syrupy drink mixes known as "bug juice"—typical fare for a long mission. There was, however, one major exception: her mess held three months' worth of frozen blueberries. Mack had a voracious appetite for blueberries and blueberry muffins, and he shared his passion with his crew. On board were also ingredients enough to fuel weekly pizza nights and a one-armed bandit to save off boredom.

There never would have been room for a slot machine on *Gudgeon* or any of the other diesel boats that went out on the first spec ops. That's not to say *Lapon* wasn't cramped, but at least each man had his own rack—no hot-bunking, no sharing. The racks were still stacked one atop another—shelves with mattresses on them—and some mattresses were still crammed in among the torpedoes, but there was some relief in having 15 square feet or so of private space that could be curtained off from the rest of the crew. The shorter guys even had room to stow a few books so long as they didn't mind designating the bottom square of their beds a bookshelf. And just about everyone had a single drawer, although that was all the space they had to store three months' worth of skivvies, uniforms, and anything else they believed they couldn't live without.

The diesel stench was gone with these nukes, as was the condensation that had plagued the diesel submarines. *Lapon* was downright comfortable, practically climate-controlled for anyone who didn't mind the constant clouds of cigarette smoke that massed despite the advanced air-filtering system. Nobody expected much more from life in their "closed sewer pipe." For most of the guys, contact with the outside would be pretty much limited to periviz and "family grams": the three- or four-line messages that wives and parents were allowed to send a few times each deployment.

Beyond that, the men's existence was charted out in a rhythm that amounted to six hours of watch, followed by twelve hours of equipment

---

sion, and that's what their commanders and crews specialized in. They were good at it, and they were aggressive. The British Royal Navy just didn't mind confronting the Soviets.

Once, a Soviet surface ship tried lining the Strait of Sicily with twin-cylinder buoys, and it seemed to U.S. intelligence that it was an effort to create an acoustic barrier—a sort of floating SOSUS net. There was great hand-wringing from the U.S. State Department to the Navy, debates about whether the United States should just go in and grab the buoys, when suddenly somebody noticed they had vanished. It turns out the British had a squadron of destroyers in Malta that went in and sank each and every one of the devices with naval gun fire.

repair, endless paperwork, and qualifying exams. Nobody was handed his dolphins, the mark of an official submariner, until he had qualified on nearly every system on the boat.

Still, sanity finds a way, and on this sub Mack was determined to help it. Mack organized nightly sing-alongs, having managed to dig up about a dozen guitar players among his handpicked crew. Tommy Cox was among them, back on board, carrying his guitar and a three-month supply of strings and picks. Cox, who had become the first spook in the navy to bother with all of the standard submariners' qualifying exams and earn his dolphins, now entertained his true crewmates with performances of "Torpedo in the Water" and a new song about *Scorpion*, as well as standard covers of Johnny Cash, Ricky Nelson, Jerry Lee Lewis, and Elvis Presley tunes.

It was no accident that Cox was back on *Lapon*. While most spooks were assigned to subs by the naval Security Group and almost never rode the same boat twice, Mack had managed to handpick his spook team just like he had the rest of his crew. He fought to keep his favorites, his core team, together. Along with Cox, there was Lieutenant Donald R. Fallon, the spook team leader. Mack decided Fallon would be a permanent member of the crew about ten seconds after the spook first boarded *Lapon*. He had spent his first nine seconds staring Mack down. The tenth second was the kicker. That's when he came up with a description of Mack that was never topped. Borrowing from the sub force's love of acronyms, he dubbed Mack "NOM-FWIC," or, in non-naval parlance, "Number One Mother Fucker What's In Charge."

Mack liked men who were bright, inventive, just odd enough to appreciate his own eccentricities, and as willing as he was to bend the rules. One of Mack's favorite acquisitions was a chief machinist's mate with the unlikely name of Donald Duck. He was a self-proclaimed hillbilly, raised in a log house in Shelby Country, Alabama. Mechanics was the family business. Duck's dad worked on buses, Duck on submarines. He never finished grade school. In fact, he had enlisted in the Navy under an illiteracy program, but he could fix anything on *Lapon*, and he was an even better scrounger than Mack. That, in particular, was an especially useful art now that the Vietnam War made materials scarce. Duck would find or steal whatever *Lapon* needed, keeping his cache of spare parts in a place only he believed to be secret.

Duck's lack of formal schooling didn't matter on *Lapon*, where most of the enlisted men had little more than a high school education anyway. This was a blue-collar crowd, but they were, as a whole, a bit brighter, a bit more inventive, and a lot more willing to put up with long months of confinement than just about anyone in the regular Navy. The officers mostly came out of the Naval Academy. In the end, the differences blurred. Rank, station, pedigree—on the best subs none of that mattered much. Maybe it was the confinement; maybe there was no other good way to run a submarine. After all, one of the first lessons any college-educated lieutenant learned was that he wasn't going to get very far without the help of his grizzled chiefs and a bunch of enlisted guys willing to engineer imaginative fixes to all of the unimaginable problems that were likely to crop up month after month at sea.

Now the crew that Mack built was about to be put to the test. One week into the trip, *Lapon* got a message, the one Mack had been hoping for: on September 16, SOSUS had detected a Yankee north of Norway. It was heading out of the Barents Sea toward the GIUK gap. A second SOSUS array then picked up the Yankee as it passed just north of Norway's Jan Mayen Island at the mouth of the Denmark Strait, which separates Greenland and Iceland. If Mack could intercept the Yankee before it made it past the gap into the open ocean, where she would be far more difficult to find, *Lapon* would be able to attempt a trail.

As Mack raced *Lapon* toward the Denmark Strait, an allied P-3 Orion airborne submarine hunter confirmed the Yankee's heading. *Lapon* arrived the next day and began a patrol moving slowly back and forth at the southernmost tip of the Denmark Strait, just southwest of Iceland.

Donnie Ray Bolling, the chief of the boat, hung a map in the crew's mess. From now on, the quartermaster would go below periodically to give the crew a look at *Lapon*'s position. If the caught up to the Yankee, he'd chart her position as well. Sharing such details with the crew was against regulation. But Mack wanted his men enthusiastic. He believed that knowing what they were attempting would make up for the lack of sleep that was about to become the rule on the boat.

Mack called for modified battle stations. Around him the control room was packed with men crammed in between charting tables, computer equipment, and weapon controls, with all their corresponding oscilloscopes, dials, gauges, and plotting gear. The pipes that hung from nearly every inch overhead and all around made the compartment seem all he more crowded. In the center of it all was the periscope stand. Two scopes sprouted out of the foot-high pedestal. Just in front of the stand, the diving officer and two planesmen sat tightly tiered in a pyramid, staring at depth gauges. From here on out, the fire control party, the sonar crews, the navigators, and the diving watch would have two imperatives: finding the Yankee and keeping the Yankee from finding the *Lapon*.

Only one day went by before the Yankee passed to the east of *Lapon*. The sound of the submarine was so faint that the sonarmen almost failed to pick it up over the clamor of nearby fishing trawlers and teeming marine life. But there it was, a slight flicker on the oscilloscope, the electronic image of the soviet submarine. This wasn't going to be easy. In the noisy waters off of Greenland, the submarine was audible in the din only when it ventured within 1,400 yards of *Lapon*.

Mack ordered *Lapon* southeast. He was going to try a "sprint and drift." The plan was to race *Lapon* at 20 knots for half an hour or so to a point where the Yankee would soon pass if she maintained her track. Then *Lapon* would slow down to 3–5 knots, drift back and forth, and listen.

The Yankee showed up, but then disappeared again. Mack was worried. The Soviets weren't keeping to their expected course. Each time the sounds from the Yankee came through, there were lost almost immediately, drowned out by the living Atlantic made even louder now by violent currents caused by a raging storm above. Mack paced about the control room, frustrated at having the crawl blindly around the ocean knowing that the Yankee was so close.

Lapon found and lost the Yankee several times over the next few days. Then, on the fourth day, the Yankee showed up again. This time *Lapon* followed, first for an hour, then for two, then for three. The Yankee's propellers spun a steady rhythm through the sonar team's headsets. Six hours, twelve hours, the Yankee was still on a steady course in front of *Lapon*. But at eighteen hours, the Yankee disappeared from the sonar screens, lost again. Mack's burgeoning underwater drama had fallen flat.

By now, most of the officers and some of the crew had gone several days with little sleep. Mack had only dozed, minutes at a time, mostly while still standing in the control room. And now, for these men, grave disappointment replaced the adrenaline rush that had already sustained itself far too long.

No one spoke the obvious. No one wanted to say that maybe it was impossible to keep track of this new, quieter generation of soviet submarine as it rode through the cacophonous ocean. No one wanted to give up.

Sharing Mack's disappointment back in Norfolk and in Washington, D.C., were Captain Bradley; Vice Admiral Arnold Schade, who was still commander of submarines in the Atlantic; and Admiral Moorer, the CNO. They had been in constant touch as Mack flashed UHF progress messages to U.S. aircraft flying overhead. The navy, in turn, kept aides to the president up to date. Nixon was following the trail in real time.

The admirals ordered all SOSUS installations in the area to listen for the Yankee. P-3 Orions also were on the lookout. But in both instances, the efforts were futile.

Mack decided to take a huge gamble. Calling his navigators and officers into the wardroom, he announced that they were going to give up trying to pick up the Yankee near the Denmark Strait. Instead, Mack was going to try to guess where the Yankee was headed next, and he wanted to try to beat her to her destination. Now Mack, his XO Charles H. Brickell Jr., the engineer officer Ralph L. Tindal, and others bent over the charts and began an intense game of "what if," putting themselves in the place of the Yankee's commander. Desperation weighed in as much as logic when they finally decided to attempt to pick up the Yankee's track several hundred miles south, near Portugal's Azores Islands.

Lapon hurried down there and then trolled about the appointed spot for three days. Too much time, Mack fretted. He made another guess and moved the sub west. Almost as soon as *Lapon* settled into her new patrol, her hull began to reverberate with the grinding of metal on metal. Mack came running into the control room. The diving officer reported that *Lapon* was losing depth.

The 4,800-ton *Lapon* had been caught in the net of a deep-sea fishing trawler, tangled in the net's metal weights and thick metal cable. The Yankee could pass by at any moment, and *Lapon* was dangling along with Sunday brunch.

It didn't take long for the fishermen to give up, or maybe they cut their net. Either way, they left the area with the greatest one-that-got-away story of their lives. But a piece of the trawler's cable had worked its way around a sonar device on the front of the submarine. There was no way *Lapon* could effect a silent trail with the dangling cable clicking across her bow.

Mack had no choice. He waited for dark, then ordered *Lapon* to the surface. Now praying that the Yankee would *not* pass, at least not now, he sent a man out onto the sail with a large pair of bolt cutters. His gamble worked—the cable was away and *Lapon* was ready when the Yankee showed up twelve hours later.

This time Mack was determined not to lose the Soviet submarine. This more southern portion of the Atlantic wasn't as loud as the waters off Greenland, but the Yankee was still quieter than any submarine a U.S. boat had ever tried to follow. It was time for a new tactic that Mack dubbed on the spot the "close-in trail." *Lapon* would tailgate the Yankee, moving no further than 3,000 yards away. More than 4,000 or 5,000 yards away, and the Yankee would be lost.

Mack's strategy was risky. Hurtling 4,800 tons that close to the massive Yankee was dangerous. Normally even surface ships try to stay about two miles apart for fear of collision. And *Lapon* had the added worry of detection. Mack just hoped that this new submarine didn't have better sonar than her predecessors. *Lapon* was so close that all someone had to do was drop a piece of equipment or slam a watertight door at the wrong time and even the soviets' outdated equipment could register an American shadow.

Just about everyone on board realized the risk they were taking, but nobody dared question Mack. Nobody had time to. It had become crucial now to figure out what the Soviet vessel sounded like when she slowed down, or turned. Until *Lapon*'s sonar team could figure out what combination of clicks or tones matched which maneuvers, both submarines were in grave danger of colliding.

Mack ordered *Lapon* to slip side to side behind the Yankee as his men set about finding answers to a matrix of questions. Once again, Mack engaged himself in a game of "what if," trying to put himself in the Soviet captain's place, wondering what he would do, and when. It was like working on a very large, very difficult crossword puzzle. One answer led to others. One blank creased several avenues of confusion. All *Lapon*'s crew could do was keep collecting information. The sonar teams began listening for any flaws in the Yankee's construction, anything that would give them clues to help them "see" the other submarine as it maneuvered.

Standard sonar would never have been enough. The Yankee was simply too quiet. But *Lapon* wasn't relying on just standard sonar. Mack had slipped aboard an added edge, an experimental sonar device designed to capitalize on some discoveries that Kelln's USS *Ray* had made in 1967 and 1968 when she trailed the November-class attack sub into the Mediterranean and then tracked a Charlie in the North Atlantic. The device worked by upgrading the way the standard system registered noise levels in the ocean. It zeroed in on certain tones, those made by the Yankee as she moved through the water, almost the way notes of music sound from a bottle when somebody blows over the top. After a fair amount of trial and error, *Lapon*'s crew realized that one particular frequency changed each time the Yankee turned. A shift to the left, and the tone was slightly higher. When the Yankee moved away, the tone lowered. If the tone changed quickly, it meant the Yankee was making a swift course change.

The one place *Lapon* couldn't follow from was directly behind. Unlike other Soviet submarines that offered an easy-to-follow din from their propellers, the Yankee was quiet enough from behind that she was rendered effectively invisible. Indeed, the Yankee might have been able to slip away entirely, even with *Lapon*'s extra sonar gadget, if not for what must have been a structural flaw. To the left, the Yankee's machinery was making more noise than any other portion of the boat.

From now on, *Lapon* was going to follow that machinery noise. If it got louder, Mack would know that the Yankee had made a left turn. If the Yankee seemed to vanish, she probably had turned right.

Ultimately the best vantage point turned out to be a little off to the side of the Yankee's stern, in either direction—with the left side being a little louder. From there the new sonar device picked up strong tones, and standard sonar registered steam noises coming from the Yankee's turbines and the clicks made by the Yankee's propeller each time it made a revolution. Counting those clicks and logging turn counts was how Mack and his crew determined the Yankee's speed.

All of this took four or five days to figure out—longer than the entire length of most trailing attempted so far against the noisy Soviet Hotel, Echo, and November subs, the HENs. But Mack wasn't going to break off. Instead, he was going to keep following, and he would figure out the mechanics as he went along. The process of trial and error spanned several watch stations, leaving it up to Mack and his engineer officer to teach each succeeding team what had been discovered over the past twelve hours.

Mack was determined not to lose the Yankee again, especially when he realized that she was headed on a track toward the U.S. Atlantic coast. He again began to forgo sleep, although he slipped in 15-minute catnaps at the helm, a trick he picked up in college from an article in *Reader's Digest*.

Days later, *Lapon* was still tracking the Yankee. Mack began to map out the Yankee's operating area, one of the most crucial pieces of intelligence he could carry home. The Soviets had settled into a holding pattern that covered about 200,000 square miles. They moved back and forth, staying between 1,500 and 2,000 miles off the United States.

Up until now, the Navy had been convinced that the Soviet Union would send its Yankees as close as 700 miles from U.S. shores. But Mack's discovery would help Naval Intelligence determine that the Yankee's new SS-N-6 missiles actually had a range of 1,200–1,300 miles.

If *Lapon* had not followed the Yankee this far, it would have been difficult for the United States to keep track of the new soviet nuclear threat, even though the Yankee plowed through what appeared to be a well-defined box. The United States would have been searching 800 miles too close to shore.

Now Mack mapped the Yankee's exact course. Choosing one area, she meandered at about 6 knots before racing to another area at

12–16 knots. Then she slowed again. Every 90 minutes, almost to the second, the Yankee changed course. Sometimes by 60 degrees, sometimes by far more.

A few times a day the Yankee went to communications depth, presumably to receive radio messages, and every night, at the stroke of midnight, she rose to periscope depth to ventilate. Between ten and sixteen times a day she turned completely around to clear her baffles, listening to see whether anyone was following. Each time the Yankee turned, *Lapon* turned with her, trying to stay behind, just off to one side, shielded in the backwash of the Yankee's own noise. (U.S. submariners also clear their baffles regularly when they are out on operations, only never according to schedule. The delicate question of timing those maneuvers was left to a pair of dice kept in the *Lapon*'s control room for just that purpose.)

Once a day the Yankee kicked out with a wild, high-speed move that *Lapon*'s crew called the "Yankee doodle" because it resembled the twisted designs on someone's desktop notepad. The Yankee would curl about, usually in a figure eight or some version of that, ending up facing 180 degrees from where she had started. Shifting to port, she would then make a 180-degree turn, then a second 180-degree turn, then a 90-degree turn, then a 270-degree turn, and end with two more 90-degree turns.

The first set of turns seemed designed to catch an intruder following close in, and the second set to catch another submarine following from farther away. All this was usually done at high speed, sometimes twice, back to back. The entire process took about an hour.

Had the Yankee's sonar been any better, the maneuver might have been effective. But the Soviets seemed to have made one key miscalculation. *Lapon* could hear the turns and get out of the way long before the Soviets could hear *Lapon*. In fact, *Lapon* sonar techs realized that their sonar seemed to have more than twice the range of Soviet sonar. In good conditions, *Lapon* could spot a surface ship from 20,000 yards away. But the Yankee would pass within 10,000 yards of the same ship before showing any reaction.

As *Lapon*'s trail fell into a routine, Mack was finally able to give up his standing catnaps. He actually went to his stateroom to lie down and sleep, though never longer than 90 minutes. He never missed a course change of a Yankee doodle. It was during one of his naps, however, that Mack made the biggest mistake of the mission, perhaps the biggest mistake of his career. The mess cook awakened Mack on the advice of a junior officer who decided Mack would rather give up sleep than his nightly order of blueberry muffins. Startled, Mack let out a roar, the cook went running and the muffins and coffee went fling. In that one moment, Mack had destroyed possibly the best perk ever offered a submarine captain: His beloved fresh blueberry muffins, split and drenched with butter. Nobody would again dare delivery, not then, not as the third week of the trail gave way to a fourth, and then an unheard-of fifth week.

By that time, *Lapon*'s three rotating officers of the deck realized they had each fallen into sync with the Soviet counterparts. Indeed, each American could identify his Soviet "partner" by slight stylistic differences in the Yankee doodles and other course changes. They named these Soviets—"Terrible Terence" and "Wild Willy" were the two most memorable—and they began to take bets on how well they could predict the Yankee's next move. Tindal won most often. The sonar crew also got into the act, interpreting the sounds they picked up from inside the Yankee. Sounds of drilling, pumps running, and other noise led to some crude jokes, mostly bathroom humor. A quick clank was automatically recorded as a toilet lid being slammed, and every time *Lapon* sonarmen heard the rushing of air over their headsets that could have been sanitary tanks being blown, they reported, quite formally, "Conn. Sonar. We just got shit on."

Every man in the crew, down to the youngest seaman and the lowliest mess cook, was getting into the act. Mack let each of them take a turn at manually plotting the unfolding course. It was heady stuff for the young crewmen. Here they were on a trail longer than any other, trailing one of the most crucial pieces of hardware the Soviets had put to sea, and they were integrally involved in the process. The excitement was extending from sub to shore. Mack had gotten to know the Yankee captain's habits well enough to predict when the soviets would go deep, and he used those moments to bring *Lapon* to periscope depth and flash a quick message to the P-3 Orions that were flying high over the Yankee's patrol area.

All continued to go well until one of the Orions almost ended the entire effort. The pilot must have come lower than he should have, because when the Yankee came to periscope depth, her crew spotted the plane and made an immediate dive. The Orion sped away. The men on *Lapon* listened to the entire drama, their sub undetected. They realized that, although the Orion had been spotted, the Soviets didn't seem to know that they were being trailed through water as well as air. That seemed true, in fact, until someone back in Washington made a big mistake.

Rumors in the sub force say it was an admiral in national aviation who leaked information to a newspaper that could threaten the mission. The leak didn't specify that *Lapon* was out following a Yankee, and it didn't even say that a soviet ballistic missile submarine was, at that very moment, wandering 1,500 to 2,000 nautical miles off the United States. But on October 9, 1969, the *New York Times* ran a front-page story headlined "New Soviet Subs Noisier Than Expected."

Whoever leaked the story was either unaware of *Lapon*'s finding or distorted them, because what the *Times* reported was far more reassuring than the truth. As Mack had found out, the Yankees were by far the quietest subs the Soviets had put to sea—although U.S. subs were still quieter.

World of the story must have made it back to the Soviet Navy and to the Yankee's captain. Either that, or he had become suddenly psychic. Within hours of the story's publication, moments after the Yankee made its midnight trip to communications depth, she broke all of her patterns. In fact, she went wild. The Yankee made a sudden 180-degree turn and came roaring back down her former path full-out at 20 knots, heading almost straight for *Lapon*. This did not at all resemble the calculated set of turns that made up the Yankee doodle. Now did it have the calm routine of the Yankee's usual slow turns, those baffle-clearing maneuvers.

This was a desperation ploy, and all-out search by the Soviets to see if they were being followed. This was the ultimate game of chicken. This was what the U.S. sub force called a "Crazy Ivan."

The Yankee came flying through the water, her image filling the screens in *Lapon*'s control room and the noise of her flight screaming through sonarmen's headsets. It sounded like a freight train running through a tunnel: "Kerchutka, Kerchutka, Kerchutka . . ."

"That bastard is coming down," someone in the control room blurted out. The men tensed, although they knew *Lapon* was still 300 feet below the Yankee as she blindly passed to starboard. Nobody missed the irony, that the Yankee, in her noisy high-speed flight, had missed her chance to detect *Lapon*. The Yankee continued to search, moving in circles for hours, but Mack countered with his own evasive maneuvers enacted by a crew who had been standing at battle stations throughout the drama. Mack refused to break off the chase. Instead, he waited for the Yankee to calm down. Then he continued the mission.

On October 13, nearly a month after the trail began, Admiral Schade sent a top-secret message to the *Lapon*: "ADMIRAL MOORER STATES THAT SECDEF AND ALL IN WASHINGTON WATCHING OPERATION WITH SPECIAL INTEREST AND NOTES WITH GREAT PLEASURE AND PRIDE SUPERB PERFORMANCE OF ALL PARTICIPANTS. I SHARE HIS THOUGHTS."

Lapon continued on, through the rest of the Yankee's patrol and then some as the Soviets took an almost straight track back home. There were no more Yankee doodles, no more Crazy Ivans. The Yankee beat a path to the GIUK gap, where *Lapon* left her on November 9.

Lapon had followed the Yankee for an amazing forty-seven days.

Tommy Cox again was moved to write, this time coming up with "The Ballad of Whitey Mack":

> Whitey's got the deck and the conn.
> Now he had quite a job to do,
> And every man on board knew,
> When the going got rough,
> In this game of "Blind Man's Bluff,"
> Somehow he'd pull her through.

Cox's lyrics were right on target. It really was Blind Man's bluff, a game far more dangerous than mere hide-and-spy operations. Mack's success marked the beginning of a new mission for the submarine force. From here on out, the fleet would be focused on tailing Soviet ballistic missile submarines at sea. U.S. attack submarines were suddenly elevated to critical participants in the nation's strategic nuclear defense. And they would lead the greatest sea hunt in maritime history. For now, as he drove *Lapon* back to Norfolk, Mack was basking in the glory that was finally his. Messages of congratulations flooded the radio channels.

Months later, *Lapon* would receive the highest award every given to submarines, the Presidential Unit Citation. Whitey Mack would win a Distinguished Service Medal, the highest personal honor the Navy awarded its officers in peacetime.

But it was one of the messages sent out when *Lapon* was still on her way home that pleased Mack more than any other accolade. It wasn't addressed to Mack or to his crew. Instead, this message was sent out to every other submarine out on operations in the Atlantic: "Get out of the way. Whitey's coming through." The order was clear. Everyone was to make way and give the *Lapon* a clear track home.

When Mack heard that, he slapped his fist in his hand, shook his head and said: "Eat your heart out, suckers. Whitey's coming through."

Becoming a Jedi, from *Warrior Soul*

CHUCK PFARRER

> The only easy day was yesterday.
>
> —Motto, Navy SEALs

When the U.S. Marines landed on the small Pacific island of Tarawa in the Gilbert Islands in November 1943, they were met with unexpected difficulties. Little intelligence could be gathered from old maps of the island and the vital data of the water's depth in the lagoon was inaccurate. When the landing craft moved toward shore, they struck the reefs hundreds of yards from shore. Marines were forced to wade through chest-deep water under merciless enemy fire as they tried to make the beach. Many drowned and hundreds more were cut down by the Japanese defenders. What was needed for any future amphibious assault was exact knowledge of the terrain and enemy defenses prior to a landing. Thus was born a group of volunteers taken from Seabee construction units that formed the first Navy Combat Demolition Units.

By the Korean War these teams had evolved into an elite group of frogmen identified as UDT or underwater demolition teams. When President Kennedy called upon the military to form a counterinsurgency force, the Navy looked to its frogmen to form naval commando units designated SEALs for Sea, Air, Land. By 1962 two SEAL Team One was operational stationed in Coronado, California and SEAL Team Two was based at Little Creek, Virginia. The mission of the SEALs was to perform unconventional warfare and counter-guerilla operations both at sea and along coastal territories. Their first test in combat came in Vietnam between 1963–1973 where they served with distinction, taking the fight to the enemy deep in his own territory where they lest expected it, capturing high ranking prisoners and gathering valuable intelligence. To the enemy Vietnamese, the SEALs became feared as "the men with green faces."

In 1980, Commander Richard Marcinko of the SEALs saw the need for a maritime counter-terrorism unit after the failed attempt to rescue American hostages in Iran during Operation Eagle Claw. What evolved was a top secret unit named SEAL Team Six. Training to become a SEAL is regarded by many as the toughest military training in the world. Chuck Pfarrer was selected for SEAL Team Six in the early 1980s and describes the unbelievable challenges he went through to earn his place among those elite warriors from his *New York Times* best seller *Warrior Soul.*

★ ★ ★ ★ ★

The supply chief was in a hurry because it was time to go home. I'd shown up late, with an inventory half an inch thick, just as he was pulling closed the steel-and-wire mesh door that separated his office and warehouse from the passageway. He grunted as I handed over my paperwork, equipment I'd need for my course in Green Team, the training cell of SEAL Team Six. The other twenty or so members of my training class had drawn their kits over the last several weeks as they arrived and checked in to the Team.

I was late for an unsurprising reason. When I received orders to Six, the commanding officer of SEAL Team Four called me in Puerto Rico and attempted to get me to decline the transfer. He said he had a great position at the Pentagon for me, an assignment that would be better for my career. As far as I knew I had no career, and I had no desire to serve at the Pentagon. I politely but firmly refused. My orders were to report aboard SEAL Six no later than September 15, and I was looking forward to the change. But through acts of either inertia or contempt, I was ordered to remain in Puerto Rico until September 14. Like Frank Giffland, I had been given one day to check out of my old command and in to my new one.

All day on the fifteenth, I had dashed around the SEAL Team Six compound, schlepping paperwork, getting ID badges, drawing weapons, parachutes, diving rigs, and radios, much to the consternation of clerks and technicians who told me this should have been done weeks ago. I learned pretty quickly that being a Green Team member didn't cut much ice at Six. None of the support guys I dealt with were even SEALs, but they all gave me a hard time. I made no excuses and asked no favors, but I soon rounded up what I needed. Supply was my last stop and the biggest haul.

There were more than two hundred items on my gear list, everything from desert cammies to arctic overwhites, ice boots to shower shoes.

The chief frowned. "When do you need this?"

"Tonight," I said. "I start training tomorrow."

He pushed open the door reluctantly, and I followed him into supply. He removed a folder from a file drawer. "We didn't think you were coming," he said.

I'm sure he would have been delighted if I'd been killed by land crabs in Puerto Rico.

"What's your operator number?" he asked.

"One-five-six," I said.

He shook his head. "We already have a One-five-six."

Before I could ask to pick a new number, like 007, the chief's eyes fell on a flat cart loaded chest-high with duffel bags. It was an individual operator's load-out, all the equipment I would need to draw. The number 205 was stenciled neatly on the bags.

"I got a full load-out right over there. You have a problem with changing your number?"

"Does it get me my gear any faster?"

"You become Two-oh-five, and you can sign right here."

We were both in a hurry. I signed, and the booty was mine. In the stroke of a pen, I was Operator 205.

"It's all there," the chief said, "all of it and then some. I just inventoried it myself."

I smiled as he locked up the supply room. Thinking I had scored, I shouldered the pile of bags on the cart and wheeled it into the passageway.

"What happened to Operator Two-oh-five?" I asked.

"His parachute didn't open," the chief said.

SEAL Six had the jack, and it showed. The equipment I'd drawn was the best of everything. I stayed up late that night, stowing the gear in my cage, a locked wire enclosure about the size of a one-car garage. Here I would keep every piece of my operational kit racked, stacked, and ready to fly. Each operator had a cage, his own personal space, warehouse, and dominion. There was little communal equipment. We all drew our own gear and were responsible for maintaining it.

I had been issued an astonishing amount of stuff. Foul-weather gear, Gore-Tex parkas, assault vests, cammies, boots, fins. Bags and sea chests full to bursting. Climbing harnesses, carabiners, chocks, jumars, and lock picks. Nomex coveralls. Custom wet suits. Flight suits. Survival kits.

Sunglasses and ski goggles. Scuba rigs, a pair of twin steel 90s for open circuit and a brand-new Draeger LAR-V rebreather. An MT-1-X parachute and an impressive number of weapons. In my personal rack in the arsenal were a CAR-15 with M-203 grenade launcher, MP5-A5 and MP-5K machine pistols, and a wicked little silenced MP5-SD. I had a personal AK-47, an H&K G3 assault rifle, an M-60 machine gun, a SAW-squad automatic weapon, a stainless-steel Smith & Wesson model 686 .357 Magnum pistol, a Beretta 92 SBF, and a blue-steel Walther PPK, just like James Bond. The armory tech was blasé as he had me sign.

"This is your basic draw," he mumbled. "If you need any other sort of weapon, or if you want modifications made, just let us know."

I reported the following morning at 0600 and met my new teammates. The twenty of us were to be the fourth Green Team processed by SEAL Team Six. Some faces I recognized and some I did not. In any case, we were surprises to one another. When we were notified of our selection, we were told to tell only those people with a need to know. Several of my new teammates were old friends. Wild Bill had been in Class 114 and was a member of my boat crew during Hell Week. Bill was an NFL-sized guy with an incredible sense of humor. He was impressively strong and born into the career of spec ops—his father was a serving colonel in the Green Berets. There were three others from 114 in my Green Team: Greg Pearlman and Chris Keller, the two hot dogs who'd swiped the jumpmaster's hat back at Fort Benning, and Vinny, a tall man built like a cross-country runner, who was quiet, intense, and dedicated. He, too, had been in my boat crew for Hell Week, and I was glad to see him. They were solid guys, good shipmates, great operators, and all would be destined to have long careers at SEAL Six.

The balance of my Green Team came from SEAL Teams One, Two, and Three, as well as the SDV Teams. Surprisingly, or perhaps not, I was the only one from SEAL Four. Everyone selected was considered top-of-the-line, the officers all former platoon commanders, and most of the enlisted former leading petty officers or boat-crew leaders. The class's sole chief petty officer was Bud Denning, a taciturn guy with a subtle and cutting sense of humor. As chiefs go, Bud Denning was one of the best.

There were three other officers in my Green Team, all of us lieutenants, and all of us would become friends for life. Sean Pikeman was our class leader, senior by a couple of years; he was fresh from SEAL Team One and a jungle deployment to the Philippines. He had been raised in Stillwater, Oklahoma; he had an Okie's level head and had played all-American lacrosse at the University of Rochester. Next was Rick Cullen, unflappable, a meticulous planner and a former platoon commander from SEAL Two. Finally, there was Moose. If the Moose didn't exist, someone would have had to invent him. Built like a linebacker, he was a high-time SDV pilot from the West Coast. Driving minisubs into Korean harbors on recons wasn't exciting enough for him, so here he was. Moose was a fascinating guy with a rigorous and accomplished upbringing. Captain and quarterback of his high school football team, he also found time to play first violin in the Seattle Youth Symphony. At Claremont College in California, he ran the 880 and majored in philosophy and religion, writing his senior thesis on the death of Eric Bonhoffer, a Lutheran theologian executed by Adolf Hitler. Moose was as impressive intellectually as he was physically. He could talk about Epictetus while he benched 350, and it was only a fool who'd try to outdrink him.

Our instructors walked in, dressed in the uniform of the day, blue jeans and polo shirts. The entire time I was at SEAL Six, I would wear a navy uniform only once. This was a civilian-clothes operation.

The training cell was led by a man with the remarkable name of Traylor Court. Court was prior enlisted, had attended OCS and gotten drafted into the command by Dick Marcinko personally. Court had a gymnast's build and was one of the operators, along with Kim Erskine, who had taken down the radio station on Grenada. Court wasn't the type to raise his voice. He commanded attention and respect.

With Court were three other instructors: Toni, a six-foot, 250-pound Hawaiian surfer; Mike Daniels, your basic triathlete sniper-cum-demolition expert; and a guy we called Bam-Bam. Bam-Bam was from Gary, Indiana, and was fond of remarking that he was the only one of his three brothers not currently in prison. Bam-Bam had been the Indiana State springboard-diving champion, and in a command where everyone was an expert marksman, he was considered one of the fastest and deadliest shots. He was also quick with his fists.

There was no welcome-aboard speech. Court made a few remarks, most notably that this was a selection course. Not only was it possible to fail; for most of us, it was likely. He predicted that half of the men assigned to this Green Team would attrite. It was a variation of my welcome to BUD/S, and I am sure everyone who heard him thought they'd be among the graduates.

Court was to prove precise in his estimate. Of the twenty of us standing in the Team room, only twelve would make it through Green Team and be assigned to assault elements on the operational team. Court went on to enumerate half a dozen transgressions for which we would be immediately canned: Accidental discharge of a weapon. Any safety violation involving diving or explosives. Use or suspected use of controlled substances. Loss or mishandling of classified material. Revealing any facts about SEAL Team Six to anyone, in or out of naval special warfare. We were specifically instructed to no longer associate with anyone back in the regular Teams. We were told bluntly: "Make new friends."

This policy was rigorously enforced and had led to the alienation of Team Six from the rest of the community. The new-friends rule was a relic of the Marcinko era, and like many other Marcinko policies we would come up against, it seemed pointless and counterproductive; but they were serious about it, so we did as we were told. There was at least a glimmer of a reason behind it: SEAL Team Six was then a black program. The existence of the Team was secret, the location of the base was secret, its budget, training, organization, and tactics were all classified. The building did not say "SEAL Team Six"—it said the name of an equipment-testing unit that did not exist. The cover was backstopped thoroughly. All of us had been processed out of the navy. At least as far as our records showed, we had all been separated from the service. Paperwork variously indicating resignation, retirement, and medical release from duty had been placed in each of our service records. We were to grow our hair long and forget that we owned uniforms. As far as the world was concerned, none of us were in the navy anymore. We were now civilians working for the phantom organization. This was what we were to tell our neighbors and new friends.

To our old teammates back at Little Creek, it would appear that we had dropped off the face of the planet. We had entered the black world. From now on the Teams would be referred to disparagingly as Vanilla SOF—plain white spec ops. As aspirant members of Team Jedi, we had crossed to the Dark Side.

There was an additional consequence of joining a black operation: compartmentalization. Green Team was firewalled totally from the operational elements of SEAL Six. We were told not to ask questions, to keep to our own cages and our own Team room, and not to fraternize with the operators, even if we had known them back in the real world. The training cell was completely segregated from the operational elements. Until we had passed out of Green Team, we were visitors. Period.

"When and *if* you graduate," Court said, "you can play with your old friends."

This culture pervaded the command. It wasn't just the support guys who gave Green Team members the short stroke. In the hallways and around campus, the members of Green Team were practically invisible. Former teammates would pass by without a nod. The no-fraternization rule went both ways. This was another Marcinko innovation. You had to earn the right to be here; until then you were nothing.

The next briefing was from the command's two counterintelligence agents, a pair of cards I'll call "Lenny" and "Dougie." It was their job to make sure the command kept a low—that is, invisible—profile. They were active-duty marines, as if you could tell. Dougie had curly hair to his shoulders and a drooping Fu Manchu. Lenny sported a goatee and an earring. They were affable enough, but their message was chilling. It was their job to discern how well our covers were working, and what the general public knew about us and the command.

"Here's the deal," Dougie said. "If I ask your next-door neighbors where you work and they tell me you're a SEAL, you're outta here."

I made a mental note: Don't chat up the neighbors.

Green Team was to be eight months long, two months longer than BUD/S. It would prove every bit as grueling. We worked six days a week, from six in the morning until five at night. We would have at least one night op a week, and we would work seven days a week when we were on the road, which would be most of the time. Individuals who attrited, were injured or deemed unsuitable would have their service records reactivated and would transfer back to the Teams. Before transfer, they would sign a security-termination agreement promising fines and imprisonment for leaking any information. Again, Lenny and Dougie would be checking.

We wore beepers and were on call to be in our cages and ready to deploy on short notice. I won't mention the time requirement, but I will say this: It was stringent enough that some people sold their houses to move closer to work.

And there was a lot of work. Traylor Court would soon dispel any notions we had about being in shape. In the woods in front of the compound, Court had erected an aerial obstacle course. Rigged through the trees were caving ladders, rope bridges, monkey bars, bits of pipe, inclined boards, and horizontal beams. Negotiating the course required a variety of rock-climbing moves: chimneying, laybacks, mantles, and countless full-body lifts. We used to say Court was trying to separate the men from the baboons, but the course had a purpose. At Six, we climbed things: the sides of buildings, oil rigs, cliff faces, and anchor chains. As I gradually gained confidence and strength, I was to fall out of Court's trees half a dozen times, but I would never fall on an operation.

We were required to swing through Court's masterpiece after our daily six-mile run, which happened after our first hour and a half of PT, which started every morning at 0600. Morning calisthenics, like the run and the aerial O-course, were led by Court in person. Not all of our cardio conditioning was roadwork or swinging through trees. We swam thousands of laps and played water rugby in the Team's indoor Olympic swimming pool. I was in shape when I got there, and I got harder. We lifted weights in a health-club-sized weight room. We did a twenty-mile cross-country run over hill and dale, forest and swamp. We swam around the island of Key West. By the end of training, I would weigh 220 pounds and be able to run ten miles in sixty-five minutes, knock out a hundred sit-ups in ninety seconds, and chin myself with one hand.

As fun as the exercise was, we were there to learn a trade, and the greater part of each day was spent absorbing the component skills required of a counterterrorist operator. We were put through an intense combat-swimmer curriculum, building on and expanding the underwater skills we'd learned in the Teams. The training required us to swim mile-long course legs underwater and affix magnetic mines to targets on time and without detection. We conducted underwater recons against port facilities and offshore oil platforms. We swam to piers, surfaced, and shot targets, disappearing back underwater and swimming a mile or two out to sea.

When I reported to Green Team, I might have been a bit jaded. I'd been in combat, I was a platoon commander, I had led numerous detachments and spent a good part of my career doing spooky stuff in Central America. I thought I'd been around the block, and I didn't expect to have the shit scared out of me. But it happened in Green Team, often. It was taken for granted that we were all experienced operators and that we would learn quickly. Some of the things we learned were just plain dangerous. In the evolutions we practiced, everything either went perfectly or people died.

"Pay attention," Bam-Bam used to say, "because if you fuck this up, it will kill you." Every day Green Team battled the combined forces of Mr. Murphy and Mr. Darwin.

We attended survival schools for desert, woodland, and arctic environments. We learned how to take over ships at pierside and under way. We attended special driving schools, learning how to do bootlegs and J-turns, how to avoid roadblocks and vehicle ambushes. We also learned how to conduct the Pitt maneuver, an offensive driving technique used to knock other cars off the road. Much to the chagrin of our instructors, we kept these skills sharp on a series of rental cars. We were taught intelligence tradecraft, studying the arcana of dead drops, load signals, and countersurveillance. We took classes on the organization and tactics of the KGB, the East German *Stasi,* and the Cuban intelligence organization, the DGI (*Dirección General de Inteligencia*).

We learned to operate and field-strip each of the weapons we'd been issued, those and about a hundred others besides. We attended shooting schools, studying combat pistol craft and police shotgun technique from national champions like Rogers and Chapman. In an exercise called an El Presidente, we would stand, hands raised, pistols holstered, with our backs turned to three man-shaped silhouettes. On command, we would about-face, draw, fire two rounds into each target, reload, and fire two more rounds into the trio. I was considered fair at this. I could fire twelve shots and reload my weapon in just over five seconds. The best operator on the team could do it in four and a half.

Combat shooting differs qualitatively from traditional marksmanship. In normal rifle and pistol craft, shooters are taught to close one eye, relax, align the target, and squeeze the trigger slowly. To rush a shot is to cheat the process. Combat shooting is, by necessity, a hasty business. When people are shooting back at you, speed is life.

We were first taught to shoot from the ready position, squared toward the target, knees slightly bent, and weight forward on the toes, a position called "the modified isosceles." Our MP-5s were secured over the shoulder and to the chest by a special assault sling. When the weapon is raised to engage the target, the sling becomes another point of stability, like a third steadying hand. On the command to fire, we would snap off safe, fire two rounds in quick succession (called a "double tap"), snap the safety back on, and return to the ready position. Initially we shot at reactive targets, armored silhouettes and dish-sized head plates. The pinging of the bullets off the metal targets and the fleeting puff of lead spatter were instant feedback, a process called "point of impact/point of aim." Eye, hand, bullet, target, brain.

Combat shooting is dynamic, not static, and we did not spend much time shooting at stationary targets. We were taught to move and shoot, shoot and move and shoot, while the targets were moving. This required a different sort of aiming, completely unlike the target-focused techniques of long-distance marksmanship. We were taught to open both eyes, keeping the scan on and avoiding target lock. There is a bit of a trick to this, especially for marksmen used to shooting at bull's-eyes printed on paper targets. Most right-handed people are right-eye dominant, and most lefties favor their left eye. The dominant eye is better exercised and slightly more acute. In traditional marksmanship, the nondominant eye is closed. We learned a technique to gray out our nondominant eye, keeping it open but using our dominant eye to process the target and align the sights. The nondominant eye maintained peripheral vision, the location of the next target and the position of obstacles. Basically, one eye scanned and the other killed.

In order to shoot accurately, we still had to acquire a correct sight picture, front and rear sights aligned, target centered over the front sight post; but in combat shooting, this process is compressed into a split second. There is no time to squeeze the trigger slowly; it is pulled rapidly and evenly. You must subtly anticipate the weapon going off, and learn by feel your own reaction to the muzzle blast and the cycling of the gun. All of this is exactly contrary to long-distance marksmanship, in which shooters are taught to relax, regulate their breathing, and squeeze the trigger so gently that they are surprised when the weapon goes off.

We often aimed on the run, or popping up from behind obstacles. Compensation for the jerk of the trigger had to be built in to the target scan, the aiming, and the firing of the weapon. Working day and night, we became masters of the fast-targeting, rapid-fire skills of combat shooting. Everything we did was timed and scored, and Green Team got smaller in the first four weeks. The class was ranked in a ratio of hits over time. Those scoring in the lowest 20 percent of our class cleaned out their cages and returned to Planet Vanilla.

Our next task was to learn the science and art of CQB, close-quarters battle. Combat shooting is an individual event; CQB is a team sport. Like everything taught in SEAL Team, we learned component skills and gradually built up to operational capability.

Sometimes called "room clearance" or "surgical shooting," CQB was developed by the British SAS and put into practice in Northern Ireland. Counterterrorism is the science of *combating* terrorism, and CQB is the reason terrorists rarely seize buildings and hold hostages these days. It is the antidote to the hostage-barricade situation, whether the venue is a building, a cave, an airliner, an offshore oil platform, or a cruise ship. In the chaotic environment of a counterterrorism rescue, the mission is to secure the hostages and neutralize the terrorists. Discipline, teamwork, target discrimination, and exceptional marksmanship make this possible.

We would learn to shoot the bad guys from among the hostages in a place called the Kill House, an indoor 360-degree shooting facility. Movable walls allowed us to configure the range into multiple compartments, and we could make floor plans to match any target. We trained first in single rooms, shooting at man-sized printed silhouettes. Some targets were depicted holding weapons, some were hostages, some held weapons and police badges. After entering the room, we had to almost instantly scan, determine the threat, and either shoot or hold fire. We entered in teams of two, four, eight, and ten, and the targets were positioned differently each time. Sometimes the lights were on, sometimes they were off. We ran the target while instructors in the control booth pumped in disco fog and flashed strobe lights. Sometimes they blared music or jet-engine noise, and always, multiple video cameras taped us so the run could be played back in slow motion and analyzed.

Each of us fired tens of thousands of rounds, running scenarios as many as fifty times a day. When we were not in the Kill House, we shot next door in an elaborate cinematic target area. Our room targets become increasingly elaborate—furniture, couches, bookcases—and hidden bad guys were added. Stapled behind the critical areas of each target was a three-by-five index card marking kill areas on the human body. For every bullet we fired that missed a card, we had to buy a case of beer.

We were soon engaging targets in multiple-room scenarios. This required an extemporaneous flow of shooters through the operational area. Room clearance requires precision, an almost Zenlike awareness of the situation, and complete mastery of the weapon. Shooting pairs grouped and split up as the Team surged through hallways and rooms. It is at this, "flow through target" that SEAL Team Six is unmatched. The extreme level of training makes this possible. It is not enough to say that we practiced multiple-room clearance. In one year the operators of SEAL Six fire more bullets than the entire United States Marine Corps. We weren't just *good* at multiple-room CQ; there is no one in the world who comes close.

As our skills coalesced, the targets became more varied and elaborate. We trained on airliners, ships, and offshore oil and gas facilities. We practiced on buses and passenger trains.

Our training evolutions became full mission profiles, with the officers of Green Team each responsible for planning and briefing operations under the watchful eye of Court and his minions. In these highly realistic training evolutions, the bad guys continued to be paper silhouettes, but the hostages were real, breathing human beings. Scattered through the targets—just as hostages would be—the volunteers were service members, members of the joint command, and sometimes they were Washington VIPs, secretaries, senators, and representatives. It was our job to penetrate, neutralize the terrorists, secure the hostages, and extract. We trained to do this all using real bullets and live breeching explosives. In Green Team, like in the real world, there was no margin for error.

There was not one operational readiness exam but two dozen. Every combination of insertion and extraction method imaginable was married to differing target sets. A big-city SWAT team has the luxury of jumping on a bus and driving to the target. We were training for operations that would take place in denied areas, an enemy's backyard. We would have to sneak in and liberate the hostages, and we would have to fight our way out. The training operations reflected this. In eight months we operated in every environment and across every SEAL mission: direct action, reconnaissance and surveillance, operations against infrastructure, counterterrorism, and hostage rescue. Sean, Moose, Rick, and I each planned, briefed, and led half a dozen missions. Failure in a training op was grounds for instant dismissal. Over half of us hung on, and eight months after we'd started, we twelve graduated after a raucous celebration on an offshore oil rig we had just "captured."

The night of our last op happened to be Traylor Court's birthday and his last day at the command. In the SEALs, there is one thing you hide from your brothers at all times: the date of your birth, because SEAL Team birthday celebrations are not pleasant. One of the Green Team instructors had leaked that it was Court's birthday, and we made sure it would be a special event. As soon as the oil platform was in our hands, together with the Green Team instructors, we turned on Court, handcuffed him, and duct-taped him to a chair.

There was a brief trial of the kangaroo variety. Charges of inhumanity, cruelty to tadpoles, impersonating a baboon, and a few other capital offenses were read. Having been found instantly guilty, Court was sentenced to a shot or a shot: After each successive charge, he was allowed to choose between a shot of peppermint schnapps, injected into his mouth from a veterinary syringe, or being shot with one of the wax bullets we used for hostage training. I'm not sure which was worse; the wax bullets were propelled by a .38-caliber pistol cartridge primer, and they hurt like hell. Of course, peppermint schnapps hurts, too. After about a dozen rounds of each, Court was released from bondage, given a pardon signed by King Neptune himself, and carried to the oil platform's flight deck to be taken back to shore. The dozen shots of schnapps had taken their toll. As we waited for the helicopter, Court had to be twice prevented from demonstrating what he called his Tarzan swan dive from the flight deck. It took half a dozen guys to get him on the helo and strap him into a seat. Court was toast, but we were finished, and when we returned to Virginia, we'd be assigned to operational elements.

Green Team was over. We were Jedi at last.

Well, almost.

★ ★ ★ ★ ★

Chuck Pfarrer would go on to Hollywood after leaving the Navy to write screenplays, including the film *Navy Seals*, *The Jackal*, and *Red Planet*. SEAL Team Six was quietly reorganized in the early 1990s under a new designation, Naval Special Warfare Development Group.

Permissions Acknowledgments

Nathan Miller, excerpt from *Proud New Frigates*. Copyright © 2000 by Nathan Miller; Reprinted with permission of John Wiley & Sons, Inc.

James Tertius de Kay, "Glory" from *A Rage for Glory*. Reprinted with the permission of The Free Press, a Division of Simon & Schuster Adult Publishing Group, from *A Rage for Glory: The Life of Commodore Stephen Decatur, USN* by James Tertius de Kay. Copyright © 2004 by James Tertius de Kay. All rights reserved.

Cecil Scott Forester, "The Battle of Lake Erie" from *The Age of Fighting Sail: The Story of the Naval War of 1812* by C. S. Forester, copyright © 1956 by C.S. Forester. Used by permission of Doubleday, a division of Random House, Inc.

H. D. Smith, "Mobile Bay" from *Under Both Flags*, edited by Tim Goff, copyright © 2003 by The Lyons Press. Reprinted with permission of The Lyons Press.

Peter Maas, Pp. 37–1 from *The Terrible Hours* by Peter Maas. Copyright © 1999 by Peter Maas. Reprinted by permission of HarperCollins Publishers.

Gordon W. Prange, "Sound General Quarters" from *At Dawn We Slept*, copyright © 1981 by Anne R. Prange. Reprinted by permission of McGraw-Hill Education.

Walter G. Winslow, "The Galloping Ghost of the Java Coast" from *Proceedings*. Copyright © 1949 by the United States Naval Institute. Reprinted by permission.

Edwin P. Hoyt, "Midway" from *How They Won the War in the Pacific*, copyright © 2000 by Edwin P. Hoyt. Reprinted with permission of The Lyons Press.

Edwin P. Hoyt, "First Blood" from *The Men of the Gambier Bay*, copyright © 2003 by Edwin P. Hoyt. Reprinted with permission of The Lyons Press.

I. J. Galantin, "Hell Below" from *Take Her Deep!: Submarine Against Japan in World War II* by Admiral I. J. Galantin, USN ret. © 1987 by Admiral I. J. Galantin. Reprinted by permission of Algonquin Books of Chapel Hill.

Dan V. Gallery, "The Capture of *U-505*" from *Twenty Million Tons Under the Sea*. Copyright © 1956 by Daniel V. Gallery. Reprinted by permission.

George Feifer, "Kamikazes" from *The Battle of Okinawa*, copyright © 1992, 2001 by George Feifer. Reprinted with permission of The Lyons Press.

Stephen Puelo, "In the Water: Gulf of Maine" from *Due To Enemy Action*, copyright © 2005 by Stephen Puelo. Reprinted with permission of The Lyons Press.

Frances Omori, "USS *Consolation*" from *Quiet Heroes*. Copyright © 2000 by Commander Frances Omori, USN. Reprinted by permission.

Thomas J. Cutler, "Nine Dragons" from *Brown Water, Black Berets*. Copyright © 1988 by the U.S. Naval Institute, Annapolis, Maryland. Reprinted by permission.

Sherry Sontag and Christopher Drew, "The Ballad of Whitey Mack" from *Blind Man's Bluff* by Christopher Drew. ISBN: 1891620088. Copyright © 1998 by Sherry Sontag and Chrisopher Drew. Reprinted by permission of PublicAffairs, a member of Perseus Books, L.L.C.

Chuck Pfarrer, "Becoming a Jedi" from *Warrior Soul* by Chuck Pfarrer, copyright © 2003 by Chuck Pfarrer. Used by permission of Random House, Inc.